Working Time in Transition

Labor and Social Change,
a series edited by Paula Rayman and Carmen Sirianni

Working Time in Transition

The Political Economy of Working Hours
in Industrial Nations

Edited by Karl Hinrichs, William Roche,
and Carmen Sirianni

Temple University Press

Philadelphia

Temple University Press, Philadelphia 19122
Copyright © 1991 by Temple University
All rights reserved
Published 1991
Printed in the United States of America

Library of Congress Cataloging-in-Publication Data
Working time in transition : the political economy of working hours in
   industrial nations / edited by Karl Hinrichs, William Roche, and
   Carmen Sirianni.
       p.   cm.
   Includes bibliographical references.
   ISBN 0-87722-757-8 (alk. paper)
   1. Hours of labor.   2. Hours of labor, Flexible.   I. Hinrichs, K.
(Karl)   II. Roche, William.   III. Sirianni, Carmen.
HD5106.W65   1991
331.25'7—dc20   90-42337

Contents

1991

Working Time in Transition

1 From Standardization to Flexibility: Changes in the Political Economy of Working Time

Karl Hinrichs, William Roche, and Carmen Sirianni

Among the pervasive changes that have been occurring in recent decades in the political economy of employment and industrial relations in Western industrial nations, changes in working-time regimes must surely count as one of the most significant. During the "golden age" enjoyed since the early 1950s by the advanced economies of the Western world and Japan, significant though gradual changes have occurred in a number of facets of working time. The length of the working week and working life were reduced in all these countries. The distribution of working hours over the day and week was altered. The flexibility accorded to employees to start and finish work as they choose was increased. The management of working time in most countries was rationalized so as to gear working hours more closely to the exigencies of production systems and patterns of demand. Moreover, the availability and attractiveness of part-time employment increased.

In virtually all countries the international recessions of the mid- and late 1970s, combined with growing international competitiveness, accelerated the pace of change and widened the scope of working-time innovations. Working time has gained a new priority on the negotiating agendas of unions and employers and in the legislative programs of governments. As Sirianni concludes in chapter 10, time has become a "contested terrain" in the transition to postindustrial society.

Contrasting Lines of Change

The recent changes evident in most of the countries covered in this volume seem to represent a radical discontinuity in the political economy of working time, with profound consequences for unions and employees. The

3

picture that emerges from recent developments in Western European nations, and over a longer period in the United States, suggests that we may be witnessing the demise of standardized working-time regulations and arrangements that were developed by unions and employers—and often underwritten by governments—over a period of more than a century. Aspects of standard working time like the eight-hour uniform working day and five-day working week are being eroded in the wake of an employer offensive against established working-time standards and regulations. From the other side, employees are also calling into question rigid regimes that tie them to fixed starting and finishing times, specified holiday periods, and linear working lives.

For increasing numbers of employees the length of the working day and working week is becoming a variable or flexible feature of employment, influenced primarily by the pattern of demand confronting the firms in which they work. Working time is still usually standardized in terms of what are sometimes known as "balancing periods"—perhaps of a month's or year's duration—over which average working hours at basic rates of pay must conform to an agreed level. However, such standards represent a departure from established patterns in many countries in setting down flexible rather than fixed levels of normal working time during any day, week, or year.

The erosion of standard working hours is also apparent in a second trend in working-time regimes: the spread of working weeks that deviate from new flexible standards of the normal working week, usually by being shorter. In part, of course, a secular trend can be identified here in the gradual long-run growth of part-time employment in many countries. Of more recent vintage are agreements between unions and employers in some countries that permit managements to offer shorter workweeks to sections of plant workforces that would hitherto have been employed on workweeks of standard duration. Other employer-initiated changes in working time that are altering the social organization of time in advanced industrial nations are the growth of shift work, the increasing popularity of late opening and weekend opening in areas of service employment, and the growing incidence of "on call" or "on standby" arrangements. These latter oblige people to be prepared to go back to work during periods of leisure, should the need arise.

Such developments represent a further encroachment of the sphere of work on periods traditionally reserved for leisure and renewal. Taken together, recent innovations raise the prospect of a radical diversification of working-time schedules and patterns. Increased diversity in working-time patterns can be expected, in turn, to affect the tradeoffs employees are prepared to make between more leisure and more pay, and their attitudes about the manner in which additional reductions in working time ought to be arranged. Ultimately, as more employees become accustomed to working variable working days and weeks, and to working during what are now regarded as "unsocial" hours, the place of work and leisure in the wider pattern of social and political life may be altered, and societal rhythms linked to traditional store opening times and the like may become unsettled.

Such developments have occurred in a number of countries at the same time that overall working hours have declined. With the exception of Japan and the United States, employees in the countries covered by this volume now enjoy significantly more leisure than they did at the start of the postwar period. They seem set to benefit further from persistent union demands for a 35-hour standard working week. Many employees have already benefited from flexible working-hours schemes that have allowed them to tailor their starting and finishing times to their leisure and family interests. The time spent at work over people's working lives has fallen, through postponed entry to the labor market and the availability, in many countries, of early-retirement options. Moreover, to a limited degree, sabbatical arrangements and parental leave are providing people with greater scope to gear the time spent at work more closely to their other social and career interests, as well as to developmental stages over the life course.

The overall pattern, then, is a complex one, whether we compare developments within or between the countries covered in this volume. Certain strands of change in working-time regimes have for many tied leisure time more closely to the demands of industrial technologies and service provision. Others have operated in the reverse direction by giving people greater "time sovereignty." In any attempt to draw up a social balance sheet, as it were, of the net prospective effects of changes in working time now under way, several questions need to be considered. First, as the 40-hour threshold, until recently defined as the standard working week, is breached in an increasing number of countries, bringing the 35-hour week into sight, will the gain in leisure time involved inevitably be at the expense of the *quality* of leisure time? The problem that may arise here is that, although the amount of time available for leisure is increasing, the times of the day, night, week, and year at which leisure can be enjoyed, as well as the duration of discrete leisure periods, may become more closely tied to the demands of industrial production schedules and the exigencies of service provision. It cannot be assumed that as the amount of leisure time increases, the character of leisure time will remain unchanged. It is quite possible that, although more leisure is available to people, their freedom to enjoy leisure as they choose could decline; relatedly, leisure patterns now established could change considerably. Specious arguments that we are entering, or have entered, the "leisure society" fail to take account of such complexities of the changing political economy of leisure. A second question that arises in any social audit of the impact of increasing leisure is whether the benefits and costs associated with increased leisure are enjoyed and borne *by the same people.* Several national studies in this volume indicate that increased leisure and enhanced job security have been gained by young and prime-age workers in some countries as a consequence of early-retirement schemes. The other side of the coin in such schemes is that these gains have been made at the expense of older groups of workers, who sometimes have reluctantly faced premature exit from the labor market, with commensurate reductions in the income available to them during their retirement. More time off for many women could mean more time to take on family burdens. More leisure for workers in some industries may mean more extended and unsocial working hours for those who provide services. The national studies presented in the volume indicate that the availability of more leisure may have important distributive effects, and that it could alter the character of the leisure now enjoyed.

The Objectives of Recent Working-Time Campaigns

In the United Kingdom, France, West Germany, Belgium, and the Netherlands changes in working time over the past decade have their roots in trade union campaigns for work sharing. In all these countries the end of the long boom brought sharp and sustained rises in the level of unemployment. Endemic high unemployment in turn led to disillusionment with established policies for economic and labor-market stabilization. Unions despaired of neo-Keynesian macroeconomic policies, and their members began to experience a deep sense of foreboding that micro-electronic technology and computerized production systems could result in catastrophic unemployment. Against such a background, unions turned to reductions in working hours as a means of widening access to the labor market. The resulting work-sharing policy called on union members to show solidarity with the unemployed and to promote social justice. In this sense, work-sharing campaigns involved, as emphasized in the chapters by Hinrichs and Roche, a "class-oriented" strategy.

Trade-unionists were urged to view the interests of the unemployed as an interest encompassing the entire working class. Other aspects of work-sharing policies, such as attempts by unions in Britain to persuade their members to refuse to "sell jobs" in "natural wastage" and productivity agreements, envisaged jobs being "held in trust," so to speak, for people who had not yet even entered the labor market.

One of the main themes of the national studies of work-sharing policies and campaigns is the degree to which their original aims were displaced during the course of the campaigns. In nearly all the West European countries where the political economy of working time was initially dominated in recent years by the question of work sharing, the issues of working-time efficiency and flexibility are gaining growing prominence. In some countries, most notably France, Belgium, and the Netherlands, the promotion of efficiency-oriented flexibility has all but eclipsed the original concern of working-time campaigns with solidarity, redistribution, and social justice. The dynamics of "goal displacement" in the conflict over working time is a central theme of several national reports in this volume. In the Belgian case, De Rongé and Molitor show how such a shift in the focus of the political economy of working time came about as a result of employers' insistence that working-time flexibility was a prerequisite for reductions in working time. This response culminated in a new employer approach that argued that working-time flexibility itself was the best means of creating and safeguarding jobs, through the competitive advantage it conferred. Such a progression in policy and response was reflected and given an underpinning by government initiatives. Having started out from a position that supported the thrust of union work-sharing policies, the Belgian state has finally embraced in the "Hansenne experiments" an approach in which the promotion of flexibility has become a major concern of public policy. In the United Kingdom working-time flexibility first came to prominence during the 1960s as part of a general concern to rationalize work through "productivity bargaining." However, union demands for reduced working time appear to have led to a new level of employer interest in the opportunities provided by flexible working-time regimes for higher levels of capital utilization and more efficient service provision. The latter are now high on employers' agendas for further rounds of negotiations on reductions in normal working hours. Chris de Neubourg shows how there has been a virtual abandonment of the original work-sharing policy in the Netherlands since 1986 because of its perceived ineffectiveness in employment terms. Employees' impatience with the cuts in real living standards involved in the Dutch approach, as well as a more general employer offensive on labor-market flexibility, also contributed to the change of direction in that country. Working-time flexibility has again emerged as an alternative to work sharing. The initial support given to union demands for cuts in working time by the Dutch government mirrors the situation in France. Here legislative initiatives by the Mitterand government in the early 1980s in support of work-sharing have given way to the promotion of flexibility; the turn-about can again be accounted for in terms of the poor employment results of reductions in working time and the "inspection effect" induced by changes in working time and work practices after the spread of a 39-hour week after 1981.

The theoretical basis of employers' concern with flexible working-time schedules is considered in detail by Karl Hinrichs in the light of the West German experience. An historically unprecedented union offensive on working time breached the 40-hour barrier in 1985. The result was a series of agreements that permitted employers in some industries to diversify working-time schedules around a new flexible standard working week; the new flexibility gave employers scope to vary actual hours worked in any week; in the engineering (metals manufacturing) industry they were also permitted to offer working weeks of different lengths to different sections of the workforce. Pressure for further cuts in hours seem certain to provoke a renewed emphasis on flexibility by employers.

The new interest of employers and governments in efficiency-oriented flexible working time is paralleled by growing interest among employees in another kind of flexibility: more choice over starting and finishing times and greater ease in moving in and out of the labor market in accordance with family, career, and wider social interests. Inevitably, employees have been very interested in the manner in which any additional cuts in working time obtained take effect. In Sweden, France, Belgium, the Netherlands, and West Germany, differences of view concerning the way working time should be reduced became a major strategic problem for union campaigns—a theme to which we will return. In two of the countries, the United States and Sweden, greater flexibility for employees, or greater "time sovereignty," was from the start the main concern of recent working-time debates and campaigns. As Susan Christopherson shows, there has been little concern to reduce standard hours further in the United States or to institute work sharing. Among employees, concepts of "family-oriented" working-time flexibility, affecting in particular the role of women in the labor force and the home, have played a major part in the debate. Christopherson views the changing political economy of working time in the United States as a development that threatens to compound the disadvantage faced by women in the labor market. More women are responding to opportunities for part-time work, while at the same time they are faced with a growing burden of work within the family.

The hegemony—and, one should say, relative success—of the "active labor market policy" in Sweden has meant that unions there have shown little interest in work sharing as a means of reducing unemployment. Instead, as Weigelt emphasizes, employee-oriented working-time flexibility has dominated the debate, being portrayed as a means of "realigning" the highly directive and collectivist policies associated with the Swedish model of economic and labor-market management. The most radical proposal for a new working-time regime tailored to the increasingly diverse preferences of employees has come from the Swedish economist Gösta Rehn.

Rehn proposes a highly flexible and individual-focused working-time regime.[1] His central concept is that of an insurance-funded entitlement to time off over the working life. A certain portion of the income credited to the fund in the case of any individual would be restricted to financing that person's retirement. The remaining entitlement could be drawn upon at the individual's discretion for continuing education, sabbatical leave, or leisure. Given the growing diversity of individual preferences regarding the use and organization of leisure, Rehn believes that a statutory entitlement to leisure, funded from general insurance contributions, would be preferable to further uniform or standardized reductions in working time, which, of necessity, may impose unwanted leisure on individuals. Rehn also argued—perspicaciously, it has turned out, as his essay on the subject was written in 1974—that employers would increasingly come to favor nonstandard flexible working-time schedules in response to changing patterns of production and demand.[2] This being so, he urged, it was better for employees and their unions to meet changing employer strategies in a "positive spirit" than to resist them in what he believed would be a "mistaken defence of values which were the *raison d'etre* of more rigid regulations."[3]

The fate of the Rehn proposals in the Swedish debate on working-time flexibility is chronicled by Ulla Weigelt. She notes that both employers and employees have adopted a relatively conservative stance on working-time innovations in Sweden—this, in spite of Swedish innovations such as "parental leave." In certain respects, nevertheless, the "conservative" strategies adopted by Swedish unions are consistent with other aspects of the overall policy of "solidarism" and the promotion of greater equality, which have been the hallmarks of Swedish union policy since the 1930s. Thus, the strong support of Swedish women's unions for a standard reduction in working time to a 30-hour week, six-hour day is consistent with a policy of promoting equality between men and women. Flexible working-time options for working mothers and the growth of part-time work are viewed in this context as institutionalizing traditional gender roles, responsibilities, and inequalities. The Rehn proposals and their champions within the Swedish labor movement have been strongly criticized on this account. Notwithstanding the political cleavages that have developed in the Swedish debate, Weigelt shows how the concept of flexibility in the sense proposed by Rehn has been gaining ground in some of the major trade unions affiliated with the Swedish Trade Union Confederation (LO).

Christoph Deutschmann's examination of working time in Japan shows how working-time regimes in that country mirror other aspects of the Japanese model of production and industrial relations. A comparatively high level of annual and weekly working time reflects the weak boundary between work and leisure that characterizes Japanese employment. Through management-orchestrated peer-group pressure, male employees are prevailed upon not to take vacations and to accept endemic unscheduled overtime. Even the time nominally available for leisure is colonized by the corporation, especially in core sector firms. Male employees are expected to socialize with colleagues and bosses in order that the ethic of commitment that binds people together in their daily work is reinforced outside the sphere of work proper.

Explaining the Timing of Hours Rounds

The work-sharing campaigns mounted during the past ten to fifteen years in West European countries are historically unprecedented in that they have achieved reductions in working time in recessionary labor markets. Never before in the countries concerned have unions succeeded in reducing normal working hours in periods of labor-market slackness and relative union weakness. The reasons for the success of these recent campaigns bear examination in comparative context.

Historically, in times of economic and labor-market slackness, unions in a number of countries have mounted pressure to reduce standard working hours in order to promote work sharing. With the exception of France and the United States, where government support did have significant impact on employment, unions in various countries campaigned for work sharing during the 1930s, but to little effect. Given the balance of power in the labor markets during the Great Depression, this was hardly surprising. As theorists of working time like Manfred Bienefeld[4] and several empirical contributors to this volume suggest, employer resistance to reductions in standard working time is usually much greater than their resistance to increases in wages. Cuts in standard hours raise the prospect of significantly increased labor costs and consequently pose a threat to international and, perhaps, national competitiveness. Because in the past employers viewed the distribution of working time over the day and week as something unalterable, the scope available to them to absorb increased costs through productivity gains appeared narrow. As well as being costly, changes in working time have always been troublesome to implement. To cut time and maintain output, managements had to reorganize production, which often raised complex issues of production scheduling and ran the risk of provoking industrial disputes if the existing division of labor or the pace of work was changed to accommodate reductions in working time.

Given management's concern to avoid conceding reductions in hours, unions have had to be particularly determined for their demands to succeed. Historically, they had been at their most determined during periods when labor markets were particularly buoyant. The major breakthroughs on working time up to the mid-1970s had occurred in periods when unemployment was low, union membership was growing, and union density was high relative to its longer-term trend. In such periods unions were capable of mobilizing determined pressure behind demands for reductions in working time. Not only did unions have the capability to press for cuts in working time, they also found the motivation to do so in the conviction that continuing labor-market buoyancy depended on restricting the labor supply. These factors might influence events at times otherwise startlingly different in character, such as immediately after the world wars and during peacetime economic peaks.

Fears of a sharp rise in unemployment following military demobilization and the running down of wartime economies provoked working-time campaigns in a number of countries after both world wars. In the immediate aftermath of the wars unions were often strong, having benefited from the benign influence of government wartime support for organization and collective bargaining. These factors tilted the balance in favor of hours rounds in the United Kingdom, for example, after both world wars. Hours rounds were not, however, a universal feature of postwar economic and social reconstruction. As the chapters on individual nations show, the United States, Belgium, the Netherlands, Japan, France, Sweden, and Germany were not affected by hours reductions in the aftermath of World War II, though most of them had been after World War

I. In these countries unions gave priority to wage increases in the late 1940s and early 1950s; in countries devastated by war unions had either been grossly weakened or outlawed altogether, and the pressing task, as they began to reform, was industrial and economic reconstruction. War casualties and the plummeting wartime birth rate often led to labor shortages, with the result that expanding the labor supply became a priority.

If union strength, combined with the prospect of a sharp rise in unemployment and the contrasting wartime experiences of different countries, provides an explanation for the occurrence of postwar hours rounds, labor-market trends and contrasting cultural and institutional traditions account for the occurrence of "peacetime" hours rounds in Western industrial nations and Japan during the long postwar boom.

The period from the end of World War II to the late 1960s or early 1970s was a time of unrivaled trade union growth in most of the West European democracies. The attainment of full employment and sustained economic growth provided a favorable context for the spread of unionization to sectors up to then characterized by weak organization. Growing union strength and security went hand in hand with the "maturation" of institutions of collective bargaining. In some countries unions or their members won new legislative rights to participate in management decision making on work organization and business policy. In circumstances of growing labor-market tightness and legislative liberalization, union leaders again gained the capacity to mobilize strong collective pressure behind their demands. This was evident, for example, in the progressively unrestrained fashion in which they pressed for wage rises in a number of countries. The motivation for a shift of bargaining priority from wage rises to reductions in normal hours in a period of prosperity is largely explained in terms of growing fear that the rapidly rising productivity and accelerating automation would permanently push up unemployment unless the supply of labor was reduced. Fear of an imminent sharp rise in unemployment coexisted with a more positive sense of material well-being that resulted from a sustained improvement in real living standards. Having experienced progressive gains in real wages, employees became more inclined to seek more leisure once they had been convinced of the threat of unemployment.

Conditions of business buoyancy during the 1950s and 1960s may also have eroded employers' resistance to demands for reductions in normal working hours.[5] The growth of mass markets for consumer products and confidence that cost rises resulting from cuts in working time could be passed on to the consumer, without a significant decline in competitiveness, made business more amenable to calls for the 40-hour week.

This is at best a partial explanation for the hours rounds that occurred during the long boom in western Europe. The economic and labor-market conditions that prevailed in the United States and Japan during the 1950s and 1960s resembled those in the countries of Western Europe. Yet no hours rounds occurred in the United States, and developments in Japan were quite distinctive. Some activity occurred immediately after the war in the hours campaign of the defeated Japanese militant workers' movement, but working-time reductions began to take widespread effect only in the mid- to late 1960s; and after the first oil crisis, working hours again increased. In neither country has there been any earnest bargaining pressure in recent years to cut working hours.

The main reason for the contrasting postwar experiences of the countries of Western Europe on the one hand, and the United States and Japan on the other, may be found in the cultural and sociopolitical nexus in which labor markets and interest organizations are embedded in these countries. As Christopherson points out, one reason American employees have enjoyed the fruits of growing labor productivity since World War II exclusively in the form of higher wages may be the relatively low density of unionization and highly uneven penetration of collective bargaining in the United States. A low level of trade union density—itself a reflection, in part, of a relatively high level of employer opposition to unionization—meant that unions had limited scope for influencing or aggregating employees' preferences for work or leisure. Highly uneven union density and collective-bargaining penetration made concerted pressure difficult to orchestrate. The political weakness of organized labor in the United States compounded the effects of its industrial weakness. Labor's political impotence meant that legislation could not be used as a substitute for collective bargaining, or as a "conveyor belt" for generalizing local breakthroughs on working time. In addition, as Benjamin Hunnicutt has argued, the triumph and institutionalization of the "new gospel of consumption" privileged wage increases over the demand for leisure.[6]

That collective bargaining structure and organization may impede generalized hours reductions is also stressed by Deutschmann in the case of Japan. Japanese collective bargaining is concentrated at the firm level. In the absence of industry-level bargaining structures, there is no tendency for breakthroughs reached in any particular firm to spill over to other firms or industries through bargaining channels. Under centralized bargaining structures working hours, like wage levels, are "taken out of competition" through standardization. In Japan, given the absence of collective-bargaining structures at the industry level or above, competition in the product market may result in some employers' increasing working hours to remain competitive.

Deutschmann also points to the role of Japanese social structure and the Japanese employment system in accounting for the "deviation" of Japan from trends in Western industrial nations. The slow and modest decline in annual working hours during the postwar long boom is attributed to low real wage levels in Japan during the 1950s and 1960s. The effect of low real living standards was compounded by the assimilation into the Japanese industrial workforce of large numbers of workers from a rural background accustomed to working long hours. Deutschmann suggests that the primary force responsible for bringing about the reductions in working hours may have been employer concern to rationalize production, curb absenteeism, and compete for scarce educated labor. Employer opposition to further reductions in working time in Japan is particularly strong, he suggests, because a weak boundary between work and leisure, implying only a nominal understanding of "standard working time," is one of the cornerstones of the "Japanese model" of employment and industrial relations. As regards employees' interest or lack of interest in more leisure, Deutschmann points to the significance of a relatively low level of public spending on education, retirement pensions, and other social benefits in continuing to predispose many toward improving their real income.

If socioeconomic and sociopolitical circumstances help explain the contrasting historical records of industrial nations on working time, we must still find an explanation for the recent occurrence of hours rounds in a number of West European countries. The problem here, of course, is that these rounds are the first recorded in a period of deep labor-market slackness and economic recession. Of the factors that have influenced hours rounds in the past, unemployment has clearly had a decisive impact on recent developments. Its impact is evident in union calls for work sharing as a means of combating mass joblessness. This time it has been the actuality more than the threat of unemployment that has led to a shift of bargaining priority in industrial relations from wages to hours. At the same time, the micro-electronics revolution has also given rise to fears that current levels of unemployment presage catastrophic or endemically high levels of unemployment rooted in labor displacement. The rising female activity rate documented in a number of chapters herein also appears to imply that labor supply might continue to increase in the face of a decline or stagnation in labor demand. There were grounds, then, over the past decade and a half for strong "negatively motivated" concern with reducing working time.

This concern has proved to be of sufficient force to countervail both union weakness in collective bargaining and the less than enthusiastic concern of employees to increase their time for leisure. Though it is incontrovertably true that unions in the West European nations covered herein—Belgium and Sweden excepted—have experienced a serious decline in membership and labor-market power since the mid- to late 1970s, it has also to be recognized that union power has become less directly dependent on membership and labor-market trends alone since World War II. The maturation of collective bargaining and representative structures at workplace level, and the enactment in some countries of legislation favorable to union organization or enshrining new rights to employment security in the legal code, have rendered union power less dependent on the business cycle or the prevailing level of unemployment.

During the second half of the 1970s and in the 1980s, periods of real wage decline were experienced in most West European countries—sometimes, indeed, as in the case of the Netherlands, this was a direct result of provisions for working-time reduction. Nonetheless, the secular trend in real living standards has been upward. The fact that working-class living standards have risen, albeit not progressively, has meant that unions have not faced the task of having to transform bargaining priorities radically, from the restoration of falling real wages to a push for additional leisure. The task, rather, has been to influence priorities as between higher real wages and more leisure.

Thus, even in a recession, unions have proved capable of mobilizing their members forcefully behind demands for reductions in working time. In the labor-market crisis of the 1930s union power and organization declined commensurately with union membership; those members who remained in employment were both relatively poorly organized and less secure than union members today. In the interwar recession, deflation and falling output, combined with mass unemployment, led to downward pressure on money and real wage levels, with the result that those who had jobs were forced to concentrate on defending existing wage levels. In such conditions union members who had escaped unemployment were an unlikely spearhead for a work-sharing campaign requiring determined pressure on employers to reduce normal hours.

Recent hours rounds are also unprecedented in another important respect: they are the first to provoke a radical response from employers to the management of working time. In the past some instances of innovation have been apparent in employers' responses to cuts in normal working hours. Roche, for example, cites cases of working-time innovation in the wake of the 1959–66 hours round in the United Kingdom. However, by and large working-time regimes in the past were viewed by employers as immutable. Why, however, should a new response have been forthcoming in recent working-time rounds? The scale of recent cuts in hours can hardly explain the new employer response. In general, the sizes of the cuts achieved have been modest, and there has been much use of phasing or gradual adjustment. If we take the United Kingdom as an illustration, since 1979 standard weekly working hours have been cut by one hour from a forty-hour standard—a cut of 2.5 percent. This compares with a reduction during the period 1959 to 1966 of four hours from a 44-hour standard—a cut of 9.1 percent. So the level and pace of the recent reductions have not of themselves provoked employer innovation. The platform from which the cuts have been made recently has been a more significant influence. As standard hours have declined, the scope available for improving productivity simply by reducing hours has declined commensurately or, in all probability, more than commensurately. Perhaps the achievement of the 40-hour standard has meant that little scope now remains for improving productivity by reducing fatigue and idle time through further cuts in normal hours. It may appear to employers that they must now adopt a proactive response to working-time management in order to offset the cost of working-time reductions.

Other factors may also have predisposed employers to rationalize working-time management. The saturation of mass markets for many standardized consumer products has led to a new vogue in "niche marketing" and product customization. Changing product policies usually involve a reassessment of existing production schedules and organization. Again, this may have influenced the management of working time, particularly as such changes in marketing and product strategy have been occurring at the same as union challenges to existing hours standards. Growing international competition has exerted further pressure on labor costs and productivity, adding to the impetus for greater flexibility in working-time management. Imitation and the transfer within and between national boundaries of technological skill and management education have also played a role in the spread of flexible working-time regimes. Of particular note in this regard is the resurgence of interest in production and manufacturing management in Western business schools and their role in popularizing Japanese styles of flexible management.

The Employment Record of Recent Hours Reductions

The contributions to this volume reflect general pessimism regarding the employment effects of reductions in working time over the past decade and a half. It has to be emphasized that estimates of the employment effects of reductions in working time are inherently problematic. This being the case, there is scope for a high degree of partisan bias in debates on the employment-effectiveness of work-sharing strategies. In all countries unions claim more ambitious targets and achievements for work-sharing campaigns than do either employers or governments. So, in assessing the employment record of work-sharing campaigns, we are inevitably dealing with the perceived or adjudged success of working-time reductions rather than with any demonstrable record that all the parties affected accept. Notwithstanding this caveat, it seems that the results of working time reductions have been disappointing for unions in all the countries in which they have occurred.

That such an outcome was inevitable had, of course, been a major strategic claim of employers wherever work-sharing campaigns were mounted. Faced with persistent claims of this kind from a party that, on the face of it, could exert control over the outcome of hours rounds, unions faced a credibility problem in their attempts to mobilize support behind demands for reduced working hours. Inherent in the problem of credibility, and central to the counterposition of employers, was the risk that hours reductions might damage competitiveness and employment by pushing up labor costs to unsustainable levels. The seriousness of the credibility problem increased where the levels of reductions sought by unions were higher. Sizable reductions in working time—under certain conditions—seemed to carry the highest potential for employment creation; at the same time they also carried the highest risk of cost dislocation and loss of competitiveness. Small reductions, implemented on a phased basis, were easier to absorb through productivity measures and were less risky, but they also had limited job creation potential. Not surprisingly, employers concentrated their resistance on demands for sizable reductions in working time. In all countries where hours rounds occurred, working-time reductions turned out to be modest when they were eventually achieved, and they were implemented on a phased basis.

But the credibility problem was only one reason why the employment effects of hours rounds were disappointing for unions. In addition to bearing the costs involved in strikes over working time—in those countries, that is, where major conflicts ensued—and foregoing wage rises or even accepting reductions in real pay, participants in work-sharing campaigns faced additional costs in pursuing union objectives. As employers were resolved to neutralize the effects of reduced hours on costs and output through productivity improvements linked with more efficient time management, those determined to abide by their unions' injunctions that lost time should be "blocked up" into new jobs faced the prospect of a second round of conflict over working time. As it was, the productivity measures sought by employers sometimes led to strikes in defense of existing work practices and working-time arrangements. These strikes could be bitter and protracted, as in the case of the exotic-sounding "flexible rostering" dispute in British Rail and the "washing-up time" dispute in British Leyland in the early 1980s. In the end, unions and shop stewards or works councilors became preoccupied in virtually all the countries involved with problems of transition to the new flexible working-time regimes advocated by employers. The initial concern to use working-time reductions as a means of forcing additional recruitment on employers practically disappeared from the negotiating agenda.

As it became clear that employers sought to diversify working-time regimes radically, unions themselves faced a further strategic problem that had not been anticipated at the outset of working-time campaigns. This problem emerges most clearly in the chapters on West Germany, France, and Belgium—countries where employer initiatives went furthest in challenging established working-time regimes. The prospect of growing diversity in working-time schedules and regimes poses a long-term threat to unions' capacity to represent members effectively. The risk is that it might progressively erode and then undermine the practice of standardizing wages and conditions, which, since the emergence of collective bargaining, has been the cornerstone of union policies. If employers become free to offer different working weeks to employees, possibly at different hourly rates, unions face the prospect of competition in the labor market over wages *and* hours. Existing differences between occupational categories in rates and conditions may become compounded by differences within categories linked with the length and location of the time worked. Standardizing rates is made more difficult when the length of the working week "reenters competition."

The mobilization problem faced by unions in promoting work sharing was rendered more serious still by the fact that those who stood to bear the heaviest costs and the highest risks associated with hours rounds also typically stood to gain least from the attainment of their employment targets. The employment effects of working-time rounds were to be of direct benefit to the unemployed. On the other hand, the costs of striking, or of holding out for job creation in the wake of reductions in hours, had to be borne by those at work—many of whom enjoyed a relatively high degree of job security. All in all, given the way in which the costs and benefits of hours rounds were distributed, the advantage enjoyed by employers in controlling levels of employment, the counteroffensive of employers on flexibility, and the strategic paralysis of unions in the face of growing diversity in working-time patterns, it is not surprising that the impact of working-time reductions on employment has been judged disappointing, even by supporters of work-sharing campaigns.

The Emergence of Pluralistic Time Preferences

Of the problems unions have faced in mobilizing their members behind demands for work sharing, those arising from the asymmetrical distribution of the costs and benefits of union policies have been considered. Other mobilization problems have arisen because of the differences that exist in the preferences of union members concerning the manner in which cuts in working hours should be taken. It is apparent from the chapters herein that working-time preferences have become more diverse. It is also clear that differences in the preferences of employees are socially patterned and reflect the wider structure of workforce stratification.

This fact emerges, for example, in Weigelt's examination of the debate in Sweden between the leading womens' unions and other sections of the labor movement on the respective merits of the six-hour day and the Rehn program as strategic objectives for the Swedish campaign to reduce working time. In most countries men have preferred to take cuts in hours in one block, on one day of the week (usually Fridays), or have supported variants of this "blocked" approach such as the "nine-day fortnight." Women, on the other hand, tend to prefer earlier daily finishing times, which allow them better to combine work with family responsibilities. More generally, as emerges in particular from the West German experience, early-retirement policies tend to be viewed more favorably by younger workers than by the older workers directly affected by their implementation. For the young, such policies increase job security at zero cost, whereas for the old they may mean premature retirement on a lower pension than anticipated. Part-time options are welcomed by growing numbers of people prepared, or constrained, to enter the labor market for less time than a full working week. Full-time workers and unions seldom welcome the growth of part-time work because of the threat it poses to the rates and conditions of full-time workers.

When working hours were longer, such pluralistic preferences were submerged by a common concern to increase time off from work. All could benefit readily by being released from levels of working time that left little room for rest or leisure. When leisure time was very limited, the task of increasing the *quantity* of leisure assumed major importance for those at work and their unions. When, as now, considerable leisure time is already available, the quality of further leisure becomes important and, in particular, the manner in which it can be scheduled if it is to be enjoyed. Such alternatives as longer holidays, later starting times, earlier finishing times, one short afternoon, a nine-day fortnight and the like become subjects of debate. When this occurs, workforce stratification begins to impinge on leisure preferences and on the strategic targets and capabilities of unions.

But it is not just a matter of having reached such a level that concern with the quality of leisure now polarizes objectives for reductions in working time. Conflicting preferences could arise in the past, as in the case of the differences between men and women in Belgium over the five-day week in 1955, reported by Molitor and De Rongé. In terms of leisure preferences, workforces have also become more stratified over the postwar period in response to changes in the labor market. As more women have entered the workforces of Western industrial nations and part-time working has risen, working-time preferences have diversified. Channels of entry into the labor market have also diversified in response to developments in education. The same holds for channels of exit from the labor market, which have been affected by firm-specific early- and phased-retirement policies and government early-retirement initiatives.

The working-time preferences of people of similar ages have diversified considerably in response to such structural changes. Greater opportunities for continuing education and greater scope for enjoying leisure—in short and long vacations—also focus people's attention on qualitative aspects of leisure. At a more general level still, the diversification of preferences is spurred by a series of sociological and sociocultural changes that have led to increased concern with "life planning." Most significant here has been the breakdown of traditional working-class communities with their strong emphasis on uniformity, as well as the growing incidence of white-collar and technical occupations in the workforces of advanced industrial nations. The significance of structural change and the broader pattern of sociocultural change for the political economy of working time are considered in virtually all the chapters. Growing diversity in employees' working-time and leisure-time preferences represents a *secular trend* in people's views on time. This raises the question of whether any other secular trends, or any cyclical trends, are apparent in the way employees view leisure.

Other Secular and Cyclical Changes in
Working-Time Preferences

There is no evidence in the chapters on individual nations of any clear and strong secular trend for employees to attribute greater priority to leisure at the margin as their real income has risen. Data on income elasticities of leisure presented by Roche in the case of the United Kingdom and Hinrichs in the case of West Germany show no evidence of any such trend. Nor is any appreciation in the social value of leisure apparent in reports on long-run trends in other countries. The "stickiness" of the annual hours of full-time workers in the United States and Japan is enough to discredit a "value-change" thesis in these conditions. Such a thesis is also rejected explicitly by De Rongé and Molitor in the case of Belgium and by de Neubourg in the case of the Netherlands.

People have indeed taken more leisure historically as their real income has risen, and they now enjoy a great deal more leisure time than their forebears at the start of the century. But this does not mean that they now attribute greater value to leisure than they did in the past, or that the value of leisure has progressively risen. A definitive quantitative analysis of the relative value at the margin of income and leisure is unobtainable because of the lack of comparative time series on hours worked and the poor state of our knowledge of general determinants of annual hours worked, as well as of the precise ways in which they influence changes in working time. On the other hand, the relative decline that has occurred in the cost of enjoying leisure time makes even more interesting the lack of any evidence of an increase in the relative value of leisure to employees.

The importance of this conclusion in sociological terms is that it goes against the grain of the influential literature on the demise of the work ethic and "bourgeois man," considered in Roche's chapter. Moreover, it warrants skepticism regarding the supposed emergence of "postmaterialist" values. Continuing this theme, Roche suggests that much of the initiative for employee-oriented flexible working-time arrangements in Britain during the 1960s and 1970s can be traced to employer strategies of recruitment and to the development of internal labor markets. Discounting the role played by supposed changes in values in the political economy of working time, Roche suggests that in the United Kingdom structural change and cyclical perturbation have been the major factors influencing the evolution of working time during the twentieth century. The U.K. experience aside, no general imperative for more leisure at the expense of more income can be identified in the countries covered herein.

If no secular or long-term trend toward an appreciation in the value of leisure can be identified, it remains to be asked whether trends in wages have affected leisure preferences in a *cyclical* manner. In a book published in 1972,

Manfred Bienefeld argued that hours rounds in the United Kingdom in the nineteenth and twentieth centuries had been critically influenced by above-trend rises in money wages.[7] Sharp rises in wages, Bienefeld argued, disrupted the normal tendency for employees to become accustomed quickly to higher living standards once they have been attained. When people have experienced sharp rises in pay, they have for a time become predisposed instead to seeking more leisure. Roche disputes the validity of the Bienefeld thesis in the British case and finds no evidence in that country of a cyclical "income effect" on employees' demand for leisure. The most that can be said about the relevance of rising wages, he concludes, is that rising real pay may be a prerequisite for the launching of earnest union campaigns for reductions in normal working hours. This conclusion seems consistent with developments in West Germany and Sweden, as reported by Hinrichs and Weigelt and in Japan, as reported by Deutschmann. No evidence for a cyclical "income effect" is presented either in the other chapters, though they do not examine this issue in any detail.

This conclusion leaves us, however, with something of a puzzle. In the countries in which they have occurred, hours campaigns immediately after the world wars emphasized the negative consequences of unchecked trends in labor supply and demand for unemployment. The issue of leisure hardly figured in union campaigns in such circumstances. The same cannot be said, however, of the rounds that occurred during the long boom in Western Europe and Japan. In these peacetime hours rounds the desirability of more leisure figured more prominently in union campaigns, though, as we have seen, the threat of rising unemployment was also emphasized in some countries at least. In what way, then, may the desire for more leisure be said to have influenced peacetime hours rounds, if not through a cyclical "income effect" on employees' preferences as between income and leisure?

Both Manfred Bienefeld and the Austrian economist Kurt Rothschild have advanced the plausible hypothesis that employees' interest in additional leisure is noncumulative. When leisure is foregone in favor of more pay, people do not thereby experience a stronger preference for leisure when next they consider how to improve their returns from work. Leisure foregone is leisure forgotten: having gone without more leisure in favor of more income, people become accustomed to their new standard of living and show the same concern as before to improve it further. The marginal value of leisure to them thus usually remains unchanged as their income rises. Rothschild's formulation of the same essential position also points toward the possibility of an "endogenous" change in preferences that may in fact *reduce* the marginal value of leisure to employees, as leisure is foregone. As employees forego more leisure—even in circumstances where they would have preferred leisure over more income but could not obtain it—they may spend more on goods and services that are "time efficient" rather than time intensive. As they grow accustomed to such goods and services, their desire for leisure may decline as compared with their initial position.[8] This indeed seems plausible as far as it goes. It implies that the desire for more leisure expressed in hours campaigns in a number of countries cannot be understood in terms of a gradual buildup of people's interest in leisure over the long periods of time during which leisure was, in fact, foregone by them in favor of income.

If we are to avoid the intellectually unsatisfying course of having to presume that periodic rises in employees' apparent interest in leisure are episodic and without social roots, two possibilities present themselves. First, the expressed desire for leisure in working-time campaigns may be little more than a subsidiary concern: a demand taken up to put a positive gloss on an otherwise largely negatively motivated concern to reduce working time. This may be an accurate enough representation of the role of leisure in recent recessionary hours rounds. Yet it hardly squares with the circumstances of peacetime rounds in a number of countries. During the long boom negative factors were weak and probably insufficient of themselves to trigger earnest demands for reduced working time. This conclusion opens up the second possibility of accounting for the place of leisure in hours rounds. The Bienefeld-Rothschild thesis neglects the role that unions may play in altering or intensifying preferences. There is no reason to suppose that unions may not be capable even of retrospectively rendering the demand for leisure cumulative by highlighting for employees the degree to which they have chosen to forego more leisure in favor of wage improvements. As all the chapters herein make clear, reductions in working hours do not "just happen" spontaneously. They occur after prolonged union campaigns in which the issues of pay and leisure and the tradeoff between them are intensely debated. Preferences past and present come into the spotlight in these campaigns; and the present import of past choices—for example, choices that may have involved a preference for more pay over more leisure—is discussed and debated. It is in this aspect of the political economy of working time, neglected in the theories of Bienefeld and Rothschild, that we perhaps find the solution to the problem of how leisure has affected the dynamics of working-time campaigns, particularly those launched during the long boom of postwar capitalism. The implication remains that irrespective of prevailing economic and social conditions, the roots of working-time campaigns during the twentieth century have primarily been negative: fear of unemployment and of what are believed to be the employment implications of momentous technological change or labor-market perturbation.

States and the "Deregulation" of Working Time

With the exception of the area of retirement pensions where states—at least in the West—continue to exercise a regulatory role, the main tendency in recent years has been for governments to "deregulate" working time. This is apparent in Belgium in the Hansenne experiments, outlined by De

Rongé and Molitor, and in the erosion of legislative controls on the employment of women during unsocial hours in the United Kingdom. More generally,
deregulation is evident in the recent support given to flexible working-time
regimes by governments in a number of countries. In Belgium, France, and the
Netherlands the new emphasis on efficiency-oriented flexibility and deregulation represents a sharp change of direction in state policy. During the 1970s
governments in these countries had sought to promote standardized reductions
in working time linked with job creation. In Britain the erosion of working-time
regulations set down in legislation is consistent with the neoliberal approach
evident in the overall strategy of Thatcher governments since 1979. In the
United States and Japan governments have historically stood further back from
employment regulation than in Western Europe.

In Japan the overall corpus of government policy has served to underwrite
a relatively high level of flexibility in working-time regimes by making leisure
expensive, both in itself and in terms of its opportunity cost in income foregone. It is because of relatively low levels of public social service provision
and a low level of public investment in leisure facilities in Japan that leisure
remains expensive and weakly delineated from work. The same broad thrust in
public and social policy in the United States has given rise to what Christopherson portrays as a "family-oriented" politics of working time. Low and declining
levels of state provision for the care of the old and young alike throws much of
the burden of looking after them onto women, at a time when increasing numbers of women are opting to work. As a result, the American debate had emphasized making working time more flexible so as to enable working women
and men to meet better their commitments in both career and family.

Only in Sweden, in the Rehn proposals, do we find the idea of employee-
oriented flexibility or "time sovereignty" being forged in terms that envisage
new legislative rights for the citizen. In other countries the dominant trend in
state policies is to weaken citizenship rights to safeguards in respect of when
work can be conducted, for how long, and by whom. In other words, the broad
thrust in state policies is to return working time to the market, where it can be
"recommodified" into a good that people are free to buy, sell, or dispense with
as they choose with little legal constraint.

The Demise of Standard Working Time

The idea that we may be witnessing the beginning of the end of
standardized working-time arrangements is the leitmotiv of the contributions to
the volume. In the future standard and inflexible working hours may come to
be viewed as a feature of a period of labor and industrial history in which
employment was successfully regulated by unions representing primarily male,
skilled, and semiskilled full-time workers employed predominantly in manufacturing. As Christopherson brings out with particular sharpness, the origins of

standardized working time are to be found in highly unionized industrial working-class communities. (In the case of the United States these communities were reinforced by ethnic identity.) If the standardized and inflexible working-time regimes now under threat originated in such a sociopolitical milieu, aspects of them were nonetheless easily incorporated into the work culture of middle-class white-collar workers as they in turn became more extensively unionized. Thus, in the final chapter Sirianni discusses growing criticism of the "male career model," characterized by a view of work as properly involving continuous and uninterrupted career progression along a linear time line. The male career model, like the model of standard working time that involved manual workers, is imperious in subordinating family life and other pursuits to the dictates of work and career. It differs from the "manual worker model" of working time, perhaps, in terms of the expectation held by employers, and accepted by employees, that advancement through corporate and professional hierarchies could be gained only on the basis of a willingness to devote time surpluses to one's career. As more part-time workers have entered the labor force and channels of labor-market entry and exit have diversified, working-time preferences have become more pluralistic, putting strain on the manual worker model and male career model of standard working time. These trends have been reinforced by the changing industrial composition of workforces and trade union memberships. The dominance of manufacturing has declined in favor of service employment and occupations; in these sectors employees are more accustomed to what in other sectors have been viewed as unorthodox working-time regimes.

As discussed earlier, the long-run decrease in working hours has also had an important effect on pressure for standardization and pressure for diversification. As Hinrichs argues, the first motive for working-time regulation historically was the need to ensure that the length of time worked was not so onerous as to damage people's health and general physical well-being. Later, employees sought further reductions to enjoy leisure. When the length of time worked was so high as to threaten health and to leave no time for leisure, standard reductions, and, relatedly, generalized standards of the length of the working day and week were easily agreed among employees. When both objectives were attained, the quality as well as the quantity of leisure time became more salient, and on this it is intrinsically more difficult to gain agreement. As employees have become more concerned about how to *integrate* their working time with their interests and priorities outside work, standard reductions and a generalized standard working-time regime have come under threat.

The success attained by unions in reducing working time has also stimulated the development and spread of shift systems and irregular work patterns, which further diversify working time in all sectors. As people gain more leisure, more money is spent on services that require other people to work during periods that had traditionally been regarded as the preserve of leisure.

It can be presumed, in the imagery used by Hinrichs, that employers have always desired flexible working hours as part of their concern to "make labor power as available as electricity by a switch or water from a tap." In recent years, however, market forces have compelled employers more strongly than in the past to realize such an objective. The growth of services, more prone than manufacturing to variable demand and possessing little scope for stocking or inventory maintenance, has given rise to structural pressure on standard working time. Growing capital intensity and growing international competition throw the economics of capital utilization and control of labor costs into sharp relief, putting the continued existence of standard working-time regimes on the agendas of employers and their federations.

As the chapters on individual nations show, these trends and developments have led to growing diversity in working-time regimes within countries. The evidence in the volume indicates that the standard working week is coming under attack in virtually all countries in which it has been firmly established. The attack is being conducted simultaneously on two fronts: by employees trying to increase their "time sovereignty" and by employers attempting to increase flexibility for reasons of efficiency. Unions by and large remain defenders of the old order—an order in which they came to prominence and from which they will find it difficult to disentangle themselves.

As Hinrichs suggests, through progressive differentiation of working-time regimes, existing working-time standards may lose their *social validity* as measures for organizing time. The idea that work should be performed during the day, leaving the evening for leisure and family responsibilities and the weekend for extended rest may be supplanted in the future by other models for the social organization of time. Irrespective of the pace at which this may occur, fixed standards, which permit little or no deviation from a five-day working week and which involve inflexible working days of equal length, seem set to disappear sooner rather than later.

As Hinrichs emphasizes, the role of standard working time in improving the position of working-class people should not be lost sight of. Strongly institutionalized standards of normal working time reduced competition between employees seeking jobs and provided unions with a lever for restricting labor supply. Normal hours standards precluded the possibility that employers might lengthen working time in response to increases in wage rates. The concept of a normal workweek also instituted the norm of a basic rate. Finally, the existence of standardization ensured that a well-defined boundary existed between employers' time and workers' time, preventing work from intruding into the sphere of leisure—in any event, without employees being compensated at premium rates.

As standard working time is eroded, these achievements come under threat. The dilemma facing unions, as discussed in a number of chapters, is how to retain the benefits of standardization while accommodating employees' concern for greater "time sovereignty" and employers' demands for more flexibility. The constraints they face as they address this dilemma are analyzed herein. The social and political implications of the manner in which the dilemma is resolved are also considered, particularly in Sirianni's theoretical contribution. This closing chapter poses the question of a democratic politics of time in terms of a basic shift in our conceptions of justice entailed by the diversification of ways in which work and other activities can be temporally organized, and it explores the institutional and cultural bases for a new economy of time based on democratic, feminist, and ecological values. Perhaps, as Michael Young has recently argued, "a new approach to time could be the key to a new enlightenment."[9] In any case, it is clear that a watershed has been reached in the history of working time in capitalist industrial nations, and that alternative approaches are on the agenda.

Notes

1. Gösta Rehn, "Towards a Society of Free Choice," in Jerzy Wiatr and Richard Rose, eds., *Comparing Public Policies* (Wroclaw et al.: Zaklad Narodowy imienia Ossolinskich/Wydawnictwo Polskiej Akademii Nauk, 1977), 121–157.

2. Ibid., 131–135.

3. Ibid., 135.

4. Manfred Bienefeld, *Working Hours in British Industry* (London: Weidenfeld and Nicolson, 1972).

5. Ibid., chap. 6.

6. Benjamin Kline Hunnicutt, *Work Without End* (Philadelphia: Temple University Press, 1988).

7. Bienefeld, *Working Hours*, chap. 6.

8. Kurt W. Rothschild, "A Note on Some Economic and Welfare Aspects of Working-Time Regulations," *Australian Economic Papers*, 21 (1982): 214–218.

9. Michael Young, *The Chronometric Society* (Cambridge: Harvard University Press, 1988), 261.

2 Working-Time Development in West Germany: Departure to a New Stage

Karl Hinrichs

Beginning in the late 1970s working hours became a prominent issue at all levels of industrial relations in almost every West European country. The reappearance of this topic on the agenda was triggered by unions' demanding reduced working hours to redistribute scarce employment opportunities when unemployment figures were rising. But, whereas the movement toward a shorter working week is proceeding very slowly in some countries (e.g., Italy, Denmark, Austria) or has already come to a halt in others, once the 40-hour threshold had been breached (e.g., France, Belgium, Netherlands), the West German metal union spearheaded a second step, to reach the 35-hour week in the spring of 1987. The collective agreement to implement the 37.5-hour week in April 1988 and a further reduction of half an hour one year later was brought about much more easily (i.e., solely by negotiations) because the major breakthrough was won in 1984 after a labor dispute unparalleled in the history of the Federal Republic.

That breakthrough in the reduction of working hours represents a novelty in three respects: (1) For the first time in their history the unions attained a working-time reduction solely by means of their own power when the labor market was actually in a crisis. Moreover, they successfully fought for full wage compensation. (2) Also for the first time, the employers not only tried to defend the status quo but brought their own substantial demands for reorganizing the working time into the bargaining process. The recognition of these counterdemands by the unions finally made a compromise possible. (3) The compromise itself represents the third novelty, since in exchange for abolishing the 40-hour week by collective agreement, it was allowed to perforate the system of standardized working hours and to depart from fixed regulations to allo-

This article is based on the results of an extensive research project (director: Professor Dr. Claus Offe) that was funded by the Stiftung Volkswagenwerk. Revised versions of the final reports are published: see H. Wiesenthal, *Strategie und Illusion: Rationalitätsgrenzen kollektiver Akteure am Beispiel der Arbeitszeitpolitik 1980–1985* (Frankfurt and New York: Campus, 1987); K. Hinrichs, *Motive und Interessen im Arbeitszeitkonflikt. Eine Analyse der Entwicklung von Normalarbeitszeitstandards* (Frankfurt and New York: Campus, 1988).

cate working hours. This means that the unions themselves called into question a major achievement of collective bargaining and that to some extent, but irreversibly, a new working-time regime has been established.

Actually, we can ascertain a fourth novelty: The obtained reduction of weekly working hours does not meet the preferences of the majority of the employees, and this is not the result of the timing of the hours round. This observation and the fact that the employers themselves actively demanded alterations in the structure of working hours lead to my main thesis: Because of its previous success, the traditional working-time policy has run up against emerging boundaries, and the developments of working time will proceed on "new rails." Thus, the 1984 collectively agreed alterations of working hours have to be interpreted as a *break in continuity*.

To substantiate this thesis I first analyze two aspects of the development of working hours since the early 1950s: the *chronometrical* (length of working time) and *chronological* (location and distribution of working hours). Then I demonstrate the altered interests of employers in the formation of working hours and the rise of a new motive on part of the employees that constitutes a highly diversified pattern of their working-time preferences. These interests and preferences were crucial for the course and outcome of the conflict on the 35-hour week issue beginning in the early 1980s, which I deal with next. The departure from the system of standardized working hours agreed upon in 1984 represents the starting point for the final section, where I model two alternative scenarios on the future development of working time.

The Development of Working Hours after World War II

The Introduction of the 40-Hour Week

Between 1918 and 1955 there was almost a standstill in the length of normal working time. As in most other countries, in Germany the 48-hour week was won during the upheaval immediately following the end of World War I. Actually, it came into effect by a (temporary) law enacted in the course of demobilization. This rigid and uniform legislation provoked employers' opposition from the beginning. During the inflationary crisis in 1923 the weakened unions had to accept a liberalization, amounting primarily to more latitude to require overtime.[1] After the Great Depression had set in, unions' attempts to introduce the 40-hour week with full wage compensation as a measure of employment policy failed. The employers demonstrated stiff resistance, and the majority of those workers still employed was unwilling to support a measure that did not guarantee success or at least relief. Their unwillingness was reinforced by income losses they already experienced as a result of short-time working hours and reductions of hourly wages.

After 1933 average working hours rose again, and in 1938 the Nazi government changed regulations enacted on the advent of the Great Depression into a working-time law (*Arbeitszeitordnung*). This law, which set eight hours per day and 48 hours per week as normal working time, is still valid in 1990. In 1950 actual working hours came close to these legal requirements. With the onset of the "economic miracle," average weekly working hours surpassed the 48-hour threshold because of an enormous increase of overtime work. The economic miracle meant an explosion of GNP (55 percent between 1950 and 1955 in real terms) and a rapid rise of wages and salaries. Real weekly earnings of workers in manufacturing grew by 31 percent (1950–1955). These vast distributional resources offered the unions a chance to start again a campaign to attain the 40-hour week. All unions organized within the Deutscher Gewerkschaftsbund (DGB) decided to give this goal top priority in collective bargaining. However, the 40-hour week claim was not a direct outflow of employees' preferences for shorter hours of work released by preceding substantial income gains. Rather, what rendered possible the peaceful introduction of the 40-hour week and accomplished the agreements within a short time were coinciding organizational interests of the actors on both sides of the labor market.[2] The continuous economic prosperity was, of course, an important prerequisite, as was the fact that there was no argument (and no necessity) to pursue the 40-hour week as a means of enhancing the demand for labor.

By the mid-1950s employees' interests in further gains in income were at least as marked as their needs for shorter working hours. Their great preparedness to work overtime demonstrated existing "income preferences." But the great majority preferred leisure in the form of the two-day "free" weekend, even at the expense of longer hours during the remaining five work days. Because of its "opportunities of scale," the two-day weekend provided a wide spectrum of desired (family) activities—especially the use of mass-produced consumer goods that came into reach gradually. For some of the employees those working-time arrangements were already established by companies independently of collective bargaining (which was also true for other occupational benefits). Insofar as the 40-hour week containing the prospect of two days off from work symbolized "progress," it met specific expectations of the constituency. Thus, the unions were able to prove their competence and to heighten their attractiveness when they managed to introduce the 40-hour week by collective agreements embracing an entire industry or the whole economy. Success on those bread-and-butter issues in collective bargaining seemed to be indispensable for maintaining unanimity within the unions and overcoming the stagnation in membership after the unions' socialist program had failed to gain acceptance by the strong bourgeois government. Thus, the unions concentrated their campaign on the "free Saturday," and within a short time they achieved broad support for the claim among the whole population.

On the other hand, the employers also shared some interest in the reduction of weekly working hours: As long as the reconstruction period was not fully completed, the recognition of unions' demands symbolizing "social progress" helped to foster the integration of unions and employees into the resurrected capitalist order and thus contributed to the strengthening of the system. Furthermore, the regulation of working hours by collective agreements was an essential element for standardizing the working conditions and for establishing stable corporatist relations. Uniform frameworks for competition were a precondition for a distributional policy oriented toward growth and stability on a high aggregate level.

Since the employers did not oppose the 40-hour week in general and the unions were willing to concede a stepwise introduction adapted to the capacities of different branches and to restrict the total amount of demands to the growth of productivity, the main conflict arose on the timing and the speed of the reduction. By high-level bargaining, the employers' associations hoped to control the process effectively, that is, to avoid radiating breakthroughs at the enterprise level and to slow down the process of reduction.

The bargaining was spearheaded by the metal industry. An industry-wide agreement was attained in July 1956. It was concluded to reduce weekly working time by three hours down to 45 in October 1956. Full wages were guaranteed. Similar agreements were reached in other branches of manufacturing and the service sector in subsequent years. In practice, this first step amounted to an abolition of work on Saturdays (or at least in every second week) and a lengthening of working hours during the remaining five workdays. The goal was now to return to the eight-hour day by approaching the 40-hour week. However, the unions had to take into account that the most urgent need of employees was satisfied, namely, the attainment of the two-day "free weekend." A situation no longer prevailed where the realization of disposable income was hampered by the lack of leisure. On the contrary, the gain accomplished in "bunched" leisure was expenditure-intensive when it was spent according to the opportunities provided. The additional leisure fostered a change in the style of consumption in favor of goods serving entertainment and the need to demonstrate status.[3] Thus, income preferences became stronger again, and the unions had to renounce their original plans to complete the introduction of the 40-hour week within three or four years. The fact that the employees' urge for shorter working hours was dwindling because they perceived that more leisure required more income forced the unions to find solutions that would make it feasible to attain the ultimate goal and to allow for perceptible wage increases. But also the employers' associations—in common with the government—repeatedly demanded moderation, as overemployment was becoming more evident.

In 1957, again in the metal industry, the second step was concluded: a mere one-hour reduction to be introduced in 1959. This agreement left a comfortable margin for wage increases (6 percent in 1958). The leading organization of German employers' associations strongly opposed a further reduction of weekly working hours at that time and tried to close ranks but failed. In 1960 the employers' association in the exceptionally prospering metal industry signed an agreement that provided for a stepwise shift toward the introduction of the 40-hour week beginning in 1962, to be completed in 1965. The agreement contained a clause that allowed for a postponement of each step if the current economic situation warranted. This arrangement helped to reduce the tensions within the employers' camp and made it possible to accept the collective agreement as a bearable compromise. In 1964 and 1966 this clause was invoked, so that the 40-hour week was eventually implemented in the metal industry only in 1967. Other branches followed with some delay. In 1971 for about 77 percent of the blue-collar workers and for 52 percent of the salaried employees the 40-hour week was already collectively agreed upon.[4]

To summarize, employees' preferences for bunched leisure acted as a starting point for corresponding demands by the unions. But, for the 40-hour week issue to have been awarded priority in the collective bargaining arena and to have been accomplished peacefully (in addition, the metal industry had no labor disputes on wage issues between 1955 and 1962), it was essential that this issue served to realize organizational motives of both labor market associations. This has to be seen against the background of the specific economic and political-institutional conditions that characterized the period of the economic miracle. One of these conditions was that intentions to make working-time reduction an instrument for enhancing employment were totally absent. The resulting employment effects were merely by-products of a reduction primarily aimed at reaping prosperity gains during and through increased leisure. The actual employment effects were not very welcomed since the scarcity of labor was aggravated thereby. Furthermore, economic conditions provided abundant distributional resources to establish the 40-hour week without perceivable expenses of annual income *increases*, and those employees exclusively preferring income were offered more than enough opportunities for working overtime.

Other Chronometrical and Chronological Developments

Besides the reduction of weekly working hours, the extension of the entitlement to vacation contributed to the downward trend of normal working hours per year. The entitlement to vacation was generalized in the early 1920s and extended in the 1930s under the Nazi regime's ideological *Kraft durch Freude* ("vigor through enjoyment"). In the 1950s the entitlement amounted to a two-week vacation (on average). This type of leisure, predominantly designated for the the sake of family and consumption, was given intensified attention already in the early 1960s when, as a result of increased disposable incomes, the mass of employees became able to take holiday trips. The shift of leisure preferences (with continued desire for wage increases) toward this type of bunched leisure retarded the reattainment of the eight-hour day when the unions reacted to this shift and strove successfully for an extension of vacation entitlements (approximately 25 percent between 1960 and 1967). However, the bulk of additional days off from work was won by collective agreements after the 40-hour week had become reality for most employees (about eight work days, or a 40 percent increase, between 1971 and 1987).[5] After the first attempt of the metal union to pave the way for the 35-hour week failed in 1978-79 (see below), a stepwise extension of vacation entitlements up to six weeks per year was concluded in most sectors. In 1987 the great majority of employees had achieved this benchmark, and different entitlements according to age and length of service have virtually disappeared. Beyond this, in some industries employees above the age of fifty and shift workers have been granted additional days off through collective agreements.[6] In conjunction with the generalization of the five-day work week, this means that in the year 1985 the average employee had to go out for work on 219 days, compared with 293 in 1950. Furthermore, shorter weekly working hours and extended vacation entitlements have resulted in an average reduction of *normal annual* working hours per employee of 26 percent between 1950 and 1985 (see Figure 2-1), that is, from 2,344 hours down to 1,734 hours.[7]

However, actual working hours per average employee have always been higher because of a varying amount of overtime worked. These fluctuations in the volume of overtime work were caused mainly by cyclical movements of the economy and the scarcity of labor that prevailed until 1974. Nevertheless, a high volume of overtime work remained after the onset of the labor-market crisis in 1974–75. In 1985 it amounted to an equivalent of about 861,000 full-time jobs. These global figures, however, disguise the great dispersion of overtime work performed by employees. Many employees never or seldom work overtime, whereas others are still working ten and more hours overtime per week.[8] This differentiation should be due to the consolidation of internal labor markets. They contribute to firms' strategies to cope with temporarily rising output by varying their staffs' actual working hours rather than adapting to those peaks by increasing the number of their employees. Firms' strategies to keep the number of personnel at a minimum level, and to aim at an improvement of an internal transfer of workers when there is no substantial and certain long-term upward development in the demand for labor, explain to a great extent why the total amount of overtime is still as high as it is.

With regard to the number of working hours per working life, enormous changes have taken place since the end of World War II: In 1950 nearly 85 percent of all males aged 15 to 20 had already entered the labor market. At the other end of working life, 73 percent of males in the age bracket 60 to 65 still belonged to the labor force in 1950. In contrast, in 1988, because of the extended duration of schooling and training, not more than 45.5 percent of the male teenagers had started their working life and fewer than 35 percent of males of the age group 60 to 65 were still employed.[9] This latter shift resulted from the flexible retirement age introduced in 1972 (since which time em-

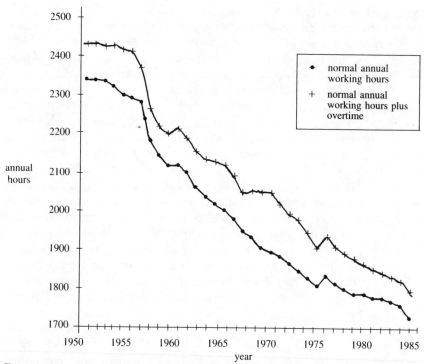

FIGURE 2-1. Average Normal Annual Working Hours (plus Overtime) per Employee, 1950–1985

Source: Calculated from (partly unpublished) data of the Institut für Arbeitsmarkt- und Berufsforschung, in Nuremberg.

ployees have been able to opt out when they are 63, and since 1980, so have severely disabled persons already at the age of 60) and from increased numbers of persons receiving a disability pension, which is to a great extent due to the worsened (re-)employment opportunities for older workers especially since 1974. The average age for retirement for males has been steadily reduced since 1973. From 62.2 years, it has dropped to 58.8 years in 1986.[10] This means that in the past decades working life has been increasingly compressed into the middle age brackets. If one also takes into account the reduction of normal annual working hours and the increased life expectancy, these developments mean that total working hours constitute a shrinking part of a lifetime: For a male employee born in 1892 working hours amounted to 20 percent; his grandson born in 1956 will spend 10.7 percent of his lifetime in occupational work, or only half as much.[11] Although those calculations are somewhat artificial and such average figures disguise the vast range of individual differences, they nevertheless demonstrate the decreasing quantitative importance of occupational work in shaping one's life. This change must certainly have been effective in transforming the subjective relationship and the meaning of occupational work and other spheres of life, especially in view of the microstructural distribution of working hours during occupational life, that is, the bunching of time free from work into the two-day weekend and several weeks of vacation.

A somewhat different picture emerges for women. They have been affected by extended periods of schooling nearly to the same extent as men, yet to a minor extent by earlier retirement. But, the *married* women's labor-force participation rate (in the age brackets 15 to 65) rose from 26.0 percent in 1950 to 49.4 percent in 1988, and in the age group 20 to 55 it has more than doubled.[12] This is due to the fact that a greater share of every succeeding age cohort pursues a durable occupational career or shortens the period that interrupts working life for motherhood. Of course, in these age brackets participation in the labor force very often means doing so on a subnormal hourly basis (see below). However, the participation of married women in the labor force is increasingly equated with performing wage labor instead of being an (unpaid) family worker. In contrast to their impact on men's lives, these developments have resulted in an enlarged significance of occupational work in women's lives and, likewise, have produced a revaluation in the relationship of different spheres of life.

The increased participation of married women in the labor force has been accompanied by a growth in part-time employment. The increased scarcity of labor following the 1966–67 recession acted as a strong "pull-effect" when firms more often offered part-time jobs to attract women not able or prepared to enter the labor market on a full-time basis because of the gender-specific distribution of family work. The doubling of the proportion of part-time employed women between 1960 and 1972—since then it has slightly, but steadily, increased (31.5 percent of all women in dependent employment)—foreshadowed the emergence of a new motive for changes in working-time patterns on the part of the employees, namely, the improved integration of working time into the individual's mode of living (see below, section on employees' preferences for flexible working hours). So far, part-time employment has remained almost purely a women's affair: 12.8 percent of all employees considered themselves part-timers in 1988, but 92 percent of them were women. However, only 7.4 percent say that they are working part time involuntarily, because they cannot find a full-time job.[13] In comparison with Scandinavian countries and Great Britain, the percentage of part-time employment in West Germany is relatively low. This is due to the relatively small service sector (the domain of part-time employment) and to the lower participation rate of married women in the labor force. The latter is caused, at least to some extent, by the joint taxation of family income and by several social security regulations that operate as disincentives for participation in the labor market as well as for employers to offer more part-time jobs.[14]

The emergence of the new motive of employees for changed working-time patterns contributed to the success of flexitime regulations. The first agreement on the introduction of flexitime was concluded in 1967. In 1972 those agreements between management and works councils were already effective for nearly 6 percent of all employees. In 1981 approximately 17 percent of all employees (among clerical workers: 36 percent) were offered the opportunity to adapt—within certain limits—the distribution of their working hours to personal needs.[15] Although very often the introduction of flexitime originated from employees' initiatives, the unions remained skeptical since at the same time flexitime served employers' interests (lower rates of absenteeism, higher productivity, fewer remunerated overtime hours, and the like). As they had with part-time employment, the unions demonstrated reluctance to attain industry-wide collective agreements on these issues because they were unable to mobilize organizational power to carry through regulations for the advantage of a very weakly unionized fraction of the labor force. If they had actually succeeded in concluding regulations by which the potential disadvantages of part-time work or flexitime for the employees in question had been altogether excluded, they would have had to fear the resistance of these very same employees when their employers, deprived of the opportunity to realize their own interests as well, would no longer offer jobs on a part-time basis or ones that enabled employees to choose starting and finishing time. In any case, the rise of flexible working-time patterns confronted the unions with a dilemma: If they ignore the spread of these working-time patterns, they will miss the chance to influence actively the state of regulations developing in individual and firm-specific negotiations and they will allow the social validity of standard working hours as a prerequisite for attaining collective progress to be undermined. On the other hand, if unions enter into collective agreements on these issues, they will legitimize working-time patterns that deviate from standard working hours, which will contradict their hitherto pursued (or at least proclaimed) goal to produce equal work and living conditions, which stance allows them to foster commonly shared interests that can be aggregated into collective demands most easily (here especially: further general working-time reductions with full wage compensation). Thus, most German unions did nothing more than express their reservations against part-time work and flexitime. It was not until 1987 that in the chemical industry a collective agreement regulating part-time work was reached.

To conclude, I briefly discuss the development of those working-time patterns that are considered "unsocial hours." The growing share of employees whose working hours are situated outside the normal pattern of Monday to Friday approximately between 7:00 A.M. and 7:00 P.M. is to a great extent a direct offspring of the reduction of normal working hours: The increase of shift work (from 12 percent in 1960 to 18.1 percent in 1975 and a —most likely— further growth thereafter) is partly due to employers' interest in maintaining (or extending) operating time when individual working hours were curtailed. Furthermore, extended consumption of services during enlarged leisure time and increased societal expectations for security, provision, and care resulted in the performance of a greater share of work during the night and on weekends (Saturday and Sunday, statutory holidays).[16] It might be said that the positive effect of reduced normal working hours has been partially diminished, inasmuch as the number of employees who suffer from psychophysical burdens related to working time (e.g., shift workers) or from restricted opportunities to spend their "off-beat" allocated leisure has increased.

To summarize, widespread but selectively dispersed overtime hours, on the one hand, and increased part-time employment concentrated among married women, on the other, have led to increasing deviations from the collectively agreed working hours. The increase in the number of working-time arrangements situated outside normal patterns has broadened the spectrum in the chronological dimension. Altogether, the diversity of actual working-time patterns has become greater during the last decades. One can expect that this markedly heterogeneous situation will result in the corresponding diversification of working-time preferences of the employees. The expectation of a very low unanimity of preferences among employees is reinforced by a growing dispersion of the age of entry into and withdrawal from the labor force and its changed structure due to the increased share of wage-earning women who have different conceptions of the relationship between work and life. Decreasing uniformity in other working conditions as well as the differentiation in spheres outside the job (see below) should also contribute to the diversification of these conceptions and corresponding preferences.

Changed Interests and Preferences

To support the main thesis of this chapter—that for employees and employers a continuation of the traditional working-time policy aimed at reducing (annual) *standard* working hours has lost its appeal or is met with growing resistance—we have to look for changes in the motives and interests that induce a different development in the future. We first consider the employers' stance toward changes of working-time regulations and then investigate employees' preferences concerning "time" and "money."

Employers' Everlasting Interest in Flexible Working Hours

It is a well-established fact that employers generally opposed workers' or unions' demand for shorter working hours. This happened even when the length of daily or weekly working hours was counterproductive, that is, they were too long to obtain a maximum of hourly output. The main reason for employers' resistance was that, in contrast to an increase in wages, a change of working hours required adaptive shifts in work organization. It overthrew accustomed practices, routines, and calculations, which in turn produced uncertainty about whether and to what extent productivity gains (exceeding the costs) would really accrue (for the sake of simplicity, we leave aside the question of the "traditionalism" of workers and the problem of wage compensation for reduced working hours). Only when an upper limit for laying claim to the laborer's time was fixed by governmental enactment (preferably internationally coordinated) or by collective agreement above the level of the individual firm was it possible to avoid problems of maintaining the relative competitive position and to introduce a more rational handling of working hours. Hence, several nineteenth-century industrialists supported the idea of standardizing the *length* of (annual) working hours.

But what the employers continued to oppose was a fixed *distribution* of a given amount of (annual) working hours.[17] That is, they opposed a day-to-day and week-to-week equal duration and chronological location of "normal" working hours that, at the same time, declared deviations and the grip on laborers' time beyond the "regular" hours or on certain days of the week and at periods of the day as prohibited or "abnormal," thus, providing a basis to bargain for remuneration over and above the regular (hourly) wage (e.g., premia for overtime, shift work, night work, or work on Sunday). Therefore, the establishment of standardized working-hours arrangements constitutes one of the major achievements of the working class. Without the existence of these arrangements, it would not have been possible for the employees to reap all the benefits of any successive working-time reduction.

We can identify four functions performed by the system of standardized working hours:

1. Inasmuch as standardization fixes an upper limit on the normal length of working hours (which can be transgressed only under certain conditions), disastrous competition among employees is prevented. Furthermore, they are protected against a premature loss of their capacity to work resulting from permanent overload. And, finally, in case of an oversupply of labor, standardization offers a lever for a collective restriction in order to redistribute scarce labor demand to more employees.

2. Working-time standards serve as a "ratchet" for further gains vis-à-vis capital within the exchange relationship. Higher wage rates will result in increased real income only when the number of normal hours are not an issue that needs to be negotiated collectively at the same time and, furthermore, when compensatory extensions of individual working hours are taboo.

3. As long as working-time standards maintain their social validity, they guarantee that employees' claims for a "full income" (albeit according to different standard wages) are respected. Social validity means that working-time standards are a fixed factor—an upper and a lower limit at the same time—for the arrangement of jobs that cannot be varied according to some economic calculus by employers. They are prevented from enforcing substandard work-

ing-time schedules and, thus, incomes below subsistence level, whereas employees do not need to prove their claim for a full-time job and a sufficient income ("family wage").

4. Eventually, standard working hours protect employees' "own" time by differentiating it from working time and thus ensure the predictability and regularity of leisure hours. The regulated, even distribution of the length of working hours and the definition of their normal chronological location ensure the autonomous disposal of the socially most valuable time periods within a societal time structure that itself ensues from standardized patterns of working hours.

In the past, employers and their associations were less hostile to union demands for shorter hours (within the framework of standardized working-hours arrangements) as long as they could anticipate that reduced working hours could be transformed into increased labor productivity per hour because of a reduced fatigue effect or because of other measures that helped to economize the utilization of labor. The productivity effect induced by shorter hours has steadily decreased, and this potential should be, in general, exhausted after the prevailing standards have been attained. Thus, one can expect that unions' claims for shorter hours will be met with stronger resistance. But, in addition, various developments cause the employers to attack the standardized working-hours arrangements as such and to take the initiative for the establishment of a new working-time regime. We can identify four developments underlying employers' attempts to break down the system of standardized working hours:[18]

1. Increasing capital intensity—in German manufacturing, approximately 500 percent between 1950 and 1984 (in real terms)—and the growing capital coefficient establish an interest in the (re-)extension of firms' processing time. This entails strategies for an enhanced decoupling of processing time and individual working time exceeding traditional shift work patterns in certain industries. The intended lowering of unit costs and increase of capital profitability aim at a *chronological denormalization*, that is, an extended grip on time (periods of the day, days of the week) hitherto outside normal working hours.

2. The establishment of a system of standardized working hours means that, as a result of the regulated and even distribution of normal working hours, employers have to bear the risk of underutilization of labor ("idleness on the job") when production falls below normal or, alternatively, have to produce (ultimately at higher costs) on stock, or to pay overtime premia when peak demand is to be met. As long as mass production of standardized goods for stable markets prevails, these passive adaptations to cyclical or seasonal fluctuations are acceptable, although far from optimal. But changes in the structure of demand and increasingly turbulent world markets require a transition to small-scale production that is more exactly accommodated to the needs of the markets. Flexible manufacturing systems, "just-in-time"-production, and other elaborated techniques of planning and cost control facilitate this transition. These changes and the opportunities provided by computerized data processing

(likewise for the management of variable and diversified working-time patterns) thus call into question the fixed distribution of working hours and reinforce the interest in a *chronological discontinuity*. To economize on labor (costs), employers pursue corresponding strategies that point to the flexible distribution of a certain amount of annual working hours.

3. Strategies aiming at a flexible and thus irregular distribution of working hours are likewise motivated by the expanding share of service work that is performed, and not only in the generic service industries. Meanwhile, approximately two-thirds of the West German labor force is employed in service *occupations*. A prevailing part of this work cannot be executed on "stock" but, rather, has to be synchronized with fluctuating demands (e.g., the presence of customers to be served). Sometimes peak demand for service work happens at unsocial hours (e.g., in restaurants, entertainment).

4. The growing heterogeneity of firms' labor forces enhances the interest in a *chronometrical differentiation* of individual working hours. To begin with, management jobs (at all levels) have increased, and these jobs are, as always, tailored fairly independently of a specific number of working hours because of certain "indivisibilities" (such as supervisory functions, responsibilities, and the like). Hence, they are, in general, synonymous with long hours. Furthermore, employers have an interest in agreeing upon working hours above the average length for those employees either if the firm has invested considerably in its "human capital" or if they represent a "rarity" on the external labor market, that is, they are difficult to recruit. On the other hand, every firm has jobs with hard working conditions where the optimum length of working time is (considerably) below the prevailing standards, and almost every firm employs workers showing reduced capability to work. Their average efficiency per hour would be higher if these employees worked shorter hours. Finally, in nearly every firm we find jobs that do not require the normal number of working hours to master the certain delimited tasks continually. Therefore, firms are interested in employing workers whose working hours meet exactly with the job requirements, that is, they wish to negotiate subnormal working hours with a corresponding earnings reduction.

All in all, these interests are directed toward:

· the departure from an evenly regulated and stable distribution of working hours (*chronological discontinuity*),
· the requirement that more employees work time schedules that run askew of the socially established time structure (*chronological denormalization*), and
· the stipulation of the number of working hours for individual employees according to efficiency criteria instead of accepting standard working hours as a "characteristic" of every worker hired (*chronometrical differentiation*).

The aim of employers' interests in flexible working hours is to make labor power as available as electricity by a switch or water from a tap, which leads to a reduction of the volume of contracted and, thus, remunerated working hours. If "internationalization of the economy" means that even the business rivals of firms producing for the domestic market exclusively are coming from abroad (and, thus, are not covered by national collective agreements), then standardized working-hours arrangements as one element of regulating (domestic) competition have to be looked upon as serious obstacles to maintaining and improving competitiveness, obstacles that have to be overcome by a new working-time policy.

Employees' Emerging Preference for Flexible Working Hours

In tracing the historical development of working hours since the early stages of industrialization, one can identify a succession of employees' motives for wanting to change working hours. The discontinuity expressed by the dominance of one motive can be described most readily by the term *extension*.

1. Although, compared with the present standards, at the early phase of industrialization work was not very intense and was often irregular, the lengthening of working hours that occurred in many trades threatened the vendibility of labor power in the long run. Therefore, the attainment of *sufficient time for recuperation from work* to secure the marketability of labor power was the first motive for changing working hours. These changes—fought for collectively by workers who had accepted their fate to be wage laborers as durable and hereditary or (initially) brought about by state legislation—were related to the *individual* as a laborer and were (predominantly) aimed at a shortening of the working *day*. The emblematic pattern of this motive was the claim for the eight-hour day.

2. Although various employer attempts to intensify work recurrently resurrected this motive, once collective norms for a shorter working day were established, a new motive for change was gradually superimposed on it, namely, the attainment of *leisure*, time free from paid work exceeding the periods necessary merely to reproduce labor power. The orientation was focused on the development and extension of spheres of life outside employment and was no longer exclusively related to the wage-dependent individual but, rather, extended to the whole *family* of the employee. Likewise, the temporal context was extended from the day to the *week* and the *year*. Symbolic figures of rationality were the 40-hour week (with a two-day free weekend) and vacation—both allowing a dissociation from everyday life (*Alltag*). Leisure for family and consumption was thus bunched. To make full use of the "opportunities of scale" provided according to the emerging forms and norms of spending leisure, rising disposable income became a perpetually necessary complement. Since the free weekend and several weeks of vacation are very expenditure-intensive and very "elastic" for spending money, the competition between shorter hours and an

alternative rise of income became intensified, and which preference got the upper hand became unclear.[19] But, as necessary as a rising income was the establishment of standardized working-hours arrangements that would protect the socially integrated (*lebensweltlich organisierte*) spheres of life outside employment (and also to secure the day-to-day reproduction of labor power) by restricting employers' grip on the total lifetime of employees and that would have regard for natural and social rhythms.

3. In order to proceed along the well-established path of further reduction of standardized working hours, employees needed a new "pattern of success" that would crystallize the spectrum of needs of all employees, but this was obviously lacking. The 35-hour week holds merely a symbolic value mediated by the union organization as an indicator of its strength and activity, but this demand does not lie "nearest to the heart of every . . . labourer,"[20] as did the eight-hour day one hundred years ago. Mobilization for supporting this claim proved to be difficult (see below) because it was the result of a further complication of the structure of motives for changing working hours: the formation of a new motive. This new motive is based on the need to harmonize (or integrate) the quantitatively extended spheres of life outside employment with those within employment. On the time axis, the frame of reference is extended beyond the year to the entire occupational *biography*; the social context includes the individual in *all primary social systems*. The context, in which working time is considered, thus becomes more fluid, and the valuation of arrangements and distributions of time less uniform. Accordingly, reasons (*Sinnbezüge*), tied to changes of working hours, are no longer aimed at solely one dimension of the working time structure. Rather, according to each worker's conception of life, different relevancies develop that define varying patterns of success. These cannot be specified concretely. The term *time sovereignty*, coined by Bernhard Teriet,[21] describes approximately the socially differentiated and individually unstable needs for a qualitative integration of time applied to the various spheres of life.

Employees' increased desire to fit working hours into more fluid life plans is one element and consequence of the individualization and diversification of people's experiences, situations, and life styles. It means that with the unparalleled rise of incomes after World War II, the expansion of the welfare state, extended schooling, and the like, class identities and class-related traditions have been fading in their importance for shaping one's life, although wage labor has become even more generalized and the inequality structure has remained almost unchanged (and new lines of inequality have arisen). But this process of "lifting the level" has led to a pluralization of life styles, a differentiation of value patterns and conceptions of life, and an enhanced competence and need to organize one's own biography.[22]

These developments require that we say farewell to the conception that working-time policy can continue to be oriented toward a "modal worker" with a certain family background. In cross-sectional perspective, the traditional "male breadwinner family" (husband is gainfully employed; wife is full-time housemaker) represents not more than about 35 percent of German households headed by a gainfully employed person, while households of singles, dual earners, and single parents have gained in importance over recent decades. Elsewhere[23] I have compiled various German and foreign surveys on the working-time preferences of employees. The combination of these surveys demonstrates quite clearly the great diversity of preferences. The needs for changes are not at all aimed at a (durable) reduction of weekly working hours. Every proposed type of reduction in working hours has its own following depending on age, sex, occupational (including working time) situation, and family background. Instead, more options for self-determination of the chronological location and distribution as well as the length of working hours are highly valued, and those who are working unsocial hours are first of all interested in normalizing their working hours, that is, overcoming the present disadvantages in regard to spending leisure time within the given social time structure.

In sum, one can no longer think of a single and collectively agreed-upon formula to change working hours that has top priority with every employee and that would be preferred to all alternative changes—including the opportunity of a rise in income. The regard given to the latter is quite important. Work still retains its instrumental function as the main source of *money* income, even though the sphere of work has been reduced in its quantitative importance for the mode of living and in its subjective significance for *Sinnstiftung*; it represents a highly differentiated experience causing dispersed orientations; and it has become dedramatized by formalized procedures of solving conflict and of applying the labor power, as well as by the welfare state's provision of security against the typical risks of wage labor.

Thus, the fundamental conflict between the preference for free time and the preference for increased wages remains unaltered in spite of the emergence of new claims: to pursue a personal life style and to shape the individual relationship between work and other spheres of life. The valuation turns even more in favor of money the more working hours are (physically) endurable; hence, further reductions are less urgent and of decreasing use-value. This change is due to the inherent characteristics of the media "time" and "money,"[24] that is to say, to their asymmetrical convertibility. If one has lots of money, one can (also) buy time (e.g., the time of commercial service producers so as to enjoy the time "saved"), whereas having lots of time does not automatically provide one with the vast range of options to obtain goods and services that otherwise have to be paid for with money. The "welfare productivity" of an additional amount of mere free time is low or even negative (it may produce boredom, or be a nuisance) if, because of structural constraints of modern patterns of family life, household activities, and urban living conditions, no productive uses can be made of it. Instead, it has to be filled with consumption activities that require a complementary spending of money. Furthermore, money is superior to time since it is less "fixed": Time cannot be saved nor can it be transferred to other persons, whereas money can be kept and spent exactly at that moment (and by anyone else) when the need is greatest and for a universe of purposes. Thus, intertemporally, free time varies in its subjective value and, therefore, the structural disadvantage of time can be lessened (and the need for money reduced) when the individual freedom to appoint the chronological location and the amount of particles of free time is increased.

Whereas the latter argument refers to the ascertained preferences for extended "time sovereignty," the former explanation helps to understand employees' reservations against working-time reductions at the expense of present income or at alternatively attainable increases of wages. From our representative survey among German employees, we found that only 15 percent of the full-time employed were ready to exchange additional free time—allocated in one way or other—for corresponding proportions of current income. Nearly 73 percent wanted to stick to their present number of working hours and 12 percent even wanted longer working hours to attain a higher income. Other surveys in the Federal Republic of Germany and abroad (e.g., in the Netherlands, Sweden, Norway, and in the United States)[25] show comparable results when the tradeoff between time and money was unequivocally accentuated. Besides the preceding explanations, further vital factors can be held responsible for the less pronounced—although *not* negligible—preparedness to forego parts of current income for additional free time: At any time, it is not very popular to fall behind an income level once it is attained. The present consumption level works as a "ratchet." Furthermore, we observed the interest in maintaining (or even better: in improving) one's own income position relative to that of others.

But the sensitivity of preferences for free time to income changes also shows when a sacrifice of *future* increases of income for more leisure is at stake: The results of a 1977 survey mandated by the Commission of the European Economic Community (EEC) proved that a slight majority of the German labor force (55 percent) preferred shorter working hours to further wage increases, 35 percent opted for wage increases, and 10 percent were undecided.[26] In 1985 the picture was almost reversed: No more than 30 percent preferred shorter working hours instead of wage increases, and 56 percent wanted higher wages (14 percent were undecided).[27] This reversal should be mainly due to the losses in real income the average employee had experienced during recent years (minus 6 percent between 1979 and 1985)—an explanation that would be consistent with the theoretical framework laid down by Bienefeld.[28]

To summarize, it is always easier for any union to aggregate income demands than claims for shorter working hours. The difficulties are aggravated when constantly present income needs are hurt and when structural developments accentuate the different valuation of time and money, that is, that an increase in leisure is attractive only in combination with substantial gains in income. But, this is only one side of the problem, since former successes in reducing standardized working hours have transformed employees' working and living conditions and thus have contributed to the emergence of a new motive for changing working hours serving the needs of an individualized labor force. That is to say, the reductions have fostered preferences for an integration of working hours into socially diversified and individually fluid life patterns. At the same time, these "successes" have also changed the conditions for the application of labor power. This means that the conflict on working hours is shifting from issues of quantity to those of quality, and thus the *manner* in which working hours are regulated (instead of merely the outcome of regulations) is at stake. For progress is attainable for both sides only outside the standardized working-hours arrangements or by their modification. While the interest of firms is to level all differences in the quality of time that result from natural rhythms or those established by the normalization of working hours, employees' needs not only point to a preservation of these time arrangements (*Zeitordnungen*) but increasingly to an adaptation of the chronological location and the (lifetime) distribution of working hours to the individualized time structures and conceptions of life. As a consequence, the continuation of the traditional policy to reduce working hours becomes more difficult at a moment when it seems to be most desirable for full-employment reasons; at the same time a need for new regulations arises, regulations that could translate the conflict on the quality of working time into new institutional forms for settling compromises.

The Conflict over the 35-Hour Week

By the mid-1970s the German public was frightened by the sudden return of stagnation and mass unemployment, evils believed to have been definitively conquered. In view of unemployment figures that were hovering around one million, the metal workers' union (IG Metall) spearheaded a first attempt to pave the way for a stepwise introduction of the 35-hour week in 1978. The struggle in the steel industry, which was chosen as the pioneering branch, was badly prepared (it was too short-dated; efforts by the union leadership were only half-hearted) and the employers' association, supported by all others in the different industries, declared the 40-hour week "non-negotiable" and was not prepared to give in. Therefore, the seven-week strike at the turn of 1978–79 ended in defeat. What was actually accomplished were additional "free shifts" for older and night-shift workers and the extension of vacation entitlement to six weeks—results not fought for originally. But IG Metall—and subsequently the unions in almost all important industries—had to accept that collective bargaining on the hours issue was not open until at least 1983.

In 1981 unemployment figures rose once more, and in 1982 they exceeded the 2 million threshold. It became evident that promoting economic growth would not be sufficient to improve the labor-market situation substantially. Thus, the reduction of working hours received growing attention again. In order not to discredit their own claim to represent the interests of all employees, the unions—and, in particular, IG Metall, making up one-third of the membership of all unions within the DGB—had to tackle the employment problem with the available tools on board. Furthermore, to abstain from measures to improve the market-power position of labor would have set in motion a vicious cycle of diminishing chances for success with regard to wages, working conditions, and job security. Even if the unions did not succeed in restoring full employment, putting into motion measures against employers' resistance that tend to lower the degree of labor abundance would serve as a demonstration of their continuous ability for collective action and thus lead to an improvement of their bargaining status vis-à-vis employers and government.

If they pursued the 35-hour week, it was unequivocally clear that the unions would encounter the continued resistance of the employers. But it would be too mechanistic to assume that the ambiguous outcome of the conflict, mentioned above, was solely due to the power asymmetry between capital and labor. To so conclude would be to ignore the contingencies of the strategic decisions of the collective actors on both sides of the labor market (and thus the possibility of a different outcome) and the dissimilar options available to each of them as associations with voluntary membership. When choosing such a perspective of strategic interactions,[29] one can mainly trace back the ambiguous result of the struggle decided in the metal industry in 1984 to internal problems of action on the side of the challenging actor IG Metall, which carried through the fight for a shorter working week for all other unions vicariously.

Although employers' unremitting resistance to a shorter working week was clear, it was also certain that the majority of employees would not support the demand for a 35-hour week for intrinsic leisure needs (see preceding section). Furthermore, it was hardly reasonable to rely on class solidarity, that is, to devalue immediate individual preferences for the sake of collective interests, as an alternative source of durable support.[30] The development of an inclusive conception of class identity is hampered by the fact that identical ways of thinking and acting, rooted in common experience, have crumbled with the fragmentation of the labor force. These fragmentations can no longer be bridged by organization's ideological attempts at unification. Likewise, it was hardly promising to accentuate the individual gains resulting from a removal of the acute threat of job loss when working hours would be reduced since unemployment risks (and experiences) were socially distributed in a highly unequal manner (apart from the fact that this "work sharing" is unsuitable for generating market power). Finally, it was also risky to trust in the 35-hour week as an "intermediate collective good,"[31] expecting that via its positive employment effect and, hence, improved market-power position of labor, it would render possible in a second step the attainment of higher individual gains (wage increases, working conditions) than could be pocketed if the status quo were maintained.

Winning support for this "investment strategy" is precarious because the immediate beneficiaries (the unemployed, new entrants into the labor market) are socially different from those who undergo the "costs" of an alternatively possible wage increase and the loss of income during an eventual labor dispute. Since the "revenues" of the sacrifices will accrue in a more or less distant future, it is uncertain whether one will still be among the beneficiaries. And since the desired employment effect cannot be contracted but, rather, is dependent on firms' reactions to the reduced working hours, it is uncertain whether the "revenues" will accrue after all (which, of course, is denied by the employers), even worse, whether beyond it further incalculable risks (foremost, a job loss resulting from the deteriorated position of one's employing firm because of the costs of that collective agreement) and disadvantages (e.g., an increased work load) will occur. Thus, the problem was not only that an abstract willingness to enter a labor dispute needed to be mobilized, but, moreover, that a concrete readiness for individual sacrifices among the employees needed to be generated.

Despite these uncertainties connected with a working-time reduction as an intermediate collective good, no less of a problematic alternative was left to IG Metall than to mobilize support in favor of the 35-hour week. The collective good of the measure was emphasized, and, hence, solidarity with the unemployed as well as with the union organization was called for. Additionally, the union attempted to awaken needs for more leisure hours and periods of rest.

Although the resistance of the employers' association (Gesamtmetall) was certain and its strategic behavior in the course of the inevitable conflict was roughly calculable for the union, IG Metall's own potency could be accumulated and proved only in the conflict itself. The willingness of the constituency to endure the conflict depended on the treatment of certain parameters by the functionaries.[32] One of these relevant parameters was the caliber of the demand: The proclaimed doctrine was to introduce the 35-hour week as *one* major immediate reduction. Only a maximalistic approach offered the possibility of showing that alternative forms of working-time reduction, namely, early retirement schemes, would be ineffective and inferior in fighting unemployment and, thus, of accentuating the dominant objective of the efforts. This was important since four other unions within the DGB had committed themselves to negotiate on early-retirement schemes and urged the enactment of an appropriate legal framework and, furthermore, since various surveys demonstrated that employees preferred early retirement and considered it the superior measure.[33] Moreover, only the prospect of a substantial gain in leisure was suitable to heighten the attractiveness of a reduction of weekly working hours among the employees. Not until the "hot stage" of the conflict had begun and the hostile attitude of the employers and federal government toward any reduction of

weekly working hours had become evident did IG Metall come to a more flexible definition of the claim. The turn to the attainable goal of "breaching the
40-hour norm" meant that the working-time reduction as such had already become an end in itself, and the instrumental relation to the original goal of
fighting unemployment was weakened. However, it preserved the possibility of
blaming the resistance of the employers for any outcome that missed the 35-
hour mark.

Another parameter relevant in the mobilization process was the employment effect of shorter working hours. From the beginning IG Metall argued
that, based on "scientific knowledge," one could expect 50 percent of the volume to be positively effective for employment, thereby making it possible to
assume a proportional employment effect for any caliber of reduction. This
argumentation absolved the union from having to make any attempts to secure
the employment effect by additional agreements (on the intensity of work,
overtime, and the like), which would have been decisive obstacles to reaching
an agreement on shorter hours. But, at the same time this meant a dilemma for
the union: The inability to tackle the prerequisites for attaining the goal (additional employment) called into question the instrumental rationality of a working-time reduction when the employers retained full autonomy over reactive
measures.

A further dilemma for IG Metall arose from its emphatic pronouncement
of the condition of a reduction of weekly working hours, namely, that it had to
take place with "full wage compensation." This doctrine was meant as a compromise between the conflicting priorities of income and employment, both
present among the constituency. To assure the employees that no agreement
that would impair the status quo would be concluded, the union had to maximize the readiness for collective action among the employees. Although it was
neither possible to accentuate the wage dimension without losing credibility for
pursuing the goal of fighting unemployment nor guaranteed that a modest wage
claim would increase the employment effect, the formula chosen amounted to a
maximization of two incompatible goals: as much working-time reduction as
possible *and* as much a wage increase as possible.

When the employers' association started to proclaim its own conceptions
for reorganizing working time, its demand for chronological discontinuity was
spared from the certain critique and rejection by IG Metall, although this type
of flexibility is nevertheless aimed at economizing on labor. The union's willingness to make concessions on this issue has to be interpreted as an attempt to
codetermine the dimension of compromise and, hence, to influence which disadvantages for the organization can be accepted when the demand cannot be
fully attained.

After the negotiations taking place at the regional level had failed in April
1984, IG Metall conducted strike ballots in Nordbaden-Nordwürttemberg and
Hessen.[34] The employers were surprised and the union was put at ease when the

vote in favor of strike action was 80 percent, that is, 5 percent above the mandate necessary for calling a strike. This "success" was not due to great enthusiasm among the membership for their union's strategy, in spite of the fact that IG Metall's tactic of presenting an ambiguous bundle of goals that left ample scope for individual interpretations and that avowals of assent by the activists made possible the necessary unity within the organization. But more important, what protected the union from a defeat already at the stage of strike balloting and intensified the readiness of the members affected to endure the following seven-week labor dispute was the intransigent position of Gesamt-metall and the partiality of the federal government in favor of the employers.[35] This political polarization and the awareness of the members that, after collective agreements had been given notice, the union could not be left standing out in the rain without also risking the status quo mobilized an unspecific but nevertheless defensive loyalty to the organization. That loyalty, to unfold its own dynamic, depended on the existence of a threatening opposition and an actual conflict.

Eventually, in June 1984 the fierce labor dispute was settled by an arbitrator. The agreement is a milestone in German working-time regulation: In April 1985 normal weekly working hours were fixed at 38.5, with full wage compensation. However, the figure merely represented a stipulation regarding the *average* working hours of all full-time employees. Additional agreements could be made at the shop-floor level on an uneven distribution of normal working hours within the week or month. It is only over a two-month period that working hours have to average 38.5 hours per week. Besides this opportunity for chronological discontinuity, agreements on a chronometrical differentiation could be concluded between management and works councils: It is possible that different sections of the workforce, different departments, and so forth, operate on different working-time schedules with the range of 37 to 40. It is merely required that the different individual working-time schedules of an enterprise's workforce average 38.5 hours. Finally, the collective agreement contained a clause that the implementation of shorter hours must not lead to a reduction of the firms' processing times. This implied a further step toward the dissociation of individual working time and firms' processing time and, thus, entailed an inroad into chronological denormalization.

For all that, this compromise helped the union to maintain unity and membership integration, because breaching the 40-hour norm was an unquestionable success. However, the reduction of merely 1.5 hours was compatible with considerable wage increases in 1984 (3.3 percent) and 1985 (2 percent) over and above the full wage compensation. By both these achievements the union militants could be satisfied, whereas the wage increase was important for those employees who gave priority to individual gains. The concession that certain parameters of flexibility become issues of bargaining was suitable to demonstrate responsibility with regard to mastering the compulsion for "modernization" of the economy—a goal never denied by West German unions. Thereby it established a platform for further, more peaceful bargaining on the working-time issue.

Nevertheless, the agreement on certain options for flexibility "according to the firms' needs" led to a "second round" of conflict, since IG Metall urged the works councils to insist upon a uniform and weekly reduction of working hours, whereas Gesamtmetall urged its members to make full use of the opportunities provided, and it accused the IG Metall of breaking its word. One important reason for rejecting shop-floor agreements on flexibility was to limit the variety of working-time conditions and, hence, to strengthen the common desire for accomplishing the next steps toward shorter weekly working hours. In reality, a great number of firms have not yet sought additional agreements on the parameters of flexibility.[36] Those agreements were found more frequently in larger firms, and often they were combined with further rearrangements of working-time schedules (e.g., the introduction or extension of flexitime or shift work). There was also a broad range in how the 1.5-hour reduction has been operationalized, although some kind of "bunching" (whole days or shifts off or early departure time every second Friday) preponderated. IG Metall and Gesamtmetall disagree on the scope of flexibility introduced,[37] but they disagree even more on the employment effect of the reduction, which virtually cannot be isolated from other factors influencing the level of employment. Though the employers' association asserts that no more than 24,000 additional jobs in the metal industry originated from this measure, IG Metall's calculations show 97,000 new jobs and a further 5,000 jobs preserved. Calculations carried out by independent research institutes arrive at figures between these two extremes.[38]

The 1984 collective agreement in the metal industry acted as a kind of model for other industries where working-time reductions were concluded subsequently. This happened, for example, in the printing, paper, and steel industry, in the metal craft business, in wholesale and retail trade, and in private insurance. As a result, at the end of 1988 for about 84 percent of the employees covered by collective agreements (that means virtually all employees), a normal workweek shorter than 40 hours was already valid or would become effective in 1989.[39] However, the possibility for chronometrical differentiation remained a unique feature of the metal industry, and it was the intention of IG Metall to abolish this regulation when the hours issue was again on the agenda at the end of 1986. From the beginning it was evident that neither IG Metall nor Gesamtmetall was interested in a new labor dispute, although the union tried to demonstrate readiness for a new battle. After a series of unsuccessful regional negotiations, a peak-level agreement on the "second step" was eventually concluded in March 1987. It confirmed the exchange formula "working-time reduction for extended flexibility" established in 1984. This agreement had to be specified in regional negotiations, so some differences evolved.

The main common results of these collective agreements were the following: Weekly working hours were to be reduced to 37.5 in April 1988 and to 37 in April 1989. The range of chronometrical differentiation was confined but not abolished altogether. The employers "kept a foot in the door," and in the future one can expect that more frequent use will be made of this opportunity where qualified employees in some categories are scarce. However, the period within which weekly working hours have to amount to 37.5 or 37 on the average was extended from two to six months. Furthermore, the union did not succeed in getting the eight-hour day recognized as the upper limit of a normal working day, and it also failed to confine the maximum number of overtime hours (ten hours per week or 20 hours per month) agreed upon in 1984. The retention of this has to be regarded as a concession to smaller firms that have greater difficulties implementing formalized flexibility arrangements, but it served the interests of larger firms as well. This, combined with the extended opportunity for chronological discontinuity, furnishes the firms with an effective device for adapting individual working hours smoothly to varying demands. In some regions the payment of a monthly salary for blue-collar workers independent of the varying hours actually worked was concluded, which removed further obstacles for applying this type of flexibility. Finally, in some regions it is possible to include Saturday in those schemes *if* the works councils agree, upon the request of the management. IG Metall failed to secure definitively that Saturday not be (re)introduced as a normal work day. It is not quite certain yet (in December 1989) if one can, however, expect that the employers will start a new attack on this "property" of employees when the collective agreements are to be given notice again in 1990, and the union will certainly demand the final step to introduce the 35-hour week. Furthermore, it is most likely that the enactment of the government's plan of a new working-time law is only postponed. This 1987 bill actively supports the idea of further flexibility of working hours, mainly by extending the latitude of collective bargaining on the concrete terms of working time.[40]

IG Metall asserts that the working-time reductions concluded in 1987 have yielded an employment effect of approximately 100,000 jobs once more. Notwithstanding the fact that these arithmetical calculations are somewhat questionable, one has to take into account the immediate effect of the opportunities for flexibility agreed upon, since the reduction of the demand for labor is the prime objective of employers' attempts to gain greater flexibility.[41] Furthermore, the volume of working-hours reduction has to be measured against the increase in hourly productivity of labor. Between 1985 and 1989 the reduction in the metal industry amounts to 1.5 percent per annum (in other industries it is even smaller), whereas one can assume hourly productivity in the manufacturing sector to be increasing by 3.5 percent per annum. This means that without a growth of production of approximately 2 percent per annum, job losses would have been unavoidable (because of flourishing exports, the growth rates were significantly higher). If, on account of its small caliber, working-time reduction has thus not become an effective instrument of employment policy, the resistance of the employers is not the only reason. It also reflects IG Metall's and other unions' correct evaluation of the persisting income needs of their employed membership.[42]

However, the 1987 agreement in the metal industry paved the way for all other unions within the DGB to negotiate on weekly working-time reduction after the respective collective agreements in the different industries had expired. And, of course, all unions have done (or will do) so, since the experiences with the early-retirement scheme (*Vorruhestand*) have been somewhat disappointing and the federal government did not extend it beyond the end of 1988.[43] It was replaced by a partial retirement scheme that seems not to be particularly attractive either to older employees or to their employers. Without exception, the unions thus gave priority to a reduction of weekly working hours. Therefore, in the final section I explore—on the basis of the development in the metal industry—what course working-time regulation might take in the future.

Time Hegemony for the Employers or Time Sovereignty for the Employees?

It is quite evident that the 1984 collective agreement in the metal industry (and those subsequently concluded in other industries) meant a departure from the tradition of general and linear working-time reductions. Accordingly, it has to be considered as highly unlikely that the arrangement and development of working hours can be brought back to its traditional track. Likewise, the employers' side will certainly not be content with the opportunities for flexibility it accomplished in 1984 and could enlarge in 1987. These agreements have perforated the standardized working-time arrangements and could, in the end, lead to a complete erosion of this major achievement of the working-class movement.

Meanwhile, the unions have accepted the heterogeneous preferences of the labor force and recognized that the need for time sovereignty cannot be satisfied merely by general working-time reductions.[44] However, they have not yet developed a conclusive position toward these issues, that is, which concessions might be made to employers' demands or which preferences of employees for extended time sovereignty should be pleaded for against opposing employer interests. When they, in default of an offensive concept, continue to "pay" small gains in working-time reduction with extended concessions for certain types of flexibility, not only will the desired effect of enlarged employment be nullified but, moreover, they will gamble away the standardized working-time arrangements that have to be regarded as a platform for extended individual time sovereignty as well as for collective progress:

1. When the employers are granted the opportunity for chronological dis-

continuity, the function of standardized working-time arrangements to ensure predictability of working hours and autonomous disposal of the employee's "own" regular (leisure) hours will wither away. This actually contradicts the ascertained preferences for more freedom of choice with regard to the chronological distribution and location of working hours.

2. The same holds true if the employers' claim for chronological denormalization to lengthen processing time is realized: If, for mere economic reasons, certain periods of the day or days of the week are no longer spared from the employers' grip on laborers' time, abnormal and, thus, unsocial working-time patterns, such as shift work, night work, or work on Saturdays or even Sundays will increase. As we know from various surveys among employees, the overwhelming majority of them are not voluntarily prepared to take up those working-time schedules, and those employees already affected prefer a normalization of working hours above all other alterations. Those working-time schedules (especially shift work in various forms) will increase the shorter the normal (or average) working hours become, since a mere cut-off of working hours (and of processing time) every working day or on Friday afternoon would contradict employers' primary interest in extending processing time. Even if daily or weekly working hours are reduced, an increase of shift work or work on Saturdays will impair the use-value of time off from work and aggravate the problems of families to synchronize desired (or necessary) activities.

3. As long as standardized working-time arrangements are a fixed measure for tailoring jobs, they guarantee that the employees will earn a full income without having to prove the actual need. If one uniform length of working time is replaced by a multitude of schedules according to firms' efficiency calculations, not only will the validity of the social norm diminish that employees *alone* may ask for shorter hours (and less pay) than normal. When firms are provided the option for chronometrical differentiation, they can assign substandard working-time schedules and corresponding incomes. The individual employee usually will be in an inferior position to resist those requests from the employer.

One can argue that employers would not impose working-time schedules meeting their interests against contradictory preferences and income needs of their employees, since any efficient productive process depends on a minimum of readiness to cooperate on the part of employees. Of course, there will also be a more or less broad margin of conformity between employers' interest in and employees' preferences for flexible working hours. But where this is not the case, the expectations that can be imposed upon employees without risking evasive reactions (e.g., absenteeism, fluctuation) increase the more replaceable the individual employee is and the more alternative candidates are available. Thus, in a situation of high unemployment that cannot be expected to be cured by exchanging shorter working hours for extended flexibility, the spreading of various forms of chronological and chronometrical flexibility will deepen traditional parting lines between segmented labor markets and will draw new ones.

4. Over and above a selective deterioration of individual working-time conditions, extended opportunities for flexibility will provoke substantial collective consequences: The participation of all employees in productivity gains secured by collective agreements is endangered when higher productivity will be compensated by the assignment of correspondingly shorter hours. Without the validity of standardized working-time arrangements, collectively agreed wage increases do not even guarantee the stability of income in every case.

5. Furthermore, an increased heterogeneity of working-time patterns following from an advance of various forms of flexibility makes it ever more difficult to interpret those patterns as deviations from standardized working-time arrangements. By progressive differentiation, these standards would lose their social validity as measures for organizing working time. If it is thus no longer possible to make the alteration of working-time standards a common goal that is broadly supported as a means of actual change, then the strategic function of standardized working-time arrangements is lost as well, that is to say, the ability for a collective limitation of labor supply is lost.

When the unions proceed along the path entered in 1984, it might be possible to attain the 35-hour week, which is already considered a "corridor station" for a 30-hour week.[45] But, under these circumstances, a 35-hour or a 30-hour week would be little more than "paper figures" because they do not determine the day-by-day or week-by-week reality for all employees and do not structure the major societal rhythms. The functions of standardized working-time arrangements would be eroded and the "time hegemony" of the employers strengthened.

Finally, I outline an alternative scenario that focuses on the enlargement of employees' opportunities for self-determination to accomplish a redistribution of working hours over the life course (as well as within the household), depending on varying needs for income and preferences or obligations to spend time in spheres outside employment. Those institutions concerned with shaping and regulating working time so far have been mainly prepared to bring about concrete, actual changes of working time—to regulate "what *has* to be." By this mode of regulation it is no longer possible to catch up with the socially diffused and individually unstable preferences of employees. On the other hand, the standardized working-time arrangements perform indispensable protective functions, and their abolition would make employees' demand for time sovereignty fictitious and collective progress impossible. Thus, to preserve the validity of these standards *and* to satisfy employees' preferences, it is necessary to switch to a mode of *procedural* regulation—to generate "meta-rules" determining which concrete conditions in the individual case might be negotiated in what manner. This would mean "guaranteed individual options" to deviate from standard hours and, inter alia, the installment of employees' rights to work less (than normal) or to a temporary withdrawal from employed work. Such guaranteed individual options can be considered as the "inverse" form of the individual decision to work longer hours (or employers' right to demand overtime).

The realization of employees' preferences for a voluntary reduction of working hours is probably more efficient for creating additional employment than any conceivable and realistic working-time reduction scheme. This would be especially so if employees are capable of presenting their *original* time preferences even when these preferences run contrary to firms' interest in applying labor power, and the employees are assured that their requests are handled in a formalized procedure and that they do not have to fear negative consequences in other aspects of their employment (e.g., job security, career prospects). Furthermore, although the readiness for an individual reduction of working hours *and* pay (or for a temporary withdrawal) is not overwhelming at the moment (see above), it is nevertheless amenable to political influence. To make the corresponding income loss less than proportional could enhance the willingness to opt for less work or a temporary withdrawal. It would be part of a supply-side policy that expands situations that entitle one to money income (so far there are only two circumstances allowing one to get command over money income: gainful employment and the claim to receive earnings-replacing benefits when certain well-defined inabilities to perform paid work occur). This policy aims to "liquefy" the transitions between full-time employment and temporal part-time work or withdrawal from paid employment when creating attractive, freely chosen alternatives to continuous full-time employment. The alternatives are those where activities considered as socially useful are performed during periods not spent in paid (full-time) work and which thus constitute a legitimate reason to receive publicly financed support.[46]

There exist various options for employees in the public services to work less. Child-rearing has been recognized as a socially useful task in the granting of certain credits with regard to the pension system and the enactment of a subsidized parental leave (up to 18 months, now). However, one can conceive of financial support for an extended parental leave if both parents successively or simultaneously reduce their working hours or interrupt their employed work, or of providing entitlements when unpaid work on behalf of elderly or handicapped persons is performed (either at home or in the context of voluntary associations delivering social services). These examples by far do not cover the potential occasions for providing subsistence to persons who are not employed or not full time employed.

The present West German government, however, seems less prepared to promote employees' entitlements for time sovereignty than it is eager to give legal support to firms' interest in deregulation and more (working-time) flexibility. Thus, the possibility of installing "guaranteed individual options" by collective agreement remains. Most paradoxically, this could be achieved only when the unions stick to the demand for further working-time reductions but change their tactics so that a compromise which establishes those individual entitlements is now given priority, namely, to working-time reductions that are combined with enlarged options for flexibility according to firms' interests.

Notes

1. L. Preller, *Sozialpolitik in der Weimarer Republik* (Kronberg/Düsseldorf: Athenäum/Droste, 1978).

2. K.-H. van Kevelaer and K. Hinrichs, "Arbeitszeit und 'Wirtschaftswunder': Rahmenbedingungen des Übergangs zur 40-Stunden-Woche in der Bundesrepublik Deutschland," *Politische Vierteljahresschrift* 26, 1 (1986): 52–75.

3. O. Neuloh, *Arbeitszeit und Produktivität. Untersuchungsergebnisse wissenschaftlicher Forschungsinstitute, Bd. 3: Betriebssoziologische Untersuchungen* (Berlin: Duncker & Humblot, 1962), pp. 16f.; K. Hinrichs, *Motive und Interessen*, pp. 131f.

4. Der Bundesminister für Arbeit und Sozialordnung (ed.), *Statistisches Taschenbuch 1988: Arbeits- und Sozialstatistik* (Bonn, 1988), tables 4.2 and 4.3.

5. Ibid., table 4.8.

6. Ibid., table 4.8; L. Clasen, "Tarifvertragliche Arbeitsbedingungen: Sechs Wochen Urlaub," *Bundesarbeitsblatt* (March 1982): 22–30; L. Clasen, "Tarif-verträge 1986: Wieder Anstieg der Nettorealverdienste," *Bundesarbeitsblatt* (March 1987): 10–14.

7. Calculated from unpublished data of the Institut für Arbeitsmarkt- und Berufsforschung in Nuremberg and H. Kohler and L. Reyher, *Arbeitszeit und Arbeitsvolumen in der Bundesrepublik Deutschland 1960–1986*, Beiträge zur Arbeitsmarkt- und Berufsforschung, vol. 123 (Nuremberg, 1988), p. 231.

8. Calculated from C. Brinkmann, et al., *Überstunden: Entwicklung, Strukturen und Bestimmungsgrößen*, Beiträge zur Arbeitsmarkt- und Berufsforschung, vol. 98 (Nuremberg 1986), tables A2 and A3, and p. 72.

9. *Statistisches Jahrbuch 1953*, pp. 43 and 123; H.-J. Heidenreich, "Erwerbstätigkeit im April 1988. Ergebnis des Mikrozensus," *Wirtschaft und Statistik* (June 1989): 327–339 (p. 331).

10. Verband Deutscher Rentenversicherungsträger (ed.), *Der Rentenzugang und der Rentenwegfall im Jahre 1974* (Frankfurt, 1975), pp. 45 and 125; Verband Deutscher Rentenversicherungsträger (ed.), *Rentenzugang des Jahres 1986 in der deutschen gesetzlichen Rentenversicherung einschließlich Rentenwegfall/Rentenumwandlung* (Frankfurt, 1987), p. 76.

11. B. Hof, "Erwerbsbiographien im langfristigen Vergleich," *IW-Trends* no. 1 (15 March 1986): 34–48.

12. *Statistisches Jahrbuch 1953*, pp. 43 and 123; H.-J. Heidenreich, "Erwerbstätigkeit im April 1988," p. 331.

13. This small share of involuntary part-time workers contrasts with the U.S. situation, cf. S. A. Levitan and E. Conway, "Part-timers: Living on Half-rations," *Challenge* 31, 3 (May/June 1988): 9–16. For the figures on the development of part-time employment in the FRG see: C. Brinkmann and H. Kohler, "Am Rande der Erwerbsbeteiligung: Frauen mit geringfügiger, gelegentlicher oder befristeter Arbeit," in W. Klauder

and G. Kühlewind (eds.), *Probleme der Messung und Vorausschätzung des Frauener-werbspotentials*, Beiträge zur Arbeitsmarkt- und Berufsforschung, vol. 56 (Nuremberg, 1981), pp. 120–146; C. F. Büchtemann and J. Schupp, *Socio-economic Aspects of Part-Time Employment in the Federal Republic of Germany*, Discussion Paper FS I 88–6 (Berlin: Wissenschaftszentrum Berlin für Sozialforschung, 1988); H.-J. Heidenreich, "Erwerbstätigkeit im Ápril 1988," pp. 336f.

14. OECD, *Employment Outlook: September 1983* (Paris, 1983), pp. 43ff; OECD, *Employment Outlook: September 1988* (Paris, 1988), pp. 20ff. and 129ff; S. Gustafs-son, *Institutional Environment and the Economics of Female Labor Force Participation and Fertility*, Discussion Paper IIM/LMP 85–9 (Berlin: Wissenschaftszentrum, 1985); K. Schoer, "Part-Time Employment: Britain and West Germany," *Cambridge Journal of Economics* 11, 1 (March 1987): 83–94.

15. For the sources of these figures see K. Hinrichs, *Motive und Interessen*, pp. 110 and 239. It is not undue to assume the percentage to have risen up to 20 at present since a further push took place in the wake of the implementation of shorter weekly working hours after 1985; cf. R. Schmidt, "Über die Notwendigkeit und die Probleme einer tarifvertraglichen Rahmengestaltung von Gleitzeitvereinbarungen," *WSI-Mit-teilungen* 40, 12 (December 1987): 735–745 (p. 739).

16. For detailed figures see K. Hinrichs, *Motive und Interessen*, pp. 109f.

17. H. Herkner, "Arbeitszeit," in L. Elster et al. (eds.), *Handwörterbuch der Staatswissenschaften*, vol. 1, 4th ed. (Jena: Gustav Fischer, 1923), pp. 889–916 (pp. 899f).

18. K. Hinrichs, *Motive und Interessen*, pp. 278ff.

19. The declining priority given to working-time reductions can be demonstrated when one compares the change of the length of normal working hours in response to a 1 percent increase of real wages for two periods (*if* one assumes wage movements to be influential for the formation of working-time preferences and that these preferences are dominating the actual development of working hours): In Germany between 1871 and 1913 the elasticity was − 0.23 (on the average). In contrast, during the period of 1950 to 1980 it was down to − 0.14 (between 1918 and the end of free collective bargaining in 1933 there was no stable upward development of wages and almost no variation in normal working hours). For more details on these calculations, cf. K. Hinrichs, *Motive und Interessen*, pp. 163ff.

20. S. and B. Webb, *Problems of Modern Industry* (London: Longmans, Green, 1902), p. 137. Even in 1987 not more than 28 percent of the employees interviewed in a representative survey preferred a reduction of weekly working hours; earlier retirement (39 percent) and a longer vacation (25 percent) found still more adherents (8 percent refused any working-time reduction); cf. Der Minister für Arbeit, Gesundheit und Soziales des Landes Nordrhein-Westfalen (ed.), *Arbeitszeit '87: Ein Report zu Arbeits-zeiten und Arbeitszeitpräferenzen der Beschäftigten in der Bundesrepublik* (Düsseldorf, 1987), pp. 92ff.

21. B. Teriet, "Die Wiedergewinnung der Zeitsouveränität," in F. Duve (ed.), *Technologie und Politik*, vol. 8 (Reinbek: Rowohlt, 1977), pp. 75–111.

22. U. Beck, *Risikogesellschaft: Auf dem Weg in eine andere Moderne* (Frankfurt: Suhrkamp, 1986), chaps. III—VI; J. Mooser, *Arbeiterleben in Deutschland, 1900–1970: Klassenlagen, Kultur und Politik* (Frankfurt: Suhrkamp, 1984), pp. 224ff; U.

Engfer, K. Hinrichs, and H. Wiesenthal, "Arbeitswerte im Wandel: Empirische Analysen zum Zusammenhang von unkonventionellen Werten und Arbeitsbeteiligung," in J. Matthes (ed.), *Krise der Arbeitsgesellschaft? Verhandlungen des 21. Deutschen Soziologentages in Bamberg 1982* (Frankfurt and New York: Campus, 1983), pp. 434–454; H. Wiesenthal and K. Hinrichs, "An den Grenzen des Arbeiterbewußtseins," *Gewerkschaftliche Monatshefte* 34, 12 (December 1983): 775–788; S. Hradil, *Sozialstrukturanalyse in einer fortgeschrittenen Gesellschaft, Von Klassen und Schichten zu Lagen und Milieus* (Opladen: Leske and Budrich, 1987).

23. K. Hinrichs, *Motive und Interessen*, pp. 242ff.

24. K. Hinrichs, C. Offe, and H. Wiesenthal, "On Time, Money, and Welfare Capitalism," in J. Keane (ed.), *Civil Society and the State* (London: Verso, 1988), pp. 221–243 (pp. 233f.); K. Hinrichs, *Zeit und Geld in privaten Haushalten* (Bielefeld: AJZ-Druck und Verlag, 1989), pp. 36ff.

25. S. E. Shank, "Preferred Hours of Work and Corresponding Earnings," *Monthly Labor Review* 109, 11 (November 1986): 40–44.

26. Cited in D. Mertens, "Neue Arbeitszeitpolitik und Arbeitsmarkt," *Mitteilungen aus der Arbeitsmarkt- und Berufsforschung* 12, 3 (1979): 263–269 (p. 265).

27. G. Nerb, "Arbeitsmarktprobleme: Ansichten der Unternehmer und Arbeitnehmer," *Europäische Wirtschaft* 27 (1986): 5–112 (p. 52).

28. M. A. Bienefeld, *Working Hours in British Industry: An Economic History* (London: Weidenfeld & Nicolson, 1972).

29. K. Hinrichs and H. Wiesenthal, "Bestandsrationalität versus Kollektivinteresse: Gewerkschaftliche Handlungsprobleme im Arbeitszeitkonflikt 1984," *Soziale Welt* 37, 2/3 (1986): 280–296 (pp. 281f.).

30. K. Hinrichs, W.K. Roche, and H. Wiesenthal, "Working Time Policy as Class-Oriented Strategy: Unions and Shorter Working Hours in Great Britain and West Germany," *European Sociological Review* 1, 3 (December 1985): 211–229 (pp. 214ff.).

31. Ibid., pp. 214 f.; K. Hinrichs, C. Offe, and H. Wiesenthal, "On Time, Money, and Welfare Capitalism," pp. 227ff.

32. For the following see: K. Hinrichs and H. Wiesenthal, "Bestandsrationalität versus Kollektivinteresse," pp. 287ff.; more extensively: H. Wiesenthal, *Strategie und Illusion*, pp. 159ff.

33. K. Hinrichs, W. K. Roche, and H. Wiesenthal, "Working Time Policy," pp. 220f. and 227 (n. 7).

34. For a more detailed description of the course of the dispute and an evaluation of the results (from a trade unionist's point of view), see G. Bosch, "The Dispute over the Reduction of the Working Week in West Germany," *Cambridge Journal of Economics* 10, 3 (September 1986): 271–290.

35. In common with the employers, the conservative-liberal government declared the unions' demand as unsuitable at best. During the "hot stage" of the struggle the government intervened twice: It enacted a law on early retirement (*Vorruhestand*) in April 1984. The timing of this enactment indicates that it was undoubtedly intended to hinder the mobilizing efforts of those unions committed to a shorter workweek. Furthermore, during the labor dispute the government influenced the decision of the Federal Labor Office to deny short-time allowances to those employees who were, so to speak, also "locked out" because their firms lacked deliveries from firms included in strikes and

(real) lockouts. At that moment this decree meant a serious burden for the IG Metall to retain unity within its membership.

36. For a discussion of the various reasons, cf. R. Schmidt and R. Trinczek, "Erfahrungen und Perspektiven gewerkschaftlicher Arbeitszeitpolitik," *Probleme des Klassenkampfs* 16, 3 (1986): 85–105. They argue that the implementation of new working-time arrangements implies a period of "incubation" (ibid., p. 100).

37. G. Bosch et al., *Betriebliche Umsetzung der 38,5-Studen-Woche: Ergebnisse einer Auswertung von Betriebsvereinbarungen aus der Metallindustrie*, WSI-Arbeitsmaterialien Nr. 12 (Düsseldorf, 1986); Gesamtverband der metallindustriellen Arbeitgeberverbände, *Sonderumfrage zur betrieblichen Durchführung der ab 1. 4. 1985 geltenden neuen tarifvertraglichen Arbeitszeitregelungen in der Metallindustrie* (Cologne, 1985).

38. For a synopsis on the different calculations see F. Stille and R. Zwiener, "Beschäftigungswirkungen der Arbeitszeitverkürzung von 1985 in der Metallindustrie," *Deutsches Institut für Wirtschaftsforschung—Wochenbericht* 54, 20 (14 May 1987): 273–279.

39. L. Clasen, "Tarifverträge 1988: Weitere Arbeitszeitverkürzungen," *Bundesarbeitsblatt* (March 1989): 17–22 (p. 19).

40. Deutscher Bundestag, *Gesetzentwurf der Bundesregierung: Entwurf eines Arbeitszeitgesetzes (ArbZG)*, Drucksache 11/360 of 25 May 1987 (Bonn).

41. Some works council members who were delegates at the IG Metall Congress in 1986 argued that they had not been able to withstand the pressure from the management to agree upon shop-floor agreements on flexibility. These agreements had nullified the employment effect of the working-time reduction (cf. "Flexi-Modelle sollen nicht verboten sein," *Handelsblatt* no. 208 [29 October 1986]: 5).

42. These needs were taken into account, since the peak agreement in the metal industry included a three-year wage contract as well, which also represents a novelty (so far, wage agreements usually covered only one year). The agreement contained an increase of 3.7 percent in 1987 and—over and above the "full wage compensation"—of 2.0 percent (1988) and of 2.5 percent (1989). Since the inflation rate remained at approximately 1 per cent, this settlement secured rising real earnings. At the same time it is of great value to employers to have certainty of labor costs for three years.

43. Until the end of 1987 approximately 140,000 employees 58 years of age or older have taken up the opportunities provided by the *Vorruhestandsgesetz* and left the labor market. This has led to approximately 60,000 substitutional hirings. These results have clearly fallen short of the optimistic expectations of the supporters of this scheme. For the figures and a discussion of the problems, cf. V. Meinhardt and R. Zwiener, "Vorruhestandsregelung solite verlängert werden," *Deutsches Institut für Wirtschaftsforschung—Wochenbericht* 55, 4 (28 January 1988): 41–49.

44. Deutscher Gewerkschaftsbund (Bundesvorstand), "Stellungnahme zur Arbeitszeitpolitik," *Gewerkschaftliche Umschau: Zeitschrift für die Funktionäre der Industriegewerkschaft Chemie-Papier-Keramik* no. 2/3 (1986): 30–32; IG Metall (Vorstand—Abt. Tarifpolitik), *Arbeitszeitflexibilisierung und Arbeitnehmerinteressen—Positionspapier der IG Metall*, Materialien zur Arbeitszeitdiskussion 2/86 (Frankfurt, 1986).

45. Kurz-Scherg, "Zeit(t)räume per Tarifvertrag. Oder: Die Renaissance der betriebsnahen Tarifpolitik," *WSI—Mitteilungen* 40, 8 (August 1987): 492–502; K. Zwickel and K. Lang, "Gewerkschaften 2000," *WSI—Mitteilungen* 40, 8 (August 1987): 455–464.

46. B. Lutz, "Notwendigkeit und Ansatzpunkte einer angebotsbezogenen Vollbeschäftigungspolitik," in L. Reyher and J. Kühl (eds.), *Resonanzen: Arbeitsmarkt und Beruf—Forschung und Politik. Festschrift für Dieter Mertens*, Beiträge zur Arbeitsmarkt- und Berufsforschung, vol. 111 (Nuremberg, 1988), pp. 275–289 (p. 285ff.). Several regulations with regard to a publicly subsidized "time sovereignty" are listed by the parliamentary group of the Green Party in their "counterproposal" to the plan for a new working-time law submitted by the federal government (see above, n. 40), cf. Deutscher Bundestag, *Gesetzentwurf der Fraktion DIE GRÜNEN: Entwurf eines Arbeitszeitgesetzes (AZG)*, Drucksache 11/1188 of 13 November 1987 (Bonn).

3   Working-Time Policies in France

Jean-Pierre Jallade

This chapter presents an analysis of recent developments and policies concerning the reduction and adjustment of working time in France. The issue is discussed in connection with employment policy and, more specifically, with the efforts made to fight unemployment and modernize the production apparatus during the first half of the 1980s. This chapter concentrates on the measures for reducing or adjusting working time in relation to the working week, the working year, and the working life, highlighting the gaps between statutory and actual duration, the intended and unintended economic and other effects of these measures, as well as the changing ideas and attitudes about working time.

Brief reference is made, first, to the historical context that is the setting for the initiatives taken in the 1980s so that the reader may judge the extent to which these initiatives do no more than extrapolate an evolutionary trend or, on the contrary, change the trend in one direction or another. The first section concentrates on the period 1960–1980 and, above all, on the period of "crisis" that began in 1974. In the second section the relationships between working time, employment, and unemployment are examined. The third section deals with the government measures taken in the early 1980s as regards the adjustment and the reduction of working time. In the fourth section the issue of flexibility in working time is examined from the viewpoints of the individual, the firm, and the economy as a whole. Future prospects for working-time policies are briefly explored in the concluding section.

Recent Trends Toward Shorter Working Time

In contemporary France the 1936 legislation introducing the 40-hour week and two weeks of paid leave per year is customarily considered as the beginning of modern policies concerning working time. Enacted by Leon Blum's socialist government at a time when the effective duration of the working week was 44 hours, this legislation has always been regarded as a symbol of great achievement by the French working class, although, according to economic historians, it may have helped thwart the promising economic recovery of the year 1937.

Trends in Weekly Working Time

Postwar trends in weekly working time are shown in Figure 3-1, which is based on effective figures concerning the average number of hours worked. Three major lessons can be learned from the figure. First, the postwar economic environment (reconstruction, rapid growth) was not characterized by a marked reduction of weekly working time, to say the least. Working time actually increased between 1946 and 1966, and then went back to the 1946 level in 1972. The turning point was 1967,[1] which marked the beginning of a rapid and steady process of reduction of effective working time for all wage earners: the 44-hour level was reached in 1972, the 43-hour level in 1974, 42 hours in 1976, 41 in 1978. Interestingly enough, the reduction of working time that has taken place since 1968 is not the result of some legislative provision but the culmination of a series of contractual agreements entered into by the "social partners" (management and labor).

Second, the figure also highlights the gap between statutory and effective working time. Indeed, it took almost half a century for the spirit of the 1936 legislation proclaiming the 40-hour week to be translated into reality, which shows that working time is not only a matter of legislation but also of economics as well. During this period, overtime bridged the gap between statutory and effective duration.

Finally, the gap between the effective working time of manual workers and that of employees has shrunk over the years. Until 1970 manual workers spent on average two hours a week more at work than did salaried employees; by 1980 the differential had been reduced to half an hour. Yet no legislative provision had been enacted for the express purpose of achieving this result, which might be explained by the economic conditions (crisis and uncertainty) prevailing during most of the 1970s.

The Working Year

The duration of the working year can be determined on the basis of that of the working week minus paid leave and official holidays. But this is only a theoretical measurement overestimating the actual duration of working time, which is shorter because of absenteeism resulting from sickness and maternity leave, work accidents, strikes, and so forth.

Paid leave (two weeks) was first introduced in 1936. After the war it was extended to three weeks in 1956, four weeks in 1963, and, finally, five weeks in 1982. This policy—rather generous by any international standards, especially those of Japan and North America—implied a notable shortening of the statutory working year. There are no time series concerning the effective duration of the working year (excluding absenteeism), but the estimates made by Doyelle[2] and the Commissariat Général du Plan[3] show that for manual workers the number of hours worked during the year decreased by roughly 10 percent

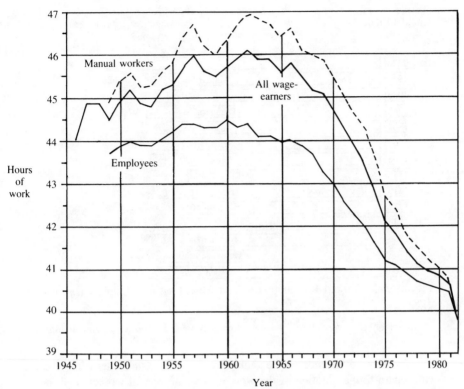

FIGURE 3-1. Trends in Weekly Effective Working Time

Source: Ministry of Labour Survey.

between 1974 (1,780 hours) and 1982 (1,610 hours). In a sample of 11 Organization for Economic Cooperation and Development (OECD) countries, France ranked seventh in 1974—with only four countries having a shorter working year—as against eighth in 1982. When all wage earners are considered, the effective working year is longer (1,700 hours in 1982) and has decreased by only 6 percent between 1974 and 1982. France currently ranks third in the same sample of OECD countries.

These data confirm the point made earlier, namely, that the reduction in working time benefited manual workers more than other workers. The word *benefit* may actually be inappropriate to the extent that this trend reflected a *steady decrease in overtime* and, as a corollary, in overtime pay, because of the adverse economic conditions prevailing between 1974 and 1982. By contrast, other wage earners (mostly employees) work somewhat longer but, more importantly, they are better protected by their statutory conditions against shorter working time and the resultant loss of pay.

Statutory working time	Effective working time	Absenteeism

Statutory		
2226	Japan 2192	34
1912	United States 1850	62
1936	Switzerland 1828	108
1792	Denmark 1695	97
1804	Austria 1652	152
1763	Great Britain 1647	116
1763	France 1639	124
1776	Italy 1631	145
1816	Finland 1624	192
1717	Belgium 1619	98
1740	The Netherlands 1609	131
1840	Norway 1608	232
1708	Germany 1580	128
1800	Sweden 1576	224

FIGURE 3-2. Annual Working Time and Absenteeism in Industry (*in hours, 1985*)

Source: Social International (Union des Industries Métallurgiques et Minières, 1986).

The large difference in the ranking of France on the international scene with regard to the duration of the working year of manual workers and that of all wage earners can be explained by the greater homogeneity of working-time arrangements in France among workers and employees, industry and services. In other countries diversity due to phenomena like part-time work in the commerce and service sectors is far greater. A typical example is the United States, which ranks second to Japan as regards the duration of working time of manual workers but eighth when all wage earners are considered.

The latest available estimate concerning the duration of the working year in industry, including and excluding absenteeism, has recently been issued by the economic institute of the federation of German employers. The data highlight the existence for the working year of a pattern (1,600–1,700 hours worked per year) that is largely common to European countries (excluding Switzerland) but that is shorter than in Japan and the United States (see Figure 3-2).

Working Life

The duration of working life is obviously affected by that of the working year but also by policies related to entry into and withdrawal from the labor market. There is no doubt that entry into working life has been gradually postponed by the steady expansion of full-time education and also by the increasing employment difficulties faced by young people. According to the 1982 census, fewer than 5 percent of young persons under the age of 20 hold stable jobs. Whether they are at school (80 percent of the 15–19 group), trainees or apprentices, in temporary jobs, in the armed forces, or unemployed, their entry into normal working life is considerably delayed in comparison with older generations.

At the other end of working life, very generous early-retirement policies have also contributed to a reduction in the number of working years. The first early-retirement scheme of significant scope was set up in 1972 by means of an agreement between employers and unions with the support of the government. Under this scheme all workers over 60 who were laid off were to be granted a benefit amounting to 70 percent of the gross wage up to retirement age (65). In 1977 the agreement was extended with the same benefit to all jobless workers over 60, including those who voluntarily quit their jobs. In addition to these wide-ranging schemes, sector-specific initiatives were taken in the late 1970s to ease out of the labor force redundant workers from 56 years of age: in the steel industry, for instance, a redundant worker stopping work at age 56 now receives continuous and improved unemployment compensation until 60, early-retirement benefits between 60 and 65, and then the pension from 65 on.

It is important to underline that all these schemes were the result of negotiations between employers' organizations and workers' unions. Agreements were possible because both parties expected to benefit from them. On the one hand, employers would get rid of aging workers more easily, while unions would secure significantly improved benefits (compared with traditional unemployment benefits) for aging workers whose jobs were threatened.

The effect of these early-retirement schemes on the duration of working life took some time to materialize, however, as the number of beneficiaries of the first (1972) scheme was always rather marginal. The 1977 decision to extend eligibility to all jobless workers over 60, thus blurring the distinction between laid-off workers and voluntary leavers, removed some of the social stigma still attached to early retirement. This decision, together with rising employment difficulties in many sectors, led many workers to opt for early retirement, which was then considered as a golden opportunity not to be missed. As a result, the number of early retired shot up to 300,000 by 1980.

Unlike the 1972 agreement, the 1977 decision gave workers the opportunity to leave voluntarily, although in many instances significant pressure may have been brought to bear on those reluctant to do so. This change was welcomed by unions as a significant step toward flexible retirement, while employers also hailed a move that enabled them to get rid of aging and costly workers.[4]

All these measures to encourage early withdrawal from active life—well before the statutory retirement age of 65—resulted in a significant lowering of the activity rates of aging workers. According to 1982 census data,[5] the activity rates of males aged 60–64 fell from 54 percent in 1975 to 39 percent in 1982; those of males aged 55–59 from 82 percent to 77 percent. A similar drop is recorded for females aged 60–64. All in all, only about one in four in the 60–64 age group was still active at the beginning of the 1980s.

Not only is the effective duration of working life steadily shortened because of late entry and early withdrawal, but other labor-market developments contribute to a decrease in average working time during working life. The most important of these factors is the rise in female employment (which has been even stronger than expected) and its consequences for part-time work. In 1982, 64 percent of adult women between the ages of 25 and 54 were active, as against 53 percent in 1975 and 45 percent in 1968. Women now account for more than 40 percent of the entire active population. Conversely, activity rates of adult males (not merely older workers) have declined more steeply than expected. It seems, therefore, that French society is heading gently toward equalization of male and female activity rates. As a result of the increasing share of females in the labor force, part-time work has been increasing steadily for more than 20 years,[6] currently providing employment for one-fifth of the female labor force. In 1984 the total number of wage earners working on a part-time basis was estimated at 1.6 million.

The increase of atypical work in its various forms—part-time employment, seasonal work, fixed-term contracts, temporary work, public service auxiliaries, home work—is another important factor that lowers the average duration of working time during working life. According to Fossaert,[7] approximately 10 percent of all gainfully employed persons are thought to be engaged in some form of atypical work. Unofficial work (moonlighting) should be added to the list to the (unknown) extent that it contributes to a reduction in the official duration of the working year.

All these phenomena (delayed entry into working life, early withdrawal, rising female employment and part-time work, atypical forms of work, and moonlighting) tend to shorten average working life, although it is very difficult to assess the extent of the change with any accuracy. In 1965 Fourastie[8] tentatively predicted that the average length of working life would go down to 42,000 hours (30-hour weeks in 40 worked weeks a year and 35 working years over a lifetime) by the year 2050. Whether or not the prediction will come true is at yet impossible to say, although it is only fair to note that significant progress toward this goal has been achieved over the past twenty years. Thus, in the early 1960s, the working life of the average French worker was an estimated 90,000 hours on the basis of a 46-hour working week for 49 weeks a year and 40 years' work. By 1985 the duration of working life had decreased by one-third to about 61,000 hours on the basis of 1,640 hours of effective work per year and 37.5 years' work—the minimum number required to receive full social security retirement benefit.

Working Time, Employment, and Unemployment

Reviewing trends toward shorter working time, as we have done in the preceding section, is one thing: explaining them is another. The most important issue is to figure out whether these trends are caused by a falling demand for labor, as a result of rising labor productivity, or are induced by supply factors related to new attitudes among the labor force. Closely connected with this issue is the readily observable fact that working time does not shorten at the same rate for everybody. As labor productivity rises, some workers have no working time at all (the unemployed) while others manage to retain theirs very adequately. In between, there exists a variety of mixed situations (those of part-timers) more or less voluntarily chosen by workers. From this stems the idea of a direct, simple relationship between working time and employment (or unemployment) and the conviction shared by many analysts in France and elsewhere, most notably in West Germany,[9] that the former can be manipulated in order to achieve results with the latter. More specifically, the key question is whether working time can be shared equitably among all potential workers to ensure full employment.

In the case of France, the relationships between changes in working time and employment in the past can be summarized as follows:

1. Up to 1962, working time increased (see Figure 3-1) while employment remained fairly stable (+ 0.1 percent per year between 1954 and 1962) and unemployment very low. This situation resulted from the conjunction of an upward pressure exerted on the demand for labor by fast economic growth with a check on supply exerted by demographic factors, essentially the low birth rates of the prewar period. Thus, the only way to respond to the increasing demand for labor was to increase working time.

2. Between 1962 and 1968 the economy kept growing fast enough to keep the demand for labor at a high level. However, at this time it resulted in job creation (employment rose by 0.8 percent per year) while working time started to decrease slowly. Clearly, this type of labor supply response was made possible by the fact that postwar "baby boom" generations were reaching adulthood.

3. Between 1968 and 1974 employment kept increasing at the same rate (+ 0.8 percent per year) and working time decreased faster than in the previous period, but neither of them rapidly enough to accommodate the fast rising supply of labor. Unemployment started to grow and reached the half-million mark for the first time in 1974.

4. Following the first oil crisis, the 1974–80 period was characterized by a slowdown in the rate of economic growth while labor productivity kept increasing at a significant rate. The rate of employment growth went down (+ 0.2 percent per year). At the same time, the supply of labor increased faster than before as a result of both the "demographic effect" and, now more impor-

tant, the rising female participation rates. Unemployment shot up to 1.5 million in 1980 despite the continuous decrease in working time.

5. During the 1980–85 period, uncertainty on the economic front led to a decline in employment while unemployment rose even further to 2.3 million (about 10 percent of the labor force) in spite of the efforts made by the government to speed up the decrease in working time (see below). Interestingly enough, rising unemployment did not deter women from entering the labor force in ever greater numbers, lending some support to the view that present rates of unemployment are, partly at least, due to supply factors. It is actually the conjunction of economic factors (i.e., slow growth and falling demand for labor) and of sociological factors (more women entering the labor force) that accounts for today's high unemployment.

An important lesson to be learned from the past with regard to the relationship between working time and employment is that it is neither simple nor obvious, because of the interference of economic and demographic factors affecting labor supply and demand. Before the 1973–74 crisis the reduction of working time proceeded without any apparent effect on the level of employment and, as from 1974, it was incapable of containing the rising tide of unemployment.

This overall conclusion should, however, be qualified by the fact that the connection between working time and employment in industry differs vastly from that in the service sector. An in-depth study carried out by the Commissariat Général du Plan[10] and covering eleven industrialized countries during 1974–82 highlights this point. According to the study, improvements in labor productivity largely explain the reduction in industrial employment, and the reduction in working time is used to limit the redundancies caused by the modernization of industry. Under union pressure, shorter working time is viewed as a defense against cutting back jobs in industry. Data show that the reduction in working time contributed as much as did industrial growth to a slackening in such cutbacks. The same conclusion had been reached a few years earlier by Boisard,[11] who investigated the reasons behind decisions to reduce working time in a sample of French industrial firms. His study emphasized the need to preserve existing jobs in firms in difficulty as one of the main justifications for shorter working time. Thus, shorter working time is a form of partial unemployment, making it possible to reduce wage costs and, at the same time, to adjust output to demand. The reduction of working time does not create jobs, but it stems the rise in unemployment.

The situation is very different in the service sector, where 1.8 million jobs were created (+ 15 percent) in the period 1975 to 1982. Two-thirds of these additional jobs are held by women, thereby confirming the well-known relationship between the "tertiarization" of industrial economies and the "feminization" of their labor forces. Since the reduction of working time is known to have been a very common practice in the tertiary sector, particularly because of the extension of part-time employment, there is some evidence to support the view that in the service sector the shortening of working time has contributed very substantially to the creation of tertiary jobs. This observation is confirmed by evidence from other countries, notably the United States, where it is now accepted that, of the very large number of jobs created in recent years, the great majority have been in the service sector. In this sector, moreover, the process has been accompanied by a sharp reduction in weekly working hours in certain branches—particularly the commercial ones—where the working week is currently less than 32 hours. It follows, therefore, that in the tertiary sector the reduction of working time has definitely contributed to the countering of unemployment through the creation of new jobs.

In contrast to industry, the reduction of working time in the service sectors was not so much the result of a shortening of the working day or week for existing jobs as of a sharp increase in the number of jobholders working less than full-time: part-timers, job-sharers, weekend workers, and so forth. In other words, it is the diversification of work schedules, which is far greater in the service sectors than in industry, that has led to shorter average working time in these sectors, rather than a general reduction of working time for all workers. Thus, the connection between shorter working time and the level of employment is much more obvious in the service sectors than in industry, It is difficult, however, to provide an accurate estimate of the number of additional jobs created in these sectors following the adoption of more diversified working-time policies: according to the Institut National de la Statistique et des Études (INSEE) calculations, approximately 20 percent of the 800,000 additional jobs created between 1975 and 1982 are believed to be the result of these policies.

The demand for diversified working schedules and shorter working time is expected to rise further in the future as a direct consequence of the increasing share of women in the labor force and the resultant increase in households with two incomes. The demand for full-time jobs, which is very strong as long as there is only one jobholder per household, is quite likely to diversify into various forms of part-time work from the time that one of the spouses holds a full-time job. To the extent that the household is the consumer unit, it can adjust its time supply to the job market in accordance with its consumption needs: between the 40 hours offered in cases where the head of the family is the sole worker and the 80 hours that the two spouses can offer, there is a whole range of possible working situations that depart from the traditional 39–40 hours a week.

This trend may lead to two opposite results: either a more even sharing of work among all potential workers, and especially among men and women, or a more acute gender-based segmentation between full and part-timers. The cultural forces militating against part-time work for men are well known. One of the most powerful ones is related to men's refusal to share domestic and child-caring work on an equal footing with women. But there are economic forces

working in the opposite direction: lower female wage rates, which understanda-
bly are considered negatively by working women, have also proved to be a
powerful instrument for women to gain new footholds in the labor market, as
employers respond to this incentive by substituting women for men in their
workforce.

The Government Initiatives of the Early 1980s

In 1981 a new, socialist government took office. Committed to a
drastic reduction in unemployment, this government promptly put into effect,
with the support of the trade unions, a vigorous across-the-board policy for
shortening working time. According to this policy, the statutory working week
was to be reduced step by step from 40 hours in 1981 to 35 hours in 1985; the
working year was shortened by granting a fifth week of leave with pay in 1982;
as to working life, it, too, was to be made shorter by means of early-retirement
policies.

Underlying this policy was the belief that shorter working time at all levels
would help reduce unemployment. Great expectations were attached to work
sharing, a trendy concept meaning that jobholders should work less to provide
more jobs for the unemployed. The structure of unemployment that affected
young people more than any other category of workers lent support to a policy
aimed primarily at "making room for all those who were excluded from gainful
employment in one way or another."

In addition to these initiatives to reduce working time, others were taken
to adjust and diversify it according to working needs. By contrast with the
political enthusiasm that surrounded the former, the latter were half-hearted and
did not benefit from union support. They were often interpreted as a favor to
employers to soften their opposition to the reduction of working time.

How effective were these initiatives?

The 35-hour Week by 1985

In early 1982 the government's will to shorten working time was put into
effect by means of an ordinance that lowered the statutory duration of the working week from 40 to 39 hours—as a first stage in the direction of the 35-hour
week planned for 1985—and introduced the fifth week of leave with full wage
compensation.

In order to appreciate the challenge that this measure represented, one
must recall the context in which the decision was taken and the conditions
under which it was put into effect. First, the statutory 40-hour week approved
in 1936 did not (as we have seen) become reality until 1982, highlighting a big
gap between legislation and actual practice or, as some say, between politics
and economics in this area. The new 35-hour-week target, set at the very time

when the 40-hour one had just been effectively implemented, was received with skepticism in many quarters.

Second, this target represented a significant acceleration of the normal trend toward shorter working time. As Thierry put it,

> In France, working time, in terms of effective working time per year was shortened by about 15 per cent in the period 1960 to 1980—i.e. in the space of 20 years—in an economy that was growing at the rate of 5 per cent a year; the 35-hour week target, taken together with the fifth week of paid leave, represents the same order of magnitude of 15 per cent, but is to be reached within five years in the context of an economy growing at a rate of 2 per cent on the most optimistic assumptions![12]

Third, the transition to the 39-hour week took place under conditions that dimmed the outlook for the subsequent stages, and this largely negated expected benefits in terms of job creation. In order to achieve its intended objectives, namely, work sharing and the reduction of unemployment, the reduction of working time ought to have been designed to enhance firms' competitiveness, thus giving them an incentive to employ additional workers.

For this purpose two conditions had to be satisfied. First, a firm policy of wage moderation (no total wage "compensation") should be pursued. According to French terminology, wage compensation is deemed to be total where the transition to the 39-hour week does not involve any drop in the monthly wage, which implies consequently a rise in the hourly rate of remuneration. Compensation is partial if it involves a slight "decline" (actually a smaller rise) of remuneration, or progressive if only the low wages are maintained.

However, this condition was not fulfilled. Whereas employers were naturally urging moderation as regards wages, the trade unions were sharply divided between those favoring total compensation (broadly the "communist" Confédération Générale du Travail, or CGT) and those which, subject to certain conditions, favored progressive compensation (the "socialist" Confédération Française Démocratique du Travail, or CFDT). Nevertheless, the negotiations between employers and unions were making headway and on the point of culminating in an agreement on partial or progressive compensation in certain branches when the government surprisingly took the decision to award total compensation. (The 39 hours were to be remunerated as though they were 40!) This (political) move necessarily had a lasting and adverse effect on wage costs and discouraged firms from creating jobs.

Second, equipment operating times should be lengthened in order to obtain a better return on the capital invested.[13] This condition was not satisfied either, because most firms reacted defensively to a measure to reduce working time that tended to ignore their specific contraints. Rather than introducing innovations in work organization geared to a more efficient use of their equipment, they endeavored to maintain their level of output with fewer hours worked;

indeed, many succeeded in doing so thanks to more efficient management and more intensive use of the workforce. In response to a survey on the reactions of industrial firms to the 39-hour week, no more than 20 percent of them stated that they had recruited people on a permanent basis.[14]

It is very difficult to assess the overall employment effect of the reduction in the yearly working time (39-hour week plus the fifth week of paid leave) enacted in 1982. According to the macroeconomic model of the INSEE, about 110,000 jobs were said to have been created or maintained as a result of the measures for the reduction in working time, a figure that many commentators consider an overestimate. This small but nevertheless beneficial effect was more than offset by the damage caused to firms' competitiveness by the resultant rise in wage costs. The latter can also be held responsible for creating "hiring-freeze" attitudes among employers.

Three lessons, it seems, can be learned from the French experiment with a reduction in working time. The first is that any uniform solution imposed from above is ineffective because it is ill adapted to the circumstances of many firms. Some of these can tap reserves of productivity and are able to shorten working time without diminishing output. Others, by contrast, have reached or are close to the limit of their capabilities; in their case an excessively abrupt reduction of working time may lead to outright extinction. Second, such a solution shows how risky it is to accelerate abruptly a trend that, in many cases, reflects certain very real economic constraints. Finally, the French experiment throws a harsh light on the practical difficulties inherent in attempts to promote work sharing by means of a reduction in the working week: if the reduction does not go far enough, it is reflected in higher productivity without the creation of additional jobs; if it goes too far, it increases the risk that wage costs will get out of control.

The lesson of the 39-hour week was soon grasped by the government. Awareness of the deteriorating position of French firms on foreign markets led to a sharp turn-about in policy towards working time, with the transition to the 39-hour week (which was supposed to mark the first stage on the road to the 35-hour week) never followed by any second stage. Nobody talks any longer about the 35-hour week, and the effective duration of the working week has been sliding gently toward its statutory duration without further government intervention, as shown in Table 3-1.

Making Working Life Shorter

During the first half of the 1980s, working life continued to shorten as a result of increasing school and university enrollments. Government policy aimed at encouraging young people to stay at school rather than look for work culminated, in 1985, in a declaration that 80 percent of the age cohort should receive full secondary education to baccalaureate level by the year 2000.

TABLE 3-1.
The Length of the Average Working Week (in hours)

	1981	1982	1983	1984
Workers	40.9	39.6	39.3	39.1
Employees	40.4	39.3	39.1	39.0
All wage earners	40.6	39.5	39.2	39.0

Source: Ministry of Labour surveys.

Whether or not this target will be met is an open question, but there is little doubt that such an initiative will tend to delay entry into the labor force.

At the same time, the difficulties faced by many school leavers in making the transition from school to work led the government to develop a wide array of "transitional education" schemes combining part-time school-based education and work experience.[15] Although the young people participating in these schemes—about half a million in 1985—are no longer students, they are not yet full workers either. And although these schemes may not have actually shortened working life per se, they certainly delayed entry to it on a full-time basis.

But it is at the end of working life rather than at the beginning that the initiatives taken by the government elected in 1981 had their strongest impact. In many ways, the early withdrawal policies initiated in the 1970s were pursued and amplified by two initiatives, namely, the so-called solidarity contracts and the lowering of the retirement age to 60, to which we will now turn.

The Solidarity Contracts. These are contracts between the government and business firms whereby the wage earners of those firms aged 55–59 are allowed to retire with 70 percent of their gross wages, provided they are replaced by new workers on a one-to-one basis. This policy, which was proposed in January 1982 and lasted for two years until the end of 1983, was a big success, especially in industry. At the end of this period 33,000 contracts concerning a population of 330,000 potential "early retirers" had been signed. The number of persons who effectively retired early as a result of the scheme was estimated at 210,000, leaving room for the recruitment of nearly as many additional workers.

The high level of benefits granted under the solidarity contracts was, no doubt, a major factor in their success among wage earners. Many employers had actually underestimated the proportion of their personnel aged 55–59 who would be ready to take advantage of the scheme. In November 1982 benefits were slightly reduced to 65 percent of gross wages up to the social security ceiling and 50 percent beyond this upper limit. As a result, the flow of applicants diminished notably.

On the employers' side, the incentives to sign solidarity contracts were also quite significant. Young workers are far less costly and more flexible than aging workers, the latter being, rightly or wrongly, considered as a barrier to the redeployment of human resources within the plant or their relocation elsewhere. Solidarity contracts were seen as an opportunity to rejuvenate the workforce and streamline the skill structure of firms. According to a survey carried out by Galland, Gaudin, and Vrain,[16] most firms using the contracts were not in poor financial straits or operating on deteriorating markets. They were, rather, firms eager to adapt their structures to changing markets and willing to promote a more flexible response to an uncertain environment.

In 1982–83 the same conjunction of interests between workers and employers was at play with regard to solidarity contracts as in 1977 with early retirement. But the former went one step further than the latter with regard to employment in that, for the first time, each early withdrawal from the labor force was systematically linked to the reduction of unemployment via the hiring of a new (usually young) worker, whereas the early-retirement policies of the 1970s had no other goal than to avoid increasing the number of unemployed. The prime objective of solidarity contracts was to free 100,000 jobs in 1982 and as many in 1983, thus allowing the employment of 200,000 new workers. By and large, this objective was achieved. But only a fraction—between 50 and 70 percent—of these new workers are unemployed, the others being new entrants into the labor force. Nonetheless, solidarity contracts have been credited with the relative stabilization of unemployment that took place in 1982–83, and work sharing proved to be much easier to implement through early withdrawal from the labor force than through the 35-hour week. This was understandable enough, since the former could be implemented at no cost to employers and wage earners (given that the financing of the schemes was borne largely by the state), whereas the latter did imply a sharing of the cost burden between management and labor in the form of higher salary costs for employers and lower wages for workers.

The very success of solidarity contracts put a heavy burden on the unemployment compensation system, which was also responsible for paying benefits to the early retired. In 1983 about half of the total outlay of the system was accounted for by early-retirement benefits, while the other half was intended for the unemployed. In spite of ever-rising unemployment contributions and increased state funding, the whole system was on the verge of bankruptcy, a situation that led the government to put an end to the scheme of solidarity contracts at the end of 1983.

Lowering the Retirement Age. In April 1983 French policies aimed at shortening working life took another apparently decisive turn with the lowering of the retirement age from 65 to 60. It is important to bear in mind, however, that approximately 60 percent of all wage earners aged 60–65 in the private sector had already retired when the decision was taken, and that the statutory age of 60 is a minimum at which people are *entitled* to retire (provided they have completed a full career of 150 semesters, i.e., 37.5 years) and not a compulsory limit at which all people have to retire. For these two reasons, the 1983 decision was not the drastic step that it purported to be at first glance; it was, rather, the culmination of a process aimed at encouraging people to withdraw early from the labor force, thereby slowing down the increase in the active population and stabilizing unemployment.

Despite the rising number of wage earners applying for retirement benefits at 60, the direct employment impact of the lowering of the retirement age will, in the short run, be relatively small because the new policy substitutes for some of the early-retirement schemes described above, and also because, in times of uncertainty firms are anxious to keep wage costs down and are therefore reluctant to replace old workers with new. But the indirect effect on employment resulting from changes in work organization of firms and on increases in productivity is expected to be considerable, though impossible to assess at this stage.

Many observers question this stance, however, pointing to the loss of valuable human resources as a result of retirement at 60. Aside from its economic aspects, the negative social aspects of such a policy are also underlined in the literature. Among them is the danger of dualism and conflict between those who are overburdened by work and those who lack socially meaningful activities.[17]

Adjusting Working Schedules

Other measures concerning the adjustment of working time have included individual work schedules, flexibility in the working week (above or below the 39-hour statutory duration), and weekend shifts. Moreover, these have been supplemented by legislation designed to promote part-time work and by further provisions to discourage temporary employment while, at the same time, strengthening the social protection of temporary workers.

As one compares moves in favor of shortening working time with those tending to adjust it, one is inevitably struck by the marked contrast in attitude on the part of the legislator: Whereas reductions in working time have been granted with confidence and enthusiasm, not to mention a clearly stated target and implementation schedule, adjustment seems to give rise to extreme governmental cautiousness and only half-hearted legislative provisions.

Obviously, the behavior of the government can be explained by the attitudes of management and labor. On one side, workers' unions were pushing for a general reduction in the working week (with full wage compensation, if possible), which in their view claimed priority over any other working-time policy. For them, an adjustment of working schedules—and in particular the spread of part-time work—ran the risk of "fragmenting" workers and of impairing the bargaining power of the unions on the general reduction of working time.

Employers' organizations, for their part, were opposed to any form of uniform working-time reduction that was imposed on them through legislation and entailed increases in salary costs. Though in no way associating themselves with government initiatives in the adjustment of working time, these organizations nevertheless displayed a more selective attitude toward such initiatives, inclined as they were to favor those likely to lead to a more flexible use of the workforce.

Up to 1983 the government's position leaned clearly on the side of workers' unions, with preference given to a general reduction of working time as opposed to individualized adjustments in working schedules. However, when the benefits to employment of its policy failed to materialize as strongly as anticipated, the government gradually reversed its position and began to devote more attention to policies for diversifying work schedules and adapting them to workers' expectations and companies' needs. No legislation across the board was needed to do this. Unions and employers' organizations were actively encouraged to negotiate new working-time arrangements at company, plant, or workshop level.

Freedom of Working Time?

Various surveys carried out in France and Europe in the early 1980s show that work will continue to occupy a central place in people's lives even though certain forms of behavior may suggest otherwise. Whether one likes it or not, it will remain "the great regulator of time . . . and, above all, it will continue to provide a principal locus and means of forging interpersonal relations and establishing one's legitimate status in society."[18] What is bound to change, however, is the traditional model of work organization uniformly applicable to nearly everybody. The demand for flexibility and the need for a better adaptation of working hours in keeping with people's aspirations and the diversity of situations are powerful influences to which innovative forms of working time should respond.

It is of course difficult to pinpoint a date marking the start of the innovative experiments with working time in France. Nevertheless, the appearance in 1980 of a book by a team of researchers who advocated *le temps choisi* ("freedom of working time") as a way to transform society was an important milestone in the development of ideas in this field.[19] Noting that "time is typically a subject of social negotiation and cannot be dealt with by ukase," the authors suggest, in effect, a policy for adapting working time in the way that would best correspond to individuals' plans for life, both at work and elsewhere. To illustrate the suggestions put forward in the book, grassroots working-time experiments in leading industrial firms were collected and publicized,[20] and to widespread astonishment, the practice of working time looked far more advanced than the theory.

There is little doubt that this research, which caused a great stir, contributed substantially to the popularization of "individualized" working-time policies that were both bolder and more innovative than earlier policies. The wider public became increasingly familiar with such notions as deferred vacations, flexible work schedules on an annual basis, part-time work on an optional basis, leave without pay, individualized work schedules, accumulated credit for hours worked, and so forth. In many cases these experiments made it possible also to verify that the potential demand for an adjustment of working time— more or less vaguely expressed in opinion polls in reply to the question "which would you prefer: more money or more free time?"—was reflected in actual decisions when the opportunity arose.

In what way was the freedom of working time consistent with the reduction in working time (the 35-hour week) advocated by the government at the same juncture?

At first glance, the two strategies shared the same overall objectives. Freedom of working time and the 35-hour week were both meant not only to reduce unemployment through work sharing but also to respond to workers' hopes for more free time. But the former had a distinct advantage over the latter as far as practical implementation was concerned, to the extent that the costs were to be borne by its beneficiaries in the form of lower wages, whereas the latter attempted to transfer part of the cost burden to employers in the form of higher salary costs.

As far as the public was concerned, freedom of working time was soon to appear much more promising than the 35-hour week. Not only did it treat any uniform, across-the-board solution of the problem of working time as inoperative, but progress in implementation was based on a network of grassroots initiatives on the part of management and labor at the most decentralized level possible (i.e., the small firm, plant, or workshop). In this respect, freedom of working time was felt to be more attuned to the growing individualist attitudes governing all spheres of social life. The extent to which these attitudes have survived the constraints imposed by economic competition during the late 1980s is, however, unclear. The supporters of *le temps choisi* came from left-of-center groups with strong ties to noncommunist unions and the enlightened elements of employers' associations. They stressed innovations and compromise at the plant level but were ill equipped to challenge the present vogue of state deregulation and privatization.

Flexibility in Working Time

In the preceding section it was shown that French attempts to reduce working time during the first half of the 1980s were either part of an overall public policy aimed at reducing unemployment or designed to adapt working time to the so-called aspirations of the labor force. What is striking about both the government's options and the state of public opinion in the early 1980s was the considerable emphasis attached to the social and cultural aspects

or working time at the expense of the economic aspects. The policy with respect to working time has been first and foremost a part of social policy and
only *secondarily* a factor pertinent to the economic life of firms. This order of
priorities has been very clear among the advocates of work sharing, who say
they want to respond to the workers' aspirations to be in control of their own
time and to reduce unemployment, without, however, jeopardizing company
competitiveness. The economic constraint of the latter is, of course, mentioned,
but it is merely a constraint, not an objective.

Since 1985 working-time policies have been characterized by a resurgence
of economic considerations and, especially, those prevailing at the level of the
firm. Enhancing firms' productive efficiency is becoming a prime objective.
Admittedly, the need to respond better to workers' claims is still in evidence,
but given a state of slow, uneven growth, a better return on capital has been the
top priority. One way of achieving this is to enhance flexibility within the firm
or, in other words, its ability to adapt to changes affecting its economic environment.

The Debate Over Flexibility

In France, as in many other European countries, there has been a lively
debate over flexibility in the first half of the 1980s. There is little doubt that the
concept has appealed to many because it expresses a reaction against rigidities
of all kinds, and especially those faced by business firms. But soon it became
clear that flexibility can be applied to many aspects of working life, including
the downward adjustment of wages, the relaxation of collective agreements, the
swift acceptance of technical change in production processes, and the ability to
adapt production to market fluctuations.

Moreover, working-time flexibility may take two forms: either employment flexibility, meaning the ability of firms to adapt the size of the workforce
to their level or activity or, alternatively and for the same purpose, variations in
the hours worked by wage earners.[21] Fixed-term temporary jobs are the most
widely used means of adjusting total working time to firms' needs. "Technical"
(i.e., temporary) unemployment is used to adjust working time downward,
while overtime and part-time work are used to adjust the total hours worked by
wage earners to their employers' requirements.

From the employer's viewpoint, it is essential for flexible working time to
result in flexible wage costs, which, ideally, should vary according to the
firm's production effort, since the ultimate objective of flexible working time is
to get rid of unproductive time worked and let market fluctuations regulate
wage costs. Needless to say, unions have considered flexibility an evil and
have advocated stability of both the workforce and working time.

The upshot of this confrontation has been that in those parts of the economy where unions are strong (the public sector and large firms in the private
sector), most wage earners have not really been affected by flexibility policies

restricted essentially to the subcontracting of very secondary services (like cleaning and surveillance) and the taking on of temporary workers in case of need. By contrast, medium and small firms where there is much market uncertainty and unions are weak welcome the possibility of flexible working time, thus giving some credence to the theory of labor-market segmentation, according to which well-protected workers in "core" activities coexist with unprotected workers in "peripheral" activities.

The Taddei Report

The debate over flexibility in wage earners' working time has naturally led to the closely related issue of flexibility in the use of capital. This point is taken up in a report commissioned by the government to a group of experts led by Taddei,[22] a member of Parliament. Its starting point is the short duration of the use of productive equipment in industrial firms (between 46 and 40 hours per week, depending on economic sector), a length of time that has declined slowly but steadily since the beginning of the crisis (1973). The report argues that this trend should be reversed because a lengthening of the duration of equipment use would enhance firms' productive capacity. Meanwhile, competitiveness would increase as a result of lower unit costs while the rate of return on capital would also rise.

Lengthening the time equipment is used would require significant changes in work organization and—this is the report's central proposal—an extension of shift work in the form of additional daily shifts that, while spreading over six days a week, would be of shorter duration to offset the possible stress resulting from unfamiliar working schedules. Additional shifts would also facilitate a reduction in traditional closings because of annual leave. The report further states, convincingly, that many additional shorter shifts could be created to operate equipment without resorting to night or Sunday work.

A key issue in the proposed strategy is clearly its effect on wage costs. On this point, it is argued that the high productivity gains resulting from the longer use of capital would make more likely both a gain in market shares following reduced prices and near total wage compensation. Thus, the wages issue—which largely explains the failure of the 35-hour strategy outlined above—is thought to be considerably alleviated, if not solved, by the present strategy.

Simulation models confirm that the impact of this strategy on job creation would be considerable. Thus, assuming that only one firm out of nine operated on the basis of two shifts of 30 hours each (instead of the traditional 39-hour shift), more than 100,000 jobs would be created in the first five years and about 350,000 after that.

The Taddei report ends with a series of recommendations related to the implementation of its proposals. Now fully aware of the counterproductive effects of any uniform, across-the-board decision in this area, the authors propose that employers and unions should start negotiating changes in the organization of work at branch and firm level. Government intervention, they say, should be restricted to providing incentives to employers to open up discussion with unions. These incentives include favorable amortization rules and lower tax rates on corporate profits as well as easier availability of subsidized loans for firms to lengthen the operating time of their equipment. Wage earners whose working time was reduced and whose schedules were changed would pay lower social security contributions.

Whether or not the Taddei proposals are implemented will depend largely on the economic environment surrounding the firm. If a firm has to contend with an unfavorable economic environment, its first concern is usually to tighten up jobs and avoid layoffs, a defensive strategy. The adjustment and reduction of working time is one way of achieving a reduction in wage costs. Employment is maintained by means of sharing the work and the total wage bill among the existing workers, but no jobs are created.

If the firm is active in an expanding sector or able to expand its share of the market, the lengthening of the use of equipment and the resulting shortening of working time will be regarded as the key component in a bold strategy for streamlining and optimizing the use of both the capital and the workforce. Such a strategy will become a means of lowering costs, producing more or better goods with the same capital, attracting market shares, and possibly—if all these endeavors are successful—creating jobs. All monographs on firms that have experimented with the reduction of working time coupled with changes in working schedules stress the close connection with a more intensive use of equipment. Here, the new time constraints resulting from the growth of shift work required by the lengthening of operating time of equipment are negotiated—and accepted—by the trade unions in return for a reduction in working time. In Boisard's words, "The time constraints are exchanged for time. The obligation to perform night work or weekend work, or to work early in the morning or late in the evening, is exchanged in return for a reduction in the total time worked."[23]

It goes without saying that, in this bargaining process, not too much heed is paid to the somewhat idealistic concerns of those who advocate the freedom of working time and schedules. The workers' hopes for more control over their time are not, of course, wholly ignored, for the progressive diversification of work schedules does, after all, offer them more options. However, when all is said and done, the reduction of working time is very often a measure granted to wage earners in order to induce them to accept an adjustment of working time that is not one of their major aims. This reduction is, therefore, not a response to a demand for free time; it is a compensation granted by employers in order to ensure that their employees agree to change their customary work schedules.

Obviously, the central role of economic considerations in working-time policies is largely attributable to the economic environment, which, in the final analysis, prevails over all else. Working time has a cost for firms (and a price for the workers!); the price varies, obviously, according to the hours of the day and the days of the week, and it is fixed by bargaining between the "social partners." These considerations are not meant in any way to deny the potency of the cultural arguments for more diversified working-time options; they are meant merely to stress that changes in existing practice have usually to be paid for.

Working Time in an Annual Perspective

The Taddei report was not expected to generate any new legislation since its proposals were to be implemented by means of decentralized negotiations between employers and unions at the branch or firm level. But it paved the way for the last—and modest—government attempt to couple the reduction of working time with flexibility in the use of the workforce.

According to the law of February 1986, employers and unions are able to sign agreements at branch level whereby weekly working time may be as much as 41 hours according to needs, provided its average duration does not exceed 38 hours *on a one-year basis*. It is also stipulated that this kind of overtime— that is, work exceeding the statutory 39-hour provision—will not receive the traditional compensation due for extra hours worked. Last, the "real" authorized overtime maximum, that is, the number of hours exceeding the (average) 38 hours a week per year, is reduced from 130 to 80 but may be compensated by an equal number of hours' leave. Monthly wages need not reflect variations in working time and may be calculated on the basis of the annual total. In those sectors where more flexibility is required, weekly working time may be as much as 44 hours provided the yearly equivalent average does not exceed 37.5.

In essence, the underlying philosophy of this law is similar to that of the Taddei report since it encourages unions to give employers the short-term flexibility they need to adapt to ups and downs in business activity, in exchange for a reduction in yearly working time. By an annual approach to working time, the law discourages the use of (expensive) overtime and enables firms to deploy the former more efficiently.

It is still too early to determine whether firms will take advantage of these possibilities. Preliminary surveys indicate that employers are keenly interested in working time in an annual perspective because it increases flexibility in the use of the workforce. Unions seem to be adopting an "understanding" stance toward this matter. Thus, in July 1986 employers and unions in the metal industry signed an agreement covering more than 2 million workers whereby weekly working time may go up to 44 hours, the yearly average being 39 hours.

This last agreement is widely believed to generate other collective agreements along the same lines in many industrial branches. Thus, working time is increasingly considered in an annual perspective by both employers and unions, stress being put more on flexibility than on overall reduction of working time.

The new government that took office in late 1986 confirmed this last point by enacting a new law in July 1987, which enhanced flexibility—weekly working time may be as much as 48 hours—while dropping the requirement concerning the reduction of annual working time.

Conclusion

French policies toward working time have gone through three stages during the first half of the 1980s. The first stage was dominated by an attempt to impose on firms, with strong union backing, a uniform across-the-board reduction in working time. The ultimate purpose of this policy was to combat unemployment by means of work sharing. It failed because wage earners proved less willing to share labor income than work. Labor costs increased, but so did labor productivity. As a result, few new jobs were created.

During the second stage the emphasis was on the diversification of working-time arrangements—a policy that often implied also a reduction in working time as in the case of part-time work. Most of these arrangements resulted from negotiations between employers and workers—often by-passing the unions—with government intervention restricted to removing legislative barriers. They were conceived as a response to workers' wishes and were granted by employers as a social bonus or an alternative to wage increases. However, they had no effect on wage rates although, in some cases, they were used by firms faced with lagging demand to bring down total wage costs.

The third stage was characterized by strong concern for a more intensive use of equipment. The reorganization of working time led to an increase in shift work and the shortening of shifts. These changes in the use of the workforce resulted from a bargaining process between employers and unions whereby the former granted such shifts to the latter in exchange for their acceptance of a new spread in shift work. They were the "social side" of a modernization process involving the use of expensive, automated technologies. For the firm, the higher wage costs resulting from more shift work were compensated by significant gains in overall efficiency and a higher return on capital investment. For the government, more shifts meant the creation of new jobs.

Obviously, these three stages have not been neatly sequential, as all three have overlapped between 1980 and 1986. But, by and large, the first stage dominated official thinking throughout the 1981–82 period, followed by the second in 1982–83, and the third began to prevail from about 1984 on.

What reasonable prospects can be envisaged for French working-time policies, taking into account the very rapid development of ideas described in this chapter? No attempt to provide detailed forecasts concerning the reduction of working time will be made here, but brief exploratory forays, based on the experience of the recent past, will be mentioned. First of all, it is likely there will be more awareness about the central importance of working-time arrangements among management. Cost-conscious company managers will increasingly scrutinize the implications for wage costs and capital productivity of new working-time arrangements. Aware of the need to adapt the pace and the nature of production to changing market conditions, they will seek flexible arrangements to minimize wage costs. The possibility of severe conflicts with unions over these issues cannot be ruled out. For such new arrangements to be accepted by workers, a first condition of success is that all interested parties should be well informed about the proposals involved. Another may be the need for limited experimentation with volunteer workers prior to full-scale implementation.

Unions have been struggling with employers on the question of shorter working time for many years. What is perhaps new in the present context is the awareness that insufficient working time may compromise competitivity *unless* it is matched by higher labor productivity or longer equipment-operating time. Thus the debate may shift toward the probable tradeoff between the length and the "intensity" of working time and unusual working schedules.

In the final analysis, both employers and unions will be led inevitably to take a closer—and more sophisticated—look at time management as part of the broader issue of human resources management. This may put a heavy demand on the traditional managerial styles prevailing in many firms. Though, at present, it is impossible to say how far and how fast new advances in working-time arrangements will spread throughout the economy, there is no doubt that the ideas of the first half of the 1980s are moving in the right direction.

The part played by the government in the shaping of working-time policies will also change as a result of recent experience. Rather than focusing on the direct but elusive relationship between working time and employment, government policies will look at working time as one way to enhance industrial and commercial competitiveness and, indirectly, job creation. The government will also be expected to play a leading part in two other important issues. The first has to do with international standards concerning working time as one way of ensuring fairness in international competition. Many things have been said about the Japanese performance on the technological front, as the rising market share of Japanese firms in leading industrial sectors is compared with the deteriorating position of their European counterparts. But working-time differentials have often been overlooked. As long as the Japanese work 30 percent longer than their European competitors, it is hard to see how the latter can stay the course. Moreover, working time is decreasing in Japan, albeit very slowly. Extrapolation of present trends indicates that Japanese working time will be at the present European level by the turn of the century! And this is a case for bringing working-time issues into the international negotiations on tariffs and trade. Be that as it may, there is no doubt that governments have a leading part to play in the setting of international standards acceptable to all.

A second area of government intervention may reflect concern for a reasonable balance between working time and nonworking (leisure) time, with the latter including the period of schooling and study between birth and entry into working life, as well as retirement. In this connection, we have seen that there are strong historical and sociological factors militating in favor of shorter working time (life), but also strong economic factors inhibiting it. *Leisure time has, somehow, to be financed out of working time*, which means that, even if the government is ready to shoulder part of the financial burden resulting from shorter working life (as in the case of French early-retirement policies), higher taxes or social security contributions will be forthcoming from those at work. Indeed, it was the high cost to society of such policies that led the government recently to discontinue them.

The connection between working time and the financing of social security is well known,[24] but the present crisis in social security budgets is attracting governmental attention. In France if has been shown that unemployment (i.e., an interrupted working life) has been a prime cause of social deficit, and it may well be that, in the near future, early-retirement policies will give way to incentives to postpone retirement until completion of a higher number of working (and therefore contributory) years.

To sum up, shorter working time is satisfactory provided it is compatible first, with successful competition (with countries, firms, or individuals) and, second, with adequately financed "leisure" time. And it is up to governments to take the necessary steps to ensure that these provisions are respected.

Notes

1. Paul Koepp, "L'évolution récente de la durée du travail," *Travail et Emploi*, 4 (April 1980).

2. Alain Doyelle, "Durée du travail, un essai de comparaison internationale," *Travail et Emploi*, 12 (April-June 1982).

3. Commissariat Général du Plan, *Aménagement et réduction du temps de travail* (Paris, La Documentation francaise, 1985), pp. 69ff.

4. Anne-Marie Guillemard, "La dynamique sociale des cessations anticipées d'activité," *Travail et Emploi*, 15 (January-March 1983).

5. Nicole Marc and Olivier Marchand, "La population active de 1975 à 1982: les facteurs d'une forte croissance," *Economie et Statistique*, 171–172 (November-December 1984).

6. Jean-Pierre Jallade, ed., *L'Europe à temps partiel* (Paris: Economica, 1982). For a summary in English, see *Towards a Policy of Part-time Employment*, Work and Social Change, 15 (Maastricht: European Centre for Work and Society, 1984).

7. Robert Fossaert, "Pourquoi et comment normaliser le travail atypique?" *Droit Social* 7–8 (July-August 1981).

8. Jean Fourastie, *Les quarante mille heures* (Paris: Robert Laffont, 1965).

9. Dieter Mertens, "Working Time Policies," in *Employment and Unemployment in Europe*, ed. Jean-Pierre Jallade (Trent on Stoke: Trentham Books, 1981).

10. Commissariat Général du Plan, "Durée du travail, emploi et chômage depuis 1974 dans 11 pays industrialisés," in *Aménagement et réduction du temps de travail*, p. 35.

11. Pierre Boisard, "La réduction des heures travaillées," *Cahier du Centre d'Etudes de l'Emploi*, 25 (Paris: P.U.F., 1982).

12. Dominique Thierry, "Peut-on trouver une problématique nouvelle du temps de travail au niveau de l'entreprise?" *Echange et Projets*, 32 (December 1982).

13. Michel Praderie and Daniel Baroin, "L'entreprise et la durée du travail: un enjeu social," *Droit Social*, 1 (January 1980).

14. Olivier Marchand, Daniel Rault, and Etienne Turpin, "Des 40 heures au 39 heures: Processus et réactions des entreprises," *Economie et Statistique*, April 1983.

15. Jean-Pierre Jallade, "La formation en alternance à la croisée des chemins," *Futuribles*, May 1986.

16. Olivier Galland, Jocelyne Gaudin, and Philippe Vrain, "Contrats de solidarité de préretraite et stratégies d'entreprises," *Travail et Emploi*, 22 (December 1984).

17. Xavier Gaullier and Maryvonne Gognalons-Nicolet, "Crise économique et mutations sociales: les cessations anticipées d'activité (50–65 ans)," *Travail et Emploi*, 15 (January-March 1983).

18. Commission of the European Communities, *Europe 1995* (Paris: Futuribles, 1983).

19. Echange et Projets, *La révolution du temps choisi*, foreward by Jacques Delors (Paris: Albin Michel, 1980).

20. Echange et Projets, "Vers le temps choisi," *Echange et Projets*, 27 (September 1981) and 32 (December 1982).

21. François Michon, "Flexibilité et Segmentation," in *Cahier du Séminaire d'Economie du Travail*, C.N.R.S.-Université de Paris I, forthcoming in *Interventions Economiques*.

22. Dominique Taddei, *Des machines et des hommes* (Paris: Documentation Française, 1986).

23. Boisard, "La réduction des heures travaillées."

24. Jean-Pierre Jallade, ed., *The Crisis of Redistribution in European Welfare States* (Trent on Stoke: Trentham Books, 1988).

4

The Chimera of Changing Employee Time Preferences: Working Hours in British Industrial Relations since World War II

William K. Roche

The period since 1945 has witnessed major changes in working-time standards and arrangements in Great Britain. Normal weekly hours for manual workers have fallen from 47 hours to 40 hours, and holiday entitlements have also increased. Significant numbers of employees have become accustomed to flexible working-hours systems, sabbaticals, and phased and early-retirement arrangements that enable them to combine the demands of work life and nonwork life more satisfactorily than was before possible. All these developments represent a significant liberation of time from the demands of work organization and economic activity. Other developments in working time since 1945, however, have had the opposite effect. The incidence of shift working has increased, causing the sphere of work to intrude into periods of the day and week customarily regarded as the proper preserve of leisure or sleep. There has been an associated growth in on-call and standby arrangements, which blur the distinction between periods of work and leisure. The management of time in work has been rationalized to a much greater degree than in the past, and working-time schedules are beginning to diversify as employers attempt to improve the efficiency of labor utilization. All these developments involve the restructuring of leisure time so as to gear it more directly to the productive and economic demands of advanced industrial society.

This chapter examines these contrasting trends in working time in Britain since 1945 and relates them to developments in the political economy of postwar British capitalism. It argues that structural and cyclical developments have been the main forces shaping the changing contours of working time. Changing priorities in the workforce concerning the relative valuation of income and leisure, or changing attitudes to traditional systems of industrial authority, on the other hand, are not regarded as having played a major role in working-time reductions or innovations.

The focus of this chapter is on developments in Great Britain. However, some statistical series concern trends in the United Kingdom of Great Britain and Northern Ireland.

Postwar Economic Prosperity and Social Values: The "Value Shift" Thesis

The issue of value change over the long boom of postwar Western capitalism has received considerable attention in social theory. Writing from the vantage point of the 1960s and early to mid-1970s, a range of scholars called attention to the "demise of bourgeois man" in the economic prosperity and social consensus of the postwar period. Most well known, perhaps, is Daniel Bell's argument that the development of capitalism brought about a contradiction between a social structure that is increasingly rationalized and bureaucratized and a set of cultural orientations that stress the enhancement and fulfillment of the self and the realization of the whole person. Bell writes with a sense of the apocalypse typical of much of the theoretical literature on the emergence of new values in the postwar growth decades: "I write . . . of deeper cultural crises which beset bourgeois societies and which, in the longer run, devitalize a country, confuse the motivations of individuals, instill a sense of *carpe diem*, and undercut its civil will."[1] Similar arguments about the demise of elements of bourgeois morality and the work ethic can be found in Habermas and Gouldner.[2] Certainly, in cultural terms the period was characterized by a diversification of values and modes of expression; and for a short period at the end of the 1960s it appeared that the postwar generation was about to engender a cultural change of seismic proportions.[3] Perhaps in such circumstances it would have been surprising if commentators had not thought that they were witnessing a "value shift," or the emergence of new values and demands in the sphere of work. The supposedly new values had much in common with the more generalized sociopolitical values that Ronald Inglehart was subsequently to describe as "post-materialism."[4] They were held to reflect a new interest in, and concern for, the quality of life, a new suspicion that material advancement alone would not herald the good society, a new wish to extend the sphere of personal autonomy and independence by challenging rigid organizational structures, and a new desire to participate in decision making and to democratize industrial no less than public power.[5] It was generally held that this value system was an "emergent" phenomenon, reflecting a widening and deepening prioritization of social or "human" values as more basic material values were realized. This new "liberal humanism," as it might be termed, was regarded as having developed out of a collective boredom with the old values rather than out of any fears that these values could not continue to be realized.

It was usually held that prevailing structures of hierarchical control in economic organizations and the structuring of economic and social life in accordance with the exigencies of production represented the great obstacles to the realization of the new liberal humanism. As the length, distribution, and organization of working time have very significant implications for the realization or frustration of such values, any significant value change should have become manifest in orientations to working time, and in practical achievements in working-time management over the postwar period.

Income and Leisure

If the work ethic can indeed be said to have decayed during the long boom of postwar British capitalism, this should be evident in the preferences of employees since the war as between additional income and more leisure. One way of estimating whether any such change in the relative value of income and leisure to employees has changed is to compare the income elasticity of leisure in prewar and postwar periods and to examine whether any trend is apparent in this measure in the decades since 1945. The income elasticity of leisure can be defined strictly as the effect of a 1 percent change in average real earnings on the percentage change in average annual hours worked per person, over a given period, other things being equal. The presumption, of course, is that rising real living standards influence the amount of leisure people take. The most reliable way to estimate the effect of rises in real wages on leisure would be to include such a variable in a general model of determinants of changes in annual average hours worked. However, because these determinants and the functional forms linking them to reductions in hours are not well understood and cannot be assumed to be linear (see the next section), and because reliable annual time series covering prewar and postwar periods are not available, no more than a rough estimate is made of the effect of rising real wages on average hours worked; the gross association is determined by dividing the percentages of change in average annual hours worked per person employed over a period of years by the percentages of change in real earnings.

Table 4-1 presents the results of this exercise, using working-hours data compiled by Matthews et al., Maddison, and Maddison and Granier. The principal difference between the hours series is that Matthews et al. and Maddison and Granier attempt to estimate annual average hours worked by employees at work, net of hours lost through industrial disputes, absences, and other factors. Maddison, on the other hand, appears to present estimates of gross annual average hours offered by employees to employers. The two series that include prewar data present prewar estimates only for selected years. From these estimates are obtained gross elasticities of -0.5 for the period from 1913 to 1937 (Matthews et al.) and -0.4 for the period from 1913 to 1947 (Maddison). These compare with postwar elasticities of from -0.1 to -0.2, obtained from Maddison's estimates for the period 1950–77, and -0.3, obtained from Maddison's estimates for the period 1950–77, and -0.3, obtained from Maddison and Granier's estimates of annual hours worked in 1960 and 1978.

Although these data do not permit an examination of the effect of the most recent hours round, they do suggest that there is little reason to suppose that leisure had a higher marginal value for employees during the postwar period

TABLE 4-1.

Real Earnings Trends and Reductions in Annual Hours Worked, 1913–1978

	Change in Average Hours Worked Annually (%)	Change in Real Earnings (%)	Income Elasticity of Hours Worked[a]	Mean Annual Changes in Real Earnings Associated with Periods for which Elasticities Are Obtained[b] (%)	Annual Changes in Real Earnings Associated with Periods for which Elasticities Are Obtained (S.D.)	Mean of Annual Elasticities of Hours Worked	Annual Elasticities of Hours Worked (S.D.)
Matthews et al. hours series							
1913–37	− 16.7	32.5	− 0.5	1.5	9.6		
Maddison hours series							
1913–48	− 13.6	37.5	− 0.4	1.7	8.3	− 0.2[c]	0.5
1950–77	− 13.9	83.7	− 0.2	(2.6)	(2.4)	− 0.3[d]	0.8
1950–60	− 2.3	28.3	− 0.1	(2.2)	(0.6)	− 0.1	0.6
1955–65	− 6.3	25.4	− 0.2	(2.9)	(2.0)	− 0.1	0.3
1960–70	− 7.2	32.3	− 0.2	(2.8)	(1.7)	− 0.2	0.3
1965–75	− 9.5	39.4	− 0.2	(3.9)	(2.2)	− 0.3	0.3

Maddison and Granier hours series					
1960–78	– 14.9	50.4	– 0.3	2.6	3.3

[a] The formula for calculating *between the time points shown* is $\dfrac{(Ht_i - Ht_x) \times Yt_x}{(Yt_i - Yt_x \times Ht_x)}$,

where H = annual hours worked, Y = real hourly earnings, and t_i, t_x are time points.

[b] In measuring *annual* elasticities, or obtaining associated summary statistics, it seems preferable to lag earnings by one year to determine the effect of changes in real earnings each year on hours worked in subsequent years. If earnings are not lagged, a small positive mean annual elasticity (0.04) is obtained for the period 1951–77. The formula used to obtain the results reported in this column is $\dfrac{(Ht - Ht_{-1}) \times Yt_{-2}}{(Yt_{-1} - Yt_{-2}) \times Ht_{-1}}$.

The results in parentheses thus relate to changes in real earnings *associated*, as per the formula, with elasticity measures over the period specified, rather than to changes in real earnings *during* these periods.

[c] 1951–77.
[d] 1951–60.

Source: All data relate to the United Kingdom.

Data on *annual working hours* are taken from R. C. O. Matthews, C. H. Feinstein, and J. C. Odling-Smee, *British Economic Growth 1856–1973* (Oxford: Clarendon Press, 1982), p. 65; A. Maddison, "Long Run Dynamics of Productivity Growth," *Banca Nazionale Del Lavoro Quarterly Review* 32 (1979): 42; "Adaptation of Working Time," *European Economy* 5 (1980): table 2.2 (Maddison and Granier series).

Data on *real earnings* are taken from G. S. Bain and F. Elsheikh, *Union Growth and the Business Cycle* (Oxford: Basil Blackwell, 1976), Appendix E; R. Price and G. S. Bain, "Union Growth in Britain: Retrospect and Prospect," *British Journal of Industrial Relations* 21 (1983).

than before World War II. What is more, insofar as other likely determinants of changes in annual hours worked have changed over these broad periods, they are likely on balance to have changed in such a way as to favor reductions in working time. For one thing, the cost of enjoying leisure has probably fallen significantly since the war with the development of mass tourism and reductions in the real cost of motor cars and such leisure-related consumer goods as radios and televisions. As is clear from a comparison of standard deviations of trends in real earnings in pre- and postwar periods, the long boom brought much steadier rises in real wages than were experienced before the war. The steady economic growth recorded from the early postwar period to the mid-1970s gave trade unions more bargaining power over longer periods with which to press for reduced hours than in the period from the early 1900s to World War II. Relatedly, the rapid rise in labor productivity after the war, when compared with the prewar trend, would have given employees more reason to believe that cuts in working time were necessary to respond to the danger of a progressive reduction in labor demand.

Table 4-1 also shows that no *trend* is apparent in the marginal value of leisure relative to wages since 1950. In other words, there are no signs of a creeping or gradual erosion of the work ethic during the long boom, such as seems to be implied in the sociological literature. (The same conclusions emerge from an examination of annual trends or moving averages in gross elasticities from 1950 to 1977, the period covered by Maddison's data.)

The complexity of the interaction between rising wages, economic growth, labor supply, and reductions in working time can be further considered by examining the circumstances of the four generalized rounds of reductions in normal *weekly* working hours that occurred in Britain during the twentieth century.

Hours Rounds during the Twentieth Century

During the twentieth century four general rounds of reductions in the normal weekly working hours of manual workers have occurred in Great Britain. As is evident in Figures 4-1 and 4-2, two of these rounds occurred after the world wars. The first postwar hours round, which occurred in 1919 and 1920, after a breakthrough by unions in engineering and shipbuilding in 1918, led to working weeks ranging from 44 to 48 hours; the second postwar round, which occurred between 1946 and 1949, introduced the 44-hour week. The most recent round was primed by a dispute in the engineering industry during 1979. By 1987 it appeared to have been virtually complete, having instituted a normal working week of 39 hours for manual workers. It is also evident from Figure 4-1 that *increases* in normal working hours disappeared in the early 1950s.

With the exception of the 1979–87 round, all general reductions in work-

Reduced Hours, 1895–1986

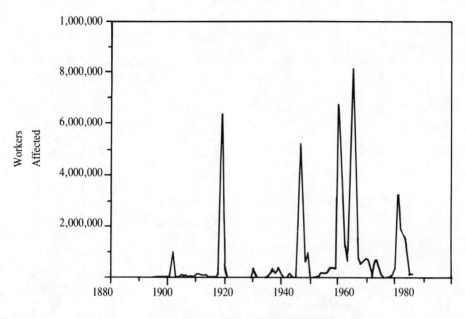

Increased Hours, 1895–1986

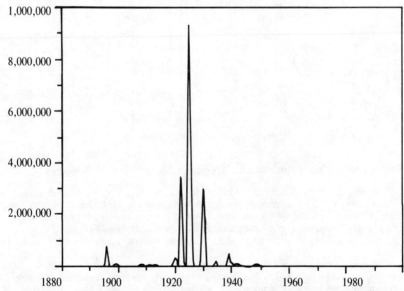

FIGURE 4-1. Changes in Normal Weekly Working Hours of Manual
Workers in Great Britain, 1895–1986

Sources: Data published annually in the *Employment Gazette* (previously the *Ministry of
Labour Gazette* and the *Ministry of Labour and Productivity Gazette*), published by the Department of Employment, London.

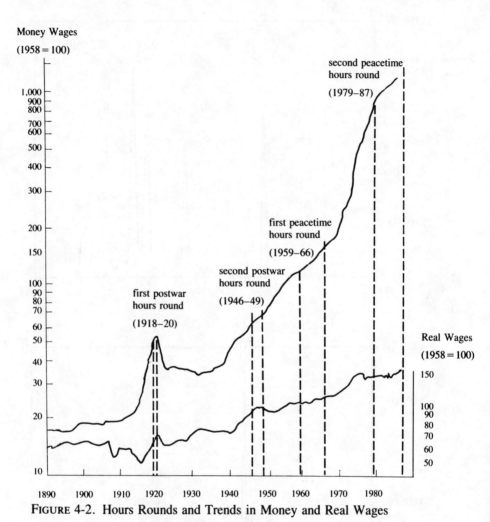

FIGURE 4-2. Hours Rounds and Trends in Money and Real Wages

Wage data for the period 1890–1984 relate to basic wage rates for manual workers in the United Kingdom. This long-running series was discontinued in 1984. Trends in money and real wages between 1985 and 1986 were derived from data on average weekly earnings of male and female manual employees on full-time adult rates in the United Kingdom.

Data on numbers affected by changes in normal working hours also relate to the United Kingdom.

Sources: Earnings data for the period 1890–1984 are taken from James Cronin, *Industrial Conflict in Modern Britain* (London: Butterworth, 1979), Appendix B, table B 7, updated from comparable series in the Department of Employment *Gazette*. Data for the period 1985–87 are taken from the *Gazette*, May 1987, table 5.4; real earnings were derived by deflating this series by the consumer price index for the United Kingdom published in *The Annual Abstract of Statistics*, 1988 (London: Central Statistics Office), table 18.6.

The hours series are taken from annual data published in the *Gazette* over the period 1895–1987.

ing time occurred during periods of economic prosperity and low unemployment. This point aside, however, the first three rounds, like the 1979–87 round, occurred against a background of widespread fears of sharply rising unemployment. In the case of the two postwar rounds, demobilization and the running down of the war economies represented a tangible threat to full employment and provided a strong impetus for cuts in working time. In the case of the first general peacetime round of 1959–66 (with some negotiating activity continuing into the early 1970s), the development of automation and a significant increase in labor supply, caused by the entry into the labor market of the postwar "baby bulge," represented a major source of insecurity in a time of full employment. The 1979–87 round, on the other hand, was a significant departure from the historical pattern. This round progressed at a time of high unemployment and economic recession. Nevertheless, other features of the socio-economic context of recent hours reductions were similar to those of previous rounds. The widespread introduction of micro-electronic technology fostered fear of permanent high unemployment in Britain, with some commentators warning of the imminent "collapse of work." The workforce was also expanding rapidly on the heels of the "baby bulge" of the 1960s and a remarkable rise in the female activity rate beginning in the same decade.

The importance of such sources of "negative motivation" in explaining the historical pattern of cuts in normal working hours in Britain has been emphasized by Manfred Bienefeld.[6] In his examination of the three twentieth-century rounds up to the mid-1960s, as well as of the nineteenth-century experience, Bienefeld argues that economic buoyancy was nevertheless a necessary condition for progress in reducing normal hours. In conditions of buoyancy employers were more reluctant to risk interruptions to production by taking a determined stand against demands for cuts in working time, though, at the same time, they could be confident that the cost of reductions conceded could be passed on to consumers through higher prices. Low unemployment had also boosted the unions' power and, with it, their determination to succeed with their demands for shorter hours.

A further feature of general reductions in working time up to the mid-1960s, according to Bienefeld, was that a sharp rise in money wages in the year immediately preceding or accompanying the hours rounds caused a shift in employees' priorities from pay rises to more leisure.[7] However, the idea of a cyclically recurring and income-induced shift in the demand for leisure fails to accord compellingly with trends in wages in the years preceding or accompanying the four twentieth-century hours rounds (Figure 4-2).[8] First of all, the Bienefeld proposition assumes a money illusion. Such an assumption appears implausible for the 1970s and 1980s, when trade unions and their members focused on real wage bargaining, and also seems dubious in the case of earlier periods of hours reductions. Second, even if we assume the existence of a money illusion throughout the twentieth century, money wage rises (like real wage rises measured in proportionate terms in Figure 4-2) were not particularly sharp when compared with their trend in the years "immediately preceding" the second postwar or the first peacetime hours rounds. Third, as can again be observed from Figure 4-2, three of the hours rounds that occurred during the twentieth century, namely, the second postwar round and both peacetime rounds, seem more closely associated with the slowing down of rising phases of longer-term trends in money wages than with their acceleration or peaks. The same holds for real wages in the case of the two peacetime hours rounds.

On the other hand, the desire for more leisure has indeed played a part in the development of union policy on shorter normal hours. As against the idea that this has occurred because of wage-induced shift in employees' priorities, we would argue that the desire for more leisure is intensified by trade union working-time campaigns that are rooted primarily in fears of job security or chronic high levels of unemployment. In part, more leisure is perceived as a way of reducing job insecurity or unemployment; in part, also, the marginal value of leisure to employees is increased as unions focus attention on opportunities for leisure that employees have forgone in past rounds of pay bargaining.

The data presented in Table 4-2 permit a rough comparison of the pace and scale of hours reductions under the two peacetime hours rounds that have occurred since 1945. Practically all manual workers covered by national (voluntary or statutory) bargaining arrangements appear to have received cuts in their normal weekly working hours during the two years up to the end of 1961. The reductions obtained were approximately two hours. Similarly, during the two years that were generally regarded as the second phase of this round, approximately 90 percent of manual workers covered by the Department of Employment's statistics had progressed to the 40-hour week. In all, this represented a fall of four hours, or 9 percent of normal weekly working hours in seven years. In the round that began to affect working time in 1980, after a major negotiating breakthrough in the engineering industry in 1979, the pace of reductions was clearly slower, while the average level of reduction of one hour represented a fall of only 2.5 percent in the 40-hour norm, which had held up to 1979 for the great majority of manual workers. Indeed, the recent hours round has taken longer to spread throughout the labor market than any other this century and has also involved the smallest reduction in normal weekly working time. It could of course be that developments since 1980 will later be seen as but the initial phase of a wider round of adjustments toward the 35-hour week. Also, it should be remembered that the estimates in Table 4-2 are based on data covering an estimated 57 to 61 percent of employees in employment in the United Kingdom at the time of the 1960s hours reductions and significantly smaller proportions of the U.K. employees at work in the period from 1979 to 1987. Although this must obviously raise questions concerning the degree to which these trends can be regarded as representative of general patterns of

TABLE 4-2.

The Progress of Collective Bargaining in the Two "Peacetime" Hours Rounds since 1945

	Manual workers affected by nationally negotiated reductions in normal hours (000s)	Estimated proportion of all workers covered by national bargaining arrangements receiving reductions in hours (%)	Average reduction per employee affected (hours)	Estimated proportion of employees in employment covered by statistics on national bargaining arrangements (%)
1959–66 hours round				
First phase				
1960	6,817	51–52	1.9	
1961	5,727	42–44	2.0	57–59
1962	1,344	10	1.6	
1963	698	5	1.2	
Second phase				
1964	4,625	31–33	1.1	
1965	8,156	56–58	1.4	59–61
1966	4,315	30–31	1.3	
Third phase				
1980	489	4	1.2	
1981	3,230	29	1.0	
1982	1,949	18	1.1	
1983	1,614	15	1.1	51–44
1984*	1,024	11	1.0	
1985*	149	2	1.0	
1986	147	2	0.8	

*From 1980 to 1983 an estimated 11 million manual workers were covered by national agreements. From 1984, however, the Department of Employment estimate dropped to 9.5 million.

Sources: Department of Employment, *Employment Gazette*; Central Statistics Office, *Annual Abstract of Statistics*: *Economic Trends.*

hours reductions in the workforce overall, it seems unlikely that the picture would be all that different in the case of other manual workers. It appears, nonetheless, that white-collar workers made significant advances in the shadow of the 1959–66 hours round.[9] In the recent round, on the other hand, there is little evidence that white-collar workers have participated to any significant degree.[10]

As indicated earlier, the two peacetime hours rounds since 1945 also differed in a variety of other respects, as is clear from an examination of their main features.

The 1959–1966 Hours Round

The round of claims for reductions in normal weekly hours served and pressed generally in the United Kingdom from 1962 to 1966 appears to have lagged behind a wider European hours movement. Pressure for reduced working hours had been building up in Britain from the mid-1950s. At the 1955 Trade-Union Congress (TUC) a motion was debated on hours reductions. It addressed the issues of technological change, the dangers of unemployment, and the desirability of more leisure. The General Council—the executive body of the TUC—opposed the idea that the TUC should "initiate a vigorous campaign." This would "interfere in the right of affiliated organizations (on policy) to decide for themselves." The General Council also believed that economic conditions did not warrant an hours movement: the economy had been experiencing a labor shortage, and a vigorous hours campaign, it was argued, would merely increase overtime.[11] The motion was voted on and defeated.

Although the 1955 motion was defeated, the hours movement gained support; by 1956 many TUC affiliates had passed resolutions supporting hours reductions and were submitting claims on a wide front. The engineering union, which had proposed the original motion, had served claims in the chemical and motor industries, meeting with "complete rejection."[12] Though several influential unions, including the National Union of Mineworkers and the Amalgamated Engineering Union, now supported the claim and stressed that because of full employment and union strength the time was opportune, General Council opposition to sponsorship continued. As Frank Cousins declared, their fear was of "going willy-nilly regardless of the consequences" for the 40-hour week.[13] However, a motion asking for the TUC's full support for affiliates in their efforts to achieve a 40-hour week was passed in 1957; by now the rationale for the hours movement was more developed and placed particular stress on the growing prevalence of labor-saving technology and the attendant dangers of unemployment. The claims for the shorter working week were encountering strong resistance from employers, which led to renewed calls for leadership from Congress. Meanwhile, unemployment rose sharply in the winter of 1958–59—passing the 2 percent mark and causing a political flurry.[14]

TUC affiliates now claimed that the British Employers Confederation was involved in orchestrating employer resistance to union demands. This indeed appeared to be the case in the printing dispute—the key dispute of the first hours round.

In 1959 ten printing unions organized into the Printing and Kindred Trades Federation (PKTF) were in dispute with the British Federation of Master Printers (BFMP) over a demand for pay increases and hours reductions. The unions argued that many sections of the trade already worked less than the 40-hour week and that their claim simply sought its extension to their part of the industry. They also claimed that more leisure was necessary because of the increased fatigue associated with new equipment and that the alleviation of this fatigue by more leisure would result in no loss in productivity.[15]

The claim for shorter hours had become PKTF policy in 1957. There was no evidence of unemployment in the industry, although some slackening in the availability of overtime was reported. As such, the claim was pressed not as "some balancing against unemployment" but "for reasons of an orthodox trade union nature." More leisure was regarded as "essential for social advance."[16] The unions were aware that their strength was enhanced by the postwar labor shortage but expected, on the basis of the historical record, that success would not be achieved "solely by negotiation across the table."[17] The print employers declared a policy of "complete rejection" of the unions' claims for pay increases, a 40-hour week, and three weeks' annual holiday.

The PKTF commenced a strategy of phased industrial action that had been endorsed by a large majority (80 percent) of members. Attempts were made, with some success, to pick off nonfederated employers by settling the claim with them before applying sanctions. The BFMP responded by offering to concede a 42.5-work week in return for a detailed 21-point guarantee on changes in labor practices. The PKTF found this offer unacceptable, and in early June 1959, 120,000 printing workers went on strike, putting regional newspapers out of action.[18] The BFMP appealed for support from all employers, clearly believing that it was acting as the employers' standard-bearer, and arguing, according to the unions, that concession to the claim would "set a pattern for a general reduction in hours all round."[19]

The dispute was eventually resolved at the end of July 1959, after what *The Times* described as the "longest series of continuous negotiation in the history of industrial relations in Britain in recent times." The unions had succeeded in their demand for acceptance of the principle of the 40-hour week: the standard working week was reduced to 42 hours in 1959, with provision for review by a judicial tribunal in 1961 should disagreement arise about further reductions.

Unions gave broad undertakings on productivity in return for concession of the claim, and it appeared that these were widely implemented at the local level with little difficulty.[20] The settlement also provided for the extension of shift working. A round of hours reductions, primed by the printing concession, spread in the autumn of 1959 and during 1960. By now, a general hours round and the 40-hour week were unavoidable. The round stretched out in two phases between 1960 and 1966, cutting four hours off the normal working week for the great majority of manual workers. The 40-hour week that had become standard by 1966 was to remain unchallenged until the late 1970s.

Thus the working-time round that commenced with the printing dispute of 1959 was the outcome of a relatively spontaneous and loosely organized campaign, which sought to trade off income against leisure in the wake of fears of technological unemployment. The printing strike, which eventually breached nationally concerted employer resistance, is comparable to the huge national engineering dispute of 1979, which precipitated the 39-hours round. The strike lasted several months in 1959 and involved 120,000 workers; 4,000 firms and 1,000 provincial newspapers were closed down by the dispute. A further feature of the dispute, besides its scale and intensity, was the high degree of concertedness with which employers in the printing industry and more generally resisted union pressure on normal hours. This unity contrasted with the reluctance of the TUC to orchestrate demands on the union side, although here, too, union pressure was very much more concerted than was common in the case of demands for pay increases. Ironically, the TUC's reluctance to lead the union campaign was rooted in large part in the same concern that provoked concerted employer resistance: fears that reductions in working time would reduce labor supply and threaten economic growth. It has also to be recognized, however, that in the 1950s the TUC had little tradition of authoritatively leading its affiliated unions. Few strategic problems were posed for the unions by the character of their demands for reduced hours in the late 1950s. The rationale for the demands, as we have seen, placed primary emphasis on adjusting labor supply in the wake of increased automation, bolstering job security, and increasing leisure. Those who pressed the demands were to benefit from them in a direct sense; and once they had been conceded by employers, little remained for the unions to do. The rationale for reduced hours in the round that began in 1979 was more complex and involved the unions in much more difficult strategic problems.

The 1979–1987 Hours Round

In 1970, when unemployment in Great Britain had reached its highest level since 1940, Jack Jones of the Transport and General Workers' Union, Britain's largest trade union, called for support for a shorter working year in order to "share the work."[21] In 1971 a motion was carried at the TUC Congress which called on the General Council to "define the action necessary in the collective bargaining and legislative spheres" to achieve a range of hours-reduction proposals.[22]

In 1973 the TUC reported that among the variety of factors influencing union policies on working time was the "increasing recognition that a higher rate of growth would not of itself solve the current unemployment problem." However, Congress's consideration of working-hours resolutions produced its most wide-ranging policy statements on working time. Shorter hours, longer holidays, sabbatical leave, early retirement, and the like were now held to be necessary to combat the increased strain and fatigue associated with the spread of machine-paced work and new performance-related pay structures, and to satisfy the demand for personal fulfillment and for a "major transition from a work-centred to a leisure-centred society."[23]

So, in the early 1970s, with a continuing rise in unemployment, unions were beginning to doubt that full employment could be realized by pursuing Keynesian demand policies alone. It appeared, rather, that the growing problem of unemployment signaled a deep recession and marked a discontinuity in economic development. This discontinuity was partly understood as a result of increased labor shedding—apparently attendant on the rising incidence of productivity bargaining in Britain—and partly remained a mystery. To combat this situation, unions reverted to the traditional crisis policy of hours reductions and work sharing. This stance was bolstered by the belief that trade unionists now adhered to a new leisure ethic. The strength of this ethic and its practical implications remained unclear.

The emerging working-time movement was contained after the return of a Labour government in 1974 and the establishment of a tripartite "social contract" between unions, employers, and the state. The social contract—at least initially—tied unions into a neo-Keynesian policy that sought to reduce unemployment through pay moderation and orthodox demand policies. Reductions in normal working hours were not regarded as an effective measure. Soon, however, the formal tripartite arrangement fell apart as inflation soared and a sterling crisis led to a change of emphasis in government policy toward control of the money supply. The problem of inflation was given priority over the problem of unemployment.

The option of hours reductions became more attractive to some unions as the social contract foundered. However, other sections of the TUC remained committed to supporting the government and sought to represent what had now become the 35-hour-week campaign as a policy that should be given priority when normal collective bargaining was resumed.

In September 1977 the TUC declared against further involvement in formal incomes policy and decided on an "orderly return to free collective bargaining." Congress was dismayed at the drift toward monetarism in government policy, which it believed would result in the continuation of unacceptable levels of unemployment.[24] Motions called for the reduction of the retirement age to 60 years and for work sharing; the Transport and General Workers' Union (TGWU) appeared to be leading the campaign. There was also condemnation of the persistently high level of overtime working in British industry. In the debates unemployment had displaced leisure almost totally as the rationale offered by most unions for hours reductions.[25] However, a new strand was introduced into the debate by Clive Jenkins, the ebullient and controversial general secretary of the white-collar union, the Association of Scientific, Technical and Managerial Staffs (ASTMS). ASTMS had been instrumental in spreading flexible working hours and early-retirement policies in the early 1970s, particularly in finance where the union was especially strong. Now Jenkins sought to convince the TUC unions—in the most graphic and forceful speech on working time recorded in the TUC debates—that a fresh approach to working time was required in the light of rising unemployment, cultural and recreational needs, and the increasing bureaucratization and routinization of work. He called for a draft General Council policy on the quality of working life and working hours.[26] This was the first real attempt to gain an institutional and policy foothold in the TUC for the idea of rethinking labor time policy in the context of profound economic and social change. Jenkins spoke with first-hand experience of the micro-electronics revolution in the services sector and was convinced that the new technology was set to transform work.[27]

In 1978, the last full year of the Labour government's life, the option of work sharing gained greater prominence. The social contract was now in ruins, although the government still sought to enforce pay control through a variety of economic sanctions. The TUC launched a major attack on overtime working and informed affiliates that the time was right to give priority to reducing working hours. Congress was confident that the international campaign coordinated by the European Trade Union Confederation would avoid the problems otherwise posed by hours reductions for the competitiveness of British industry.[28] Congress agreed to the ASTMS proposal that a comprehensive study should be made of the future of work and leisure. It also prepared to lead the new campaign, a role it persistently refused to adopt in the previous hours movement. The penultimate social contract white paper acknowledged the build-up of pressure for shorter hours but pointed out that reduced hours were welcome only if unit costs were not affected. Despite TUC pressure, hours could not be reduced outside the government's pay limit.[29] The unions were now in open disagreement with the Labour government on working time: the reduction of working hours was now a central issue in unions' negotiating policies. When Prime Minister James Callaghan outlined government policy on hours reductions to TUC in September, he was interrupted by shouts from the floor.[30] Elements of an "alternative economic strategy" were now beginning to emerge in union policies. The nascent strategy combined Keynesian policies for demand-induced investment with import controls and shorter working hours. But it appeared, nonetheless, that the hours movement would have to succeed against government policy, and in economic conditions that had never before witnessed a successful general round of cuts in working time. The major breakthrough was to occur in 1979 in the national engineering dispute.

The 1979 engineering dispute was one of the most serious conflicts in British labor history. The series of stoppages it involved affected 1.5 million workers and resulted in the loss of 16 million working days.[31] In 1978 the Confederation of Shipbuilding and Engineering Unions (CSEU) included demands for a planned reduction of the working week to 35 hours over an agreed period and for improved holidays in a claim submitted to the Engineering Employers' Federation (EEF). The key union in the CSEU, the Engineering Section of the Amalgamated Union of Engineering Workers, or AUEW(ES), was to become the main force behind the claim and the subsequent industrial action.

The claim was based on comparability with white-collar workers in engineering and a range of occupations. Comparisons were also made with European countries.[32] The EEF, rejecting the claim, stressed the cost implications of hours reductions and disputed the unions' use of comparability and their analysis of the productivity effects of a reduction in hours. However, during negotiations they proposed remitting the claim to a joint working party on the harmonization of conditions between blue-collar and white-collar employees in the industry. The CSEU regarded this as a delaying tactic. For their part, the employers believed that there would be little firm rank-and-file support for strike action. The wage demand included in the claim was restricted largely to increasing the national minimum rate for the industry. This meant that a large proportion of engineering workers would not gain monetarily from a strike victory. The dispute would be fought largely on "conditions." Although all stood to benefit from hours and holidays concessions, there was no tradition of strong support for such conditions disputes in the engineering industry.

The dispute came close to being settled before strike action on terms that included the remission of the hours issue to a joint working party. This was apparently avoided because of a fortuitous change in the political balance of the National Committee of the AUEW(ES) in favor of the union's left-wing faction.[33]

Following the failure of conciliation talks to produce a settlement, the CSEU embarked on a series of one-day stoppages in August 1979. The one-day strikes were successful and commanded a very high degree of membership support. The CSEU strategy amounted to a nationally coordinated campaign of local stoppages. Shop stewards were permitted to negotiate "exemptions" with employers who agreed to settle on the unions' terms. This strategy of "picking off" employers anxious to avoid stoppages proved very successful and was used by the unions to weaken EEF resolve. After the series of one-day stoppages came a program of two-day stoppages at the end of August. The only tactical move left to the EEF when it became clear that rank-and-file support was holding was to orchestrate a lockout. This option, however, was not pursued. A close-down by the public corporation Rolls Royce failed to damage union solidarity, while employer solidarity was waning and the number of employers negotiating exemptions with the CSEU was on the increase. In September a settlement was finally reached, which provided for the reduction of normal weekly hours to 39 by 1981 and extra holidays. The CSEU had succeeded in breaking the 40-hour week barrier for a significant section of the manual workforce.

During 1980, under the influence of the engineering settlement, hours and holidays concessions were gained by unions across a broad front. However, few agreements contained provisions to limit overtime, a central TUC objective. Provisions for the reduction of the cost impact of settlements through productivity improvements were, however, common. By December 1980 the new round had been firmly established. A TUC *Progress Report* in December 1980 declared that the 40-hour week and four weeks holidays "barriers" had been "comprehensively breached." Almost half of the 10 million or so full-time manual workers in the United Kingdom had now moved below 40 hours. The most common reduction was to 39 hours. However, the vexing question of limiting overtime was now of central concern.[34]

In July 1980 the TUC issued a checklist to affiliates to assist negotiators in cutting actual working time and to urge them to link the introduction of new technology to reduced working time.[35] In 1981 the main employers' body, the Confederation of British Industry (CBI), issued advisory proposals to members on the handling of reductions in working time. The CBI dismissed union claims that reductions in normal hours would ease unemployment and that employees were interested in more leisure. The CBI also stressed that cuts in hours should be offset by genuine productivity concessions.[36] A subsequent attempt by the CBI and TUC to agree on a joint statement on technological change and working hours failed. However, following the initial breakthrough in the engineering industry—as was the case in the aftermath of the 1959 printing dispute—employers put up little further resistance to cuts of one hour in the normal working week and extra holidays.

While the 1979–87 recessionary round of reductions in working time represents an unprecedented achievement for British unions, it appears for the time being to have taken the momentum out of the campaign for the 35-hour week and to have had little impact on employment. These shortcomings reflect the broader goals of the 35-hour week campaign—when compared with the campaign conducted in the mid 1950s—and the strategic problems they posed for British unions in the recessionary conditions of the late 1970s to mid-1980s.

In the 1950s campaign for the 40-hour week, cuts in working time were presented as a means by which employees at work might reduce labor supply to match the putative reduction in labor demand that would result from increased automation. Against a background of rising real wages, more leisure could be presented in a positive light, and those who stood to gain more leisure were at the same time the immediate beneficiaries of greater job security. Moreover, a lax approach to overtime by the unions provided those who preferred more income to more leisure with a means of more than offsetting the effect on wages of reduced normal hours. Relatedly, once the hours reductions were achieved and the labor supply thereby reduced, it was assumed that the benefit of increased job security would arise more or less automatically, without union involvement in company decision making. In all these respects the 35-hour-week campaign was different. In the increasingly slack labor markets of the late 1970s and early 1980s there were few "positive incentives," so to speak, to interest employees in more leisure. Considerable bargaining pressure was required to maintain real wages, and real living standards entered a plateau period for the first time virtually since the 1950s. As such, the success of the working-time campaign depended primarily on whether those in employment were prepared to identify with the unemployed and to use their bargaining power in the first instance to share work with the unemployed. In marked contrast with the 40-hour week campaign, this time the emphasis was placed on the relationship between working time and social inequality. The issue of job security, which had been at the heart of the 1950s campaign, was now developed on the wider canvas of the implications of current employment trends for social inequality, including inequality within the working class between those at work and the unemployed. Irrespective of the fact that the ideological appeals of the 35-hour-week campaign diverged little from the reformist and incrementalist tradition of the British labor movement, the campaign's success depended to a significant extent on the degree to which trade union members were prepared to identify, or conceive of, their interests broadly in class terms. In the first instance, of course, the campaign sought to persuade them to identify with those already unemployed. However, union members were also expected, in effect, to hold existing jobs "in trust" for future incumbents by resisting agreements that proposed to phase out jobs through "natural wastage." Finally, as we have seen, the campaign stressed the divisive implications of current labor-market trends and urged union members to resist the injustices that would result if such trends were to continue unchallenged. The essential difficulty confronting the 35-hour-week campaign is that such objectives represent in important respects a series of "collective goods." That is, the class-relevant benefits flowing from the campaign are indivisible: all can expect to benefit from them, whether or not they have contributed to their realization.[37] However, the costs of pursuing the policy are also quite asymmetrically distributed. Those in employment, and particularly trade unionists in well-organized bargaining units, must bear the heaviest costs, whereas those in poorly organized bargaining units and the unemployed bear less or none of the costs associated with the campaign. Moreover, an active insistence on the TUC's principle that cuts in normal hours should be translated into new full-time jobs, or into "stays of execution" on job losses in the pipeline, is likely to impinge so strongly on managerial prerogatives that it will succeed only if unions are prepared to back it with strong bargaining pressure and possibly even industrial sanctions.[38] Moreover, the extent of industrial reorganization and the degree of effort intensification that may be required to support the costs of a recruitment-focused adaptation to cuts in working time may conflict with customary standards and skill boundaries. Only in the case of a significant additional thrust forward toward the 35-hour week, as distinct from phased small reductions in working time, could employers be expected to adapt "voluntarily" by expanding recruitment. So it is hardly surprising that employers have sought to adapt to the 39-hour week by extending overtime working and seeking productivity concessions, or that the unions have not been able to offer much resistance to the *principle* of such an adaptation.

In the engineering industry, where the surge of hours bargaining commenced, the fall in normal hours that resulted from a shorter working week and longer holidays was offset largely by unilateral and joint reviews of work practices, leading to improvements in the efficiency of manpower utilization. Resulting measures included the reorganization of shift rotations and the curtailment of breaks and rest periods.[39] The pattern elsewhere appears to have been similar.[40] Despondently, the TUC passed a motion on economic policy at the 1982 Congress that included a call for "an end to the policy of selling jobs for cash."[41] To make matters worse, as the British hours round was proceeding, productivity bargaining was coming back into vogue, as employers sought to use the recession to force changes in working practices on employees in return for wage increases under annual pay rounds. The working-time policy was thus facing an employers' offensive on productivity only partly related to progress on hours but intensified by the 35-hour-week campaign.

The concept of resisting the depletion of job stocks by objecting to proposals for "natural wastage" of work force levels (particularly as part of new technology agreements) has also failed to register success. Here, trade unionists are expected to identify with those who might seek such jobs in the future and to resist such financial incentives as may be offered for workforce depletion. Again, the class dimension of this expectation is evident; but also again, however, many unions have felt unwilling or unable to implement the policy.[42] While union-sponsored measures for overtime control are by no means unknown, the TUC's policy of limiting overtime has not met with any significant degree of success. As is clear from Table 4-3, overtime working has not fallen to any significant degree since 1980. Levels of overtime working are, of course, sensitive to the business cycle. A dip in the levels worked in the early 1980s reflected a cyclical downturn in the economy rather than the influence of the working-time campaign, as the TUC itself recognized.[43]

Notwithstanding, then, the unprecedented achievement of British unions in cutting normal working hours in a recession, the working-time campaign has so far met with limited success in terms of the size of the reductions achieved and their effect on job creation and retention. This could in itself reduce confidence

TABLE 4-3.

Average Working Hours of Full-Time Manual and Nonmanual Employees in All Industries and Services, 1970–1985

	Full-Time Manual Men			Full-Time Nonmanual Men			Full-Time Manual Women			Full-Time Nonmanual Women		
	Total hours	Normal basic	Overtime	Total hours	Normal basic	Overtime	Total hours	Normal basic	Overtime	Total hours	Normal basic	Overtime
1970[a]	45.8	40.2	5.6	39.1			38.4			37.1		
1975[b]	45.3	39.9	5.4	38.7	37.3	1.4	39.4	38.6	0.9	36.6	36.3	0.4
1980[b]	45.0	39.8	5.7	38.7	37.2	1.6	39.6	38.5	1.1	36.7	36.3	0.4
1985[c]	44.5	39.1	5.4	38.6	37.0	1.6	39.5	38.0	1.5	36.6	36.1	0.5

[a]Employees aged 18 and over.
[b]Employees aged 21 and over.
[c]Employees on adult rates.
Source: New Earnings Surveys (London: Her Majesty's Stationery Office), compiled from annual reports for years shown.

in the campaign and retard progress toward the 35-hour-week target. On the other hand, by 1986 approximately 10 percent of all manual workers covered by national collective agreements had achieved normal hours of less than 39 hours a week.[44] These workers could yet become the bridgehead for further general reductions in the normal working week below the current 39-hours standard.

Trends in the Management of Working Hours during the 1960s

Any attempt to examine trends in the management of working hours in Britain is hampered by the paucity of general studies and data. However, from the sources available, several trends in the management of working time since the war are apparent.

The nineteenth century had witnessed attempts by management to "rationalize" working time by establishing a clear barrier between work and leisure, between the "employer's time" and the "worker's time." This involved the suppression of precapitalist or communitarian working practices that combined work and play and allowed a casual approach to the utilization of time. As Hearn puts it: "At the core of the pervasive efforts to establish worker discipline was the attempt to change the worker's conception and experience of time. If the transition to a mature industrial society was to be successful, time had to be compartmentalized, artificially regulated and synchronized to the mechanics of technology."[45] Nevertheless, patterns of time use reflecting *worker preferences* for weak boundaries between work and leisure continued into the twentieth century. During the 1960s a major attempt was made to rationalize working time as part of a wider strategy to increase management control of labor practices in a number of industries. This led to the abolition of traditional practices such as "welting" or "spelling" in dock working, which involved each work gang's dividing itself into two groups that worked one hour on and one hour off.[46] Employers in shipbuilding also complained to an industrial relations inquiry about chronic inefficiency in time use in the industry and union acquiescence in the practices responsible.[47]

But cases like these, in which important aspects of working-time utilization remained dramatically beyond employer control, pertained to industries in which the control and standardization of work practices proved exceptionally difficult. With the spread and development of factory production, employer control of working time in most industries was extensive, if heavily bargained. The dominant pattern was one in which unions defended regulations on working hours, starting and finishing times, rest periods, and meal-times, and the like— established by collective agreements, or legislation, or custom and practice— against employer incursions. From the nineteenth century British employers had been offered advice on optimal working hours by liberal economists. To this stream of advice was added, in the twentieth century, the ideas of the industrial welfare movement and various research agencies. Both world wars had given rise to research on working time. Management organizations such as the Institute of Personnel Management sought to ensure that this research would be utilized in the management of working time.[48]

With the growing popularity of productivity bargaining during the 1960s, employers sought to intensify control of working time. Many "inefficient" time practices that proved particularly disruptive to production were modified or eliminated—at least formally. Many productivity agreements, across a range of industries, sought to control or eliminate what remained of "leisure in work." Productivity bargaining involved in essence the negotiation of pay rises in return for union concessions on working practices. In theory, productivity deals were intended to be self-financing and to represent significant exercises in constructive joint management. The notion of productivity bargaining and the rationalization of "inefficient" labor practices received strong support from the National Board for Prices and Incomes (NBPI), established by a Labour government in 1965 as an instrument for controlling pay rises. In productivity agreements in a number of industries, and sometimes at the urging of the NBPI, rest periods were shortened, tea breaks were abolished, employees agreed to take refreshments on the job, and meal times and starting and finishing times were more strictly enforced. However, instances of the liberalization of time control, such as the abolition of "clocking in" regulations, were also to be found.[49]

Apart from the elimination of leisure in work, many productivity agreements sought to extend work into what had traditionally been regarded as leisure time. Indeed, the traditional conception of the standard working week was being rendered increasingly irrelevant as more employees began to work newly designed and technology- or demand-optimized patterns of working time. Productivity bargaining was used in electricity generating to "stagger" the working day and to bring starting and finishing times into closer harmony with the technical requirements of power generating.[50] Again in electricity supply, and in airlines and newspapers, the time horizons over which working hours were required to average out to a stated norm ("balancing periods") were altered to achieve greater flexibility in matching labor supply to the demands of product or service markets.[51] The NBPI itself encouraged this concept in plant bakeries, arguing that "a five day 40-hour week had little real relevance to actual working in the industry."[52] Working time also intruded further into leisure time through the spread of "call in" arrangements in several industries. These allowed employers to summon employees back to work to cover for absences or in emergencies when they had left the factory, or were on a rest day or holiday. Again, the NBPI supported a variant of such on-call systems in the fire service.[53]

The extension of shift work and the introduction of greater flexibility into shift schedules were also important features of many productivity agreements.

The postwar period had witnessed a sharp increase in the incidence of shift working. In the early 1950s between 12 and 15 percent of manual workers in manufacturing industries were on shift; by 1968 it was estimated that this had increased to 25 percent.[54] Many productivity agreements extended shift work beyond process-type production—its traditional situs.[55]

Some idea of the relative importance of changes in working-time regulations in productivity agreements can be gained from McKersie and Hunter's examination of productivity agreements recorded by the Department of Employment. Of the 73 agreements recorded for the period from 1963 to 1966, 36 included provisions for the "re-arrangement of working hours." This placed changes in working time second in a league of productivity bargaining issues over the period. Of the 4,091 productivity agreements recorded for the period from 1967 to 1969—during the operation of formal incomes policy in Britain—945 involved alterations in working-time regulation. However, working-time issues had slipped back to fifth place in the "issue league."[56] Of course, productivity bargaining also gave rise to reductions in normal working hours. Such reductions were achieved either as the main objective of bargaining, or as a spin-off from changes in the location of working time.[57] In its first report on productivity bargaining the NBPI attacked the widespread reliance on systematic overtime working in British industry. The board regarded it as an example of "weak managerial control."[58] The need to reduce overtime and regain managerial control "over the pace of work" was a favorite theme of the NBPI.

Although some productivity agreements were negotiated at industry level, the bulk of productivity bargaining was concentrated at plant level. Research by McCarthy and Parker has shown that shop stewards were heavily involved in bargaining over working time. Of the 1,600 shop stewards they surveyed in the late 1960s, 75 percent had participated in bargaining over issues of working time, and 49 percent negotiated on such issues as a matter of standard practice.[59] While the NBPI sought to influence labor time policies in a number of the cases in which it intervened, a general report on working hours, overtime, and shift working appeared in 1971. The board noted that the two subrounds of the 1960s hours movement reduced actual working hours for male manual workers by about half the fall in normal hours, leading to an upward drift in overtime.[60]

Although the board again supported measures to reduce overtime, it did not believe that further reductions in normal hours were likely to be helpful in this regard. The report presented a model "hours of work policy" aimed at encouraging enterprises to engage in systematic appraisals of the effects of change in working hours on their costs and profits.[61] Consistent with the NBPI proposals to extend the growing practice of subjecting the amount and pattern of working time to more systematic control, the board also recommended that employers should consider whether new patterns of working time were viable both for employees in general and for part-time employees, especially married women.[62] Declaring against incomes policy, and turning instead to legislative curbs on union power to solve Britain's "industrial relations problem," the Conservative government, returned in 1970, abolished the NBPI in 1971.

The explosion of productivity bargaining during the 1960s fostered two central developments in working-time policy: attempts to reduce or abolish what remained of "leisure in work" and an intensification of the postwar trend to use capital more productively by extending work into what were traditionally regarded as normal nonwork or leisure periods and by diversifying working-time schedules or regimes. The NBPI in general encouraged these trends. No major innovations in adapting working hours to the preferences of employees appear to have arisen, although the NBPI—otherwise skeptical that employees had become more interested in leisure—made some suggestions on this issue in its general report of 1971. The 1960s, in sum, witnessed widespread attempts to control working time and diversify its location through a range of innovations in shift cycles and flexible working-time schedules.

Trends in the Management of Working Time since the 1970s

Few major innovations in the management of working time seem to have occurred during the 1970s; at any rate, the pace of change and rationalization did not accelerate. Productivity bargaining, which had been a significant contributor to developments during the 1960s, went out of vogue. The eclipse of productivity bargaining reflected, in part, a shift to less interventionist forms of incomes policy and also, in part, growing employer skepticism regarding its effectiveness in fostering permanent changes in working practices and attitudes. On the union side, too, rising unemployment called productivity bargaining into question. Some union leaders now began to view the job-shedding proposals common in productivity agreements as a contributor to unemployment.

New Earnings Survey data indicate that the incidence of shift working continued to rise during the 1970s and into the 1980s. It is clear from Table 4-4 that significant changes have also been occurring in the gender and industrial distributions of shift working. Among full-time manual men, the highest level of growth in the incidence of shift working between 1973 and 1986 has occurred in nonmanufacturing industries. Levels of shift working among full-time manual women appear to have more than doubled over the same period. Again, the sharpest rise has occurred in nonmanufacturing industries. These data suggest that the incidence of shift working is rising most rapidly in areas of employment growth such as services. An important consequence of this trend is that the overall decline in the incidence of shift working that would have occurred as a result of falling employment in manufacturing industries associated with continuous process technology will be offset by the growth of shift working in areas of rising employment. In short, the development of a service econ-

TABLE 4-4.
Levels of Shift Working among Full-Time Manual Men and Women

	% of All Full-Time Employees Paid Shift Premia			
	1973	1975	1980	1986
Full-Time Manual Men				
All industries and services	18.4	22.8	23.0	23.7
Manufacturing industry	22.6	23.9	24.8	24.8
All nonmanufacturing industries	14.4	21.7	21.5	22.8
Full-Time Manual Women				
All industries and services	6.3	9.6	11.5	13.8
Manufacturing industry	5.2	5.6	7.1	8.9
All nonmanufacturing industries	12.8	15.4	16.7	19.0

Note: Data relate to full-time employees on adult rates.
Source: New Earnings Surveys (London: Her Majesty's Stationery Office), compiled from annual reports for years shown.

omy in employment terms is consistent with an overall rise in the incidence of shift working among employees.

A rise in the incidence of shift working leads to a rise in the incidence of standby and call-out arrangements, which, like shift working, cause working time to intrude into periods customarily regarded as the preserve of leisure or rest. Standby allowances are usually paid when employees are regarded as being on call and are expected to be prepared to report for work, should the need arise. Call-out allowances are paid to employees who report to work outside normal working hours. Some collective agreements guarantee a minimum overtime credit on call-outs and specify rest periods after long hours of call-out duty.

Although representative data on trends in the incidence of shift-related benefits are unavailable, commentaries on trends in benefits and premia in British industrial relations suggest that a dramatic growth in time-related elements of compensation occurred during the 1970s and this may have reflected the emergence of a broader conception of shift working. If such a broader conception of shift working indeed gained prominence during the 1970s, it is important to consider whether this in turn might have reflected a growing tendency for employees to place a higher marginal value on leisure foregone in the working of unsocial hours, or to experience a greater sense of disutility concerning work done during inconvenient or "unsocial" hours.

The primary reason for any increase in the incidence of payment for work during inconvenient and unsocial hours, over and above the increase in the incidence of shift working, would seem to be the growing recognition such payments were accorded by incomes policy. The first "official" acceptance of the notion that employees working unsocial hours had a right to additional payment was contained in Stage 3 of Edward Heath's pay policy, introduced toward the end of 1973. Provision was made in the pay code for increases over and above the pay limit for those working unsocial hours. This was defined as work undertaken "between 8 P.M. and 6 A.M. on any day, or hours worked on Saturdays, Sundays or public holidays which did not attract overtime payments at premium rates."[63] Doubtless, allowances were already paid for unsocial hours working, although how prevalent this practice was is not clear. It seems reasonable to suggest that the inclusion of such a clause in the pay policy had a major "inspection effect" on unsocial hours working and led to a sharp rise in the incidence of special premia. In its *Sixth (Quarterly) Report* the Pay Board noted that between November 7, 1973, and June 30, 1974, unsocial hours payments had been included in 563 settlements, affecting 1,450,000 employees.[64] This amounted to approximately 6.5 percent of employees in employment. Thus, it is reasonable to assume that the rising incidence of "unsocial hours premia" is best understood as one aspect of a wider tendency for conditions premia, fringe benefits, and "perks" to expand under incomes policy, as means of obtaining disguised or indirect pay increases. Having gained an institutional foothold, unsocial hours payments would have spread as part of the normal "imitative" operation of collective bargaining. By 1979 commentators were regarding the "plethora of unsocial hours payments which had arisen as reflecting a broader conception of shiftworking."[65] It can be concluded, nonetheless, that rather than being attributable to an endogenous change in the marginal utility of leisure, or the marginal disutility of unsocial hours working, the "plethora of unsocial hours payments" reflected a tendency for collective bargaining to focus on fringe benefits as a means of surmounting the constraints imposed by incomes policy on wage negotiations.

Two leading attempts to restructure working hours during the 1980s, one in banking, the other in retailing, can be explained in terms of changing patterns of consumption. In August 1982, 34 branches of Barclays Bank opened for business on Saturday mornings. Saturday working in British banking had ceased in 1969 when the banking unions finally succeeded in winning their demand—developed during the late 1950s—for a 35-hour, five-day working week. The return to Saturday opening was prompted by the decline in clearing banks' share of the personal deposits market, caused by increased competition from building societies. Other clearing banks have also experimented with extended or changed opening hours, but Barclays was the first to press ahead with an extensive change in the face of opposition by banking unions. By mid-1985 the main clearing banks had succeeded in introducing Saturday opening. An attempt to legalize Sunday opening in retailing in England and Wales, prohibited in most branches of retailing by the 1950 Shops Act, failed in February 1983 when a Shops Bill was rejected on second reading in the House of Commons. This was the seventeenth occasion on which the 1950 Shops Act had been challenged through a private member's bill. A subsequent challenge to the legislation also failed.

The radical diversification of working-time schedules that occurred in Germany after the metalworkers' union breakthrough on normal hours in 1984 has no counterpart in Britain. Innovations in working-time scheduling have occurred along the lines of developments in West Germany (see Chapter 2, by Hinrich). However, these are still few and are regarded by researchers as, at most, "prototypical."[66] An important survey of trends in flexibility in British industry by Atkinson and Meager concluded that flexible hours scheduling was still more an aspiration than a reality in manufacturing and service industries, with the exception of the growing use of part-time employment.[67] On the other hand, it seems likely that pressure for such innovations will intensify. Employers have made it clear that further reductions in normal working hours will be conceded only in return for flexibility in the management of working hours. A general concern in British industry to improve labor flexibility will probably have a strong impact on the management of time in service industries characterized by variable demand across the day, week and year. It has also been suggested that the widespread introduction of micro-electronic technology will ultimately lead to a radical diversification in working-time schedules.[68] These developments are likely to set Britain on the "German road," so to speak, toward the disappearance of a working week of standard duration for a large proportion of the workforce.

Part-Time Working

One of the most important aspects of increased diversification in working-time schedules is the remarkable rise, indeed revolution, in part-time working. As Mallier and Rosser have pointed out, virtually the entire growth of employment, in terms of numbers of jobs available, in the period since the war can be accounted for by the development of 2.57 million new part-time jobs, employing women.[69] Part-time employment has been largely confined to women.

Table 4-5 presents data on the rise in part-time employment. Total employment grew during the 1960s but had dropped back to near its 1951 level by 1978. (By the end of 1982 it had fallen further, to less than 20.5 million.) However, levels of part-time working increased dramatically among males and females. Though the level of male part-time employment is low in absolute and proportionate terms, it has nevertheless grown more rapidly than female part-time employment. Between 1951 and 1981 the proportion of total employment accounted for by part-time females increased from 3.4 percent to 17.8 percent. The degree of concentration of female part-time employment in service industries has also increased, although part-time working by women was always in large part a service industries phenomenon. The proportion of total service

TABLE 4-5.

Trends in Part-Time Working in Great Britain, 1951–1981

	1951	1961	1966	1971	1973	1975	1977	1978	1981	1986
Total employees (000s)	22,133	23,339	24,857	21,648	22,182	22,213	22,619	22,253	21,148	16,104
Male part-time (000s)	45	174	373	584	665	697	702	704	709	450
Female part-time (000s)	754	1,892	2,748	2,757	3,163	3,551	3,681	3,679	3,759	4,138
Proportion of all part-time employees who are female (%)	3.4	8.1	11.1	12.7	14.3	14.3	16.0	16.3	17.8	25.7
Proportion of female part-time workers in services (%)	72.6			80.0	80.9	82.6	84.0	85.0		

Source: Sample Census of Population, Great Britain, 1951, Table 2.5; 1961, Summary Tables, table 36; 1966 Economic Activity Tables, table 3; Department of Employment (DE), Gazette, July 1979, p. 673, table 4; Census of Employment Reports for 1977 and 1978 in DE, Gazette, March 1980, February 1981, and December 1982; Labour Survey data for 1986 in DE, Gazette, April 1987.

employment accounted for by part-time women increased from 8.9 percent in 1951 to 24.2 percent in 1978.

Of considerable sociological interest is whether a concomitant of growing female part-time employment has been an intensification of the employment disadvantage experienced by women. It might be that gender-specific second-ary labor markets have become more pronounced as employers have recruited greater numbers of part-time women, in response to progressively higher wages and more extensive employment rights among full-time women, or that part-time females have become more concentrated in low-paying occupations and industries. An intensification in the employment disadvantage of part-time women would show up in the first instance in a worsening in their hourly earnings ratios relative to full-time women workers.

Although the hourly earnings and hourly rates of part-timers continue to be lower than those paid to full-time workers, the ratios of the average earnings of all manual women (1950–68) and full-time manual women (1972–78) to part-time manual women have not changed all that much over the period of the great expansion in part-time working (see Table 4-6). As dualist tendencies might have been expected to intensify in the increasingly slack labor markets of the 1970s, the absence of significant movement in the full-time to part-time ratios for this period is noteworthy. In interpreting these data, it should be remem-bered again that they reflect changes in the employment distribution of women across occupations and industries as well as changes in full-time to part-time wage ratios within occupations and industries. Moreover, the ratios relate to average earnings for women in all industries and services and may disguise significant changes in relative pay within and between particular industries and occupations. However, the data suggest that part-time women do not appear overall to have become increasingly "marginalized" in terms of their hourly earnings relative to all full-time workers or full-time women. Against this, there are important differences between full-time and part-time workers in enti-tlement to occupational fringe benefits, allowances, and premia of various kinds. Although the extent of these differences is unknown, it is reasonable to assume that they have grown with the expansion of the "system of occupational welfare." Part-time workers seldom qualify for membership in occupational pension schemes and are seldom paid overtime at premium rates for additional hours worked, other than those in excess of the normal hours of full-time workers.

Secondary employment, however, involves more than lower relative earn-ings. Further problems are apparent: first, lower employment security, in the sense of disproportionate vulnerability to cyclical unemployment; second, what might be termed "second-class industrial citizenship," or denial of protection under the evolving system of employment legislation; and third, a high level of flexibility in labor deployment and utilization, and the absence of organiza-

TABLE 4-6.

Ratios of Average Hourly Earnings of All or of Full-Time Female
Manual Employees to Those of Part-Time Female Manual
Employees, 1950–1978

	All: Part-time Female Employees		Full-Time: Part-Time Female Employees
1950	1:0.97	1972	1:0.90
1955	1:0.95	1973	1:0.92
1960	1:0.95	1974	1:0.92
1961	1:0.94	1975	1:0.94
1962	1:0.94	1976	1:0.92
1963	1:0.94	1977	1:0.92
1964	1:0.94	1978	1:0.91
1965	1:0.94		
1966	1:0.94		
1967	1:0.94		
1968	1:0.94		

Source: British Labour Statistics: Historical Abstract, 1886–1968, tables 47–49;
New Earnings Survey, Department of Employment, *Gazette*, July 1979, p. 675.

tional controls on the "effort bargain." It is obviously very difficult to assess
trends in such aspects of employment. Nevertheless, it may be useful to examine the employment situation of part-time female workers within this framework, but in a rather more static sense.

An econometric study of part-time workers in the trade cycle between
1961 and 1974, conducted by Joshi, investigated whether married women who
had chosen to opt out of paying social security contributions (mainly part-time
women) represented a secondary labor force in the orthodox economic sense of
constituting a category "not continuously attached to the labour force, but a
flexible, auxiliary element in it."[70] She found that only the youngest group of
opted-out women (aged 25–35) experienced disproportionately large cyclical
movements in employment. The employment of women aged 45–49 was remarkably cyclically stable but more seasonally volatile than average. It should
be stressed that Joshi's study included only those whose earnings brought them
above the floor at which social security contributions cease to be payable. As
she recognizes, this probably excludes groups whose labor-market participation
might be highly sensitive to cyclical changes. Indeed, as we will see, there is
evidence that employers and part-time workers sometimes agree to keep working hours below a level that would generate earnings above the floor. A survey
of 764 establishments by Bosworth and Dawkins conducted in 1979 suggests
that part-time employment *is* especially cycle-sensitive.[71]

Although the "industrial citizenship" of part-time workers is less extensive
than that of full-time employees, their rights have become more clearly defined

under employment legislation introduced during the 1970s. Looked at in a different way, however, this legislation institutionalizes a second-class industrial
citizenship for part-time employees. All employees working 16 or more hours
with specified lengths of service are regarded as having certain rights in regard
to areas such as unfair dismissal, maternity leave, redundancy, as are all employees who work from 8 to 16 hours per week and have five years of continuous service. Nevertheless, it has been estimated that 1 million part-time employees are excluded from the main provisions of employment legislation.
Moreover, constraints on the detection and processing of part-time employees'
grievances are also considerable. A large proportion of part-time workers are
employed in industries where trade union organization is notoriously poor and
management decisions are notoriously unregulated.[72]

The relatively free hand enjoyed by employers of part-time workers in
regard to determining the "effort bargain" would appear to be an important
attraction of this type of employment. Research suggests that part-time employees may allow, or may be prepared to accept, a high degree of flexibility in
the organization and scheduling of their work, especially in sectors where trade
union organization is poor. The detailed regulation of the effort bargain encountered where collective representation is highly institutionalized appears to
be absent from a large proportion of part-time employment systems. In a study
of part-time working in retailing, Robinson and Wallace found that employers
could adjust work schedules to minimize quickly the cost impact of changes in
tax and social security contribution, and that management enjoyed a high degree of general flexibility.[73] A trade union study of cooperative retailing has
shown that working-time schedules were organized to fix earnings at just below the floor at which social security contributions became payable; this involved a small financial saving for employees but a more significant saving
for employers.[74] However, in the survey of 764 establishments by Bosworth
and Dawkins, referred to earlier, only 4 percent of all the reasons given by
employers for recruiting part-time staff referred to the flexibility of part-time
workers.[75]

There is survey evidence that part-time employees have different priorities
than full-time workers. Brown et al. surveyed 764 male and female economically active people in Newcastle-upon-Tyne in 1979.[76] They found that there
were "clear differences" between part-time and full-time workers' orientations
to employment. What they describe as "convenience features" dominated the
priorities of part-time workers when they were looking for a job. Next in order
of priority came economistic and intrinsic features.[77] If part-time employees are
prepared or feel constrained in this way to trade economistic and other employment dimensions against the convenience element of part-time work, it becomes possible to understand how a British General Household Survey found
that 56 percent of part-time workers were "very satisfied" with their jobs, compared with 39 percent of full-time employees.[78] The same issue gives rise to

conceptual problems in treating cyclicality and seasonality as prime indicators of the secondary market situation of part-time employees. If convenience factors receive a high priority and part-time employees are concerned to optimize work and nonwork activities, subject to a strong constraint against work's becoming inconvenient for nonwork and family activities, it may be that many part-time workers *expect* to participate only in activities that are seasonal or cycle sensitive. In other words, it may be necessary to consider the possibility that at least part of the barrier against part-timers' moving out of "secondary employment" reflects employment priorities, and more specifically, working-time preferences that are, so to speak, distinctive or group-specific and rooted in sex roles and stereotypes in the family that have not changed appreciably, even though the female activity rate has risen dramatically.

The possibility that the rise in part-time employment may be attributable to employer and management strategies in the face of a growing "ossification" in "core" sectors of the labor market has already been considered. Although the data relevant to such a thesis are suggestive, there is firm evidence that much of the growth in demand for part-time workers can be attributed more simply to the growth of sectors in which part-time working is particularly suited to production. Part-time work tends to be particularly important in occupations and industries requiring part-day working, certain kinds of shift work, and work during unsocial hours. Developments such as the lengthening of opening hours in retail distribution and the introduction of the "twilight" shifts have increased the demand for part-time workers. The expansion of the service sector has greatly increased the number of productive activities prone to daily, weekly, and longer-term fluctuations in demand, and which can often most "efficiently" be staffed by employing a high proportion of part-time employees. This is reflected in the reasons given by management for employing part-timers, as reported in the survey of Bosworth and Dawkins. No less than 70 percent of all the reasons given for employing part-time workers referred to uneven demand and the unsuitability of full-time employment.[79]

So, on the demand side, the diversification of working-time schedules attendant on the growth of part-time employment can be explained in large measure by structural change in the British economy and the process of deindustrialization. The emergence of a ready supply of part-time employees, particularly females, may well reflect changes in the values of women with regard to their position in the family and attitudes to economic dependence, as well as, more recently, rising unemployment among spouses. But such value changes are not usefully understood in terms of changes away from a fulcrum defined by economism. To the extent that they were partly instrumental in involving a progressively greater number of women in the labor market, such value changes would appear to have increased the number of employees prepared to apply an economistic calculus to the issue of working time, albeit qualified by the demands of home life.

Employee-Oriented Flexible Time Initiatives

The 1970s and early 1980s also witnessed changes that appeared to make patterns of working time somewhat more flexible or penetrable to employee choice. Perhaps the liberalization of working time, evident in such developments as flexible working hours, gradual retirement, sabbatical leave, job sharing, and compressed-week working, indicates that changes in employees' values or priorities have been of greater significance than appears to be the case when we limit ourselves to an analysis of the emergence and development of reduced working-hour campaigns, or of trends in the management of working time. Although there is indeed evidence of the liberalization of working-time patterns, it is doubtful whether this reflects any independent "leisure push," so to speak, on the part of employees or their unions. And in any case, as we will see, the incidence of many of these liberalizing initiatives appears very limited.

The practice of granting sabbaticals has certainly become more common in British industry. By the 1980s it had become widespread in "creative" fields such as journalism and in executive management and administration.[80] The use of compressed working weeks has also gained in popularity.[81] Instances where early retirement is offered as a reward for good attendance are also reported, as are various timekeeping incentive schemes.[82] Though job sharing was known in banking from the early 1960s, it appears to have become more widespread since the early 1970s.[83] Of course, flexible working-hours schemes also spread widely following the acceptance of the idea in public administration in 1975 and the introduction of flexitime in insurance and finance from the mid-1970s.[84]

The main impetus for the development of measures like sabbatical leave and early retirement seems to have come from the growth of "internal" labor markets and the attendant expansion of occupational welfare systems. As such, these innovations form part of packages of fringe benefits and welfare measures designed to retain members of core workforces. Thus, it is not surprising that sabbatical leave has become more common in administration and media organizations, and among executive grades in industry and the services. Schemes for gradual retirement, which usually allow employees to work shorter hours in the years, or, more commonly, months before retirement, originated in management-sponsored initiatives restricted to managerial and white-collar staff.[85] More recently, apart from being more common, such schemes tend to include all employees and to be introduced by agreement with unions. However, gradual retirement, like pre-retirement preparation, is far from widespread. In Parker's survey of retired workers, conducted during 1977, only 6 percent of those interviewed said they had received any pre-retirement assistance.[86] However, there is evidence that such schemes are growing in popularity since the late 1970s.[87] Although flexible hours schemes have aroused growing interest since the latter half of the 1970s, it appears that they have been restricted to a tiny minority of employees. In 1976 it was estimated that only 1 percent of the workforce participated in flexitime schemes.[88] Lee conducted a survey of the attitudes of 40 unions to flexitime in 1975 and 1981.[89] Though there appeared to be greater interest among both white-collar and blue-collar unions in 1981, and though more blue-collar unions had published views on flexitime, only the largest blue-collar unions had been involved in flexitime negotiations, whereas 73 percent were either "reserving judgment" or unfavorably disposed. Lee concluded that flexible working hours remained largely a white-collar phenomenon: almost all those working flexitime were white-collar staff.[90]

Job sharing was first practiced on a systematic basis during the 1960s by the clearing banks, in response to clerical staff shortages in central London.[91] Alternate-week schedules were offered to attract married females back to work. job sharing is now also found in finance, medicine, and administration. In the main, schemes tend to be restricted to routine clerical and secretarial posts. There appears to be a widespread view among managers that job-sharers cannot be given the same degree of responsibility as full-time workers.[92] Supporters of job sharing argue, on the other hand, that it can be applied at all levels of the occupational structure, and that the principle of responsibility for the job, inherent in full-time working, can be transferred to shared jobs. Indeed, lobbyists for job sharing frequently regard the measure as a strategy for normalizing part-time working, not alone by splitting the pay and benefits of full-time jobs on a pro rata basis, but also by transposing the overall career structures of full-time jobs to part-time employment.[93] Certainly, where practiced, job sharing does involve such a pro rata division of full-time pay and benefits and is thus more advantageous than part-time working. However, this feature probably makes it unattractive to large employers of part-time workers, such as retail chains, who offer part-time jobs that might otherwise be suited to job sharing, within prevailing conceptions of its proper scope.[94] Thus job sharing, stricto sensu, has yet to gain widespread acceptance in Britain. And even the more limited or restricted type practiced is unlikely to gain a foothold among the large employers of part-time workers, unless unions mount a campaign to replace part-time working by job sharing, or legislation normalizes part-time employment. However, the British government has expressed strong opposition to European Economic Community (EEC) proposals to improve the rights and conditions applying to part-time working, and although there are isolated instances of action by local organizations, unions have shown little interest in job sharing.

There are no systematic data on the extent of job sharing in Britain. Of the 152,000 employees of three large clearing banks (Lloyds, Barclays, and National Westminster) that employed job-sharers in 1980, 2,800, or less that 2 percent, were employed on job-sharing contracts.[95] In all cases where it occurs, job sharing appears to have originated in employer initiatives, and the typical job-sharer is a married female clerical worker. Initiatives in which full-time employees opt to split and share their jobs in order to enjoy more leisure have yet to arise on any significant scale.

In late 1982 the Conservative government surprised many commentators, employers, and trade union leaders by announcing plans to introduce what they called a "job splitting" scheme during 1983. Unlike job sharing, which aims to normalize part-time working and entice more people into the workforce, job splitting is designed to encourage employers to divide *existing* full-time jobs and fill them by recruiting from among the registered unemployed. Again, there are examples of private or voluntary job-splitting schemes. GEC Telecommunications introduced such a scheme in Coventry in 1981, avowedly as a corporate response to the high level of unemployment among school leavers in the city. The West Midlands Metropolitan County Council also introduced a scheme, with the same objectives, in 1981.[96] In both schemes job sharing is regarded as a temporary status and, in effect, as a source of work experience that might prove valuable to those involved in the search for full-time employment. The state scheme, which began in January 1983, offers employers who split jobs to recruit unemployed workers a cash payment for each job split. The rules of the scheme, in effect, debar the participation of married women and make it unlikely that those approaching retirement or facing redundancy will become involved. Thus, the main participants are likely to be unemployed school leavers.[97]

It can be concluded, therefore, that the greater flexibility in working hours and working lives evident in schemes that allow employees a greater measure of choice in their starting and finishing time—and in schemes that allow them to take leave in mid-career, maintain a career while sharing a job, and stagger their eventual retirement from work—has yet to become a reality for any significant proportion of employees. Moreover, where such schemes occur, they are likely to have originated in employer initiatives to recruit or retain particular types of available workers. In short, the job-sharer who works flexible hours, takes a sabbatical in mid-career, and retires early on a reasonable pension after a gradual exit from the labor market remains, so to speak, very much a character of employment science fiction. Nevertheless, one white-collar union, ASTMS, already a pioneer in working-time innovations, aspires to a situation in which "core" or obligatory working time periods will not longer exist, and in which employees will be able to "come and go as they wish."[98] This is in essence the approach to working-time management advocated by Swedish economist Gösta Rehn. Examples of minor experimentation in such "time bank" arrangements are not unknown in Britain.[99]

The Determinants of Changes in Working Time in Modern Britain

From our analysis of income elasticities of leisure, the emergence and dynamics of working-time rounds, and trends in the diversification and distribution of working time, we conclude that *structural change* rather than *value change* has been the primary determinant of changes in working-time patterns over the postwar period. The tendency for working time to intrude into traditional leisure periods, as employers adapt to changing patterns of consumption and new technologies, appears to have affected the quality of life of more employees than have countertendencies toward the liberalization of working time. Of course, time spent at work has declined very significantly over the postwar period. Yet this decline, as we have seen, would not appear to manifest any shift, or even gradual change, in the relative valuation of work and leisure. Rather, the surges of bargaining activity aimed at reducing normal working hours, far from reflecting a spontaneous avowal of leisure, were in large measure a product of widespread concern about rising or chronic unemployment against a backdrop of rapid technological change. Indeed, in the recent campaign for the 35-hour week, additional leisure tended to be regarded as a necessity that could and should be transposed into virtue to prevent a further rise in unemployment. What perhaps has been most remarkable about the course of working time over the postwar period is the limited degree to which people have tried either to liberalize time at work or to seek "liberation" from it. After all, up to the mid-1970s this was a period of great economic prosperity, which witnessed significant developments in industrial and social citizenship. Notwithstanding the theorizing of sociologists and political scientists, none of these developments, nor the rising prosperity with which they were associated, appear to have released new social values impinging on working-time levels and regimes.

To judge from studies of orientations to work, however, the new values appear to be just as elusive at a more general level.[100] Attitudinal data on working time also confirm that little dissatisfaction has been evident concerning the length of time people work per se, or the working time regimes to which they are subject. The British General Household Survey investigated attitudes to working time in 1974, 1975, and 1976. In 1974 respondents' views on the general statement "the hours (of work) are good" were measured on a seven-point scale, ranging from "very true" to "not at all true." Of the men surveyed, 66 percent answered in the scale range 1–3; only 16 percent answered in the range 4–7, and only 3 percent stated "not at all true." Levels of satisfaction expressed by female respondents were even higher.[101] Replies in the following two years were even more positive, with roughly 80 percent of respondents stating that they were very satisfied or fairly satisfied with their hours of work.[102] When reasons for satisfaction were requested, the replies showed a large degree of expressed satisfaction with starting and finishing times, the suitability of weekly hours, and the reasonableness of overtime arrangements—although the latter dimension was lower on the scale of satisfaction.[103] Of course, such data must be interpreted cautiously, especially in the light of the reductions in normal hours negotiated since 1979.

Although there are many proponents of work and management restructuring, practical achievements in this area are rather undramatic and hardly attest to a new employee challenge to hierarchy and organizational rigidity. It is difficult not to conclude from a sober assessment of survey and case study data, including the data adduced in this study, that new social values in the sphere of work and at the boundary between work and leisure are a chimera. This is not to say that adherents to such values, with distinct social bases, cannot be identified, or that some such values have not become more compelling in the wider social lives of employees. It has to be concluded, however, that the radical potential envisaged for such values, the new prioritization within economic organizations as well as in the relationship between work and leisure, have scarcely been realized. The new values were believed to be momentous precisely because they appeared to involve a generalized orientation to social activity, and to receive the support of central and powerful social groups.

The effects of structural change and cyclical perturbation in the political economy of British industrial relations on working-time patterns are more readily evident. First, changes in patterns of consumption and the application of new technologies were instrumental in increasing the incidence of shift working and in changing the distribution of working hours across the 24-hour and weekly cycles. Second, the same developments were largely responsible for the rise of "off-duty duties," such as the standby and call-in. Third, incomes policies have played an important role in facilitating adjustment to such trends by exhorting the rational management of working time. Fourth, the development of internal labor markets and attendant occupational welfare systems appears to have fostered employee-oriented flexible working-time arrangements such as flexitime, sabbatical leave, and gradual retirement. And fifth, major changes in technology and associated changes in investment, labor market demand, and supply and wage trends have been of major importance in explaining the emergence of working-time campaigns and the initiation of working-time rounds.

Value change may well have had an effect on the female activity rate. However, here value change was congruent with broader structural changes that increased the tendency for employees to offer traditional leisure periods to the market, or to economize or exchange nonwork time, much as they economize or exchange effort. Thus, to paraphrase Marx, many of the traditional boundaries set by "morality and nature, age and sex, day and night" have indeed been broken down by the development of capitalism. As yet, there is no evidence of the kind of postindustrial morality that might serve to reconstruct the boundaries between working time and "free" time by liberalizing and "liberating" the time spent at work by the great majority of employees. If such a morality should arise, it is likely to reflect a response to necessity and the collapse of work as a general institution. The historically unparalleled advances enjoyed by wage and salary earners over the postwar period have had little overall effect on working-time values and preferences

Notes

1. D. Bell, *The Cultural Contraditions of Capitalism* (London: Heinemann, 1976), p. 28.

2. See J. Habermas, *Legitimation Crisis* (London: Heinemann, 1976), pp. 117–130. A. Gouldner, *The Coming Crisis of Western Sociology* (New York: Basic Books 1970). See also S. Brittan, *Capitalism and the Permissive Society* (London: Temple Smith, 1973).

3. See B. Martin, *A Sociology of Contemporary Culture Change* (Oxford: Blackwell, 1981).

4. See esp. R. Inglehart, "The Silent Revolution in Europe: Integenerational Change in Post-Industrial Societies," *American Political Science Review* 65 (1971): 991–1017; and "Post-Materialism in an Environment of Insecurity," *American Political Science Review* 75 (1981): 880–899.

5. See, for example, L. E. Davis and A. B. Cherns, eds., *The Quality of Working Life* (New York: Free Press, 1975); C. L. Cooper and E. Mumford, eds., *The Quality of Working Life in Western and Eastern Europe* (London: Associated Business Press, 1979); S. Barkin, ed., *Worker Militancy and Its Consequences, 1965–75* (New York: Praeger, 1978); C. Levinson, ed., *Industry's Democratic Revolution* (London: George Allen and Unwin, 1974).

6. M. Bienefeld, *Working Hours in British Industry: An Economic History* (London: Weidenfeld and Nicolson, 1972).

7. Ibid., chap. 7.

8. For a more detailed examination of the Bienefeld thesis, see W. K. Roche, "Leisure, Insecurity and Union Policy in Britain: A Critical Extension of Bienefeld's Theory of Hours Rounds," *British Journal of Industrial Relations* 25 (1987): 1–17.

9. W. K. Roche, "Crisis in the Labour Market and Working Time Policy: Explaining 'Hours Rounds' in Britain," University College Dublin, Department of Industrial Relations Working Paper No. 6, pp. 19–20 and p. 37, n. 19.

10. Ibid., p. 19.

11. *TUC Report 1955*, p. 399 (all *TUC Reports* are published in London).

12. *TUC Report 1956*.

13. Ibid., p. 481.

14. See A. Deaton, "Unemployment and Politics in Britain since 1945," in B. Showler and A. Sinfield, eds., *The Workless State* (Oxford: Martin Robertson, 1980), pp. 67–68.

15. *The Paper Worker* (journal of the National Union of Printing, Bookbinding and Paper Workers) 19 (Feb. 1959).

16. *PKTF Annual Report for 1957* (May 1958).

17. Ibid., p. 34.

18. *PKTF Annual Report for 1959–60* (1960).

19. Ibid., pp. 32–34.

20. *PKTF Annual Report for 1961–62* (1960), pp. 110–141.

21. *TUC Report 1970*, p. 664.

22. *TUC Report 1971*, p. 527.

23. *TUC Report 1973*, p. 293–294.

24. *TUC Report 1977*, p. 219.

25. Ibid., pp. 466–475.

26. Ibid., p. 552.

27. See C. Jenkins and B. Sherman, *The Collapse of Work* (London: Eyre Methuen, 1979).

28. *TUC Report 1978*, pp. 285–286.

29. *Winning the Battle against Inflation*, Command Papers 7293, (London: Her Majesty's Stationery Office, July 1978), pp. 627.

30. *TUC Report 1978*, pp. 29 and 521.

31. P. Edwards and H. Scullion, "The Local Organization of a National Dispute: The British 1979 Engineering Strike," *Industrial Relations Journal* 13, no. 1 (1982): 57.

32. See M. J. Rice, "The 1979 National Engineering Dispute," (M. A. thesis, University of Warwick, 1980), pp. 51–52.

33. Ibid.

34. *TUC Progress Report*, No. 6, Dec. 1980, and TUC, *Unemployment and Working Time* (Feb. 1981).

35. *TUC Report 1981*, pp. 265–267.

36. CBI *Working Time—Guidelines for Managers* (1981).

37. See Karl Hinrichs, William K. Roche, and Helmut Wiesenthal, "Working-Time Policy as Class-oriented Strategy: Unions and Shorter Working Hours in Great Britain and West Germany," *European Sociological Review* 1 (1983): 211–229.

38. For the TUC's advice to affiliates on "time blocking" see *TUC Annual Report 1980*, pp. 265–267.

39. Income Data Services (hereafter abbreviated to IDS), *Productivity and Working Time*, Study 312 (April 1984).

40. See M. White, *Shorter Working Time*, Report No. 579, and *Case Studies of Shorter Working Time*, Report No. 589 (both published by the Policy Studies Institute, London, in 1980 and 1981, respectively); Trade Union Research Institute, *Working Time in Britain* (London: Anglo-German Foundation, 1981); IDS, *Productivity and Working Time: Industrial Relations Review and Report*, No. 288 (Jan. 1983).

41. *TUC Annual Report 1982*, pp. 543 and 543–554.

42. K. Robins and F. Webster, "New Technology: A Survey of Trade Union Responses in Britain," *Industrial Relations Journal* 13, no. 2 (1982): 6–12.

43. *TUC Campaign for Reduced Working Time: Progress Report*, No. 11, p. 4.

44. "Recent Changes in Hours and Holiday Entitlements—Manual Employees," *Employment Gazette*, March 1987, p. 131.

45. F. Hearn, *Domination, Legitimation and Resistance* (London: Greenwood Press, 1978); see also E. P. Thompson, "Time, Work Discipline and Industrial Capitalism," *Past and Present*, Dec. 1967.

46. See M. Mellish, *The Docks after Devlin* (London: Heinemann, 1977), esp. chap. 2.

47. Royal Commission on Trade Unions and Employers' Associations, *Minutes of Evidence: The Shipbuilding Employers' Federation* no. 48, paras. 7811–19; and for a discussion of "leisure in work" in shipbuilding, see R. Brown et al., "Leisure in Work," in M. Smith et al., eds., *Leisure and Society in Britain* (London: Allen Lane, 1973). For a discussion of "leisure in work" in police work, see M. Cain, *Society and the Policeman's Role* (London: Routledge and Kegan Paul, 1973).

48. For an examination of the ideas of the marginalists on working time, see C. E. Dankert, "Shorter Hours in Theory and Practice," *Industrial and Labour Relations Review*, Jan. 1962, pp. 307–322. For the ideas on working time of a prominent welfarist see, B. Seebowm Rowntree, *The Human Factor in Business* (London: Longmans, Green, 1925), chap. 2. The IPM, having reviewed the research evidence on working

hours in a publication of 1945, recommended to members that they "watch how changes in hours, rest pauses or shift arrangements react upon the employee's health, sickness, accident rates and general efficiency"; B. J. Cohen and M. Towy-Evans, *Working Conditions and Employee Services* (London: IPM, 1945).

49. See R. B. McKersie and L. C. Hunter, *Pay Productivity and Collective Bargaining* (London: Macmillan, 1973). T. Cliff, *The Employers' Offensive: Productivity Deals and How to Fight Them* (London: Pluto Press, 1970). See also NPBI, *Pay and Conditions in the Building Industry*, Cmnd. 3837 (Nov. 1986); *Pay and Conditions of Workers in the Exhibition Contracting Industry*, Cmnd. 4088 (June 1969). For evidence of the liberalization of working time, see McKersie and Hunter, p. 37. However, cases where "clocking in" was introduced for white-collar workers could also be found; see NPBI, *Salaries of Certain Staff Employed by British Insulated Callender Cables Ltd.*, Cmnd. 4168 (Sept. 1969).

50. See NPBI, *Pay of Electricity Workers*, Cmnd. 3045.

51. McKersie and Hunter, pp. 132–135.

52. J. Mitchell, *The National Board for Prices and Incomes* (London: Secker and Warburg, 1972), p. 138.

53. NBPI, *Fire Service Pay*, Cmnd. 3287 (May 1967); the use of the "call in" in industry is discussed in McKersie and Hunter, pp. 134–135.

54. W. P. Colquhoun and P. Rutenfranz, *Studies of Shiftwork* (London: Taylor and Francis, 1980).

55. McKersie and Hunter, pp. 134, 230–234.

56. Ibid., chaps. 2–3.

57. Ibid.

58. NPBI, *Productivity and Pay during the Period of Severe Restraint*, Cmnd. 3167 (Dec. 1966), p. 9.

59. William E. J. McCarthy and Stanley R. Parker, *Shop Stewards and Workshop Relations*, RCTUEA, Research Paper 10 (London: Her Majesty's Stationery Office, 1968), pp. 21–22.

60. NPBI, *Hours of Work, Overtime and Shift Working*, Cmnd. 4554 (Dec. 1970), p. 17.

61. NPBI, *Hours of Work*, appendix F.

62. Ibid., pp. 50–54.

63. IDS, *Study* No. 207 (London: 1979), p. 3.

64. Pay Board, *Sixth (Quarterly) Report*, cited in IDS, *Study* No. 110 (Nov. 1975).

65. See IDS, *Study* No. 207, p. 3.

66. Examples are reported in *Industrial Relations Review and Reports* (hereafter abbreviated IRRR), 385–386 (Feb. 1987) and 389 (March 1987).

67. J. Atkinson and N. Meager, *Changing Working Patterns—How Companies Achieve Flexibility to Meet New Needs*, Institute of Manpower Studies and National Economic Development Organisation (London, 1986).

68. N. Blandy, "New Technology and Flexible Patterns of Working Time," *Employment Gazette*, Oct. 1984, pp. 439–444.

69. T. Mallier and M. Rosser, "The Changing Role of Women in the British Economy," *National Westminster Bank Review*, Nov. 1979, p. 54.

70. H. Joshi, *Secondary Workers in the Cycle*, London Government Economic

Service, Working Paper No. 8 (London: Department of Health and Social Security, 1978), p. 1.

71. D. Bosworth and P. Dawkins, "Women and Part-time Work," *Industrial Relations Journal* 13, no. 3 (1982); 32–39.

72. Ibid., p. 35.

73. O. Robinson and J. Wallace, "Part-time Employment and Low Pay in Retail Distribution in Britain," *Industrial Relations Journal* 5 (1974); 41.

74. Trade Union Research Unit, *Working Time in Britain* (London: Department of Employment, Anglo-German Foundation, 1981), chap. 5; and see Department of Employment *Gazette*, July 1982, p. 245.

75. "Women and Part-time Work," p. 34.

76. R. Brown et al., *Changing Attitudes to Employment?* (London: Department of Employment Research Paper No. 40, 1983).

77. Ibid., chap. 5.

78. Reported in Department of Employment, *Gazette*, July 1982, p. 285.

79. Bosworth and Dawkins, "Women and Part-time Work," p. 34.

80. See *IRRR* 199 (May 1979), and 238 (Dec. 1980).

81. See *IRRR* 223 (May 1980).

82. See *IRRR* 164 (Nov. 1977); 186 (Oct. 1978); and 188 (Nov. 1978).

83. See *IRRR* 225 (June 1980); 255 (Sept. 1981).

84. See *IRRR* 199 (Jan. 1976).

85. B. Casey and G. Bruche, *Work or Retirement* (London: Gower Press, 1983), p. 29.

86. Stanley Parker, *Work and Retirement* (London: Allen and Unwin, 1982), chap. 3.

87. See *IRRR* 266 (1980).

88. See IDS, *Study* No. 119, p. 2.

89. R. A. Lee, "Trade Union Attitudes to Flexible Working Hours," *Industrial Relations Journal* 14, no. 1 (1983): 80–83.

90. Ibid., p. 83.

91. See *IRRR* 225 (June 1980), p. 6.

92. Ibid.

93. See Equal Opportunities Commission, *Equal Opportunities for Women* (London: Her Majesty's Stationery Office, 1983).

94. See *IRRR* 287 (Jan. 1983), pp. 6–7.

95. From data in *IRRR* 277 (June 1980).

96. *IRRR* 287 (Jan. 1983).

97. Ibid.

98. See IDS, *Study* No. 84 (1974), p. 2.

99. See B. McEwan Young, "The Shift towards Shiftwork," *New Society*, July 15, 1982.

100. R. Brown et al., *Changing Attitudes to Employment?*

101. See F. Butler, "Pay and Hours—How Satisfied are You?" *Employment Gazette*, Sept. 1977, pp. 906–915.

102. Ibid., p. 909.

103. Ibid., p. 911.

5   Where Have All the Hours Gone? Working-Time Reduction Policies in the Netherlands

Chris de Neubourg

In its review of working-time reduction policies in the Netherlands after World War II, this chapter emphasizes the period since 1973 and argues that working time was reduced in the Netherlands mainly because there was a society-wide consensus among the labor unions, employers' organizations, and political parties about the need to redistribute employment and unemployment. The reductions of working time did not satisfy the need of workers for more leisure. On the contrary, workers' support for the policy of working-time reduction never was convincing. It is therefore not surprising that it disappeared as a major issue in the negotiations between workers and employers and in the political debate. Emphasis nowadays, rather, is laid on wage claims and labor-market flexibility.

Developments in working time since 1870 are discussed first. It is argued that reductions in working time after 1963 are the result of long-term trends and cyclical movements rather than the outcome of deliberate policy decisions. Union strategy and its economic, social, and political context are discussed in the second section. Working-time reduction practices since 1973 are reviewed in the next section, and their effects on employment, social inequality, and attitudes are emphasized. Conclusions are summarized in the final section.

Working-Time Developments, 1870–1983

The average number annual hours worked per employee in 1970 amounted to only about 60 percent of those for 1870, indicating that there has been a substantial drop in labor input per employee over the past century. In Europe (except in France) this downward trend was even more pronounced during the postwar decades. In comparison with the development of the average annual hours worked per employee, the decline in average weekly hours worked by full-time workers was especially pronounced in the late nineteenth and early twentieth centuries. After World War II (or, more specifically, after the factual application of the 40-hour working week), however, the average weekly hours for full-time workers remained surprisingly stable. Two main factors explain the decline in the average annual working time while the average weekly working time remained more or less stable: first, the increase in the number of voluntary part-time employed, and second, the decrease in the average annual number of days worked per employee.

The number of part-time employed has risen dramatically during the past decades in the majority of the advanced capitalist economies.[1] The rise in part-time employment was especially marked during the 1970s in the Netherlands. In the other countries part-time work was already popular before 1973, having increased mainly during the 1960s. In 1981 in the Netherlands one-fifth of the workforce worked on part-time schedules. A striking though not unexpected feature of part-time employment is the overrepresentation of women. However, it has to be noted that the number of male part-time workers is not negligible in the Netherlands.[2]

From Table 5-1 it can be seen that the number of days worked per year has also declined in the Netherlands, even over the short period of observation, by ten or more days. A substantial reduction in the annual days worked is realized by the introduction of the free Saturday. In the Netherlands this was accomplished in 1961.

The components of the downward trend in the average number of days worked per employee per year are also illustrated for the Netherlands in Table 5-1.[3] As the table illustrates, the number of hours lost because of public holidays and vacation has risen and absence from work because of illness or incapacity has increased significantly. Other components that affect the annual number of days effectively worked are of minor importance—days lost because of bad weather and industrial disputes.

The growing number of part-time workers, together with the decline in the number of days worked annually are responsible for the downward trend in average annual hours worked per employee, while contractual weekly working hours remained constant.

The accelerated decline in annual hours worked in the 1970s is also to be attributed to a cyclical reaction. This reaction is related to the behavior of employers. In the downswing of the business cycle employers prefer reducing hours of work over laying off workers. Taylor explains that this reluctance to dismiss workers (labor hoarding) will be important "until forecasts about the likely course and duration of the recession are more certain."[4] There are several sound reasons for a slow and prolonged reaction of employment levels to changes in output, including legal and institutional constraints (contractual agreements), technical constraints (indivisible production processes), and economic constraints (such as the costs of hiring and firing workers and retraining costs). The adjustment of hours of work by employers is very important, espe-

TABLE 5-1.

Average Work Time in Netherlands, 1960–1982 (per employee per year)

	Days Worked	Hours off for Holidays or Vacation	Hours off for Illness or Incapacity
1960	250.6	174	112.6
1965	220.6	173	102.1
1970	217.6	188	146.4
1975	208.9	234	176.8
1980	204.1	253	191.2
1982	195.2	249	—

Source: Eurostat, "Labour Force Sample Surveys" (Luxembourg, 1973–1983; unpublished, kindly provided by Eurostat).

Note: Working days calculated as the number of days in a year minus Saturdays, Sundays, public holidays, vacation, and days lost because of illness and personal reasons, bad weather, and industrial disputes.

cially when a recession is persistent; in March 1932, 63 percent of the manufacturing employees were on involuntary part-time work in the United States.[5] The way this reaction actually works out varies internationally. In the countries where a temporal reduction in the working week is legally easy (e.g., in Belgium and the United States) or is allowed but not easy (e.g., in the other European Economic Community [EEC] countries) it results in a reduction in the weekly hours of work offered by employer (short-time) or, complementarily, in a rise in the number of persons involuntarily on part-time schedules for economic reasons. In countries where overtime is commonly used to deal with output fluctuation, this cyclical reaction is reflected by the volume of overtime. Overtime is relatively unimportant in the Netherlands. Short-time work, however, is used, contributing to the recent decline in the average annual hours worked per employee. Consequently, the downward trend in annual working time per employee is accelerated by cyclical pressure on the number of hours worked.

The total number of hours worked by individual workers over the life cycle, however, is determined not only by the number of hours worked during each year but also by the number of years worked. Since working-time reductions were mainly introduced during the past ten years in order to reduce overt unemployment by means of a decrease of labor supply, it is not correct to leave reductions of working time over the life cycle out of consideration. In the Netherlands as well as in other countries government policy stimulated early retirement and other forms of withdrawal from the labor force.[6] It is clear that the diminution of labor supply by means of a reduction of working time over the life cycle has been enormous since 1870. This reduction of lifetime working time is mainly due to the prolonged stay in education of the younger age groups and to the development of pension plans and other old-age facilities.

Having reviewed general information on working time that is useful in judging its recent reductions, we should keep two observations in mind. First, the average annual working time has declined in the past century, and its decrease has accelerated during the 1970s without deliberate policy actions. Second, the recent working-time reduction is not to be attributed to changes in the weekly (contractual) working time for full-time workers.

Union Strategy and Its Economic, Social, and Political Context

Up to and after World War II, discussions of working-time reduction concentrated on reducing the working week as well as the working day. Not until the introduction of the 40-hour working week did the reduction in annual working time (in the form of longer holidays) and the reduction in the number of years a person works during a lifetime (in the form of early retirement and the raising of the school-leaving age) become the subjects of discussion. Before World War II the concept of holidays was virtually unknown. It was not until after the war that holidays were being gradually introduced.[7]

From the second half of the nineteenth century until the beginning of World War I drastic reductions in weekly and daily working times took place everywhere. At the beginning of these developments, 78-hour working weeks of six 13-hour working days were commonplace in most countries. However, large differences among the various branches of industry did exist.[8] Especially in those branches of industry with many qualified laborers who were well organized, agreements were made on shorter working days at an early stage.

However, still in 1890 excessively long working hours occurred, for example, in the brick factories in Friesland, where people worked 16 hours a day.

A Dutch survey conducted in 1904 showed that night labor, overtime, and Sunday work occurred especially in those branches of industry that already had the longest working hours. Examples include bakers, dock workers, and mates of river vessels, who had working days of more than 13 hours and did not even have a weekly day of rest. In contrast, for instance, typographers, who had relatively favorable working hours, were also favored with an ingenious shift system for night work.[9]

This survey also pointed to the different ways in which people experienced working either long or short hours. Those who—at that time—already worked fewer than 10 hours (a very small group of people) stood out from the rest by showing more devotion to their work, greater intellectual capacity, and a more intelligent way of working, whereas the large group of laborers who worked more than 13 hours a day led "a totally demoralized, dipsomaniacal, sick and miserable existence."[10]

At the end of the nineteenth century unions' objectives were, therefore, to come to a uniform arrangement about working hours in all branches of industry. The first efforts to lay down legally the daily working hours were related only to women and children. For instance, the Dutch Labour Act of 1889 stipulated that children under 12 years of age were not allowed to work;[11] the work done by children up to the age of 16, as well as work done by women, was limited to a maximum of 11 hours a day; night work for both categories was forbidden. In most countries working time was actually reduced by means of unions' campaigns.

It was not until 1919 that the eight-hour working day (six-days a week) had been generally accepted. From that time in virtually all countries the eight-hour working day had been made legal (except in England). However, in practice this did not make much difference. It was to be a short-lived joy; with the worsening of the economic situation in the 1920s, employers exerted pressure upon the laborers to work longer days. Obviously, the laws were not strong enough to prevent this from happening, and working time rose sharply. Indeed, in some branches of industry 12-hour working days again occurred.

In the late 1920s working time was being cut back gradually, and by 1930 it reached 48 hours a week again. The union fight had been fought. From that time onward the point at issue was the introduction of a five-day working week: the free Saturday. In the light of mass unemployment, motives changed as well. Whereas the goals of the introduction of the eight-hour working day were the improvement in morality, cutting back of excessive drinking, improvement in education, and the betterment of laborers' health, in the 1930s the fight for a 40-hour working week was aimed at the reduction of unemployment. Arguments that were used at the introduction of the eight-hour working day (working-time reduction improves productivity so it can be adopted without a fall in wages) were now, of course, odious. Attempts to use the 40-hour working week as a means of fighting unemployment came to nothing. After World War II working time rose again, and the fight of the trade unions to obtain a 40-hour working week was continued. The old argument—the shortening of working time could be paid out of the increase in productivity—had again become topical. As the labor market was tight, the trade unions had to prove that (especially) a reduction in working time would not create new jobs, so that it would not have an effect on total production. The motivation simply restricts itself to a greater need for leisure time: time for hobbies and for children. By the early 1960s most employees had a free Saturday afternoon, and by the late 1960s and early 1970s the free Saturday had come into force nearly everywhere. For most countries this also meant that the 40-hour working week had become a fact.

In the Netherlands the change from a Saturday afternoon off (the 45-hour working week) to a free Saturday meant that people had to work an extra half an hour on the other days, so that in 1971 the working week was fixed at 42.5 hours.

In the Netherlands and western Europe generally, after the 40-hour working week had been introduced, trade unions concentrated on the extension of holidays. In most countries holidays varying from four to five weeks are nowadays normal. The developments following World War II especially, which took place during a period of strong economic growth, have progressed without many conflicts. In the light of rapidly increasing productivity, employers had little difficulty in conceding trade unions' demands. In general, working-time reductions have had little effect on employment.

In discussions of working-time reduction as an instrument of employment policies, two conflicting arguments were used. On the one hand, it was argued that working-time reduction could be paid out of a rise in productivity, so that wages would not have to be reduced. This would keep purchasing power and, consequently, sales at the same level. On the other hand, it was insisted that working-time reduction could *not* be paid for from a productivity rise because if it were, any effect on employment would be undone.

After 1975 unemployment rates rose sharply and were not expected to decline at the same pace as they had increased. This change led the Dutch labor unions to the conclusion that a redistribution of (un)employment by means of a general and drastic working-time reduction was inevitable. In their view, unemployment could be brought toward an acceptable level only by a reduction of the working week to 32 hours. The largest, and politically most influential, socialist and confessional unions agreed on this general point. The claim for a drastic reduction of the working week by eight hours (one day) was adopted by the Social Democrat Party (PvdA). A moderate reduction of working time was also advocated by the Christian Democrat Party and the conservative governments before and after the elections of 1986. The defenders of this type of social policy referred to the specific labor market features of the Netherlands.

In comparison with other countries in the Organization for Economic Cooperation and Development (OECD) and more specifically with other European countries, the Dutch labor market is characterized by two special features. These features warrant, according to the unions and a large group of policy makers, a reduction of working time in order to combat unemployment. First, the Dutch unemployment rate is among the highest in the OECD and is higher than the unemployment rate in any of its trade partners. Second, Dutch labor supply grows and will continue to grow faster than labor supply in other European countries because of a faster growth of the population at working age (older than 16) and a more pronounced increase in female labor-market participation. The latter has to be attributed to the extremely low female labor-market participation in the past.

The timing of Dutch labour force growth is significant, however. The overall activity rate was and still is very low by international standards, at only 52.1 percent in 1985. But, uniquely among the countries studied, aggregate participation increased by more than 3 percent after 1979. The low Dutch participation rate reflects extremely low female participation; in 1975, only one in four women aged over 15 years was in the labor force. Over the next ten years, however, female participation surged, to 35 percent in 1985. Until 1979 this growth was relatively slow but it has accelerated in the 1980s. Low female labor participation helped offset the effect of rapid population growth, so that until 1975 the Dutch labor force grew broadly in line with developments in the other European countries. Like them and unlike countries with very fast labor force growth, the Netherlands achieved economic expansion in the 1950s and 1960s through strongly rising labor productivity.

The combined effects of high population growth and an increasing female participation rate became visible after 1975. It was partly mitigated by a pronounced decline in the male participation rate (due to prolonged full-time education, more early retirement, and a growing number of people classified as disabled) and by a decline in the average number of hours worked per worker. Nevertheless, high fertility rates in the 1960s and a big increase in the proportion of women working or wanting to work resulted in a rapid growth of the labor force from 1975 onward. This came after a long period of modest labor force growth, and at a time when the industrialized countries were facing severe economic recession.

The number of employed declined in the 1970s and remained more or less stable in the 1980s. A strong increase in labor supply and an unemployment rate already high, combined with the expectation that employment growth will be moderate, form the rationale behind the wide-scale consensus in favor of working-time reductions in order to keep unemployment "manageable." The (conservative) governments had an additional reason to advocate working-time reduction. The recovery of profitability in private enterprise and the reduction of the budget deficit had been made the main targets of government policy. Working-time reduction with a corresponding decline in real wages could contribute to the realization of these targets both directly and indirectly. A decline of the real wage costs contributes to both. In the large state-financed sector, declining real wages result also in a decline in total social security payments. Moreover, the government hoped that increasing overt unemployment, which resulted partly from its nearly deflationary economic policy, could be mitigated by a redistribution of employment and unemployment and thus by a reduction of labor supply measured in hours.

At first employers had been reluctant to give in to the unions' demand and the government's plea for shorter working time. They feared increasing nonwage costs and losses of production as a result. However, they were tempted by the decline in wage costs and the prospects of increased profitability. Moreover, they saw possibilities for urging more flexibility in working-time arrangements, both in the legal settlements and in negotiations with the unions.

In November 1982 an agreement between the organizations of employers and employees was signed at the central level. It was agreed that working time would be reduced in order to raise profits and to reduce unemployment. The next section of this chapter gives more information on the practical implementation of this intention.

By the end of 1984 the Central Bureau of Statistics estimated that 72

percent of the nation's workers experienced some form of working-time reduction. However, in 1985 and especially in 1986 working-time reduction was
gradually abandoned by the labor unions and the political parties as the most
important policy instrument to combat unemployment. Three major reasons explain that change in positions.

First, working-time reduction did not generate as many new jobs as its
defenders had hoped (for some estimates, see the section below on the effects
of reductions). This was mainly due to underestimated secondary effects on
labor productivity and final demand and to organizational problems. The profitability of private enterprise, nevertheless, was raised, although this cannot be
attributed solely to working-time reduction.

Second, inflation was brought back to nearly zero percent per year. Since
the working-time reduction was to be paid for out of the price compensation
mechanism in wage adjustment (automatic wage indexing), no inflation implies that financing further working-time reductions would be troublesome.
They can be financed only by diminishing nominal wages or by raising wage
costs.

Last but not least, workers' support for working-time reduction was never
convincing, and it declined further because of the disappointing employment
effect. It seemed in 1982 that only 40 percent of the full-time workers were
prepared to reduce their working time; another 40 percent by no means wanted
to work less. Moreover, only 19 percent of the full-time workers were prepared
to reduce their working time if doing so meant a corresponding decline in their
real wage.[12] In 1985 opinions were similar, although a growing number of
workers declared that they would be prepared to work one hour less only if
guarantees were given that employment would be raised correspondingly.[13]

The impossibility of giving such guarantees and the apparently small employment effect of previous working-time reductions made working-time mea-
surements increasingly unpopular. All the civil servants and some other groups
of workers have already faced a decline of nominal wage. These workers scorn
the idea of further working-time reductions and their corresponding wage cuts.

Employers, on the other hand, increasingly tend to emphasize the flexibility aspect of working-time arrangements. Therefore, this issue can be expected to become more important, both in negotiations between employers' and
workers' organizations and in labor-market policy.[14]

Recent Working-Time Policy in the Netherlands

Since 1945 an employer has been able to request a license for
employees to work short hours on the ground of the special labor law: Buiten-
gewoon Besluit Arbeidsverhoudingen 1945 (BBA). The main conditions for
obtaining a license are that economic activity in the firm has to have fallen to

an "abnormally low level" and that this fall is temporary. Where a license has been granted, the employees concerned are regarded as partly involuntarily unemployed and are entitled to receive an unemployment benefit of 80 percent of their most recent salary. In most collective agreements it is arranged that the employer supplements this to 100 percent. Especially since the first oil crisis this approach has widely been used. In 1974 the number of workyears lost by working short hours was 4,873, which rapidly climbed to a peak of 17,916 in 1975. The number of workyears lost went down to 695 in 1979 and climbed in 1980 to the level of 2,414. The importance of this arrangement thus paradoxally declines as unemployment rises. According to Lukkes, this is because "the cabinet from the period 1973–1977 was, far more than the succeeding cabinet, inclined to use this measure to inflate the official unemployment figures."[15] It seems more plausible, however, that since 1976 the belief in the temporary character of the "fallen economic activity" had diminished, and the need was felt to introduce more structural measures to reduce working hours.

All the same, it was not until 1980 that other measures were taken to reduce working time. Then a measure was introduced by the government to stimulate employers to create part-time jobs by means of a subsidy arrangement. This measure was abolished by 1982 because it appeared that it did not influence employers' decisions; the part-time jobs for which subsidies had been granted would have been created anyway, without subsidies. Criticism from the women's movement focused on the fact that subsidies were granted for the creation of part-time jobs in the traditional female professions in the service sector and thus did not have any emancipating effect.

Furthermore, the role of the government has been restricted to guaranteeing an unemployment benefit until the age of 65 to persons who become unemployed at 60 years of age, and to stimulating measures to reduce working hours on the sector level. In this latter context the government is working on a revision of the legislation on working hours, which dates from 1919. In 1985 the government reduced the working time of civil servants to 38 hours per week. The additional employment that compensates partly for this reduction in working time is paid by a decline in nominal wages.

The majority of the collective agreements since 1975 (agreements between unions and employer's organizations at a sectoral level) contain a provision on early retirement. This is also financed by a decline in real wages (no more, or less, wage indexing). These provisions stipulate that retiring workers should be replaced by younger workers. The collective agreement for the metal industry, for example, allows workers to retire at the age of 60 or 61. Employers agreed to employ more young workers for 32 hours per week in order to compensate for the quitting older workers.[16] By the end of 1984, 60,000 workers (1 percent of the labor force) made use of the possibility of retiring before the age of 65 (the figure for the country as a whole).[17]

In November 1982 an agreement was settled between the central unions of employers and employees in the Stichting van de Arbeid (labor foundation). This agreement exposed the desire of both employers and employees to reduce working time in order to raise profits and reduce unemployment. Employees were prepared to pay for the reduction of working time by waiving their price compensation (automatic wage indexing). Specific conditions were to be settled in the separate collective agreements.

Since this central agreement was reached, most collective agreements include some form of working-time reduction, ranging from a few days a year to a 36-hour working week. The greater part, however, includes arrangements for the 38-hour working week, which is now settled for about 1.3 million employees in the private sector (this is approximately 50 percent of the total number of employers in the private sector). For almost half of these arrangements, a study will be done on the possibility of introducing the 36-hour working week at a later date. Arrangements on the 36-hour working week already concern approximately 200,000 employees in the private sector, mainly in the graphics industries and the tobacco, alcohol, and food industries. Usually, employees pay for working-time reduction by waiving their price compensation. Furthermore, agreements have been made on other forms of working-time reduction, like early retirement (see above) and involuntary part-time jobs for youths.

In most agreements where some form of working-time reduction has been arranged, introduction occurs by means of so-called *roostervrije dagen* (unscheduled holidays), which rotate among employees or are taken collectively. In the first case, production time usually stays at 40 hours a week; in the latter case, production time is reduced by the same amount as working time.

In the graphics and printing industries the collective agreement foresaw a 5 percent reduction of working time (two hours per week) in 1984 and a further reduction of two hours per week in 1986. Employers promised to create 1,800 additional part-time jobs for young workers; 800 of them would also be offered training. Workers in the building industry received three additional unscheduled holidays. In that industry, working-time reduction had gone up to 5 percent by April 1985. The age for early retirement was lowered from 62 to 61, and new jobs for younger workers would be part-time by definition (32 hours a week). It became common practice to employ workers younger than 26 years for 32 hours per week. This practice is also adopted by the government.[18]

On the company level few experiments have been carried out. As has been mentioned, most firms introduce working-time reduction by means of unscheduled holidays. This was the case, for example, in the Port of Rotterdam. Unions and employers agreed to reduce working time by 10 percent in order to preserve 335 jobs. The costs were paid partly by the employers and partly by the workers (50 percent each). The working-time reduction was introduced by giving the workers 22 extra days off.

Of course, other forms of working-time reductions were introduced in some other firms.

The Swiss pharmaceutical corporation Ciba Geigy proposed a reduction of the working time by 15 minutes per day for workers at their plant in Maastricht. The unions rejected this proposition, and the court found it in violation of the collective agreement. DAF Trucks (6,000 employees), on the other hand, where the 36-hour working week was introduced in August 1983 because of lack of sales, first experimented with a reduction by day. After research into the financial consequences of the 7.2-hour working day, it was concluded to be too expensive. Now production personnel work eight hours a day again and receive 23 extra days off in return. Some small firms such as Chemco (a chemical firm with 340 employees) and Phenolpers (a grinding firm with 125 employees) are experimenting with a compressed working week; employees work four days of nine hours a week (36 hours) while production time is lengthened to 45 hours a week (five days of nine hours). The tobacco concern Niemeyer (700 employees) uses the 36-hour working week to increase flexibility over the year; starting on January 1, 1987, production time was lengthened to 45 hours a week and employees worked 45 hours a week in the peak periods (five days of nine hours) and 27 hours in slack periods (three days of nine hours). In this way no employees have to be dismissed, but new jobs are not likely to have been created.

In September 1986 the Economic Institute for Medium-sized and Small Enterprises (EIM) published the results of a large-scale survey on the working-time reduction practices in small business corporations.[19] Since we know from French experiences that the most important bottlenecks in working-time reducing processes are found within the smaller firms,[20] the results of this survey are highly significant. In the Netherlands there are 168,000 enterprises with fewer than 21 employees, employing about a quarter of the Dutch workers. Only 37 percent of these firms reduced working time; the others met too many problems to create a plan or did not even try to.

In the majority of the small firms working time has been reduced (mostly in 1983 and 1984) by 5 percent: 57 percent of the firms choose unscheduled holidays; in 23 percent the working time was reduced by working less on one specific day during every week; and in 16 percent working hours are cut every day. Operation time is reduced in 40 percent of the firms.

It is striking that 54 percent of the firms said that serious problems were encountered. Among the problems most often cited were planning and communication difficulties and a deterioration in the service extended to customers. One out of ten firms faced a serious increase in production costs. In another survey among firms in the graphics industries, it appeared that the shortage of skilled typographic workers was a serious problem. It was said that in 1986, 1,560 vacancies existed because of the introduction of working-time reduction.[21]

The Effects of Working-Time Reductions

The Effects on Employment and Unemployment

In 1984 research was published on the employment effects of working-time reduction by the Ministry of Social Affairs and Employment.[22] The survey covered 583 firms with more than 20 employees. The results were rather disappointing. In almost 80 percent of the firms some form of working-time reduction was realized or planned. Of these, 48 percent maintained the same production time, 45 percent reduced their production time, and the other 7 percent did not know at the moment of questioning what they were going to do, or lengthened their production time. Furthermore, in 17 percent of the firms where working-time reduction arrangements had been made, new jobs were created, and in another 26 percent new jobs were expected to be created. In 7 percent of the firms jobs were said to have been saved, and in 6 percent of the firms jobs were expected to be saved. However, in 4.5 percent of the firms jobs were lost, and in another 4.5 percent jobs were expected to be lost in spite of the working-time reduction.

Asked for the reasons for these low employment effects, 35 percent of the firms ascribed it to productivity growth, 22 percent to overcapacity, 15 percent to the reduction of production time, and 9 percent to reorganizational problems. It appeared that especially where production time had been reduced, employment effects were low. On the basis of this research the reemployment rate can be estimated at 20 percent to 25 percent. As the survey excludes small firms, where employment effects will be lower (see previous section), we might safely take the lower limit of 20 percent. Combining this percentage and the numbers of employees for which a 38-hour working week has been agreed upon (mentioned above), the total employment effect in the private sector would amount to about 20,000 new full-time jobs.

For more than half of the 600,000 employees in the semipublic sector (hospitals, welfare institutions, and the like) the 38-hour working week has also been arranged. They have been promised a reemployment rate of 80 percent of the hours lost. On the basis of this figure, the employment effect would be almost 15,000 new full-time jobs, but it is questionable whether this will be realized.

Our estimate of an employment effect of approximately 35,000 new jobs in the private and semipublic sectors is close to the official estimate of 55,000 *saved and new* jobs used by the Minister of Social Affairs and Employment, on the basis of calculations by the Central Planning Bureau (CPB). For its own 700,000 employees the government had introduced the 38-hour working week on August 1, 1985. The reemployment rate is set at 70 percent. If it is realized, the employment effect in the public sector can be estimated at 25,000 new jobs.

The government uses the figure of 150,000 full-time jobs to the end of 1985 for the total employment effect of all variants of working-time reduction.

This figure consists of the 55,000 jobs in the private and semipublic sector, the 25,000 jobs in the public sector, plus a further 20,000 jobs as the employment effect of early retirement and 50,000 jobs caused by the long-term growth of involuntary part-time work. This latter trend in part-time labor is, however, in no way stimulated by the government and can even be said to have remained in spite of government policies.

Estimates for the long term (the year 2000) made by the CPB and the Organization for Strategic Labor Market Research (OSA) reveal that the employment effect would be 330,000 to 370,000 workyears if working time is reduced by 15 percent, and 550,000 workyears if it is reduced by 20 percent.[23] However, these estimates are partly based on simulation, using questionable assumptions. Moreover, both studies calculate the effects of a rigorous cut in working hours. Given what has been said above, in the section on union strategy, it is highly uncertain whether this reduction will be realized in the decade to come.

Working-time reduction is believed in the first place to cushion overt unemployment. However, it cannot be assumed that unemployment will diminish with the same number of persons as the number of newly created jobs, for two main reasons. First, working-time reduction leads to an increase in labor supply, and second, it is likely that more people will take second jobs or that moonlighting will grow as an effect of working-time reduction.

It is well known that the real unused stock of labor resources is considerably larger than registered unemployment.[24] This has to be attributed to the "discouragement effect" and to the fact that in most countries not all unemployed are registered. It is clear that a working-time reduction would activate a part of this potential nonregistered labor force. On top of this effect, an increase in labor supply has to be expected because of the fact that real income per salary earner diminishes when wages are reduced proportionally with working-time. reduction (additional workers). Siegers estimated recently that the combination of the encouragement and the additional worker effect absorbs about 30 percent of the employment increase resulting from a rise in labor supply represented by the inclusion of married women in the Netherlands.[25]

Empirical estimates of the unemployment effect of working-time reduction are available only from macroeconomic models. They reveal that unemployment would diminish by, say, 1 percent on the short term.[26] To summarize the empirical information on the (un)employment effects of working-time reduction in the Netherlands, it may be said that working-time policy did not create a growth in employment that can be assumed to lower overt unemployment considerably.

The Effects on Social Inequality

Working-time reduction in the Netherlands is mostly discussed under the assumption that gross wages would be lowered proportionally. Under this assumption, changes in the income distribution that are attributable to working-time reduction are inevitable. There are no empirical data at our disposal to judge the significance of these changes. However, the Social Cultural Planning Bureau did conduct a simulation study in order to estimate the distributional aspects of working-time reduction.

In this study working time is assumed to be reduced by 20 percent. Given a proportional decline in gross wages, this implies a gross wage reduction of equally 20 percent, leading to a net decline of 15 to 16 percent. However, the decline is not the same for various groups. Although it is assumed that all wage earners, including those working for the minimum wage, are facing a similar decline in working time and income, there are three important groups that are excluded from the reductions or that are affected in another way: the self-employed, social security benefit receivers, and the retired who are living on a pension. The self-employed are assumed not to reduce their working time. Dutch social security benefits are directly related to wages, that is, when wages change, social security benefits are accordingly adjusted nearly automatically.

An important element in the impact of working-time reduction on income distribution is the fact that more persons are employed and therefore earn more than before. This implies not only a redistribution of employment but also the redistribution of income. The income of households wherein no members hold additional employment after a working-time reduction is lower than it was before. If a member of a household gets a job, having been unemployed or out of the labor force before the working-time reduction, household income may increase or decline less. Taking all the other (e.g., tax) effects into account, it is possible to estimate average changes in some household categories.

When working time would have been reduced by 20 percent in 1981, a wage-earner family would have faced a decline in net household income of 9.9 percent. A family income based on self-employment would have been increased by 1.3 percent, whereas beneficiaries of social security and retired living on a pension would have been confronted with a diminishing of income of, respectively, only 1.9 and 11.4 percent. It is easy to conclude that working-time reduction increases income inequality, if measured as the difference between the highest and lowest household income category. Moreover, it appears from simulation exercises that nearly 920,000 households would fall below the social minimum income (poverty line), while for 42,000 the income will increase from below to above the social minimum. As a whole, households would face a fall of 13.3 percent in income, while only 8 percent of the families will see their income increased.[27]

However, there is another type of social inequality that may be affected by a working-time reduction, namely, the inequality between men and women. Although, there is no empirical evidence on this point, it may safely be assumed that after working time is reduced, more women would have the opportunity to hold a job. This means that a more equal distribution of paid work would result. However, this does not automatically imply that unpaid work (within the household) is also more equally distributed between men and women. From empirical research, we know that a marginal reduction of the working day hardly affects the division of labor within the household. If men work fewer hours (5 or 10 percent less than 40 hours per week), they generally use this time for leisure, mainly sleeping, reading newspapers, and watching television.[28]

To summarize: one effect of working-time reduction policies is that income inequality is increased, especially between the self-employed and wage earners and between retired people living on a pension and other workers. The division of paid labor between the sexes becomes more equal, although this is unlikely to change the division of labor within the household significantly in the short term.

The Effects on Social Priorities and Attitudes

Leaving aside the question of whether working-time reduction has had effects on social priorities and attitudes, it may be asked whether working time was reduced because social priorities and attitudes had already changed. Two types of attitudes are most relevant in this context, namely, attitudes toward work and leisure and those toward the division of labor between the sexes.

In the Netherlands working-time reduction since 1975 was introduced mainly to deal with specific problems in the labor market. Although the labor unions and the employers' organizations agreed in 1982 to reduce working time in order to cushion overt unemployment and to raise profitability, only a minority of the workers (19 percent) said (in 1982) they were prepared to work and earn less (40 percent of the workers were prepared to work fewer hours without a wage loss). However, 40 percent of the workers in no way wanted to work less. It can therefore safely be concluded that the reduction of working time was not "caused" by a shift in workers' preferences for more leisure.

The same conclusion holds for the attitudes toward the division of labor between sexes. Although, feminist organizations urged a drastic working-time reduction in order to redistribute paid and unpaid work between the sexes, these propositions were not matched by a significant change in opinions on the value of household work. In other words, as with the labor unions, the organizations are well ahead of their members and do not represent the opinions of their average members.

There are no grounds for arguing that working-time reductions in the 1980s have changed attitudes toward work and leisure and toward the division of labor between the sexes. Working-time reduction strategy has been abandoned by the labor unions for various reasons. One of those was said to be the lack of support by their members. Table 5-2 reflects some changes in attitudes toward work and working-time reductions: it lists the answers to questions posed in regular national surveys by the Social Cultural Planning Bureau. From

TABLE 5-2.
Opinions on Work and Working-Time Reduction, 1963–1983 (*percentages*)

	1963	1975	1977	1979	1981	1983
What gives you more satisfaction?						
work	—	20.0	21.1	19.9	21.8	22.5
work and leisure	—	64.0	62.7	60.1	59.2	58.2
leisure	—	16.0	16.2	19.6	19.1	19.3
Do you have enough time for leisure?						
yes	72.0	80.9	—	83.6	85.5	83.7
no	28.0	19.1	—	16.4	14.5	16.3
Does not want fewer hours	—	—	—	41.8	39.3	42.1
Does not want more holidays	—	—	—	41.6	39.5	41.6

Source: Sociaal Cultureel Planbureau, *Rapport 1984* (The Hague: Government Publishing Office, 1985).

Note: — = not available.

the figures, it is clear that work satisfaction (as opposed to satisfaction with leisure) grew rather than diminished between 1975 and 1983. It is striking that a growing number of respondents say that they think they had enough time for leisure (72 percent in 1963 versus 83.7 percent in 1983). The number of persons who indicated that they didn't want to work fewer hours rose between 1979 and 1983, while the number of those not wanting longer holidays was stable over the same period.

Opinions on household work changed somewhat between 1981 and 1983 (see Table 5-3). It is, however, surprising to find that, on the one hand, more housewives say that housework is often both a thankless task and dull, but that, on the other hand, the number of housewives who think the opposite is also rising (the percentage of housewives who answer "now and then" diminishes). It is, however, questionable whether these small changes in attitudes are the result of working-time reductions. There are good grounds for arguing that changes in sex-role definitions and in the division of labor between the sexes are rather autonomous.[29] It may nevertheless be assumed that the growth of part-time employment may reinforce attitudinal changes in the same way as appears to have happened in Sweden.[30]

Summary and Conclusions

The average number of annual hours worked per employee diminished significantly in the Netherlands as in other nations during the past hundred years. Before World War II this decline resulted from both a significant decrease in the number of days and hours worked per week and from the introduction of more and longer holidays. After the achievement of the 40-hour working week, the average number of annual hours worked per employee was

TABLE 5-3.
Opinions on the Character of Household Work
(*percentages*)

	1981	1983
Housework is a thankless task:		
often	15.8	17.4
now and then	28.1	24.8
seldom or never	56.1	57.8
Housework is dull:		
often	16.8	17.9
now and then	28.8	26.2
seldom or never	54.4	56.0

Source: Sociaal Cultureel Planbureau, *Rapport 1984* (The Hague: Government Publishing Office, 1985).

further reduced because of the increase in part-time work, longer holidays, and absences from the job.

After 1975 the unemployment rate rose sharply in the Netherlands, as in many other countries. Moreover, the Dutch labor supply grew and will continue to grow faster than the labor supply of most other European countries. Employment, however, declined in the same period. These features formed the rationale behind the consensus in favor of working-time reductions.

In 1982 an agreement between the labor unions and the employers' organizations was signed at the central level. As a result, working time was reduced by two weekly hours on the average for many workers. By the end of 1984 the Central Bureau of Statistics estimated that 72 percent of all workers experienced some form of working-time reduction.

In 1985 and especially in 1986 working-time reduction was gradually abandoned by the labor unions and the political parties as the most important policy instrument to combat unemployment. This change of opinion has to be attributed to three reasons. First, the (un)employment effect of the working-time reductions was small. Second, inflation was reduced to nearly zero percent, rendering the financing of further reductions troublesome. Third, workers' support was not strong, and it declined further because of the small employment effects of the policies.

Working-time reduction policies in the Netherlands cannot be said to be the consequence of a latent wish for more leisure by workers. Nor did it cause a significant change in preferences for work or leisure. Its effects on social inequality are difficult to establish, although an increase in income inequality is not unlikely.

Judged from workers' opinions and from the programs of labor unions and political parties, it seems most plausible that working time will not be reduced further in the years to come. Employers' organizations and labor unions are currently discussing wage claims and labor-market flexibility. These are now set to become the major issues in Dutch collective bargaining.

Notes

1. For details see C. de Neubourg, "Part-time Work: A Quantitative International Comparison," *International Labour Review* 124, 1 (Jan. 1985): 559–576.

2. The reasons for these international and intertemporal differences are interesting but fall outside the scope of this contribution. For more details see ibid.

3. For an international comparison, see C. de Neubourg and L. Kok, *Arbeids-tijdverkorting* (Utrecht: Het Spectrum, 1984); L. Kok and C. de Neubourg, "Working Time: Length, Past and Future," in A. Kleinknecht and T. van Veen, eds., *Working Time Reductions and the Crisis of the Welfare State* (Maastricht: Presses Interuniversitaires Européennes, 1986), pp. 12–80.

4. J. Taylor, "The Unemployment Gap in Britain's Production Sector 1953–1973," in G. D. N. Worswick, ed., *The Concept and Measurement of Involuntary Unemployment* (London: Allen and Unwin, 1976).

5. H. A. Millis and R. E. Montgomery, *The Economics of Labor*, vol. 1: *Labor's Progress and Some Basic Labor Problems* (New York: McGraw Hill, 1938), p. 477.

6. An extensive discussion is given in C. de Neubourg, *Unemployment, Labour Slack, and Labour Market Accounting: Theory, Evidence, and Policy* (Amsterdam: North Holland, 1988), chap. 5.

7. By 1920, a holiday of three to six days was normal in the manufacturing industry; civil servants were entitled to 12–18 holidays.

8. There were also large regional differences. In the country people worked much longer hours than did people in cities.

9. J. E. van Dierendonck, "Historisch Overzicht," in P. J. Verdoorn, *Arbeidsduur en welvaartspeil* (Leiden: Stenfert Kroese, 1947).

10. Ibid., pp. 115–116.

11. In 1874 this had already been stipulated in the "Kinderwet van Houten."

12. J. Dorenbos, Th. Schepens, and A. Vissers, *Arbeidstijd en arbeidstijdverkort-ing Onderzocht*, (The Hague: OSA, Government Publishing Office, 1985).

13. OSA *Arbeidsmarktsurvey* (The Hague: Government Publishing Office, 1986).

14. Chris de Neubourg, *Unemployment and Labour Market Flexibility: The Netherlands* (Geneva: ILO, 1990).

15. P. Lukkes, *Tijdelijk korter werken in Nederland*, no. 22 (Groningen: Geografisch Instituut Rijksuniversiteit Groningen, Sociaal Geografische Reeks, 1982).

16. Catz argues that this kind of regulation is in various ways lucrative for employers. First, they have to pay lower wages for younger workers than for older workers. Second, they do not have to replace all the quitting workers. Third, young workers are employed only for 32 hours per week and thus are involuntary part-time workers. See F. Catz, "De vele slagen om de arbeidstijd," *Tijdschrift voor Politieke Ekonomie* (Sept. 7, 1983).

17. Ministerie van Sociale Zaken en Werkgelegenheid, *Herverdeling van werk, een internationale vergelijking* (The Hague, 1986), p. 23.

18. This explains partly why the growth of part-time employment was spectacular in the Netherlands in the period 1979–85 (see above).

19. G. Th. Elsendoorn and C. C. P. M. van Ginneken, *ATV in kleine bedrijven* (Zoetermeer: EIM, 1986).

20. O. Marchand, D. Rault, and È. Turpin, "Des 40 Heures aux 39 Heures: Processus et Réactions des Entreprises," *Economie et Statistique* 154 (April 1983): 3–15.

21. KVGO, "Tweede fase ATV: een brug te ver?" *Repro en Druk* 35 (1986): 3.

22. L. T. D. (Loon Technische Dienst), *Werkgelegenheidseffecten van verschillende vormen van arbeidsduurverkorting in 583 bedrijven* (The Hague: Ministry of Social Affairs, 1985).

23. C. P. B. (Centraal Planbureau), *De Nederlandse Economie op Lange Termijn* (The Hague: Government Publishing Office, 1986); OSA (Organisatie voor Strategisch Arbeidsmarktonderzoek), *OSA Rapport 1985, Werk voor Allen* (The Hague: Government Publishing Office, 1986).

24. C. de Neubourg, "The Dough, the Doughnut and the Hole: Unemployment, Labour Utilisation and Labour Market Accounting," in D. Bosworth and D. F. Heathfield, eds., *Working Below Capacity* (London: Macmillan, 1987).

25. His conclusion that the additional worker effect has practically no influence seems to be rather misleading, since he uses cross-sectional data to estimate the effects. These data have two important shortcomings. They do not account for the cumulative effects of succeeding years with diminishing real wages and the supplementary income reduction imposed by working-time reduction. Second, they do not reflect the effect of a forced income reduction imposed on the mass of the workers (in contrast to a chosen income reduction by part-time workers only). His results are likely to underestimate the observed effects. J. J. Siegers, *Arbeidsduurverkorting en het Arbeidsaanbod door Gehuwde Vrouwen* (The Hague: Ministerie van Sociale Zaken, 1983).

26. See L. Kok and C. de Neubourg, "Working Time."

27. Sociaal en Cultureel Planbureau, *Berekend Beleid* (The Hague: Government Publishing Office, 1985).

28. W. Knulst and L. Schoonderwoerd, *Waar blijft de tijd. Onderzoek naar de tijdsbesteding van Nederlanders*, Sociaal en Cultureel Planbureau, Sociale en Culturele Studies 4 (The Hague: Government Publishing Office, 1983).

29. See L. Kok and C. de Neubourg, *Projecting Labour Supply: Methods, Theory and Research* (The Hague: OSA Government Publishing Office, 1986).

30. See C. de Neubourg and C. Caanen, *Employment, Unemployment and Labour Market Policy in Small Open Economies* (The Hague: OSA, Government Publishing Office, 1987).

6 The Reduction of Working Hours in Belgium: Stakes and Confrontations

Annik De Rongé and Michel Molitor

In Belgium the reduction of working hours is a demand that for a long time has been at the heart of conflictual relations between unions and employers. Until the 1950s union demands sought the modification of the living conditions of those in employment. In the 1950s the unions, in exchange for a reduction of working hours, accepted elements of employers' arguments and compromised to raise productivity.

The demand for a reduction of working hours regained prominence in the 1970s. This time, the objective was to alleviate unemployment through work sharing. Opposition from employers to this union objective, combined with the dynamic of industrial relations and macroeconomic evaluations of the effects of a significant reduction of working hours, has progressively transformed the demand itself. If the unions have continued to demand the reduction of working hours, a new theme has been added to this demand: the *modification* of working hours, that is, the flexible reorganization of work, which in fact would result indirectly in a reduction of working hours.

It appears to us that flexible working hours is a new development in the compromise between employers and unions, which has historically centered on reducing working hours in exchange for productivity increases. In this context, the role of the government in its pursuit of a policy of flexibility and use of labor legislation has been decisive.

"Winning More Time for the Workers": From the Beginnings of Industrialization to 1940

The process of industrialization began very early in Belgium, which by the middle of the nineteenth century was one of the most industrialized countries in the world after Great Britain.[1] Economic liberalism characterized this period until about 1886. No social legislation was enacted because all labor laws and regulations were considered an attack on the freedom to work and to enter into binding contracts. Among the ruling classes individual effort was regarded as the only way out of misery for the masses.

In this context, the number of working hours was the prerogative of employers. In 1863 an official enquiry showed that the working day was 12–14 hours long for adults and children—the latter might be under nine years old. Very long working hours, subsistence wages, and no political representation formed the general climate in which the first workers' leagues were formed. The leagues subsequently grouped together in 1885 to create the Parti Ouvrier Belge (POB).

The struggle for the reduction of working hours was first concentrated, therefore, on women and child labor. The campaigners for working-time regulation stressed physiological and moral arguments, whereas the opponents relied mainly on ideological arguments (the freedom of heads of households to dispose of their labor as they choose) and also upon economic (competition) and social (the family need for extra wages) arguments.

In 1889 the first law regulating woman and child labor was promulgated. It outlawed work for children under the age of 12, introduced a 12-hour working day for boys (between the ages of 12 and 16) and for girls (between the ages of 12 and 21). A six-day week was also introduced for girls.[2] From this point, further changes in working hours were negotiated in collective bargaining between employers and trade unions. Hence, the first law regulating working hours for adults—a 1909 law introducing a nine-hour day for miners—in fact merely confirmed the results of previous negotiations between unions and employers. However, the principle of promulgating laws and regulations remained important, since it instituted a minimum set of rules applicable to all.

A second characteristic of the workers' movement for the reduction of working hours must also be underlined. Although physiological and moral arguments were still used (more rest, better hygiene, the promotion of family life, the reduction of alcoholism), they were now surpassed by economic considerations. The modernization of the economic structure and increased productivity now became the core of trade unions' arguments in favor of the reduction of working hours. The last argument to be used concerned the link between the reduction of the working day to eight hours and the alleviation of unemployment. Demands for the reduction of working hours have thus never been expressed in anticapitalist terms in Belgium. The employers' position regarding the reduction of working hours is also based on strictly economic arguments: the danger of a deterioration of competition between firms, increases in production costs, increases in taxes and decreases in production. However, there is no conflict of principles. Employers and the unions bargained in conflictual manner, but within a climate of consensus on economic principles.

It needs to be stressed that since the beginning of the twentieth century the two large union organizations that exist in the Flemish and French-speaking communities in Belgium have had different attitudes to the question of the reduction of working hours.[3] Although there is unanimity on the necessity for this reduction, opinions vary with regard to the means to be used. At certain times the socialist unionists contested the matter, whereas on other occasions the Christian unionists took the initiative. The links between the unions and the political parties—closer in the case of the socialists than the Flemish Christians—may explain these differences. The timing of demands by the different federations has been related to the composition of government coalitions.

Nevertheless, in 1919 the two union confederations declared themselves in favor of the eight-hour day, but the CSC judged the moment inopportune, since it might thwart the postwar reconstruction efforts. The CSC therefore declared itself in favor of free negotiations at firm level in each sector rather than legislation.

During this period many conflicts erupted. One of the most important occurred in 1919 in the metal products manufacturing factories; the principal demand was the eight-hour day. The spread of this strike caused the government to create a *commission d'arbitrage*. This resulted in the creation of the first Commission Paritaire.[4] It is interesting to point out that this body, which is a favored concertation tool in Belgium, originated in confrontations concerning working hours. A second Commission Paritaire was created 15 days later, this time in the mining sector. Thus the mining and metal products manufacturing sectors were the pioneers of all demands in reduction of working hours, and so it has continued till today.

In the beginning of 1921, 55 to 65 percent of the workers had an eight-hour working day and a 48-hour week. At this moment a law was judged necessary because the remaining workers (the majority in medium-sized or small firms) were not strongly unionized, such that negotiation would not be feasible. Here we find a characteristic element of the industrial relations system in Belgium: the most militant sections of the workforce pressure employers, negotiations ensue sector by sector via concertation, and then finally a law confirms the existing situation by generalizing it to sectors or firms scarcely touched by workers' organizations.

It should be noted that article 13 of this law stipulated that "the reduction or working hours resulting from the present law can in no circumstances result in a reduction of wages." This is an aspect of the law to which we will return. The law regulating the eight-hour day provoked a strong employer counterattack aimed at neutralizing its effects. The employers instigated many bills that aimed at a return to the previous situation; these were rejected, though a few became objects of social conflict.

The reduction of the working week to 48 hours coincided with the growing success of Taylorism. The reorganization of labor produced a change in wage payment, particularly the introduction of piece rates. The workers' movement eventually changed its attitude to these innovations, although in 1919 it had opposed them by strikes. In the same way, the union confederations eventually supported increased mechanization. Although the employers claimed significant production losses, these occurred only in firms where the labor process had not been modernized. On the other hand, it is impossible to evaluate the effect of reduced hours on unemployment, particularly as this did not constitute the principle demand.

The situation changed, however, during the 1930s crisis when the claim for the 40-hour week was presented as a demand. In 1929 Belgium's unemployment figure was 13,000, and by 1934 it had reached 235,000. In 1930 the CSC proposed a reduction in working hours to 45 hours per week without a reduction in wages. In 1931 the Socialist Party demanded a 40-hour week. At its congress in August 1932 the CSC went as far as to demand a 36-hour week without a reduction in wages. However, the arguments used varied in accordance with the level of economic activity at the time. In 1932 the demand was for a 40-hour week to achieve an "equitable sharing of work available between all workers." In 1936, however, when unemployment had considerably decreased, the 40-hour week was demanded as a means of improving standards of living.[5]

The first national Conference for Employment was held in June 1936, on the initiative of the government of national unity.[6] A few hours of negotiations proved sufficient to obtain a substantial rise in wages and six days of paid holidays. However, the 40-hour week was obtained only in those industries or sections of industry where working conditions were unsanitary, dangerous, or arduous. This solution was immediately ratified by parliament in the form of an outline law that determined the general principles but that could be ratified only by royal decree. The Commissions Paritaires were responsible for sectoral implementation of the law. This outline law was very rarely applied, so rarely, indeed, that until World War II skirmishes occurred between employers and trade unions without profoundly changing working hours.

After the war, however, the entire system of industrial relations was thoroughly altered. At the end of the war employers' organizations and the trade unions reached an agreement concerning a *pacte social* (social contract). This was designed to establish the basis of a new system of social relations so as to facilitate the resumption of production. In the pact were elaborated various mechanisms of representation of workers at different levels of economic activity, a system of social security, and a wage policy. There was no new agreement concerning working hours; this matter was still regulated by the prewar legal dispositions. The emphasis of the new social contract on social security, worker participation, and wages was facilitated by workers' organizations, which gave their priorities to purchasing power in the wake of wartime economic conditions.

1945–1975: Management by Concertation

After 1945 a system of institutions and practices that governed collective labor relations progressively emerged. Belgium has a pluralistic system of trade unions. Two confederal organizations dominate industrial relations, however, the CSC and the FGTG. These were joined in 1956 by a small third organization, the CGSLB (Centrale Générale des Syndicats Libéraux de Belgique).[7]

The general framework of industrial relations is largely based on contractual agreements and legislation that, since 1968, has delimited the essential mechanisms and has really only confirmed widely spread precedents. The sectorial Commissions Paritaires play an essential dual role in the industrial relations framework as both negotiator and conciliator. It is in this context that the most important collective agreements emerge. The Conseil National du Travail, a bipartite body composed of employers and the unions, is authorized to negotiate collective agreements of a more general nature.[8] These have often had an impact similar to common collective agreements applicable to all occupations in all sectors. Thus there exists a hierarchy among collective agreements. General collective agreements define minimum employment conditions. It is then possible for the various sectors, and then the various firms, to negotiate more advantageous agreements in varying circumstances. This practice was to change in 1981 when a common collective agreement, as defined above, fixed an upward limit to what could be agreed in negotiations.

The concept of concertation was itself progressively elaborated in the 1960s, principally at the national level. Progressively, during the years of the economic crisis the practice of tripartite concertation has become an object of criticism by employers and by governments, each party reacting against constraints on their capacity to make decisions. As a result, the practice has been greatly weakened.

Priority Accorded to Wage Demands

In 1945 Belgian economic recovery proceeded rapidly, the production infrastructure having been relatively little affected by the war, and so there occurred little modernization of the means of production. One of the consequences was a rise in unemployment beginning in 1947; by 1952 and 1953, 7 percent of the active population was unemployed.

Demands for the reduction of working hours were, however, shelved. It is interesting to note that between 1947 and 1954—a period of great conflict—hardly any strike occurred because of conflict over working hours. However, in 1953 the topic reemerged, linked this time to an increase in productivity. The economic situation had by now improved. The year 1954 marked an important turning point in the system of industrial relations in that it involved a confirmation of the largely consensual basis of the relations between the social partners. Employers and trade unions signed a common declaration on the subject of productivity. Increased productivity was deemed to be the key element in firms' competitiveness and also the necessary prerequisite for the improvement in the workers' standard of living. Wages were increased and working hours were to be reduced. Wage increases appeared to be accorded priority by the majority of workers. Nevertheless, in 1954 most trade unions demanded the 40-hour week on principle, while in practice they accepted a transitional period to the 40-hour standard. As will become clear, this divergence between the position of the union organizations and the demands that appeared pervasive among workers was to be repeated. It is interesting to specify the positions of the two trade union confederations, since they define different conceptions at a macro-social level. The CSC emphasized the demand for a five-day week and did not insist on the 40-hour week. The plan for society that underlay this attitude was one of greater autonomy and greater participation in private life, conceived principally as family life. Of course, this demand was phrased in terms of economic arguments such as the reduction of fixed costs on Saturdays. The FGTB centered its arguments on the 40-hour week, spread out in a five-day or six-day week, depending on the possibilities available.

The employers were not against the reduction of working hours in principle, though they doubted the suitability of the moment chosen and the wisdom of unilateral reduction without prior agreement with their competitor countries. The unions argued from an economic point of view and started negotiations in the Commissions Paritaires. A few strikes broke out, without immediate effect in terms of reducing working hours, but they did manage to popularize the demands in the eyes of the public. The demand for a reduction of working hours then became a political stake *between* union organizations. At this moment, they stood opposed to one another over other issues connected with governmental policies (namely, legislation concerning schooling and education).

After a period of severe social tension, a compromise was nevertheless reached after a meeting between social partners. Experts were given the task of determining the probable effects of a reduction of working hours. After many ups and downs, time scales were fixed in different sectors for a reduction of working hours, following an examination of the situation by three experts. The experts' report emphasized the positive aspects of a reduction in working hours (especially the anticipated reduction of absenteeism) and contended that the issue of profitability was linked more to investment and production structures than to working time. In short, it was argued that a reduction in working hours need not of itself lead to a loss in profit. It then became possible to reach an agreement that pleased everyone, especially employers who were able to avoid a general strike.

On October 29, 1955, an agreement was reached bringing about the realization "in an orderly fashion, methodically and step by step of the 45-hour week. This was eventually to be spread over 5 days, taking into account the difficulties particular to each sector, the viability of firms and national competitiveness."[9]

Concertation as a Priority?

One of the principal characteristics of the agreement was the flexibility of the measures adopted. Decisions taken in the Commissions Paritaires allowed overtime for those "not particularly attached to their leisure time."[10] This, incidentally, led the trade unions to demand a law that was not introduced until 1964, although by then the 45-hour week had practically become general.

However, both the social climate and the economic conjuncture were favorable to the agreement, and it was implemented without painful disruption or competitive problems. Surveys carried out at the time show great satisfaction on the part of men, particularly concerning free Saturdays. On the other hand, women felt negative about increased working hours per day as the system changed from an eight-hour day, six-day week to a nine-hour day, five-day week. Before the 1964 law was even voted on, new demands, such as that of the FGTB for a 40-hour week without a reduction in wages, appeared. But a settlement was reached by means of extra holidays; in 1963 the third week of holidays was obtained easily.

But the organs of concertation fulfilled their roles well and managed to achieve a collective agreement applicable to all occupations in all sectors, and one that planned a modulated reduction of working hours.[11] The sectors were permitted to negotiate one hour in 1969, another hour in 1970. The aim was to reach a 42-hour week in 1972, 41-hour week in 1974, and finally a 40-hour week in 1975. Actually, most sectors were working a 40-hour week by January 1, 1974, without any major conflict. (See Table 6–1.) An auxiliary collective agreement was thus signed at the Conseil National du Travail to spread the 40-hour week to firms unaffected by any previous agreement. One can see that since 1956, the reduction of working hours has not been the object of strikes but has been resolved by means of concertation. For 22 years (from 1956 to 1978) the number of days lost due to conflict on working time was negligible.

The Crisis: 1975–1986

The effects of the economic crisis on unemployment really began to be felt in 1974. Unemployment rose from about 90,000 in 1974 to 162,000 in 1975 (judging from the numbers receiving full unemployment benefit). The rate of increase was such that in 1983 there were 500,000 unemployed—almost 12 percent of the labor force.

In 1975 the leaders of the trade unions began demanding a 36-hour week, with immediate and universal effect, as a means of fighting unemployment. The topic of work sharing became the subject of very different approaches by trade unions and employers. Unions insisted upon a sharp reduction in working

TABLE 6-1.
Average Weekly Working Hours of Blue-Collar Workers in Belgium,
1970–1985

1970	42.7	1980	35.7
1975	37.1	1981	35.9
1976	38.5	1982	34.9
1977	37.1	1983	35.1
1978	37.6	1984	35.7
1979	38.1	1985	35.7

Source: Emploi et chômage (Brussels: Eurostat, CEE, 1987).

hours to be balanced by new recruitment; employers emphasized flexibility, in particular, through increasing voluntary part-time work. At the same moment, the government sponsored legislation modifying the link between salaries and the cost-of-living index. This link, which had been automatic since 1948, was now judged to be inflationary. The protests of the workers focused on this point, thus leaving behind plans for a reduction of working hours that had not received wide support among those at work.

The trade unions, however, achieved unanimity, and they presented a common front in February 1977, declaring for a reduction in the working week to 36 hours that would involve additional recruitment. It was their position that the reduction had to be rapid so that its employment effects could not be neutralized by a reorganization of the labor process. The unions also agreed upon a strategy of strikes that would cut across all sectors, alternating by provinces, one day per week. These strikes, known as the "Friday strikes," were focused upon the distribution of labor: the 36-hour week, multiple jobbing ("moonlighting"), and overtime. However, they were also used to show disapproval for measures adopted by the Tindemans I government (a Christian Socialist–Liberal coalition). The strikes were very successful and brought about the resignation of the government.

The trade unions restated their wish to reach a 36-hour week by 1980 through a collective agreement covering different occupations in different sectors. After much fruitless bargaining, the employers hardened their tone. They refused to negotiate a reduction of working hours at a national level. Various measures concerning part-time work were willingly sanctioned by the Tindemans II coalition government (a Christian Socialist–Socialist coalition with two communitarian parties).[12]

In spite of a significant campaign disseminating information at firm and sectoral levels on the initiative of the larger union organizations, the majority of union members were not committed to the demand for a 36-hour week. The economic climate of the time did not appear to favor the possibility of a significant reduction of hours with full wage compensation. Moreover, past experience suggested that reductions of working hours had never given rise to distinct increases in employment. These two elements largely contributed to the weakening of the union demand and the undermining of its credibility.

Certain nonindustrial sectors nevertheless managed to obtain agreements reducing working hours. In 1977 department stores signed an agreement for a 39-hour week and shortly afterward a plan for a 36-hour week. Similarly, banks, insurance companies, gas and electricity boards, and wholesalers signed agreements to shorten working hours. Bleeckx remarks that only agreements in banks and the department stores contained specifications concerning overtime, although their impact was limited and was perhaps little more than a reflection of the demand for labor in these sectors at that time.[13] The hypothesis that agreements on a reduction of working hours were used more to protect those actively working than to share work between those working and the unemployed is already revealed in these agreements.

The first industrial sector to propel itself against the 40-hour barrier was the petroleum sector. There, however, an agreement was finally reached after conflict and government intervention. The agreement provided for a 38-hour week, without wage decreases, from January 1, 1979, onward. Similarly, in the iron and steel industry conflict led the government to propose a settlement that planned the introduction of the 38-hour week in July 1979.

Agreements multiplied at sectoral and firm levels, sometimes preceded by conflicts, as at Philips, FN, DAF, Bell, Agfa-Gevaert, and Renault. In March 1978, following a three-week strike in Ford's factories in Genk, the union organization failed in its objective of obtaining the 36-hour week plus the recruitment of an additional 1,000 employees. The strike ended with the acceptance of an employer offer of wage increases and bonuses. Here again economic demands dominated the objective of solidarity. The 38-hour week was generalized throughout metal products manufacturers, nonferrous metals, the public utilities (after a wildcat strike in 1978), and other sectors to such an extent that in 1978 a third of the private sector was working less than a 40-hour week. It should be pointed out that these agreements were accompanied by stipulations maintaining wages at the same level. Belgium was now in the forefront of working-time change and served as a social guinea-pig for competing countries.

In 1978 the social partners resumed negotiations in an effort to achieve a collective agreement covering all occupations in all sectors. The various stands taken proved once again to be incompatible. The employers proposed a 5 percent reduction in working hours in the form of an increase in paid holidays accompanied by greater flexibility (in regard to shift work, overtime, and the like). Part-time work was also encouraged. The trade unions adopted a firm stance on a 36-hour week before 1981. Given the gap between each side, a general agreement was not to be reached until 1981.

A new industrial dispute broke out in 1979 with the Ateliers de Constructions Electriques de Charleroi (ACEC), which was a union stronghold. ACEC was also a pioneering firm within the metal products' employers' organization (Fabrimetal). The strike was centered on claims for a 36-hour week and a wage increase. Three months of strike activity led to an agreement conceding the gradual introduction of a 36-hour week.

It was at this moment that the first Martens government (a Christian Socialist–Socialist coalition) took the initiative in proposing a reduction in working hours to a 36-hour week before the end of 1981, accompanied by an obligatory new recruitment rate of 3 percent. The state agreed to take upon itself the burden of part of the social security contributions involved. The refusal of the social partners to accept the proposal led to a new government initiative favoring all firms with less than a 38-hour week.

It can be suggested that the unions simply sought a reduction in working hours as a technique to share out work, without asking questions about the social and cultural context in which this reduction might take place. Many of the agreements provided for an increase in holidays (which could have little effect on the level of employment) instead of a weekly reduction in working time (which could have been more likely to lead to extra recruitment). Different surveys have shown that more holidays was the preference of an important percentage of employees, who were disinclined to accept weekly reduction on the grounds that this would have meant a reorganization of work as well as an increase in productivity levels.

Gradually the employers abandoned their defensive position and started a large campaign focused upon the theme of a reestablishment of company profitability. The stress by employers on the economic problems of firms and the necessity to control production costs more effectively so as to increase competitiveness pointed up the growing attraction of modifying working hours as an alternative to reducing them. The position of employers was that the uninterrupted use of productive capacity that would result from the reorganization of work could engender a surplus, which allowed the financing of new jobs.

The government, however, wanted to force the social partners to restart collective agreements covering different occupations and different sectors, but in a completely different direction to the previous agreements. The strategy deployed is quite interesting. It proposed a law that limited free collective bargaining and that could be applied if the employers and the trade unions were not able to reach agreement.

Under such political pressure, an unprecedented agreement along these lines was reached. Whereas in the past collective agreements covering different occupations and sectors fixed minima that sectorial agreements, or agreements at the level of the firm, could go beyond, the 1981 agreement fixed maxima for negotiations at a lower level. This was "self-censorship" in negotiations, particularly in those concerning reductions in working hours. In other words, where the 38-hour week was already in use, the new agreement only allowed negotiations for either a maximum of a 2 percent increase in wages or a maximum of a

TABLE 6-2.

Average Annual Working Hours for Salaried Workers in Belgium, 1972–1984

1972	1,790	1981	1,552
1975	1,616	1984	1,537
1978	1,593		

Source: Emploi et chômage (Brussels: Eurostat, CEE, 1987).

one-hour reduction in working hours over two years. Now only the balance of power at the firm level counted, and this explains why where the trade unions were not strong, the 40-hour week remained, whereas in sectors or firms that had been at the forefront of trade union disputes on working time, hours of work remained fixed at a 37-hour week. (See Table 6-2.)

The effects of this round of working-time reductions on employment were very feeble. In fact, in many cases this was not a real concern. Unemployment had peaked, the economic situation was very worrying, and the state of public finances was catastrophic. In these worsened circumstances the employers' position gained greater prominence among the public authorities and also among sections of the workforce. The aim of restoring profitability among firms, it was claimed, implied flexibility and deregulation.

The new Martens V government (a Christian Socialist–Liberal coalition) began its term in office by a devaluation and a freeze on the price index. It did not, however, confront the problem of a reduction in working hours. In 1982, according to Eurostat sources, the length of the working week offered to workers in Belgium was 39.9 hours, or the lowest level in the European Economic Community (EEC). Meanwhile, the trade unions' united front broke up; only the FGTB led actions and protest strikes, but these did not lead to any change in policy by public authorities.

Secure in its position, the government defined a policy combining past formulae for reducing working hours and original experiments. It was thus that in 1982 it adopted a new formula commonly known as "5-3-3," which involved a 5 percent reduction in working hours, accompanied by a recruitment rate of 3 percent and—for the first time ever in the history of reducing working hours in Belgium—a 3 percent decrease in wages. The objective was the creation of 75,000 jobs through negotiations at the sectoral level and at the level of individual firms.

A few agreements planned to link a reduction in working hours to a change in work organization, specifically, to allow for team work, night shifts, or even weekend shifts. We shall return to this point later. It is important because it illustrates the type of compromise concerning flexibility that the trade unions had to accept. It is a moot point to what extent the demands for a reduction in working hours acted as catalysts for flexibility, deregulation, and even—as will be suggested below—disorder.

The opportunities presented to firms to combine the reorganizations of work with modifications of working hours is well illustrated by a legislative measure (*l'arrêté 179*) that came into force in the beginning of 1983. This *arrêté* was aimed at facilitating firm-level agreements on experiments concerning the modifications of working hours with the view of redistributing available work. The new juridical disposition authorized the negotiation of experiments in spheres such as the reduction of the length of working hours, flexible hours, working hours without breaks, part-time work, job sharing, shift work, short working week, weekend work, dispersion of leave over the year, seasonal working hours, working at home, breaks in one's career, flexibility of working hours, and leave at the end of one's working life. The measure had been implemented in a certain number of experiments that met with varying degrees of success with the workers involved.

In 1984 the government launched a new "rehabilitation plan" that, among other reforms, provided a freeze on wages. There was no longer any talk of reductions in working hours, but the legislation concerning part-time work was improved. The Fédération des Entreprises de Belgique (FEB) launched a campaign for the creation of 100,000 part-time jobs. This formula was presented as a means of creating jobs by increasing flexibility in work organization.

The most original, given its aim of social experimentation, was the Hansenne experiment, named after the minister for employment who set it up. The motive behind the experiment was very clear. As the originator Hansenne explained, working hours are one of the most fundamental social issues. A century and a half of working-class struggle has resulted in a whole armada of rules and regulations that limit and constrain. One could not hope to reduce unemployment without creating new types of reductions in working hours: solutions allowing for less individual work and more collective work.[14]

In fact, these experiments sought to reorganize the working time of firms with a view to redistributing the work available. The legal text contained a provision for encouraging the creation of new jobs by means of new forms of work organization in firms. This was an experimental system that allowed deviations from legally established rules. In other words, the problem of working hours, weekly closing time, night shifts were all to be resolved without legal constraint at the firm level. This decree thus allowed the employers to lengthen production time, to react in a more subtle manner to market variations, to anticipate future reductions in working hours, and even to reevaluate certain investments.[15] These experiments have, as yet, remained very limited, in fact often limited to one or the other department, frequently maintenance. After the trial period it is planned that certain experiments will be prolonged indeterminately. In these cases not only will the number of working hours be specified firm by firm, but the very legal framework of work will be individualized, making it possible to deviate from both laws and collective agreements existing at national as well as sectoral levels.

In January 1987, 65 firms employing 26,000 workers participated in these experiments, leading to the employment of approximately 900 additional persons. The majority of these experiments took place in Flanders, in the north of the country where union attitudes were more pragmatic and employers more modern than in the south. They have generally been better accepted by the workers participating voluntarily than by the unions themselves. The unions continue to show a notable reserve, primarily because of the progressive erosion of the juridical basis for the protection of labor that the experiments engender. Certain of these experiments have been well accepted by the public: for example, the opening of the large shops on Sundays and the extension of opening hours of certain public services. The public response has further weakened the union position.

We have already considered the second approach to flexibility as involved in the response by employers to generalized reductions in working hours: namely, cuts in working time on a voluntary basis and involving reductions in wages. Despite problems of quantification, the analysis of Leroy and Godano brings out a certain number of issues.[16] In the years 1977–83 the percentage of the active population working part time went up from 5 to 10 percent; the percentage for men rose to 3, from 0.7 percent in 1977 (see Table 6-3). The increase in the popularity of part-time work was due to many different factors. First, legislative incentives were important. Following pressure from employers and starting from 1982, part-time workers enjoyed the same rights to social security as those working full time. Similarly, various programs for reemploying the unemployed became more oriented toward part-time work under the influence of public policies. These programs were for the most part aimed at young people. It is difficult to escape the conclusion that this was a kind of preparation for the flexibility (and the temporary nature) of a growing number of jobs both in public services and in industry. There also existed, second, a social demand for part-time jobs, primarily in the case of women. The trade unions admitted that they had underestimated the demand for part-time work. Nonetheless, they remained totally opposed to the expansion of part-time work,

TABLE 6-3.
Part-Time Employment in Belgium, 1984
(percentage of all workers)

	Men	Women	Total
Blue collar	2.1	21.8	7.3
White collar	5.1	23.1	13.5
Public sector	3.1	15.2	7.5
Total	3.2	20.9	9.6

Source: Bulletin de l'IRES (Louvain-la-neuve, Oct. 1985).

TABLE 6-4.

The Number of People on Early-Retirement Pensions in Belgium, 1976–1987

1976	5,136	1982	108,120
1977	24,634	1983	126,273
1978	42,936	1984	136,046
1979	63,303	1985	141,607
1980	74,809	1986	186,333
1981	90,055	1987	197,247

Note: The data indicate the number of people affected by the early retirement pension system as of June 30 each year. The same person could be counted for a number of years until reaching the age of 60 (for women) or 65 (for men).

Source: Bulletin mensuel de l'Office national de l'emploi (Brussels, annual).

regarding it as a development that threatened to slow down reductions in working hours for everyone.

The third approach to flexibility, early retirement, has not lacked followers in Belgium (see Table 6-4). The solution that met most of the requirements of flexibility was early retirement by agreement (*prépension conventionnelle*). This was imposed upon the workers by a collective agreement and affected laid-off workers who were over 60 (men) or over 55(women). Private agreements could depart from this age requirement by settling on a lower age. In fact, this often proved the case. Each year the age criteria were modified in response to the layoff needs of the various firms. The technique involved reducing the early retirement age until the numbers corresponded to the reduction in manpower sought. Between 1976 and 1985 more than 500,000 workers were affected by this measure. This formula, though not very popular among the old workers on whom it was imposed, has generally been well accepted by younger workers, who saw it as a way to enhance their own job security.

This was no longer, of course, a reduction of weekly working hours but, rather, a reduction in working hours over the lifetime. Though not without negative effects at a personal level, it proved a popular formula among the trade unions, which saw it as a substitute to layoffs. Unions have not always, then, reflected on the contradiction between the goal of solidarity involved in the reduction of working hours and the concrete effects of policies of early retirement.

A fourth direction toward flexibility is voluntary choice in working hours, which is legally sanctioned to allow for new recruitment. This is apparent in recent rules and regulations on breaks in careers, early retirement, and sabbatical leave, which give financial encouragement to those who benefit from them.

It is obvious that other measures favoring flexibility in the organization of production, such as subcontracting, fixed-term contracts, and increases in the number of people holding jobs of a precarious nature have the effect of individualizing situations and of rendering all collective actions or demands extremely difficult or ineffectual (given the heterogeneous and varied nature of these demands). In the long run, indeed, they may undermine social legislation on labor entirely.

The unions failed, then, to impose the demand for a reduction of working hours in the terms through which it had been formulated. Progressively, modifications of hours developed in response to two objectives: flexibility in work organization and job creation. It appears that though the first has been achieved, the second has not.

Toward an Explanation

Demands for reduction of working time are linked to the development of the workers' movements, but over the course of time they have acquired a quite different meaning. Until World War II more time off was a priority for the workers' movement, and this demand combined cultural aspects (a new freedom of life style), social aspects (justice), and economic aspects (labor costs). Immediately after the war demands for reduction in working hours lost their priority; the emphasis was instead placed upon wages and social security.

The theme of reduced working hours reappeared in the 1950s but was the object of competition between trade union organizations involved in competitive relations at a sectoral level and at firm level. Nevertheless, the demands were concerned above all with employment objectives, and then with wage increases. Negotiations centered upon the themes of productivity and wages, and demands for reduced working hours intervened only as a tertiary concern. The argument employers advanced to oppose the reduction of working hours was in fact remarkably the same over time. Reductions in working hours without a decrease in labor costs would diminish output and damage competitiveness. Only significant increases in productivity would allow a reduction in working hours and wage rises. It was in this context that it was possible to say that a reduction in working hours might modernize work organization.

In these circumstances reductions in working hours were defended in economic terms as involving an increase in the relative value of work done. Elements of a cultural problematic also emerged during discussions concerning the ways and means of reducing working hours. Thus in 1954 the CSC justified demands for a 40-hour, five-day week in terms of the need to improve family life.

Furthermore, during this period the objective of the demands remained a distant goal. It was only nine years later, in 1964, when a law rendered it obligatory, that the 45-hour week was achieved in most sectors. It must nevertheless be stressed that even if negotiations were centered on economic arguments, the ideas that people had about reductions in working hours, especially in the case of older sections of the working class, were expressed in terms of a social conscience. Thus the surveys conducted during the large strikes in the winter of 1960–61 showed that political demands for structural reforms were translated in the workers' experience into demands for reductions in working hours. One can therefore suggest that reductions in working hours had a double meaning at this time. It was defined in economic terms by the trade unions and in social terms by the workers themselves. When emanating from the concrete experience of work, demands for a reduction in working hours assumed the form of a protest against both the organization of work and its duress. It was only later, in the 1960s, that cultural considerations appear to have gained considerable weight in arguments regarding the concrete forms that reductions in working hours should take.

Under the pressure of sectoral and then general agreements, reduction in working hours progressed smoothly (at 1.26 percent per year between 1965 and 1970). Fernet has shown that two cultural factors dominated in this round: changes in life style and consumption: "As women increasingly went out to work the weekend became an indispensable period for the family unit."[17] The social demand itself was only a form of adaptation to new constraints. One cannot yet talk of demands compelled by new definitions of the place of work in a person's life. Such demands were formulated later and only by a minority fraction of the trade unions or by militant groups that were scarcely representative of the aspirations of the majority of workers.

As we have seen, demands for reduction in working hours were relaunched by the trade unions at the beginning of the period of economic crisis. Faced with the progressive deterioration of the labor market, a significant reduction in working hours was looked upon as a means of reabsorbing some of the unemployed into the labor market. This was the theme of the campaign led by the trade unions on "reduced working hours and compensatory recruitment." This campaign did not attain its goals. The reductions in working hours achieved were not followed by an increase in the level of employment.

Between 1975 and 1981 the trade unions were obviously weakened in their attempts to negotiate by the uncompromising attitudes of the employers, who insisted on the need to decrease wages in order to restore competitiveness. Nevertheless, in the course of their various actions the unions also encountered obstacles intrinsically linked to the world of wage-labor. The poor results obtained must also be linked to the divergence between the stated demands of the trade unions and the unstated demands of their members. The demands for reduction in working hours of 1975–1985, as phrased by the trade unions, were elaborated in terms of distributive justice: sharing the jobs available. These demands were the result of previous trade union experiences—especially in the 1930s' crisis when the same demands were made—and of the concern of the unions to intervene in the labor market.

Time has shown that the unstated demands of the wage earners were, in fact, quite different. In many cases a reduction in working hours was linked with a concern with life planning. Soon this demand became subordinate to demands for jobs. The increasing scarcity of jobs combined with the preoccupation of life planning led to a greater tolerance of new job forms and new working-time schedules. Despite the possibility there was for developing different modulations of reduced working hours, for example, the differential distribution of working hours over the whole of a person's occupational life, unions were unable to negotiate a generalized model. Without doubt, the problem was at least in part due to the tension between the reduction of working hours seen as a collective concern by the trade unions and the increasingly varied interest and preferences of their members.[18]

Within the context of economic crisis, the trade unions saw reductions in working hours as a means of combating unemployment. The popularization of this demand and the mobilization of workers presumed a collective interest in fighting unemployment. However, the chances that collective interests exist are fairly low when it is remembered that the probability that people might become unemployed varied widely. The difference between sectors (the unemployment level in August 1981 was 2 percent in banking and 36.6 percent in the clothing industry), between different regions (9.5 percent in Antwerp; 22.6 percent in Mons), or between the sexes (12 percent for men; 25.4 percent for women) were such that the fight against unemployment could not easily be perceived by many workers as a collective concern. The trade unions had always encompassed very varied interests, but they normally managed to overcome the tensions by resorting to concepts of solidarity and social justice substantiated by a collective experience of social struggles or by class consciousness.

In the context of recent working-time campaigns these concepts were insufficient to prevent the effects of diversification. Moreover, what was defined as a collective interest could be in total opposition with private or individual interests. It might be advantageous for particular categories of wage earners to negotiate something other than reductions in working hours, or to negotiate forms of reductions that would serve not the collective aims but, rather, the individualization of working conditions.

Two other factors intervened to reduce the effectiveness of demands for reductions in working hours. The first concerned the effect on wages of reductions in working hours. Over a long period of time the unions demanded reductions in working hours with full wage compensation. This demand made negotiations with the employers more difficult. However, the idea that a significant decrease in working hours should be accompanied by a wage restraint, and even in certain cases by a decrease, did emerge. This new constraint, which appeared in government policies, further undermined the credibility of reductions in working hours in the eyes of many workers.

Another problem arose from the very conditions of concertation. As Bleeckx has shown, reductions in working hours affected more than just the work situation; all sorts of other domains were affected as well. The rules for concertation between employers and unions, however, limited negotiations to the field of work itself, and this excluded the intervention of other social actors who have broadened the debate and could probably have helped to unblock the situation.[19]

When negotiations were held, they were conducted in an uncoordinated manner, and the absence of any credible general perspective focused the attention of negotiators on what was immediately useful and necessary for those directly involved[20]—hence, the lack of social or cultural innovation in the agreements on working time. The absence of a unifying vision encompassing the economic, social, and cultural dimensions of workers' existence and the dynamics of concertation are factors that heavily constrained the popularization of demands for reductions in working hours and reinforced the internal divisions of the various organizations, as well as increasing the heterogeneity of their members' conceptions of their own interests.

The Weight of Economic Logic

We have seen that negotiations about time were limited to negotiations concerning working hours and that those involved viewed the question strictly in the context of the needs of trade union and employers' organizations. The state has traditionally played an auxiliary (by legislating) or a mediating role. It is obvious, however, that the state has become increasingly involved in the problematic of working hours without fundamentally changing the terms of the debate.

If here and there one can discern social, political, or cultural aims, it cannot be denied that in reality the logic has been strictly economic. In Belgian history demands concerning working hours have been mediated by economic concerns. At the beginning of the twentieth century the modernization of the trade unions strongly linked the modernization of technology and work to a reduction in working hours, insisting even on the contribution of Taylorism. Then, in the middle 1950s, unions and employers agreed on the ways productivity should be shared to such an extent, indeed, that one could read in 1957 that "union leaders are now aware of the fact that increases in productivity constitute an indispensable prerequisite for a choice between an increase in leisure time and extra income."[21]

Since the middle of the 1970s and the effects of the crisis on jobs and unemployment, the consensual basis of agreement between social partners has shrunk considerably. Flexibility has become an objective in itself for employers. Progressively, it is this theme that is the subject of negotiation, along with the experiments made possible by government initiatives.

A shift has occurred away from the issue of reducing working hours— where the trade unions have a strong position—to issues of work organization, where the employers hold the upper hand—especially in Belgium, where this is a question of management prerogative. In times of economic growth demands for reductions in working hours arose more in the context of wage policies than in the context of a transformation of the place of work in people's lives. During periods of economic crisis and unemployment, reductions in working hours were viewed instead as work sharing.

When reading trade union texts, one gets the impression that the actual aim of reducing working hours can be assimilated to matters of simple techniques, for the place of work in society is never questioned. In the same way, employers' organizations treat demands in financial terms without going into questions concerning industrial policies or the reorientation of production toward areas with high added value. Moreover, such systems as the Hansenne experiments or early-retirement schemes make use of public funds, which underlines their fragility.

Conclusions

It appears that in recent years Belgian unions have progressively lost their hold on the demand for a reduction of working hours, elaborated as a response to the crisis of employment. By seeking *a unified approach* to reductions in working hours, they have assumed a defensive position relative to social experiments from outside, such as variable timetables, the Hansenne experiments, or part-time work. This is especially the case because these experiments were undertaken in reply to explicit demands on the part of some workers. The unions constantly viewed the question of reductions in working hours as an approach capable of improving the job situation. Employers simply refused to negotiate these demands in the terms formulated by the unions. The attitudes of different governments varied.

Initially, the government and then employers became preoccupied by the need to adapt work to the new necessities of production and proposed a certain number of new formulae for reorganizing working time. The unions adopted a very restrictive attitude—varying between a wait-and-see policy and outright refusal—toward the new proposals. They could not see in them any echo of their own concerns. The fact that negotiations were increasingly decentralized strengthened the insularity of the politics of working time. As Bleeckx has claimed: "Isn't it extraordinary that the declared goal of a better distribution of the work available has been practically completely hidden at these levels of negotiation and that there exist practically no guarantees of worksharing in this sphere?"[22] Finally, it must be asked whether the fate of demands for the reduction of working hours for everyone has not revealed the very heterogeneity that now characterizes preferences regarding working hours and time in general.

We shall conclude with a paradox: The reduction of working hours, which has been a central theme for mobilization of the working-class movement, is today presented by trade unions in nearly identical terms to those used in the

1930s. This, in spite of the fact that the technical and organizational conditions of production have been transformed, along with the general cultural context of work. In this context, one of the major difficulties of the trade unions has been their tendency to reply to new yearnings with old suggestions and formulas.

Notes

1. For the descriptive sections, we have used two works of references: B. S. Chleppner, *Cent ans d'histoire social en Belgique* (Brussels: Université de Bruxelles, 1972); G. Maes and K. Van Rie, *De Werkdag* (Antwerp: EPO, 1985).
2. This law included several provisions, one of the most important of which was that of 1914 outlawing child labor.
3. There exist in Belgium two large union confederations: the Fédération Générale du Travail de Belgique (FGTB) with a socialist tendency, and the Confédération des Syndicats Chrétiens (CSC). These confederations bring together at the national level sectoral organizations (engineering, textile, etc.) and regional organizations. The occupational tradition is very important in Belgian trade unionism, and the sectoral organizations possess a large degree of power in trade unionism. There exists a third national confederation, the Centrale Générale des Syndicats Liberaux de Belgique (CGSLB); this is of lesser importance. The rate of unionization in Belgium is very high: global unionization is estimated at 80.7 percent; the rate of unionized industrial workers is 96.2 percent; the rate of unionized employees is 42.8 percent; the rate of unionization in the public service is 68 percent. See J. Neuville and E. Arcq, "The Evolution of the Rate of Unionization in Belgium," *Courrier Hebdomadaire, Centre de Recherche et d'Information Socio-Politique* (Brussels, Jan. 30, 1987).
4. The Commission Paritaire is an official organ of bargaining, established at the sectoral level. It brings together equal numbers of representatives of worker organizations and of employers in the sector under the presidency of a civil servant of the Labor Ministry. The Commissions Paritaires have a predominant role in the elaboration of collective agreements and in the prevention or management of labor conflicts.
5. Chleppner, *Cent ans d'histoire*, p. 240.
6. We will see later that these conferences also played an important role in the Belgian system of consultation and bargaining.
7. In 1985 the CSC numbered 1.2 million members, the FGTB 1 million, and the CGSLB less than 150,000.
8. The Conseil National du Travail (CNT) is a national organ composed of representatives of employers' organizations and workers. Its function was originally consultative. Since 1968 it has had the power to conclude collective agreements applying to all occupations at the national level.
9. The official text is cited in *La réduction de la durée du travail*, Conference of the 23rd and 24th February 1957 (Brussels: Bibliothèque de la Société Royale d'Economie de Belgique, Edition de la Librairie Encyclopédique, 1957).
10. Ibid., p. 208.
11. An agreement valid for all the sectors of the economy often defines the minimal general conditions upon which the employers and the trade unions agree. It does not exclude the possibility that agreements more advantageous to the workers might be

negotiated at sectoral or firm level. One exception to this rule has been made by the 1981 agreement that limited subsequent negotiations.

12. The Belgian political scene is characterized by the existence of traditional *familles politique* (socialists, Christian Socialists, and liberals), which were the original basis of relatively stable political parties. The linguistic tensions have led, in the north as in the south, to the arrival on the scene of new political parties with aims strictly regional or communitarian: Volksunie, Rassemblement Wallon, Front Democratique des Franco-phones. These have experienced considerable success in the 1970s.

13. F. Bleeckx, "La concertation et les enjeux du temps: régulation ou dysfonctionnement?" *L'aménagement du temps de travail: un enjeu social prioritaire*, Dossier de l'Institut du Travail, no. 3 (Dec. 1981).

14. A. Hansenne, interview in *Trends-Tendances*, no. 206 (May 1985).

15. In Ibid.

16. R. Leroy and A. Godano, "Travail à temps partiel: une nouvelle statistique," *IRES, Service de Conjoncture* (U.C.L.), no. 96 (March 1985).

17. A. Fernet, "Heur(t)s et malheurs de la réduction de la durée du travail," *La Revue Nouvelle* 76, no. 4 (April 1983).

18. Hypothesis borrowed from K. Hinrichs, W. K. Roche, and H. Wiesenthal, "Working Time Policy as Class-Oriented Strategy: Unions and Shorter Hours in Great Britain and West Germany," *European Sociological Review* 1, no. 3 (Dec. 1985): 211–229. The authors utilize the perspectives developed by M. Olson, *The Logic of Collective Action* (Cambridge, Mass.: Harvard University Press, 1965).

19. Bleeckx, "La concertation."

20. Ibid.

21. Société Royale d'Economie Politique de Belgique, *La reduction de la durée du travail*.

22. Bleeckx, "La concertation."

7 Trading Time for Consumption: The Failure of Working-Hours Reduction in the United States

Susan Christopherson

In the 1920s Americans looked forward to a decrease in working hours and increased leisure. Time had been carved out of long wage-work hours by dint of political battles in the workplace, and these victories represented not just more "free" time but an increase in total wages. For some workers these victories meant more. According to an International Ladies' Garment Workers' Union official, "the great movement for limitation of hours that is sweeping over the trades, employing hundreds of thousands of women will bring working women the great boon of Time—time for rest, time to play, time to be human."[1]

In the later 1980s working hours are again a matter of political debate in the United States, but the issues being discussed are considerably different. Workers are pressing to rearrange rather than reduce work time. The original political basis for achieving working-time reductions in the United States differed significantly from that in Western European industrialized countries because of the character of American capitalism and its labor force. The nature of the early political bargains subsequently led American labor to emphasize increases in wages and consumption over hours reductions. Although the nature of labor demand and union strength reduced hours of work for many workers from the 1920s to the 1960s, work time is now increasing in the contemporary American workforce, albeit in the form of "flexible" jobs.

The regulation of working hours from the 1920s to the mid-1960s was constructed out of industrial bargaining power that did not translate into a national political consensus to restrict working hours apart from wages. The emphasis on earnings rather than shorter hours also financed a way of life in which the family rather than the state was primarily responsible for what many Europeans would consider social welfare services. The weakly formulated standard of a 40-hour week began to crumble as the character of the U.S. economy

Research for this paper was partially funded by a National Science Foundation Grant.

changed in the mid-1960s. To maintain their standard of living, Americans are now working more. An emerging political consensus, at whose center is a "family-oriented working hours flexibility," is intended to solve some of the social problems emerging from significantly increased wage work and the continued private responsibility for reproduction of the workforce and care of people who cannot work.

The American Limits to Working-Time Regulation

Several tenets have informed the politics of working hours in the United States. One is the doctrine of freedom of individual contract, which presumes the equal rights of capital and labor in negotiating wages and hours of work. Under this doctrine, the interests of individuals take precedence over the interests of classes of individuals. One early antagonist of state intervention to reduce hours of work described time as the one element of production that laborers and capitalists have in common. Workers who seek legislation to regulate hours of work are asking to be deprived of the "freedom" to dispose of their own time.[2] That this is a strongly held belief across capital and labor was demonstrated by a recent article about the widespread increase in child labor law violations in the United States. A 16-year-old interviewed about his 48-hour (part-time) work week in a fast food operation was quoted, "This is America. I should be able to work as many hours as I want."[3] Other teenagers interviewed looked forward to stricter enforcement of the laws as a way to protect themselves from employers who required them to work long and unsocial hours in order to keep their jobs.

Historically, American workers who fought to reduce hours of work had to have a common sense of grievance as well as significant bargaining power in order to overcome legal constraints against "class" bargaining over wages and worktime. The first legislation regulating work time was initiated on behalf of women and children, presumably "interestless" workers who lacked the ability to contract freely.[4] Two methods of work-time regulation thus developed in the United States, a relatively weak regulation based in protective legislation restricting the hours of women and children and a stronger regulation based in collective bargaining through which trade unionists negotiated directly with their employers. Because legislative remedies were so restricted by the courts and by the ideology of laissez-faire capitalism in the late nineteenth and early twentieth centuries, unions of working men, particularly craft workers, tended to avoid legislative politics in favor of collective bargaining in the workplace.

The second feature of the American political economy shaping the politics of work time is the ethnocultural diversity of the population and its division by industry and region. Historically, workers embedded in strong cultural communities with a way of life that required time apart from work were able to draw on community support and strengthen their position vis-à-vis the employer.

Thus, reduced working hours were originally achieved in labor markets with large numbers of skilled workers with substantial bargaining power and with strong ethnocultural communities that valued personal and social time. The preeminent example of this regionally based work-time bargain was New York City, where skilled working men achieved a ten-hour day by 1828 and where collective action by women garment workers was successful in achieving a five-day week in the mid-1920s.[5] In contrast with the conventional argument that ethnocultural communities inhibited collective action by the workforce, they were, in reality, the wellspring of collective action.[6] The limitation of working hours was won region by region, industry by industry.[7] As a consequence, capital faced significantly different production politics in different regions of the United States. Whereas industrial workers in northern cities achieved working-hours reductions as well as higher wages by 1920, the South and West remained largely unregulated.

In some respects, it was the very success of these ethnic community-based industrial movements in northern cities that stimulated the adoption of uniform national standards for working hours as well as minimum wage and working conditions. As early as the 1920s a consensus emerged between capital and labor on work hours and wages because northern firms had a strong interest in equalizing competitive conditions across the country. Southerners and westerners, in contrast, opposed national legislation to establish labor standards.[8] The consensus extended only to those industries in which workers were organized and not to the workforce in general. As a consequence, the initial legislation establishing fair labor standards covered only one-fifth of the existing workforce.[9] Needless to say, few of the workers covered were women or minorities, and only goods-producing industries were regulated.

In goods-producing industries the combination of collective bargaining and legislative "equalization" across regions led to increasingly higher wages and shorter hours. By the mid-1930s workers in these industries had achieved a 36-hour "standard" working week. This does not mean that they were working 36 hours, however, for the standard simply delimited the point at which overtime began, and most workers worked overtime. Thus, earnings increased even faster than did hourly wages.

The politics of work time from the 1930s to the mid-1960s was based on a set of assumptions about how to stimulate and maintain economic growth. It was generally assumed that the Depression was caused by "underconsumption," or lack of demand. Thus, ameliorative policy measures were directed at implementing a Keynesian strategy to stimulate the economy. The New Deal solution, however, differed quite dramatically from that preferred by the unions. The unions advocated work sharing, or the reduction of work hours for already employed workers with the expectation that this reduction would create more jobs. The Roosevelt administration preferred and adopted a job-creation strategy. This choice represented a defeat for organized labor but a predictable defeat. Organized labor represented only a portion of the workforce, and a job-sharing policy would tend to improve wages and working hours in certain industries and regions (the industrialized North). The job-creation strategy favored by Roosevelt was more appealing politically and practically because it could potentially affect a broader cross-section of the workforce and of the population. The adoption of a jobs strategy to stimulate the economy in many ways marked the end of the period of hours reduction in the United States.

The American Keynesian solution combining job creation with collective bargaining over wages rather than hours culminated in the postwar bargaining agreements. These agreements reinforced the tendency initiated during the 1920s and 1930s to emphasize increased consumption over any decrease in working hours. While in Western European countries with high levels of national unionization, countries like Sweden and the Netherlands, increases in wages and declines in working hours were balanced, in the United States 75 percent of the increased standard of living between 1948 and 1975 was translated into increased wages rather than decreased hours of work.[10]

Three features of American industrial politics thus influenced the wage and work-time bargain in quite distinctive ways. First, working-class culture remained ethnic culture, and its political power remained concentrated by region and industry. Reductions in work time were largely a regional phenomenon rather than national in scope. Second, whereas in many European countries labor power was translated into national legislation with collective bargaining as an additional source of power for industrial workers in goods-producing industries, collective bargaining was the primary source of political power over working conditions for American workers. If they did not have collective bargaining power, they did not have political power as workers. Finally, American workers have historically favored using hours restrictions and the delimitation of standard work hours as a way to increase earnings through overtime pay. This is possibly attributable to the differences in cultural values and experiences of the workforce and to the agrarian origins of much of the industrial workforce. Increased income was a strategy everyone could agree on, whereas decreased hours alone were a potential source of conflict.

The Social Side of the American Wage and Work-Time Bargain

The wage and work-time bargain struck by the unionized mass-production workforce in the 1950s and 1960s in the United States also facilitated a particular gender division of labor between home work and wage work, one in which a reasonably well-paid male worker supported a family with a dependent wife. The nature of postwar employment contracts made work for women difficult unless they were willing to work full-time and possibly overtime. Men have historically preferred decreasing working hours through a short workweek with longer workdays, leaving full days available for leisure pursuits or for earning additional income. Women, on the other hand, prefer short workdays because of their responsibilities for domestic work and childcare. Since postwar bargaining agreements emphasized wages and overtime pay for long hours rather than decreases in working time, women with children, particularly young children, found it difficult to take full-time work. In addition, as Elaine Tyler May has described in *Homeward Bound* (1989), the male breadwinner–female housewife model that characterized the postwar era in the United States was an aspect of a general retreat to family life and the home. The nuclear family replaced the ethnic community as a source of personal identity. At the same time the power of ethnic communities to provide social security and political bargaining power waned. The suburbanized nuclear family was left to its own resources. During the 1950s and 1960s, however, these resources were quite significant, and consumption replaced other values, including a value on nonwork time. "Commodities would solve the problem of the discontented housewife, foster pride in the provider whose job offered few intrinsic rewards, and allow children to 'fit in' with their peers. Consumerism provided a means for assimilation into the American way of life: classless, homogeneous, and family centered."[11]

Women did enter the workforce in the 1960s but overwhelmingly as part-time workers. Women were able to take part-time jobs because those jobs were in unregulated sectors of the economy where nonstandard hours could be negotiated by employer and employee. The new female entrants into the labor force were those at the end of the then traditional childbearing years—most were over 35. (The labor-force participation rate of women 45–54 grew from 34 percent to 48 percent between 1950 and 1960.) Since many of this first wave of married female workforce entrants were the spouses of men employed full time, their part-time jobs paid for increased consumption. For a brief period the supplementary income provided by these primarily working-class and lower middle-class women decreased household income inequality in the United States.[12]

The Origins of the Contemporary Time Crisis

In the early 1970s the social and political arrangements underpinning the mass-production economy in the United States began to come apart under the pressures from the increasing international competition, the restructuring of the global economy, and the rapid growth in the U.S. labor force. In the new international division of labor, the United States became a service economy dominated by business services for industries serving global markets and producing throughout the world. The jobs in goods-producing industries that had provided the base line for work-time regulation declined precipitously and declined in exactly those regions in which their industrial bargaining power had been most significant.[13] Industrial jobs grew in the relatively less regulated South and West, and less regulated service jobs replaced industrial jobs in the Northeast.

The U.S. labor force grew 3 percent per year in the 1970s, notwithstanding efforts to control the labor supply by encouraging early retirement among the protected segment of the male workforce and extending educational time for the "baby boom" generation. As the workforce expanded and diversified, unionized labor was forced to stand behind provisions to extend to the workforce as a whole some of the wage benefits obtained by the mass collective worker. Hence, the "forced translation" of the 1970s that led to a general inflation-based economic crisis.[14] However, the set of wage and work-time bargains made by the mass-production workforce and partially extended to the labor force as a whole began to deteriorate as employment declined in the sectors in which the workforce had bargaining power and dramatically increased in the largely unregulated service sector and among those segments of the workforce that had been excluded from the wage and work-time bargains of the postwar period.

In the wake of this crisis, with growing demand in service jobs, young married women went into the workforce in large numbers. The labor-force participation rate of women 25–44 years of age grew from 48 percent to 71 percent between 1970 and 1985. Among mothers of minor children, the labor-force participation rate rose from 40 percent in 1970 to 59 percent in 1984. By 1986, 54 percent of women with children under six years of age were in the labor force.[15] It is this group of young, and now reasonably well-educated, mothers who have expanded the labor supply. The combination of an increased number of single-earner households plus the decline in male earning power transformed female employment patterns. Most women in the United States are now lifetime wage workers, albeit frequently in "flexible" jobs. The most recent data show that 66 percent of women of working age currently hold jobs or are actively seeking them. Among women college graduates, this figure is 81 percent. At the same time, the proportion of working men in the population continues to decline.[16]

In the 1980s organized labor represents only 17 percent of the U. S. workforce, the lowest percentage among advanced industrialized countries. Unions are less powerful in representing the interests of their members and certainly with respect to the interests of the workforce as a whole. Overall, the bargaining power of the workforce to determine work time has declined as jobs have been created in nonunionized unregulated sectors, organized around flexible or contingent jobs that are more responsive to changes in the demand for a good or service.

Contemporary Trends in Working Hours and Work Distribution

The contemporary United States evidences some striking and difficult-to-interpret employment patterns. Prominent among these are two trends, first, an increase in total work hours, and second, a redistribution of wage work among a much larger portion of the population. In contrast with the 1960s when total work hours decreased and leisure increased by 10 percent, Americans in the 1980s are working longer hours and have less leisure time. Women have increased their hours of paid work by approximately six hours per week, and there has been little change in the work hours of American men, who have historically worked more than 40 hours per week. Per capita work hours were 14 percent higher in 1986 than in 1965; 71 percent of working-age adults in the United States hold jobs, and the percentage of people holding second jobs or "moonlighting" jumped 20 percent between 1980 and 1987.

With the exception of the Japanese, Americans spend more hours and days at work than their counterparts in other industrialized countries. While the West Germans, Dutch, and British average slightly longer hours than Americans (40.3 hours to 40.6 hours in 1983), average American work hours are dramatically undercounted because of the larger number of part-time workers in the workforce.

Americans also have significantly less vacation time and paid leave time than their counterparts in Western European economies. Paid holidays are lower in the United States than in all but two Organization for Economic Cooperation and Development (OECD) countries.[17]

Since the mid-1970s this trend toward increased wage work by Americans has been disguised by the forms increased work has taken—a proliferation of temporary and part-time jobs whose work hours can be more easily adjusted to changes in demand than those of permanent, full-time workers. They include part-time jobs and temporary jobs and, to some extent, independent subcontractors. As the United States has been transformed from a manufacturing-oriented to a service-oriented economy, large service firms have increasingly begun to hire workers on flexible work schedules. On the supply side, the increasing number of people, including students, the semiretired, and women with children wanting other than full-time, full-year jobs has expanded the supply of potential workers. Employers have altered labor-deployment patterns in order to use these workers who are, in many respects, less expensive to employ than full-time workers.

From 1973 to 1979, 12.5 million jobs were added to the U.S. economy. Another 14.5 million jobs were added in the 1980s. Nearly a quarter of these jobs were part-time, and approximately 66 percent were filled by women. One out of every six U.S. jobs, or about 19 million total, is a part-time job. Although the United States has a lower percentage of workers in part-time jobs than the United Kingdom or Sweden, the share of total labor input (in terms of hours) by part-time workers is higher in the United States. This is because the yearly average number of part-time workers understates the dimensions of the part-time work experience in the United States. A much larger proportion of the workforce is employed part-time at some point during the year than is indicated by the average number of part-time jobs. In 1985, for example, the number of people who worked part time for a portion of the year was double that of the annual average number of part-time workers.

Although part-time jobs are the most numerous of flexible or contingent jobs, other forms of employment are expanding more rapidly, particularly temporary work. The use of temporary workers is particularly prevalent in those situations, such as general clerical work and data entry, where the pattern of demand is not predictable and in work where generalized rather than firm-specific skills are required. Temporary work contracts can take a number of forms, including (1) a short-term job; (2) a long-term job with no employment security, lower pay, or no benefits; or (3) a structured internal temporary worker pool (most common in large public institutions, such as universities and in hospitals).

In the United States temporary "industry" more than 1 million workers are employed as temporaries at any one given time but, more significantly, at least 6 million people work as temporaries at some time during any given year. Average annual employment in the industry increased from 340,000 in 1978 to well over 1 million in 1988. The temporary-supply industry is growing at three times the growth rate of service industries and eight times the rate of all non-agricultural industries.[18] Between now and 1955 the temporary-help industry is projected to grow 5 percent annually in comparison with a 1.3 percent growth rate for all industries. The temporary industry employs only a small portion of temporary workers in the United States. The largest portion are "direct hires," employed as on-call workers in large firms and, more and more frequently, in the public sector. The U.S. federal government is one of the largest employers of temporary workers and under revised regulations can hire "temps" up to four years without providing benefits or job security. Approximately 300,000 workers in the executive branch, including the postal service, are currently employed as temporary workers. Among the private firms with their own in-house temporary labor services are Standard Oil, Hunt-Wesson, Beatrice Foods, Hewlett Packard, and Atlantic Richfield (ARCO).

The role of the temporary or on-call worker is beginning to change as this type of work distribution becomes more prevalent. More firms are restructuring work to use a "permanent" temporary labor force to do certain jobs. Rather than a part-time phenomenon, temporary workers are more frequently employed on long assignments, for weeks and even months.[19] The director of a law firm continuously using temporary workers exemplified this trend in stating, "We concluded we were better off maintaining a staff for minimal demand. We can satisfy short-term increases with temporary help. It's more cost effective and better management." And, according to the president of a major temporary agency, "Our business has changed from a replacement and fill-in service to an effective tool for managing labor costs."[20]

There is at least some evidence that many of the full-time jobs created in the United States since 1982 are, in fact, jobs with no expectation of continuous or long-term employment.[21] The information on the vast majority of these jobs is quite limited because, as of yet, no public agency collecting statistics on the workforce differentiates among jobs based on the character of the employment contract. Thus, available information is largely anecdotal or based on firm surveys.[22] Among the few firm surveys that shed light on this phenomenon, the 1986 Bureau of National Affairs survey of 442 firms indicates that 90 percent use short-term hires and on-call workers. The data in this survey allowed Abraham to calculate that the use of temporary workers is probably twice as large as that represented in the temporary industry.[23]

Temporary workers are similar to the part-time workforce—they tend to be young and female. The best available information on the characteristics of this workforce, from the May 1985 Current Population Survey, indicates that 64 percent of temporary workers are women and that one of three of them is between 16 and 24 years of age. Blacks are also overrepresented in the temporary workforce. They constitute 20 percent of the temporary workforce in comparison with 10 percent of the workforce across all industries.

The trend toward more "flexible" jobs is also demonstrated by a decrease in the number of people who work a 40-hour workweek in the United States. Both longer and shorter workweeks are growing. For example, the number of women working more than 49 hours per week increased 50 percent between May 1979 and May 1985.[24]

The year-to-year variation in work hours is also increasing. The average year-to-year change in work hours during the 1970s was nearly 320 hours (the average for men workers). Variation in work hours ranged from 280 hours per year for white women workers to 350 hours for black workers.[25] Thus, fewer adult Americans hold stable full-time jobs and receive pay for 40-hour workweeks.[26]

Recent evidence suggests that despite the proliferation of flexible jobs, more and more American women are moving from part-time or temporary work into jobs that require them to work full-time. In the United States, this frequently means more than 40 hours per week since they are in salaried rather than waged positions and work in industries in which work time has not historically been regulated. Growth in voluntary part-time work is stagnant, while the number of full-time women workers and involuntary part-time workers is increasing. Women across all age groups increased their hours of paid work by about six hours a week between 1975 and 1985.[27] This is, of course, part of the general trend toward increased wage work and represents the way in which Americans have adjusted to economic change. Increased work hours have enabled Americans to maintain household incomes at levels comparable to the boom period of the 1960s and early 1970s despite the fact that average (adjusted) hourly wages have declined 7 percent since 1973 and weekly wages 15 percent.

The trend to increased work time throughout the population as a whole and particularly the more recent trend toward increased full-time wage work for women has, however, led to a social crisis that also emanates in the wage and work-time bargain made by Americans in the postwar era. Americans not only chose consumption over reduced hours of work, they chose private consumption rather than social consumption. With assistance from a minimal welfare state, Americans chose to provide for health and welfare through private wages and in the family rather than through state-provided social services. This solution depended on a high level of earnings and a full-time "service provider" in the household. As American women increasingly work full time to maintain household incomes, their other role has not diminished but, rather, is expanding. This is the source of the contemporary time crisis in American society.

Individual and Social Costs of Contemporary Working Time

Possibly because of a history of relatively unregulated work time and dependence on private effort, Americans have accepted the need to work more without question. The lack of political opposition to changes in the distribution of work may also stem from differences within the population in the effects of additional work effort on total income. The ability to maintain income by increased wage work differs among individuals and types of households. Middle-class families with two full-time wage earners (and possibly an employed teenager) have been able to maintain or even increase their total earned income. Households headed by single women, however, find it impossible to earn enough even with increased work hours. They make up an increasing proportion of the poverty-level population. Overall, increased working hours have failed as a solution to decreased individual hourly wages. The number and proportion of the working poor has increased in the United States.

Despite Americans' apparent acceptance of the necessity for increased work time, there are a series of political issues that have arisen as a larger portion of the population has moved into the workforce. The emerging politics of work time in the United States focuses primarily on the social costs perceived to be associated with increased work time by women and young people still in school. Wage work by women is associated with a range of social "costs." First, there is growing concern that young children are not being cared for properly. This concern is exacerbated by fears about the future of the American labor supply. Invidious comparisons are made between the working American woman and the Japanese woman who stays home to educate her children. Recently, the comparison between Japanese and American women was extended to the effects on the quality of the American workforce of a decline in childbearing among educated American women.[28] Some policy analysts have gone so far as to indirectly attribute divorce or family dissolution to increased work by women.[29]

Increasing work by teenagers is criticized in much the same vein. However, there is no evidence thus far to substantiate whether teenage workers are working more hours to buy cars and records or to supplement or replace family income.

An analysis of the sources of the contradictory pressures on American workers, particularly women workers, is almost completely absent from political debates on issues emerging in a society that has been moving toward authentic full employment but that still maintains an ethic of private service provision. For example, the recent restructuring of health-care provision to reduce costs includes the development of elaborate home-care equipment and the early release of all but acutely ill patients. It is assumed that care will be provided by family members at home. And, with the aging of the American population and a lack of adequate socially provided care facilities, it is assumed that care providers must come from the family. Although the need for child care is now given some attention, it is only one of a range of service work demands that are increasing.

The ability to replace time with commodities is also beginning to be seen as limited, since many consumption decisions have become more complicated and themselves require time if the products are to effectively satisfy needs.[30] And, ironically, the increase in so-called labor-saving devices in the household has not been to increase productivity but to increase the time spent on housework.[31]

The greatest burden of combining wage work with purchasing, domestic work, and home care falls on women. And, although American women are working longer hours and are progressively moving into continuous full-time work, the time they spend on care of children and other relatives and housework has only marginally decreased. A survey by a large U.S. insurance company, for example, found that one out of every five employees over age 30 provides some care to an elderly parent. Of these employees, 8 percent spend 35 hours or more a week on this care, and the average is about ten hours. The majority of these caregivers are women, even when it is the husband's parent who needs care.

The average woman had five to six hours' less free time per week than the average man. Men also spend their time differently, with significantly more time devoted to paid work and educational opportunities. In a society in which upward mobility increasingly depends on increased skills, women do not have time to pursue further education or job training.[32]

The Costs to Employers of Multiple Role Workers

However difficult the situation is for the individual worker, it is not the total increase in women's work hours that has stimulated a desire to develop alternate work schedules. "Unanticipated lost time is the problem," according to employers of workers whose productivity is affected by their multiple responsibilities. The primacy of productivity in the workplace was central to a recent widely cited report, "Work and Family in the United States." "Our national interest will best be served if we can enable working parents to concentrate on their jobs without neglecting their families."[33]

Policy initiatives are essentially concerned with ameliorating the negative effects of increased total work time on the job—effects that include job turnover, absences, tardiness, and decreased productivity. That this has become a very real problem for employers is indicated by a number of national surveys, including one by *Fortune* that indicated that 41 percent of working mothers report absenteeism due to family responsibilities. It is these interests that are shaping political solutions to the work-time, home-care crises.

A Family-Oriented Politics of Work Time

There is remarkable unanimity among American policy makers about the nature of the problem and about the boundaries within which solutions can be posed. Even progressive unions, such as the Service Employees International Union, whose membership is made up of women workers and workers who provide professional care to children, the elderly, and the ill, shy away from proposing collective solutions that would free women from some of their family responsibilities. The types of political solutions now being formulated are consistent with historical limits on social or collective solutions in the United States.[34] First, they originate with the employer and the individual. These benefits come (as have all benefits in the United States) as a consequence of employment rather than as a right of citizenship. Second, they must not impose costs on the employer or must at least be cost effective.

Now that productivity is being negatively affected by the dual responsibilities of workers, employers are becoming more aware that work time accommodations are the best way to make the relationship between family, home, and workplace "more efficient." Family-oriented policies advocate the restructuring of work time so that workers can more adequately manage the burdens of care and still be productive in the workplace. For employers, this accommodation represents a least-cost solution that maintains large numbers of relatively inexpensive women workers in the workforce and avoids the costs of state-supported care for children, the ill, or the elderly.

The most prominent of these solutions is that of flexible work time or flexitime, which would allow workers to set their own hours within limits, in order to carry out their family obligations, such as visits to a physician or care of a sick child. These tasks would be allocated to the employee's personal time rather than requiring an absence from work. The employee would then be expected to make up the work time. What this would mean, in effect, is an institutionalization of private responsibility for socially necessary work and longer total work hours for women workers, who shoulder most of the responsibility for care of children and other relatives.

Approximately 12 percent of American workers are now on flexible schedules, and this number is expected to substantially increase because it offers employers a low-cost solution to the dilemma posed by the need to employ women workers and the need to provide for the care of nonworking citizens.

Conclusions

In the early 1970s Americans responded to economic change and a threat to their standard of living as individuals rather than collectively. They began to work more and adjusted to employers' demands to tie work time and earnings to the exigencies of the market. In the process, they created the myth of the "flexible" American worker. The American response to recent economic change has been characterized by substantial and largely unquestioned sacrifices of time and security and by continued private provision of socially necessary work.

The contemporary politics of work time in the United States can be understood only with respect to a broader set of concerns facing U.S. policy makers. Foremost among these is a perceived need to increase the productivity and decrease the cost of a service workforce while at the same time minimizing the social (and tax) burden of caring for nonworking citizens. This politics has both a material and ideological basis. Materially, the United States had become a service economy, with significantly different labor-demand conditions than those that characterized a manufacturing-based economy. Ideologically, the American response to socioeconomic stress derives from two sets of assumptions. First, there is the historical rejection of collective approaches to socially necessary work, such as child care, which in the United States has always been considered a private responsibility. Second, the recent debates over flexible work are significantly influenced by ideas about "the family" and fears about a diminution of its functional role.

The contemporary politics of work time in the United States differs from that of most Western European countries in the problems it addresses and in its proposed solutions. These differences derive from current labor demand but also from enduring features of the American political economy. American unions have always had a limited and politically weak role in regulating the conditions under which the vast majority of Americans are employed. This political weakness has been exacerbated by the transformation of the U.S. economy to a service economy. Second, social securities, such as access to health care, have historically been linked to employment rather than provided as a right of citizenship. And the socially necessary work of caring for non-working people, including the sick, elderly, and children, has always been primarily a private responsibility. These conflicts have contributed to the aura of crisis that surrounds the working-hours debate. The policies that are being proposed to resolve these conflicts are clearly within the American tradition—private solutions to what are not only private but also social issues. They show every indication of continuing to exacerbate inequalities of time as well as wages and to contribute to what Scitovsky has so accurately described as "the joyless economy."

Notes

1. J. S. Poyntz, *ILGWA Journal* (Feb. 15, 1919): 6, cited by B. Hunnicutt, *Work Without End* (Philadelphia: Temple University Press, 1988).

2. S. Fine, *Laissez Faire and the General Welfare State* (Ann Arbor: University of Michigan Press, 1956).

3. *New York Times*, June 15, 1989.

4. J. Baer, *The Chains of Protection* (Westport, Conn.: Greenwood Press, 1978); Fine, *Laissez Faire and the General Welfare State*.

5. Hunnicutt, *Work Without End*.

6. M. Davis, *Prisoners of the American Dream* (New York: Verso Press, 1986); D. Walkowitz, *Worker City, Company Town* (Urbana: University of Illinois Press, 1978).

7. R. Ratner, "The Social Meaning of Industrialization in the United States," *Social Problems* 27, no. 4 (April 1980):448–461.

8. Ibid., 448–461.; J. Rayback, *A History of American Labor* (New York: Oxford University Press, 1959).

9. Hunnicutt, *Work Without End*.

10. J. Owen, "Workweeks and Leisure: An Analysis of Trends, 1948–75," *Monthly Labor Review*, Aug. 1976, pp. 3–8.

11. E. T. May, *Homeward Bound* (New York: Basic Books, 1989), p. 172.

12. N. Paulson, "Change in Family Income Position: The Effect of Wife's Labor Force Participation," *Sociological Focus* 15, no. 2 (1982):77–91.

13. B. Bluestone and B. Harrison, *The Deindustrialization of America* (New York: Basic Books, 1982).

14. E. Alliez and M. Feher, *ZONE* 1,2 (New York: Urzone, 1988).

15. U.S. Bureau of Labor Statistics, *Employment and Earnings, Characteristics of Families: First Quarter* (Washington, D.C.: U.S. Department of Labor, 1988).

16. *New York Times*, Aug. 1, 1988.

17. Office of Technology Assessment, Congress of the United States, "Technology and the American Economic Transition" (Washington, D.C.: Government Printing Office, 1988).

18. F. Carre, "Temporary and Contingent Employment in the Eighties: Review of the Evidence" (Washington, D.C.: Economic Policy Institute, 1988).

19. Thomas J. Plewes, "Understanding the Data on Part-Time and Temporary Employment," in *Flexible Workstyles: A Look at Contingent Labor* (Washington, D.C.: Women's Bureau, U.S. Department of Labor, 1988).

20. S. Oates, "Temporary Employment Industry Booming," *San Francisco Chronicle*, Aug. 7, 1985, sec. F, p. 6.

21. L. Uchitelle, "America's Army of Non-Workers," *New York Times*, Sept. 27, 1987, sec. 3, p. 1.

22. Bureau of National Affairs, "The Changing Workplace: New Directions in Staffing and Scheduling" (Washington, D.C.: Bureau of National Affairs, 1986); D. Mayall and K. Nelson, "The Temporary Help Supply Service and the Temporary Labor Market," Report Submitted for the Office of Research and Development, Employment and Training Administration, U.S. Department of Labor (Washington, D.C.: Government Printing Office, 1982).

23. K. Abraham, "Flexible Staffing Arrangements and Employers' Short Term Adjustment Strategies," *National Bureau of Economic Research Working Paper* 2619 (Cambridge, Mass.: NBER, 1988).

24. S. Smith, "Growing Diversity of Work Schedules," *Monthly Labor Review* 109, no. 11 (Nov. 1986); Office of Technology Assessment, Congress of the United States, "Technology and the American Economic Transition" (Washington, D.C.: Government Printing Office, 1988).

25. G. Duncan, "Years of Poverty, Years of Plenty" (Ann Arbor: Survey Research Center, University of Michigan, 1984).

26. A multitude of reasons are advanced for these tendencies in the U.S. economy. One of the most common explanations roots increases in the demand for flexible labor in recent short-term business cycles that have increased interfirm competition. In order to remain competitive, firms must circumvent the regulatory structures in national economies that inhibit rapid adjustment in the quality and quantity of labor. The growth of forms of work, such as part-time and temporary work, that fall outside the employment security system are the consequence (Organization for Economic Cooperation and Development, "Flexibility in the Labor Market: A Technical Report" [Paris: OECD, 1986], p. 112). These rigidities are, in turn, associated with high employment. There is, obviously, a basic contradiction in this explanation. The proportion of flexible workers in an economy is a measure of both its capability to adjust speedily (as in the case of the United States) and of its inflexibility since flexible workers are used to avoid rigidities in the form of nonwage benefits. If one accepts the argument that structural rigidities produce more part-time and temporary jobs, then the case of the United States is an anomaly. The United States has by far the least "rigid" employment security system and the largest flexible workforce. It is the very lack of employee protection and bargaining power, particularly among women and minority workers and particularly in services, that has enabled employers to utilize workers flexibly.

Another explanation is supply-based, attributing the increase in flexible work forms and particularly in part-time work throughout industrialized countries to women's moving into the workforce in greater numbers and to their desire for part-time jobs. Thus, increasing part-time work is a function of increased female labor-force participation. Although on an international level, this correlation looks plausible—female labor-force participation is increasing and part-time work is increasing—there is no clear pattern. Britain, France, the United States, and Germany, to take examples of societies where female labor-force participation has increased, all have different patterns in female labor-force participation over the life cycle, in the sectoral distribution of women workers, and in the percentage of part-time versus full-time women workers (Veronica Beechey, *A Matter of Hours: Women, Part-Time and the Labor Market* [Minneapolis: University of Minnesota Press, 1987]). The industrialized countries, including the United States, that have shown the fastest gains in female labor-force participation are those characterized by growth in service-sector employment but also those in which female labor-force participation was lowest in 1960. Those countries showing the slowest growth in female labor-force participation are those in which women made up a large segment of the manufacturing workforce and which had relatively high female labor-force participation rates in the period following World War II (Thierry Noyelle and Thomas Stanback, "The Postwar Growth of Services in Developed Economies," Report to the United Nations Conference on Trade and Development [Geneva: UNCTAD, 1988]).

Both these demand and supply-based explanations explain firm and individual decisions within a severely limited ahistorical economic rationality. They do not explain why, for example, firms are faced with this choice at this moment or why women would want to go into the workforce when that previously had not been the case.

27. Another indication of the redistribution of work in the American workforce is evidence of a decreasing unemployment rate among the employed population but a continuing hard-core population of "discouraged workers," people who say they want work but are not seeking jobs or who work less than half the year and earn under $10,000. This group is estimated at between 10 million and 20 million people and excludes the majority of nonworkers who remain out of the workforce for reasons of health, education, or retirement. Uchitelle, "America's Army of Non-Workers." Although the U.S. unemployment rate has fallen from 9.5 percent in 1983 to under 6 percent in 1988, this statistic measures only the status of those who are actively in the workforce. Despite apparent labor shortages and a declining unemployment rate, the number of discouraged workers has remained sizable and stable since the recession of the early 1980s.

28. R. Herrnstein, "IQ and Falling Birth Rates," *Atlantic* 263, no. 5 (May 1989):73–79.

29. J. Schachter, "Women Seen Closing the Wage Gap," *Los Angeles Times*, Feb. 8, 1989, pt. 4, p. 3.

30. T. Scitovsky, *The Joyless Economy* (New York: Oxford University Press, 1976).

31. J. Vanek, "Time Spent on Housework," *A Heritage of Her Own*, ed. N. Cott and E. Pleck (New York: Simon and Schuster, 1976):499–506.

32. Office of Technology Assessment, "Technology and the American Economic Transition."

33. Economic Policy Council of the United Nations Association of America, *Work and Family in the United States: A Policy Initiative* (New York: United Nations Association of the United States of America, 1985).

34. See F. Block, "Social Policy and Accumulation: A Critique of the New Consensus," pp. 13–31, and T. Skocpol, "America's Incomplete Welfare State: The Limits of the New Deal Reforms and the Origins of the Present Crisis," pp. 35–58, in Martin Rein, Gösta Esping-Andersen, and Lee Rainwater, eds., *Stagnation and Renewal in Social Policy* (New York: M.E. Sharpe, 1987).

8 The Worker-Bee Syndrome in Japan: An Analysis of Working-Time Practices

Christoph Deutschmann

As is well known, Japanese working hours have continued to be quite different from normative standards and average actual conditions in most other developed industrial countries. First I review these peculiarities of the Japanese working-hours system. Second, I offer an explanation dealing with the economic as well as the sociological aspects of working hours. In particular, I examine how working hours are influenced by the Japanese system of industrial relations and personnel management.

The Japanese System: An Overview

The Japanese working-hours system can be seen in two aspects: (1) A truism: By international comparison, working hours in Japan are long. (2) There is no clear and formal distinction between working hours and leisure. Male employees, in particular, are engaged in many "grey" activities of neither work nor nonwork character, such as socializing with colleagues after work or on weekends, nonpaid overtime, and small-group activities.

The Extension of Working Time

According to figures published by the Japanese Ministry of Labor, yearly effective working hours per production worker in Japan amounted to 2,168 hours in 1985. The corresponding figures for other major industrial countries were: 1,924 hours (United States), 1,952 hours (Britain), 1,643 hours (France), 1,659 hours (West Germany).[1] The reasons for this large gap in the extension of working hours can be briefly summed up in three points.

In Western Europe and the United States employees are enjoying—as a rule—five-day weeks. In Japan the five-day week is still an exception, which is granted to only 28 percent of all employees in enterprises with 30 employees or

This paper summarizes some of the results of the author's two-year research stay at the Faculty of Economics of Tohoku University, which was made possible by a fellowship of the Japan Society for the Promotion of Sciences. The author thanks all colleagues at Tohoku University, and especially Professor Tokunaga Shigeyoshi, for their kind help.

more (in 1986).[2] Moreover, many Western European countries have cut average standard weekly working hours below 40 hours since 1980. By contrast, average scheduled weekly working hours in Japan amounted to 41 hours and 40 minutes per employee (44 hours and 26 minutes per firm) even in 1984. In particular, many small and very small firms maintain weekly scheduled working hours of more than 45 hours and a full six working days per week, although effective working hours are not so different between large and small firms because of a relatively higher amount of overtime in the former.

Under the pressure of "social dumping"–reproaches from abroad, the Japanese government has repeatedly announced efforts to shorten working hours by legal measures. According to the most recent of these initiatives, the reform of the labor standards law in 1988, the general introduction of the 40-hour week is expected to take place gradually in the 1990s.

Overtime is much longer in Japan than in other major industrial countries. In 1985 it amounted to an average 14.8 hours per employee every month. Monthly overtime hours of male employees alone were far in excess of 20 hours. By contrast, West German employees worked only 5.6 overtime hours on average in 1985, in spite of their relatively short regular hours.[3] One important reason for the high amount of overtime in Japan must be seen in the fact that the rate of extra payment for overtime is very low by international comparison. Even large firms pay, as a rule, an extra payment of no more than 30 percent of the basic wage for overtime on regular workdays as well as on holidays (except night work). The corresponding rates in the United States and Western Europe amount to 30–50 percent (normal workdays) and about 100 percent (holidays).[4]

Annual paid vacations are much shorter in Japan than in any other major industrial country. In Western Europe paid annual holidays (not including national holidays, i.e., legal holidays other than weekly rest) vary between four and eight weeks, while in the United States they amount to about two weeks. In Japan holidays other than weekly rest are not guaranteed by law but by collective-bargaining agreements on the company level; their average number per employee (approximately 17) is relatively large by international comparison. Paid annual vacations, however, are very short. Legally they vary between 6 and 20 days, according to seniority, with 14.9 days granted per year to the average employee. But only 7.5 of these days are in fact taken (in 1986). Firms exert considerable pressure on workers (by means of moral pressure of the work group, by financial sanctions, and the like) not to make full use of their holidays. Staffing standards are often calculated under the assumption of a less than 100 percent rate of holiday utilization. Moreover, even if holidays are taken, they are taken mostly in order to cover absences due to sickness. Because of the poor level of sickness compensation in most Japanese firms, it is a widespread practice to count days taken for sickness as a part of one's vacation. Thus absences due to sickness may be hidden, to a large degree. Japan's fantastically low rate of absenteeism does not necessarily reflect a higher morale of workers. First of all, it results from the fact that in Japan paid annual vacations are virtually nonexistent.

What is peculiar to Japan is not only the actual extension but also the long-term trend of working hours. Whereas in most other countries the postwar process of shortening hours began immediately after the war during the 1950s, Japan experienced an extended period when working hours were prolonged, a period that followed the defeat of the militant workers' movement during the first postwar years. Working hours rose to a maximum of 2,433 yearly hours per worker in 1960. It was only after 1960 that Japan joined the international trend toward shorter working hours. Moreover, whereas the declining trend of working hours continued even after the "oil shock" in 1974 and 1975 in Europe, average scheduled and effective hours in Japan rose once again.

"Grey" Activities between Work and Leisure

The peculiarities of Japanese working hours, however, are not confined to the measurable aspects of working time. Statistical measurement of working time presupposes a real world in which working hours are clearly separated from nonworking time by a number of organizational and technical devices, such as time recorders, work schedules, controls of performance, and the like. The real rhythm of work always differs to some degree from these formal provisions, but the difference is particularly large in Japan. Just as the formalization of organizational positions and roles is much less pronounced in Japanese enterprises than in Western ones, and just as the contractual element of the employment relationship is far less emphasized,[5] the working-hours regime is much less formalized. According to an empirical survey of the Japanese Institute for Research on Industrial Work (Sangyo Rodo Chosa Sho) on methods of attendance control, only a minority of large enterprises (37 percent) had time recorders. In most cases, attendance is confirmed personally by supervisors, putting a personal stamp on the duty record. By and large, blue- and white-collar workers are treated equally in this respect. Only in the medium and small firm sectors was the percentage of companies that had installed time recorders higher.[6]

Effective attendance at the workplace and in the social milieu of the firm, in fact, is even much higher than the statistical figures on working hours indicate. The deviation from the formal work schedule starts in the morning before official work begins. In many firms employees are expected to show up half an hour or even one hour before scheduled time in order to do cleaning work, other preparations, or to participate in the morning ceremony and in the obligatory gymnastic exercises that often take place outside scheduled time.[7] On the other hand, very few employees terminate their work at scheduled time. Permanent overtime is a normal phenomenon in Japan; even in 1975—the year of the most severe crisis of the Japanese economy after the war—average monthly overtime per worker amounted to 10.6 hours. According to data provided by the Federation of Electrical Workers (Denkiroren), monthly average overtime in 25 electrical machinery firms investigated between January 1983 and July 1984 never fell below 19.6 hours per employee.[8] When planning daily production targets, many firms presuppose a considerable amount of permanent overtime. Attempts by the Ministry of Labor to correct these practices have met fierce resistance by the employers.[9] Another factor contributing to the high level of permanent overtime is the "just in time" system of production, which often enforces time-consuming improvisational efforts of workers in order to correct irregularities of the production flow. As Richard Schonberger has put it: "In Japanese plants output *rate* is not important; as we have seen, the rate can be interrupted at any time for a line stop—and it can also be interrupted for correcting defectives. While the rate is not important, the daily schedule is, and if there are numerous line stops and reworks to perform, the workers may need to stay late to meet the daily schedule."[10]

In addition to permanent overtime, irregular overtime has to be taken into account. In many firms overtime schedules are communicated only on the same day, so that employees do not know in advance when they can leave work. Irregular overtime often is not paid, as in the case of office workers who are expected not to leave before everybody else in the group (in particular, the superior) has finished his work,[11] or in the case of small-group activities, which also take place outside scheduled hours and often without extra pay.[12]

The overtime workload differs considerably by qualification, tasks, hierarchical level, and, in particular, by sex. Male employees put in many more extra hours than female workers; characteristically, Japanese labor-standard law provides upper limits for overtime only for women (albeit these limits have been relaxed by the Equal Employment Opportunity Law of 1987). The high amount of overtime of a male employee, in turn, confirms, as we shall see more in detail later, his internal status as a "permanent" and "regular" worker.

But the social duties of a permanent worker are not the end of his work responsibilities. After work he is expected to join his superior and his colleagues in going to a bar for drinking and socializing. These socializing activities not only take place at least once a week, but also on Sundays and weekends (for excursions, playing golf, sports, and the like). The firm supports them with considerable sums of money in order to promote mutual understanding and emotional ties at the workplace.[13] Moreover, many companies have appointed so-called recreation monitors—people who are responsible for preparing and organizing joint recreational activities.

As a consequence, male employees spend not only their working hours but almost all their active time in the social milieu of the company. This applies also to married workers, who have to postpone their family obligations if required to do so by the firm. There is no clear separation of work and leisure, no taboo against the firm intervening into the private sphere of employees. These "grey" aspects of the actual practice of working time in Japan appear even more important than the mere quantitative differences between working hours in Japanese and Western companies.

The Economic and Social Aspects of the Japanese System

So far I have reviewed the characteristics of the Japanese working-hours system that appear to be most striking from the standpoint of international comparison. Of course, this review is far from complete; there remain many aspects that might deserve closer attention (for example, shift work). Nevertheless, I will limit my empirical considerations here in order to develop some explanatory arguments. I first consider the economic background of the Japanese working-hours system, and then the industrial relations and social and cultural context.

Economic Background

Orthodox economic theory attempts to explain the level of working hours by two groups of variables: first, the factors determining employers' decisions on working-hours schedules, and second, working-hours preferences of employees. According to the first line of argument, the most important factor is productivity. Employers will schedule the workday in such a way as to achieve maximum productivity per hour. In general, it is assumed that with increasing working hours, productivity per hour will increase at first and then, after reaching a certain amount of daily (weekly) working hours, will decrease again.

With regard to working-hours preferences of workers, the most important variable is real wages. The influence of real wages on working-hours preferences is conceptualized, as is well known, by the terms *income* and *substitution* effects. As long as the level of real wages is low, the substitution effect will dominate, thus creating a desire for longer working hours as real wages rise. As real wages continue to rise, however, the income effect will increasingly dominate and consequently lead to a decline of the level of preferred working hours.

How far can these considerations contribute to explaining the level of working hours in Japan? Productivity in Japanese industries rose much faster in the postwar era than it did in Western Europe and the United States.[14] On the other hand, the speed of working-hours reduction (after 1960) surely was faster in Japan than in the United States, although starting from a much higher level. But it was hardly faster than in Western Europe.[15] A lag in productivity can hardly be cited in order to explain the gap in the level of total working hours that remains between Japan and the other industrial countries in the West.[16] Thus, orthodox economic theory of employers' preferences does not seem to contribute much to the explanation of Japanese working hours.

What about the theory of working-hours preferences of employees? Truly,

Japanese real wages were much lower than those in Western industrial countries during the 1950s, but since then they have risen rapidly, and today the
Japanese real wage level is roughly equal to that of Western Europe, although
still lagging behind that of the United States. Thus, again, economic analysis
appears to be not very relevant to our problem. However, international comparisons of real wage levels are a complicated matter. Even if the dollar equivalent
of the wages in two countries is roughly equal, there can be large differences in
real purchasing power. It has often been pointed out that several basic items of
the average family budget are comparatively more costly in Japan than in other
industrialized countries, especially those in education, housing, and leisure activities.

Koshiro[17] has suggested that the high cost of housing and leisure can be
attributed principally to the scarcity of land in the overpopulated urban areas of
Japan. This explanation appears somewhat incomplete. Although the importance of scarcity of land cannot be denied, at least equal consideration must be
given to the lack of investment in social capital by the state in Japan. Traditionally, Japanese governmental infrastructure policies have put much emphasis
on the requirements of economic growth and largely neglected those of social
welfare, thus causing a lack of cheap housing and recreational facilities. Governments in Western Europe (especially social democratic ones) have invested
comparatively much more in the building of public parks, swimming pools,
cultural and social facilities, and housing programs, and they have subsidized
education to a much higher degree than has the Japanese government.

Lack of state intervention in the field of social infrastructure surely is one
of the most important factors decreasing the real value of household income in
Japan, and this, without doubt, contributes to the widespread inclination among
Japanese employees to increase their real income by putting in extra hours in
whatever form is available (e.g., overtime, moonlighting, work of housewives). On the whole, however, economic and political economic considerations like these do not seem sufficient to explain the characteristics of the Japanese working hours outlined above. It remains an open question, for example,
why Japanese unions were not more effective in raising excess payment for
overtime to the current international standards. Obviously, it is necessary to
supplement economic theory by a sociological analysis of industrial relations
and of the Japanese management system.

Industrial Relations and Social Background

In analyzing the industrial relations and social background of Japanese
working hours, I proceed in two steps. First, I start with the common orthodox
Marxist assumption of class conflict, according to which employers tend to
extend or intensify working time, whereas workers struggle for shorter and less
intensive work. I then examine the specific obstacles to the shortening of working hours that arise from the particular decentralized structure of industrial rela-

tions in Japan. In the second step of my argument I reconsider the basic assumption of this orthodox argument itself and ask: How strongly have Japanese unions and employees been interested in shortening working hours at all during the postwar era?

My first argument is based on the presupposition that employees and unions are vitally interested in and eagerly striving for a reduction of working hours. It can be shown that, even this being granted, reduction of working hours remains a difficult and cumbersome matter under conditions of the decentralized, firm-centered structure of industrial relations prevailing in Japan. The particular obstacles against working-hours reduction that are created by this structure can be made clear if we compare the Japanese system with working-hours policies under more centralized systems of collective bargaining, such as those of West Germany, Sweden, Norway, Denmark, and the Netherlands, which have been most effective by international comparison in reducing working hours. The centralization of collective bargaining results in a high degree of standardization of working hours and work conditions in general, and it can easily be shown that standardization of working hours (i.e., setting an equal norm for different branches and occupational groups) greatly facilitates its shortening. Or, to put it the other way around: The fragmentation of collective bargaining and differentiation of working hours and work conditions, as in Japan, severely impedes the progress of working-hours reduction. This can be attributed mainly to three causes:

First, a centralized system of collective bargaining makes it easier to transfer agreements on shorter working hours achieved in branches and firms with strong unions to more weakly unionized branches and firms. Since agreements are binding on all firms of an industry, the centralized system forces both sides, unions as well as employers, to coordinate and balance different interests of members (arising from different market conditions, enterprise sizes, employment structures, and the like) internally before reaching a settlement. As a rule, however, the decision-making process in unions and employers' organizations is, in fact, dominated mostly by large and highly unionized firms whose members are often highly overrepresented in the negotiating bodies on both sides. Of course, compromises with regard to medium and small firms are made, but in principle the system forces medium and small enterprises to keep pace with the improvement of working conditions and, in particular, with the reduction of working hours in large enterprises.

In Japan there is no such institutionally guaranteed spillover effect. Since negotiations are generally made separately in every firm, collective-bargaining agreements on shorter working hours do not spread automatically. Whether the spread takes place or not is largely dependent on the situation in the labor market. Under conditions of scarce labor supply, firms must be eager to offer work and working-hours conditions at least not worse than those of their competitors in order to attract new personnel in sufficient quality and quantity.

When the supply of labor is abundant, however, firms no longer need to compete for better working conditions. Indeed, it seems that the actual development of working hours in Japan since the 1960s can to a large degree be explained by the competition of firms for recruitment of high school and university graduates in the labor market. However, after the oil crisis of 1974–75, when the situation in the labor market changed, the downward trend of working hours did not continue. In fact, there was even a slight rise in scheduled as well as in actual total hours.

Second, under conditions of centralized bargaining the determination of working hours becomes independent of the influence of competition in the product market. Working hours are an institutionally fixed datum for all enterprises. Thus, technically backward firms with low productivity that face the danger of being eliminated from the market cannot resort to forcing longer working hours (or substandard wages) on their employees. Under the conditions of a decentralized system like Japan's, however, this might be quite possible, at least insofar as there are no countervailing factors arising from the situation in the labor market of the kind I have just considered. The situation in Japan is aggravated by the fact that there is no legal limitation of working hours for male adult employees. The practice of long hours (and low wages) may be considered one of the most important reasons for the survival of a large sector of small and very small enterprises in Japan.

Third, there is still another reason why, under conditions of enterprise bargaining, it is much more difficult even for unions in large companies to achieve shorter hours than under conditions of industry-wide bargaining. This has to do with the important question of the relationship between content and institutional levels of bargaining. Quite naturally, employers tend to react to every reduction of working hours by organizational and technical measures aimed at increasing productivity in order to offset, at least in part, the productivity losses resulting from shorter hours. However, although working-hours questions, because of their general and relatively abstract character, can easily be negotiated on industry-wide level, productivity questions are by their very nature firm specific and can be generalized only to a very limited degree. Thus, under conditions of the centralized system employers have no possibility of countering working-hours demands of the unions directly by demanding union consent to productivity-increasing measures. A second bargaining process on the enterprise level is needed in order to carry out organizational and technical rationalization steps that compensate the shortening of working hours. Under conditions of the decentralized system as in Japan, on the other hand, employers can link acceptance of working-hours reductions directly to unions' acceptance of productivity measures. Indeed, this has been the normal practice of working-hours negotiations in Japan. Good illustrations include the negotiations on an increase of annual holidays in the four leading companies in the steel industry in 1969–70 and the conflict over the introduction of the 40-hour week in the large brewery companies, which lasted from 1963 to 1968. In both cases unions had to accept rather tough productivity measures, such as a reduction of staffing levels, the introduction of new shift systems, the shortening of breaks, and so forth before reaching an agreement on working hours.[18] Thus, when Japanese unions consider entering into negotiations on working hours, they have to anticipate delicate compromises deeply intervening into work conditions and everyday work habits of their members. So, in many cases unions may abstain from demanding shorter working hours because the disadvantages of the tougher productivity regime to be expected outweigh the advantages of more leisure.

So far I have argued that Japanese unions, when trying to promote shorter working hours, are confronted with several specific obstacles arising from the firm-centered system of bargaining. Now I shall turn to the second step of my argument by posing the more fundamental question: Do Japanese unions really want shorter working hours at all? There are indeed authors who have doubted this, like Tsujimura: "Unions have in the past occasionally made an issue of working hours, but only as a kind of appended demand; their basic demands have consistently concerned wage rates."[19] Is it true that Japanese unions in their collective-bargaining policies have pursued mainly "monetary" interests?

Surely the answer is not simple if one is considering the entire postwar period. In the first years after the war Japanese unions, just like European unions after World War I, very militantly fought for shorter working hours and very often succeeded in cutting weekly working hours below the legal standard of 48 hours. But there is little doubt that the working-hours issue dropped to the bottom of union priorities at the beginning of the 1950s when the postwar boom began. This cannot be attributed to the changed political climate alone, but also to socioeconomic reasons, of which, as Fujimoto has pointed out, two were particularly important. First, Japan at that time was really a "cheap-wage country" with real wages of about one-tenth of the U.S. level and between one-third and one-half of the European level. Under these conditions unions had no choice but to fight primarily for wage increases. Second, the change of the social structure of the working population was important. Because of rapid industrialization, large numbers of the rural population joined the industrial labor force, while still retaining agrarian conservative habits and ways of thinking. These first- or second-generation industrial workers still did not have any clear consciousness of the difference between work and leisure and the time-related nature of wages. Their attitude toward work and remuneration was determined by the principle of subsistence, not by the level of hourly wages. They were used to working long and hard and did not feel themselves attracted by the pleasures of leisure.[20] The traditional attitudes of first- or second-generation industrial workers surely was one of the major obstacles against a movement for shorter working hours in Japan during the 1950s. This may provide an important explanation why working hours continued to lengthen during the

1950s and why the process of shortening working hours in Japan began so late and from such a high initial level.

But it remains an open question why the progress of reduction of working hours was so slow even after the urbanization of the working class had been largely finished. One should have expected that in Japan, as in Western countries, the progress of industrialization would lead not only to an adoption of increasingly efficient, time-saving methods of work organization but also to the rationalization and modernization of workers' attitudes toward work. If this had taken place, long working hours would have been rapidly replaced by short and efficient working time.

There is no doubt that this process did take place to some degree in Japan, as shown by Yamamoto. For example, effective utilization of the assembly-line production system in the automobile industry made it necessary to reduce absenteeism and to ensure steady, intensive and disciplined work behavior. Work and leisure had to be concentrated and clearly separated from each other, and this was one of the main motives for the introduction of some paid summer holidays at Nissan in 1956. For similar reasons, Matsushita began to introduce the five-day week already in 1982.[21] However, in spite of the rapid technical progress and intensification of work in Japanese industry, "modernization" of work organization and working-hours systems developed comparatively slowly. Theoretically, there had been much euphoria in Japan with regard to scientific management in the 1950s and 1960s, but in practice Japanese enterprises introduced it much more hesitatingly than did Western enterprises[22] and, at the same time, their resistance to shortening of working hours was much stronger. On the other hand, for workers, too, the "rationalization" of work attitudes seems to have developed rather slowly.

The rapid progress of working-hours reduction in Western countries cannot be attributed simply to strong union pressure, for it was also closely interconnected with the spread of scientific management. Scientific management reorganizes work according to the principle of maximum saving of time. This is achieved by the minute division of labor, by the separation of conception and execution of tasks, by the formalization of work organization, and by the clearcut definition of responsibilities, content, and quantity of work. The clear-cut definition of tasks also requires a clear-cut definition of time. Taylor himself always insisted that work hours should be devoted to work and rest hours to rest, each being clearly separated from the other. This system allows for intensive but short and calculable working hours, and this in principle was the basis on which compromises between unions and management concerning the shortening of working hours could be achieved.

The Japanese system of personnel management, however, has remained different. Of course, in Japanese firms there also exists a formal division of labor, but in practice there is often no precise definition and separation of individual tasks. Within the work group there is frequent job rotation, and responsibilities are not assigned to the individual but to the group as a whole. At the same time, the personnel allotment is calculated very restrictively. As a result, there arises very strong group pressure on every individual worker not to be absent, even not to take holidays in order to avoid creating additional strain on colleagues.

While in fact leaving ultimate power clearly in the hands of managers (I am following here the argument of an essay by Tokunaga),[23] the system evokes the perception of individual work autonomy and harmonious cooperation between superiors and subordinates. Given the lack of formalized responsibilities, the maintenance of this atmosphere of "harmonious commitment" is a vital functional prerequisite of the Japanese system. At the same time the system secures efficiency by fostering competition among group members. Merit rating and promotion depend on the judgment of the supervisor or the section chief, and in order to be evaluated favorably, workers first of all have to demonstrate loyalty and cooperativeness. The most elementary indicator of cooperativeness, of course, is attendance at the workplace and readiness to work at any time, even outside working hours (sometimes even without pay).

Indeed, given the high frequency of job rotation, workers need much time to learn and to adapt themselves to new jobs and work environments. The need for time flexibility is enhanced by such production management techniques as "just in time" production and "total quality control," under which system workers may stop the line in the case of quality problems. Under these conditions, time flexibility is needed if workers are to meet the daily production target.[24] Last but not least, much time is needed to build group ties at the workplace, which are so important; workers achieve this socializing with superiors and colleagues in bars and restaurants after work and relaxing together on Sundays and holidays.[25]

Japanese management does not content itself with standard performance but demands priority of work over private life. Appointments outside the firm, holiday plannings, private interests, and the like have to canceled or postponed if required by the firm. Most Japanese regular workers hardly have a chance to lead an independent private life, even a family life, outside the social subculture of the firm. Since overtime in many cases is unscheduled, employees cannot count on rejoining their families after work at a particular time, nor can they engage in any regular duties or commitments outside the company.[26] The irregularity of time requirements results in a social isolation of work groups in the firm from the outside world, which in turn reinforces the moral pressure of the group on each of its members.

Maybe we are now able to understand better why Japanese unions have been so hesitant to take up working-hours issues. Of course, in spite of the harmonious image of Japanese personnel management, labor-management relations generate much conflict in Japan, as in other industrialized countries. For the unions it is quite possible to express discontent in the area of wage issues without threatening the principal cooperative relationship between labor and management. Unions may also achieve reductions of regular working hours if they are ready to make concessions on productivity questions. Demanding effectively shorter and strictly scheduled working hours, however, would be disruptive to very basic principles of Japanese management. By such a policy, unions implicitly would claim that the private time schedules of workers should have priority at least equal to the time requirements of the firm. This would seriously challenge the high standard of commitment firms demand from their employees. Since Japanese unions are interested in maintaining a cooperative relationship within the firm, they have carefully avoided industrial action over working-hours matters. The official working-disputes statistics of the Japanese Ministry of Labor (which have been published annually since 1965) reveal that disputes over working hours have never made up more than 3 percent of the total of labor disputes.

Admittedly, changes toward a more leisure-centered style of life have developed in Japan, too, especially in the so-called my-home movement in the 1960s and the early 1970s. Management had to make constant efforts to prevent its spread. As Noda puts it: "Company executives consider competing for the employees' spare time—against the threat of affluence, ownership of automobiles and shorter working hours—as a key management issue. For this reason they make every effort to incorporate the spare time activities of employees within the range of activities provided by the company."[27] The introduction of quality control circles, for example, must be seen also in this context. These policies of management seem to have been fairly effective up to now, especially under the changed economic and labor-market conditions since the oil crisis.

Conclusions

My conclusion with regard to the possibility of closing the large gap between working hours in Japan and in Western industrialized countries in the foreseeable future is rather pessimistic. I have argued that there are three structural conditions underlying the present pattern of working hours in Japan: First, the continuing income preference of Japanese employees, which to a considerable degree is due to the lack of state intervention in social infrastructure; second, the enterprise-centered structure of industrial relations; and third, the "holistic" style of Japanese personnel management. Unless there is basic change in these structures—and presently I do not see signs of a change in the near future—I think that there is no realistic reason to expect that future administrative guidelines and union campaigns for shorter working hours will be more effective than they have been in the past ten years. To be sure, there is no lack of declarations of intentions for shorter working hours on the part of unions as well as on that of the Ministry of Labor. But here we must distinguish clearly between *tatemae* ("principle") and *honne* ("real intention"); it seems that those declarations are to be interpreted largely as expressions of the former, not of the latter. In fact, the point is not simply a "lack of power" of Japanese enterprise unions in the field of working hours. Their inclination to promote shorter working hours appears to be weaker than that of (at least) European nations.

Notes

1. Nihon Seisansei Honbu, *Katsuyo Rodo Tokei* (current series 1988), p. 176.

2. Statistics used herein are compiled from the yearbook of labor statistics of the Japanese Ministry of Labor and Nihon Seisansei Honbu, 1988, p. 136, and 1986, p. 130, if not indicated otherwise.

3. C. Brinkmann, et al., *Überstunden: Entwicklung, Strukturen und Bestimmungsgrößen*, Beiträge zur Arbeitsmarkt- und Berufsforschung, vol. 98 (Nuremberg, 1988), p. 64.

4. Takeshi Fujimoto, *Nihon no Rodo Joken* (Tokyo: Shin Nihon Shuppansha, 1984), pp. 71f.; Chuo Rodo Iinkai Jimu Kyoku, *Chingin Jijo Chosa* (Tokyo: Roi Kyokai, 1984).

5. Hanami Tadashi, *Labour Relations in Japan Today* (Tokyo: Kodansha, 1979).

6. *Romu Jijo* 637 (July 1985): 19.

7. C. Deutschmann, *Arbeitszeit in Japan* (Frankfurt and New York: Campus, 1987), pp. 97f.

8. Denkiroren, ed., *Rodo Handobokku 1985* (Tokyo: Denkiroren, 1985).

9. Komuro Hoju, "Koyo Keitai Rodosha Seikatsu no Henyo to Rodo Jikan Kisei no Hoteki Sha Mondai," *Rodo Ho* 135 (1985): 16–30.

10. R. J. Schonberger, *Japanese Manufacturing Techniques: Nine Hidden Lessons in Simplicity* (New York: Free Press, 1982).

11. J. P. Alston, *The American Samurai: Blending American and Japanese Managerial Practices* (Berlin: W. de Gruyter, 1986), p. 157.

12. Deutschmann, *Arbeitszeit in Japan*, pp. 110f.

13. *Japan Times*, March 5, 1989.

14. Fujimoto, *Nihon no Rodo Joken*, pp. 79–82.

15. According to a calculation of Lecher, average shortening of annual working hours per employee amounted to 1 percent in Japan and 0.8 percent in the European Economic Community (EEC) countries during the period 1960–73. During 1973–78 the corresponding figures were 0.6 percent (Japan) and 0.8 percent (EEC). Cf. W. Lecher, "Arbeitslosigkeit und Arbeitszeitpolitik im internationalen Überblick," *WSI-Mitteilungen* 36; no. 4 (April 1983): 262.

16. On the basis of an econometric analysis, Sakurabayashi has shown that in spite of the rapid increase of productivity in postwar Japan, the amount that working hours were shortened did not correspond to the principle of optimum productivity. Cf. Sakurabayshi Makoto, "Saitei Chingin to Rodo Jikan Tanshuku no Keizai Koka," *Teikyu Keizai Gaku Kenkyu* 17; no. 1 (1984): 157.

17. Koshiro Kazutoshi, "Labor Productivity and Recent Employment Adjustment Programme in Japan: Are We Workaholics?" in Japan Institute of Labour, ed., *High-*

lights in Japanese Industrial Relations (Tokyo: Japan Institute of Labour, 1983; first ed., 1978).

18. Matsusaki Tadashi, *Nihon Tekkogyo Sangyo Bunseki* (Tokyo: Nihon Hyoransha, 1982), pp. 190f. Chuo Rodo Iinkai Jimukyoku, *Rodo Kyoyaku Jitsumu Hyakka, Sangyo Rodo Chosasho* (Tokyo: Roi Kyokai, 1982), p. 150.

19. Kotaro Tsujimura, "The Effect of Reductions in Working Hours on Productivity," in Nishikawa Shunsaku, ed., *The Labor Market in Japan: Selected Readings* (Tokyo: University of Tokyo Press, 1980), p. 671.

20. Takeshi Fujimoto, "Nihon no Rodo Jikan to Rodo Undo," *Rodo Jikan to Shokumukyu: Shakai Seisaku Gakkai Nenpo Dai* 11 (1964): 107.

21. Yamamoto Kiyoshi, *Nihon no Chingin, Rodojikan* (Tokyo: Yuhi Kakusen, 1982), pp. 157–212.

22. Michael Y. Yoshino, *Japan's Managerial System: Tradition and Innovation* (Cambridge, Mass.: MIT Press, 1968), p. 202.

23. Tokunaga Shigeyoshi, "Nihon no Roshi no Saikento-Hitotsu no Hihanteki Kenkai," *Nihon Rodo Kyokai Zasshi* 6 (1984): 9–19.

24. Schonberger, *Japanese Manufacturing Techniques*, p. 61.

25. T. Rohlen, "The Company Work Group," in E. Vogel, ed., *Modern Japanese Organization and Decision-Making* (Berkeley: University of California Press, 1975), p. 90.

26. To be sure, this applies mainly to employees of larger firms. It may be less true in the case of small firms, where promotion chances (and consequently also competition for promotion) are more limited. Cf. Kobayashi Kenichi, "Japanese Style Labor-Management Relations and Employment and Industrial Relations in Small and Medium Enterprise," *Journal of International Economic Studies* 1 (March 1985): 53–71. And perhaps the attitude toward work is more instrumental here.

27. Noda Kazuo, "Big Business Organization," in Vogel, *Modern Japanese Organization*, pp. 140f.

9 On the Road to a Society of Free Choice: The Politics of Working Time in Sweden

Ulla Weigelt

In Sweden as in all the other Western countries, a discussion is in progress on the future of working hours. Ever since the beginning of the 1970s, this discussion has been largely dominated by the demand for a six-hour working day and a 30-hour working week, a demand that emerged as women began entering employment in earnest. The idea of using working-hours reductions or other working-hours arrangements to combat unemployment has had only a marginal bearing on the discussion. Nor have employers' demands for greater flexibility done much in recent years to influence the debate, which instead has tended more and more to focus on individual demands for freedom of choice and flexibility. Thus far, Sweden differs a great deal from other Western countries. To explain the difference, one has to analyze both the working-hours question and other related issues, for example, the structure of Swedish welfare policy, relations between the labor-market parties, employment growth, and so forth. In this chapter an attempt is made to highlight factors that make Sweden relatively unique, especially in regard to working time.

Full employment has been one of the overriding aims of Swedish economic policy. The number of persons in employment has steadily risen, and unemployment in recent years has not assumed the serious proportions to be seen in so many other Western countries. The growth of employment has been accompanied by an extensive structural transformation of the labor market. Industry provided about 40 percent of all employment in 1950. Today the figure is 30 percent. The public sector has increased its share of employment from 20 percent in 1950 to 38 percent in 1987. Thus, more than one employee in every three today works in the public sector.

The national system of social insurance has been steadily expanded in compliance with a basic model presupposing that members of the community will earn their livelihood. Payments from the pensions system, health insurance, parental insurance, and the like are proportional to the earned income of the individual. In recent years the general system of social insurance has been supplemented by collectively negotiated insurances to fill the gap between general insurance and earned income in various situations.

The public sector and the comprehensive system of social insurance are financed out of income taxation, various indirect taxes, and employers' contributions. A Swedish employer generally pays about 40 percent of an employee's wages in social security contributions. The rate of taxation for the individual employee in middle income brackets is about 40 percent. Marginal taxation rates are steeply progressive in higher income brackets, reaching about 75 percent at incomes of SEK 200,000.

Sweden's economic policy since the beginning of the postwar period has been based on an integrated model of equitable pay policy, structural rationalization, and active labor-market policy. The theory underlying the Swedish model was constructed by Gösta Rehn and Rudolf Meidner. Up until the mid-1960s this economic policy model operated for the most part as expected, resulting among other things in rapid structural change. This in turn presupposed a high level of external mobility in the labor market, which meant a notable increase in geographical mobility, especially as regards migration to the big cities. The security of individual employees was derived mainly from the active labor-market policy, which facilitated retraining and migration.

High external mobility generated problems in the form of housing shortages in the big cities and a drain on the rural population. When Swedish industry began losing market shares at the end of the 1960s and when industrial employment diminished, acceptance of the policy of rapid structural change was reduced. This was part of the reason for a realignment of the Swedish model, whereby attention was concentrated on in-company conditions and on labor submarkets, so as to restrain the negative impact of rapid structural change. The security given to the individual by labor-market policy was supplemented by security of job tenure.

This change of direction led to new legislation on job security, codetermination, the occupational environment, worker-directors and the like. The principal rule of the Security of Employment Act heavily circumscribes the ability of employers to make use of fixed-term contracts. These are permitted only in a number of specified instances, for example, for temporary replacements. The Co-determination Act gives unions extensive influence on corporate decision making, partly by imposing a duty of negotiation and information on employers regarding all important issues. And the Work Environment Act has increased the requirements to be met by the physical and psychosocial working environment. This legislation was combined with a number of educational measures and also with an expansion of research into working conditions in Sweden. A completely new research institute, the Institute for Working Life, was set up to supply employees and union organizations with the knowledge they required in this field. Employers were then considered—as indeed they still are—to have a head start, for example, in questions of management and organization.

The purpose of working-life policy was to lay the foundations on which employers and employees together could tackle long-term questions of structural adjustment, and also to give employees a great deal of influence on processes of change, for instance, the introduction of new technologies and work organization (working hours included).

Working-life policy, conjointly with labor-market policy, is now being ascribed progressively greater importance as a factor influencing the stability of the Swedish labor market. International comparisons have shown that the flexibility and adaptability of the Swedish labor market are relatively unique. Swedish companies invest in long-term functional flexibility so as to be able to adjust to economic and technical developments. Educational measures have been given high priority both by the labor-market parties and by the government. Forms of flexibility that are common in other countries, for instance, fixed-term contracts, work on call, and subcontracting, hardly exist in Sweden, nor are they compatible with current Swedish legislation.

Similar lines of demarcation also exist where the flexibility of working hours is concerned. Swedish law entitles a full-time employee to avail himself or herself of rules concerning part-time work and leave of absence that entitle him or her to revert to full normal working hours. In other countries, flexible working hours have developed mainly for reasons of employment policy or purely in response to the demands of production economics. Whereas other governments have tried to solve unemployment problems by means of various measures in the working-hours context, the Swedish government has continued in recent years to pursue an active labor-market policy.

In many countries technical progress and new production requirements have necessitated overhauls of working-hours legislation. Deregulation in the working-hours sector has not infrequently resulted in a shift of power in favor of employers, thus heightening tensions between employers and union organizations. No such painful process of adjustment has been necessary in Sweden, because Swedish working-hours legislation was already modernized at the beginning of the 1970s.

Some Basic Facts on Working Hours Developments in Sweden

Developments until 1970

At the beginning of the twentieth century the working week in manufacturing industry averaged about 60 hours. Legislation coming into force in 1920 provided the first statutory confirmation in Sweden of the principle of an eight-hour working day and a 48-hour working week. Initially this act was regarded as a stopgap measure, and it did not achieve any real impact until the early 1930s. The 48-hour week then became standard practice for those employees coming within the purview of the act, namely, industrial workers. The eight-hour day, on the other hand, remained uncommon, since the majority preferred working slightly longer between Monday and Friday and slightly less on Saturdays. Corresponding improvements for other groups were achieved partly through collective bargaining and partly through legislation (in the case of agricultural workers, retail employees, and hotel, restaurant and cafe employees).

The working-hours question was examined again at the end of the 1940s, but without any agreement on changes to be introduced. One inhibiting factor was the labor shortage prevailing at the beginning of the 1950s. In the mid-1950s a royal commission was appointed to investigate the feasibility of making the normal working week 40 hours. The commissions' recommendations led to legislation gradually reducing weekly working hours to 45, from 1960 onward. The next working-hours commission was appointed in 1963 to consider a further reduction of weekly working hours. In the 1966 pay talks agreements were reached on shorter working hours for a large number of sectors. The commission therefore recommended that legislation be brought into line with these collective agreements, so as to establish a normal working week of 42.5 hours. In 1968 the same committee recommended a statutory 40-hour week, and it submitted the draft version of a general working-hours act that could be applied to all categories of employee. The General Working Hours Act, the provisions of which included a 40-hour working week, was passed by the Riksdag (parliament) in 1970.

Arguments put forward by the Working Hours Commission in favor of a general working hours act included laying the foundations for more flexible working hours and for a finer adjustment of work input to conditions at the individual workplace. The commission took the view that a strictly regulated maximum number of working hours per day was no longer needed and that weekly working hours ought more commonly to be computed as average figures for a period of more than one week. Another important consideration was that in this way the purview of the legislation could be extended so as to include groups that had hitherto been excluded, for instance, the majority of all private salaried employees, national government employees, and employees in medical and social services.

The 1970 General Working Hours Act was entirely discretionary, that is, it could be overridden by collective agreements concluded or approved by a main union organization. Another important factor that did a great deal to influence developments was that the act did not specify a maximum number of hours per day.

At the beginning of this century there were certain limited holiday benefits that had been provided by collective agreements. It was not until 1937 that holiday legislation was passed in Sweden, providing two weeks' holiday per annum. Legislation passed in 1951 and 1963 increased annual holidays to three and four weeks, respectively, and a five-week annual holiday was introduced in 1977.

Statutory working-hours reductions and longer holidays helped, among other things, to reduce inequalities between manual and salaried workers in Sweden. Many salaried employees in both the private and public sectors were already working a 40-hour week much earlier than this. Ever since 1970, therefore, manual and salaried workers, with occasional exceptions, have had the same normal working week, that is, 40 hours. Great differences still exist as to holidays, with the result that demands for equalization are still being voiced in present-day discussions of working hours.

Developments since 1970

Statutory weekly working hours have remained unaltered since 1970. Working-hours legislation was revised at the beginning of the 1970s in such a way that it was amalgamated with the provisions concerning the disposition of working hours previously contained in workers' protection or work environment legislation. The 1983 Working Hours Act also includes a number of provisions on part-time work.

Collective agreements have reduced the working hours of employees on shift work or with otherwise irregular or unsocial working hours. Workers on continuous triple shift have had a normal working week of 35–36 hours since 1975. The working hours of double-shift workers in industry have also been reduced during the 1980s, in such a way that for every working week completed they receive two hours' compensatory leave. Where conventional daytime employment is concerned, shorter normal working hours—under national federation agreements—apply only to banking and insurance, where the working week comprises 38.75 hours.

Reductions of normal working hours, however, account for only some of the changes undergone in actual working hours since 1970 (see Table 9-1).[1] The main reason for the reduction of actual working hours since 1972, the year when the 40-hour week was fully implemented, is above all the rapid growth of part-time employment during the 1970s. The proportion of part-time workers in the employed population rose from 17 percent in 1970 to 25.6 percent in 1982, since which time it has declined somewhat.

The growth of part-time employment coincided with a steep rise in female employment participation. The employment participation rate for women aged 16–64 rose gradually from 62.6 percent in 1970 to 81.1 percent in 1972, which is only a few percentage units short of the male participation rate. The swiftest increase has been reported for women with children under seven years old, as is confirmed by Figure 9-1.

Several factors contributed to the rise in women's economic activity: for example, the abolition of joint taxation of married couples, the expansion of the

TABLE 9-1.
Average Actual Working Hours per Week for Employed Persons in Sweden,
1970–1985

	1970	1971	1972	1973	1974	1975	1976	1977
Men	43.5	42.9	41.5	41.2	41.2	41.0	40.9	40.5
Women	32.8	32.5	31.0	31.6	31.6	31.5	31.2	30.9
Total	39.3	38.8	37.6	37.4	37.3	37.1	36.9	36.4

	1978	1979	1980	1981	1982	1983	1984	1985
Men	40.2	40.1	40.0	39.9	40.0	40.1	40.4	40.5
Women	30.8	30.9	30.9	30.9	31.1	31.2	31.6	32.0
Total	36.3	36.1	36.0	35.9	36.0	36.1	36.4	36.6

Note: Because of changes of definitions and methodology in the labor-force sample surveys, no comparable data are available for 1986 and 1987. Data based on the persons at work during the survey week.

public sector, and new educational developments during the 1950s and 1960s. The growth of women's gainful employment can also be viewed as a manifestation of the equal-opportunities policy that became distinctly apparent during the 1960s. But the almost explosive rise in part-time employment came as a virtual surprise to politicians and trade unions.

Part-time employment has changed since the beginning of the 1970s. For example, part-time employees today work more hours per week, on average, than used to be the case. The number of part-time employees working fewer than 20 hours per week is steadily declining, while increasing numbers are working relatively long part-time hours (30 per week). This is partly due to deliberate efforts on the part of the trade union organizations to secure minimum working hours, so as to ensure that part-time employees will participate in as many social benefits as possible. (The minimum qualification for unemployment insurance is 16 hours per week, and similar restrictions apply to a number of nonwage benefits governed by collective agreements.)

There is also another reason for the shift in favor of longer part-time hours. Looking back on events during the 1980s, one finds that most employees have sustained a loss of real earnings as a result of economic developments. Real hourly earnings, in other words, have declined. Households have offset this loss of purchasing power by stepping up their work input. Among other things, this has meant that part-time women employees have increased their part-time hours or switched to full-time work. Developments in this direction have probably been influenced by the tax reform introduced in 1983, which meant higher taxation rates but less marginal taxation for part-time employees.

Registered unemployment during the early 1980s was very high, by Swed-

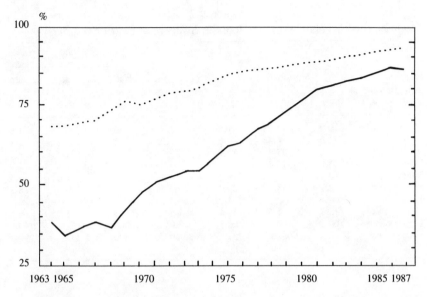

..... Women without children under 7 years of age.
_____ Women with children under 7 years of age.

FIGURE 9-1. Relative Employment Participation Rates for Women aged 25–54, with and without Children under 7 Years of Age

Source: Ministry of Labor, unpublished, 1988.

ish standards, culminating in 1983 at 3 percent. The growth of overt unemployment was accompanied by a growth in the number of part-time unemployed, that is, persons working part time but willing and able to work full time. This rise in part-time unemployment has continued since 1983. For the past several years the Swedish government has been allocating special funds to combat part-time unemployment. Table 9-2 shows the breakdown of employees' normal weekly working hours between various input levels. The term *working hours* as used here applies to both principal occupations as well as secondary ones (moonlighting). Persons whose normal working week falls short of 35 hours are classed as part-time employees.

Another factor influencing working hours since the beginning of the 1970s has been the development of absenteeism. Several laws were passed in the 1970s entitling employees to leave of absence for various purposes, for instance, parental leave (see the section below on statutory leave). Apart from illness and holidays, parental leave is the dominant cause of absence in the Swedish labor market. During 1987 women with children under seven years old had a relative absence rate of 33.3 percent.

These absence rates, of course, help to make average working hours per

TABLE 9-2.
Normal Weekly Working Hours in Sweden, 1987 (*in thousands*)

Hours/week in main and sideline job	Men %	Women %	All %	Of whom employees %	Sector		
					Nat'l gov't %	local gov't %	private %
1– 8	0.9	2.1	1.5	1.4	0.8	0.8	1.8
9–19	1.0	4.4	2.6	2.5	1.2	3.2	2.4
20–29	3.0	23.3	12.7	13.3	9.3	21.8	9.5
30–34	1.8	15.4	8.3	8.8	7.0	14.8	5.9
35–39	8.7	11.7	10.2	10.8	11.5	11.4	10.4
40	62.7	35.7	49.7	52.6	62.0	39.4	58.2
41–44	6.6	3.0	4.9	5.1	5.0	2.8	6.3
45+	15.2	4.5	10.1	5.5	5.3	5.5	5.5
Total percent	100	100	100	100	100	100	100
Total number (000)	2,256	2,081	4,337	3,940	403	1,238	2,298

employee and year in Sweden very low compared with other countries. Figure 9-2 shows changes in working hours per employee, with allowance made for absenteeism.

During the 1970s a declining trend was observed in overtime work in Sweden. The 1984 upturn brought a relatively steep rise in industrial overtime. This can be viewed in relation to the fall in real earnings earlier during the 1980s and the taxation reform of 1983. Overtime in the Swedish labor market during 1987 comprised 2.5 percent of the total number of hours worked. This overtime, however, was very unevenly distributed, both between different branches of the economy and different industries. Under the Working Hours Act an employee cannot be ordered to work more than 200 hours' overtime per annum. Much the same limit applies in the collective agreements that have been concluded on the subject of overtime and that thus override the statutory provisions.

General retirement age was reduced in 1976 from 67 to 65 years, at the same time as the principle of flexible retirement age between 60 and 70 was reaffirmed. Persons aged 60 or over are now entitled to what is termed early withdrawal of pension. The rules are considered unfavorable, however, because the rate of pension benefits is gradually reduced until normal retirement age. Only a very small percentage of people in the relevant age group have availed themselves of this option. Early retirement is also possible on grounds of re-dundancy and illness. A person who has been unemployed for a prolonged period can be awarded a permanent disability pension from the age of 60. The number of such pensions awarded on grounds of redundancy has risen steeply

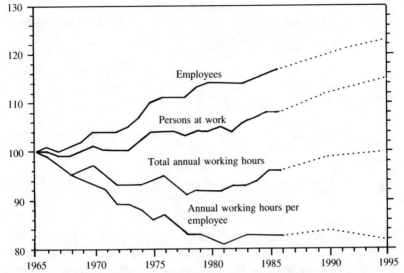

FIGURE 9-2. Employment and Working Hours in Sweden, 1965–1995
(index 1965 = 100)

Note: The forecast for the period ending 1995 was prepared by Statistics Sweden. Data concerning annual working hours refer to the total number of working hours for the entire economy.

during the 1980s, in connection with the radical restructuring of the mining,
shipbuilding, and steel industries.

Employers and unions have in many cases circumvented the provisions of
the Security of Employment Act on the order of dismissals by dismissing elderly workers in connection with structural changes. Once they have drawn on
unemployment insurance benefits for the maximum number of days, they are
awarded permanent disability pensions on grounds of redundancy. The system
is currently being reviewed because of the heavy expenditure that it involves.
The award of a permanent disability pension on grounds of illness or redundancy does not, in contrast to early withdrawals, influence future entitlement to
an old-age pension. Table 9-3 shows the number of persons aged 60–64 with
permanent disability pensions of various kinds, compared with the total population in each age group. (See also Table 9–5. Partial retirement schemes are
discussed below.)

Figure 9-3 shows changes in the working-hours inputs of different age
groups of the population in 1970 and 1983. Work input in the younger age
groups is declining because of prolonged youth education.

The extent of irregular and unsocial working hours was charted in special
surveys during 1974 and 1982.[2] Daytime hours, that is, those between 6:45

TABLE 9-3.

Persons Aged 60–64 with Disability Pensions and Early Withdrawals of
Pension, December 1986

	Age					
	60	61	62	63	64	60–64
All persons with disability pensions	17,379	21,259	24,728	28,066	30,388	121,820
Persons with disability pensions for labor-market reasons	811	2,119	3,583	4,476	5,089	16,078
Persons with early withdrawals of pensions	1,084	1,689	2,268	3,492	4,551	13,084
Population	88,911	91,470	92,197	93,366	93,438	459,382

A.M. and 5:45 P.M. Monday to Friday, were worked by 70 percent of all
gainfully employed persons in 1982, as against 67 percent in 1974. The proportion of shift workers (using a relatively strict definition of triple and double
shift work) fell slightly, from 4.9 percent in 1974 to 3.8 percent in 1982. The
working-hours arrangement that grew most was roster work, which rose from
7.5 percent to 10.6 percent in 1982. Roster work occurs, for example, in medical services, commerce and transport, and 32.2 percent of roster employees in
1982 had night work. The proportion of employees with staggered daytime
working hours fell from 10.6 percent in 1974 to 7.6 percent in 1982. A very
small proportion of employees (0.6 percent) worked on Saturdays and Sundays
only. Of these, 75 percent were aged between 20 and 24 and 98 percent worked
part time.

Flexibility within the Framework of Laws and Collective Agreements

In most cases the organization of working hours at the individual
workplace in Sweden is decided at a number of different levels. First of all,
The Working Hours Act imposes certain restrictions:

- Normal working hours must not exceed 40 hours per week or an average
  of 40 hours for a period of not more than four weeks.
- Night work between midnight and 5:00 A.M. is prohibited (though there
  are general exceptions).
- An employee must have continuous weekly rest of 36 hours per seven-
  day period.
- A rest break must be taken after five hours' work.
- Overtime must not exceed 48 or 50 hours per four-week period or month
  and 200 hours per annum.

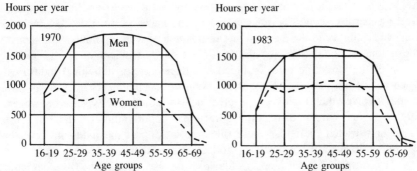

FIGURE 9-3. Annual Working Hours in Sweden for 1970 and 1983, by Age Groups

As of 1983, deviations from the provisions concerning night work and overtime have been permissible by means of short-term local agreements (valid for one month).

In cases where the Working Hours Act is entirely overridden by collective agreements, the agreements usually include corresponding restrictions. The agreement for manual workers in the engineering industry, for example, includes rules making it possible for average working hours to be computed on an annual basis. Collective agreements also open up the possibility of more extensive deviations, for example, from the rules concerning night work and overtime.

Agreements at the industrial level usually include rules on overtime compensation (a question not governed by statute) and compensation for unsocial working hours. Many industrial agreements also include what are known as guillotine rules, to be applied when the parties at local level are unable to agree on any other disposition of working hours. These guillotine provisions normally indicate the times between which working hours may be distributed and the forms in which shift work or its counterpart is permissible. The guillotine rules may be termed a relic of the days when working hours were fixed at industrial level, but they are of course a practical aid to the settlement of local disputes. In some cases the disposition rules of the agreement for an entire industry preclude any local deviations.

In most cases nowadays, the more detailed design of working hours is settled locally at the workplace level. Both precedent and statutory provisions in Swedish labor law make the disposition of working hours a matter to be decided by the employer. But the employer is required in all circumstances to negotiate with the local union organizations before making a decision. The employer's powers of discretion in this respect are, of course, restricted by the statutory provisions or collective agreements applying within the employer's field. Whatever the provisions that apply, Swedish employers have comparatively generous scope for maneuver, which makes it possible for them to achieve flexibility in the duration and disposition of working hours. In practice, the union organizations have the last word on the subject of flexibility, by virtue of the guillotine rules included in agreements for individual industries. Then again, time classed as unsocial in collective agreements, as well as shift work, involves the employer in a great deal of additional expense on wages. However, one cannot disregard the fact that opportunities of flexibility are fairly unrestricted in fields where rules are lacking at the industrial level or where employers are not bound by collective agreements.

No conspectus is currently available of the use made in the Swedish labor market of the opportunities for flexibility that have now been described. There are a few examples of markedly deviating working hours, for example, 12-hour shifts for 24-hour operations in industry and, more recently, in connection with CAD-CAM technology. One has the impression, however, that both employers and employees are relatively conservative and are disposed to retain traditional working-hours patterns, for both cultural and social reasons. This is particularly true in sectors of the labor market—for example, manufacturing industry and construction—that are thoroughly organized and dominated by men. The rules of the engineering agreement concerning the computation of average weekly working hours on an annual basis are considered, at least by the employees, to have been introduced in order to facilitate the advance working of odd days between major festivals. On the other hand, this agreement does not seem to cater to the employers' interest in varying working hours according to fluctuations in demand.

At the central level, the trade union organizations are trying to restrict irregular and unsocial working hours, and these efforts are sometimes at variance with demands from employees to be allowed to work during odd but better paid hours. There have been instances of local union branches' opposing the change from shift work to daily working hours, against the wishes of both employer and central union organization.

Retail trade today presents a wide variety of working hours. Since the abolition of statutory opening hours at the beginning of the 1970s, shop working times have been extended to include late evenings, Sundays, and public holidays. Sweden has more in common with the United States than with other European countries where shop opening hours are concerned. At the same time, retail employees have been able to secure very good rules of compensation for work during odd hours.

Under the 1977 Holidays Act, which is also discretionary, employees are entitled to five weeks' paid holiday for every qualifying year completed. The Holidays Act also entitles employees to carry forward one week's holiday per annum for a period of up to five years. Public employees and certain private-sector salaried employees are entitled by collective agreement to longer holidays and sometimes also to more favorable qualifying conditions. The disposition of holidays can be decided in several different ways. The amount of influence exerted in this respect varies a great deal from one sector of employment to another and also between manual and salaried workers.

Individual opportunities for flexibility have been expanded in Sweden since the 1970s through several enactments on leave of absence. These enactments entitle the individual to adapt his or her working hours to personal circumstances.

The most utilized and best known of these enactments is the Parental Leave Act, which entitles both parents to full-time leave of absence from work until their child is 18 months old, and also entitles them to work 75 percent of normal working hours until the child is eight years old or has completed its first year of school. This leave of absence, however, compensates only partially for loss of earnings. At present, parents can share 360 parental insurance benefit days between them, of which 270 days carry a rate of benefit equaling 90 percent of regular earnings and 90 days confer a guaranteed rate that is the same for everybody. The 360 paid days can be drawn in the form of full, half, or quarter-days.

Utilization of parental leave in connection with childbirth can be observed through the benefit-day statistics produced by the National Social Insurance Board.[3] These show that paid leave of absence following childbirth is taken principally by women. Of the 27 percent of married fathers who took parental leave during the child's first 18 months (children born in 1981), two-thirds were on leave for not more than two months. The higher the mother's income, the larger is the percentage of fathers taking parental leave. The husband's income seems to make less difference. One study showed that men sharing leave of absence acquired greater understanding for the child and its needs later on during its formative years.[4] These fathers, consequently, participate more actively than others in the education and upbringing of their children.

There are no other particulars available concerning the numbers of people who directly avail themselves of statutory entitlement to part-time work. The labor-force sample surveys convey a picture of the overall extent of part-time employment among, respectively, men and women with children under 18. Men with children under seven years of age are seldom employed part time and, moreover, to no greater extent than men without children. On the other hand, a definite majority of mothers of young children are employed part time. These mothers work part time a good deal more often than women without children under seven (see Table 9-4).

This, of course, is a state of affairs which, from the viewpoint of equal opportunities, has frequently been called into question. What is more, the differences are augmented by the fact that men with children under seven work more overtime than do other groups (cf. Table 9-2). There is hardly any deep resistance on the part of employers to part-time work by fathers of young chil-

TABLE 9-4.
Hours Usually Worked per Week in 1987
by Gainfully Employed Men and Women
with Children under 7 Years Old
(*percentages*)

Hours per week	Men	Women
1–19	0.5	6.6
20–34	3.2	54.7
35–39	9.7	8.3
40	62.6	24.6
41+	23.9	5.7

dren. Instead, the opposition apparently comes from male colleagues. This is particularly apparent in manual occupations where men predominate. Parents are also entitled to paid leave of absence in order to look after sick children for up to 60 days per child annually. Men account for roughly 40 percent of all benefit days.

Another important component of statutory leave is the entitlement of employees aged 60 or over to partial pension. This is conditional on the employee's having previously worked at least 20 hours per week and on the reduction of working hours in connection with partial retirement amounting to at least five hours. The employee has to reach a personal agreement with the employer concerning part-time employment; the statutory provisions are concerned only with entitlement to compensation. When the reform was introduced, the compensation rate was 65 percent. This was reduced to 50 percent in 1981 but restored to 65 percent in 1987. Table 9-5 shows, among other things, the percentages of eligible persons exercising their right to partial pension.

The Education Leave Act entitles employees to full-time leave of absence or part-time work for longer or shorter periods. The educational activities need not be connected with the employee's work. The only stipulation is that they must be scheduled. The act does not provide loss-of-earnings compensation. Its original purpose was to provide educational opportunities for the undereducated, but primarily it is believed to have been utilized by relatively well-educated persons who are accustomed to educational activity. The act has come in for a great deal of criticism from employers, partly because educational leave can continue for several years. The labor-force sample surveys indicate that only about 1 percent of all employees are partly or wholly absent from work because of educational activity.

In addition to this legislation concerning leave of absence, there are a number of enactments, but these are more limited in duration and have had less

TABLE 9-5.
Persons Electing to Receive Partial Pensions, 1977–1986

Year	Total (*thousands*)	Percentage of Eligible Employees	Self-Employed Persons (*thousands*)	Percentage of Eligible Employees Who Are Self-Employed
1977	32	12		
1978	42	16		
1979	49	22		
1980	68	27	2	6
1981	65	24	3	8
1982	62	22	3	8
1983	55	20	2	7
1984	47	17	2	6
1985	38	13	1	4
1986	32	12	1	4

Source: National Social Insurance Board.

noticeable impact on total work input. They include, for example, entitlement to leave of absence in order to take part in voluntary activities in school and entitlement to leave of absence for shop stewards to attend trade union activities and trade union education.

The legislation on leave of absence provides certain opportunities for the parties to conclude collective agreements that deviate from the statutory provisions. These facilities have not been utilized, and so in practice there are two distinct codes of rules at workplaces: one governing collective working hours, and another governing individual deviations.

It is a debatable point whether the enactment of the leave of absence legislation reflected a consistently thought-out model of working-hours organization. The enactments were successively introduced during the 1970s, a period when the government and the Riksdag embarked on a wide-ranging regulation of labor-market conditions. Some enactments, such as the Educational Leave Act, were passed during the Social Democratic term of office ending in 1976, whereas, for example, the Parental Leave Act was passed during the nonsocialist period of office, between 1976 and 1982. And, in fact, it is only during the 1980s that working-hours questions have come to be discussed more systematically and holistically. Previous decisions to reduce the retiring age, prolong schooling, or introduce legislation on leave of absence were usually made separately, without much consideration for the impact of one alternative on other measures. What is more, several policy decisions were made without any investigation of the actual preferences of different groups or the population generally.

As a result of the government's and Riksdag's making increasing provision for individual demands for flexibility, the trade union organizations were able, well into the 1980s, to maintain their traditional line of standardized solutions for working hours.

The Working-Hours Debate during the 1970s and 1980s

Soon after the introduction of the 40-hour week in Sweden, a discussion ensued concerning a rapid reduction of normal working time to a six-hour day or a 30-hour week. The idea came from the Social Democratic Union of Swedish Women, who looked on the six-hour day as a means of attaining full equality between men and women both at work and in the family. When the debate began, social attitudes were still dominated by the developmental optimism generated by the rapid economic growth of the 1950s and the 1960s. The six-hour day quickly gained the ear of the Social Democratic Party and the big union organizations. The Swedish Trade Union Confederation (LO), which represents manual workers in Sweden, had already come out in favor of the six-hour day at its 1976 congress.

The Social Democratic Party made the six-hour day part of its program following a congress resolution in 1975. The Central Organization of Salaried Employees (TCO) also adopted the principle of the six-hour day or 30-hour week at its 1976 congress. And SACO/SR, the central graduates' organization of higher level salaried managers and professional staff, endorsed the principle of the six-hour day in a working hours program adopted by its congress in 1979.

In 1974 the then Social Democratic government appointed a Committee for the Study of Working Hours (DELFA), whose tasks included the collection of research material on previous general reductions of working hours.[5] The government supported the long-term target of a 30-hour week but at the same time declared that "the parties must decide the rate at which this long-term objective is to be achieved and how general reductions of working hours are to be balanced against other working hours reforms and against other improvements in living standards."

Developmental optimism was subdued during the mid-1970s, in the economic aftermath of the oil crisis, and the six-hour day tended more and more to assume the character of a long-term objective. At the same time, interest in the six-hour day was so powerful as to effectively overshadow other demands for working-hours reforms in the course of general debate. Throughout the 1970s the Social Democratic Union of Swedish Women emphatically opposed "separate solutions" in the matter of working hours, for example, for parents of young children. Misgivings were voiced, for example, in connection with the gradual expansion of parental insurance by Social Democratic and nonsocialist governments during the 1970s.

The growing number of parents of young children in the employment sector called for a rapid expansion of child care services. The difficulties involved in achieving full public coverage of child care needs were probably one of the reasons why the women's movement gradually accepted the need for separate working-hours arrangements for parents of young children.

The climate of debate changed toward the end of the 1970s, when the nonsocialist government was able to carry through its proposals entitling parents of young children to reduced working hours without any unduly vociferous protests from the groups that had previously been adamant in their demands for a universal six-hour day. And it was during the 1970s that the practical difficulties entailed by both parents combining parenthood with full-time employment became increasingly apparent. At the same time, progressively greater attention came to be paid to the children's needs, since many children were spending more than ten hours a day in child-care institutions or with private sitters.

The demand for a universal six-hour day was originally viewed as a means of counteracting part-time employment among women. The rapid growth of part-time employment during the 1970s was regarded as a growing threat to the promotion of equal opportunities. The parliamentary Equal Opportunities Advisory Committee appointed during the 1970s undertook a study of conditions for part-time employees, which resulted in a number of specific proposals aimed at improving their status.[6] These included demands for minimum working hours and demands for the general entitlement of part-time employees to longer working hours or full-time employment.

Opinions often differed a great deal as to whether the increase in part-time employment meant an ongoing consolidation of women's position in the employment sector or the opposite. There were also many divisions of opinion regarding the causes of part-time employment, for instance, as to whether it was voluntary or whether certain employers were only recruiting part-time labor or were forcing women to change from full time to part time.

Attitudes concerning part-time employment have gradually become more balanced. A study during the early 1980s showed that most people working part time were doing so by choice.[7] Quite contrary to what many people had believed, it was found that the growth of part-time employment during the 1970s had resulted from the entry of previously nonemployed women into the labor market as part-time workers. At the same time, a closer analysis of movements in the labor market showed that the proportion changing from full time to part time during the 1970s was offset by an equally large proportion changing in the opposite direction. The group reducing their working hours mainly included women who had had their first or second child. Those changing from part time to full time included many women around age forty who no longer had young children to look after. These findings corroborated the conclusion that part-time work was a means for women to keep in touch with the labor market and to combine parenthood with economic activity. Part of the expansion of part-time employment during the 1970s could also be attributed to purely demographic factors, that is, to an unusually large proportion of women of childbearing age during the period in question.

Studies that approach the problems of part-time employment in economic terms show that developments could also be attributed to purely private economic considerations.[8] The progressive nature of taxation rates, with heavy marginal taxation of full-time employees in middle income brackets, coupled with certain income-related transfers (e.g., the housing allowance), made it beneficial to many families for only one spouse to work full time. Economic considerations, however, do not account for the fact that it was (and is) mostly women who reduced their working hours. There is only one possible explanation: sexual stereotypes.

Gösta Rehn's proposals for flexible working life were drafted at a time when the debate on the six-hour day was in full swing. Whereas in other countries those proposals lent powerful impetus to the debate, in Sweden they remained relatively unknown throughout the 1970s. Besides, some of Rehn's proposals—for example, those concerning educational leave and recurrent education for the working population—were already included on the political agenda. His essay "Towards a Society of Free Choice," written in 1974, was not translated into Swedish until 1985.[9]

By the end of the 1970s the working-hours debate in Sweden had almost ground to a halt. Activities in the trade-union organizations were at a low ebb, as was reflected by the activities of DELFA itself, which practically ceased to exist. The work-sharing debate that began in the European Economic Community (EEC) and elsewhere attracted a certain amount of interest. The review of working-hours legislation that took place between 1978 and 1982 was unaffected by any demands for changes in normal working hours. The proposals resulting from that review were concerned with the computation of overtime and with provisions governing additional time worked by part-time employees. The concept of additional time was introduced partly in order to prevent employers' using part-time workers as contingency reserves by varying their working hours according to fluctuations in demand.

After the 1982 parliamentary elections, a Social Democratic government was returned to office following six years of nonsocialist rule. Rising unemployment was the paramount election issue. In 1983 the government issued new terms of reference to DELFA, which at the same time was also made to include parliamentary representatives.[10] The terms of reference included the question whether working hours measures of different kinds could be used to combat unemployment. This question was prompted more by a desire to supply necessary knowledge to public opinion than by any intention of gathering arguments to justify any such redirection of employment policy. (The main organizations in the labor market have firmly rejected demands for work sharing ever since the 1930s.)

Berit Rollén, undersecretary in the Ministry of Labor, who took over the chair of DELFA in 1982, had played a very active part in the debate on the six-hour day during the 1970s. As DELFA chair, she saw to it that the scope of the working-hours debate was appreciably widened. This involved reviving thoughts of a six-hour working day and taking in such new issues as flexibility. Under Rollén's leadership, DELFA helped to bring about a new and very lively discussion of working hours, not least within the union organizations. She herself derived progressively more inspiration from Gösta Rehn and was instrumental in getting his report for the Organization for Economic Cooperation and Development (OECD) translated into Swedish and published by DELFA in 1985. In this way she has also been one of Rehn's main advocates within the Social Democratic Party. She was heavily criticized by the League of Social Democratic Women on this account.

Between 1983 and 1985 DELFA issued 16 debate publications of its own concerning working-hours questions and organized a succession of conferences on various subjects.[11] At the beginning of 1986 Berit Rollén resigned as undersecretary of state at the Ministry of Labor and relinquished her chairmanship of DELFA, and DELFA was gradually disbanded.

In 1984, because of the poor rate of economic growth, the government appointed a Pensions Committee to study the general supplementary pensions (ATP) system in Sweden and the workings of the flexible retirement-age system. In addition, so as to facilitate a pay settlement, the government appointed a new Holidays Commission in 1985 to suggest ways of equalizing holiday benefits between different categories of employees.

At the beginning of 1987, following a protracted internal discussion, the government appointed a Working Hours Committee to undertake a complete assessment of the various demands existing for working-hours policy measures. These include questions relating to both pensions and holidays, as well as demands for general reductions of weekly working hours and longer parental leave. The committee has also been instructed by the government to investigate what are termed "alternative working hours reforms," including Gösta Rehn's system.

Current Demands for Working-Hours Policy Measures

In 1984 DELFA conducted a survey of employees' attitudes to various working-hours reforms. One finding is that about one-fifth of all full-time employees would be prepared to consider reducing their working hours with a corresponding reduction in pay and that one-fifth of all part-time employees would like to work longer hours. About 45 percent of all full-time

TABLE 9-6.
Employees' Preferences Concerning Daily Working-Hour
Reductions (*Percentages*)

	Preferred a Shorter Week	*Of Whom* Preferred a Daily Reduction
Full-time employees		
Men	62.0	34.0
Women	71.2	42.6
Part-time employees	28.0	27.4
Men	26.7	26.6
Women	28.2	28.0
All employees	55.3	36.0
Men	59.7	33.8
Women	50.6	38.7

Note: Employees who wanted reduced working hours accepted either a corresponding reduction of pay or of future wage increases.
Source: DELFA, Report No. 7.

employees prefer a shorter working week to higher pay. This means that more than two-thirds of all employees would be prepared, one way or another, to reduce their working hours.

The same survey shows that more than one-third of all employees who want shorter working hours would prefer a shorter working day. Women are more interested than men both in a total and a daily reduction of working hours, as can be seen from Table 9-6. About a quarter of all employees wanting shorter working hours preferred longer holidays. Men predominate in this respect. Earlier retirement age was advocated above all by elderly persons, and especially by elderly men.

The results of the DELFA survey came as rather a surprise to the union organizations, which for several years had been restraining demands for shorter working hours, in view of the decline in real earnings. This led to a discussion concerning the relevance of such attitude surveys and also to initial moves by the unions themselves to chart their members' preferences. Another surprising result was that interest in reductions of daily working hours proved to be a good deal less than had previously been believed, and also that the lines of demarcation were not class-related but tended more to be bound up with the age and sex of employees.

The graduates' organization, SACO/SR, is the first of the three big organizations to have abandoned the demand for a six-hour day, partly in view of the highly variable preferences of its members. SACO/SR's current standpoint is that the organization must promote flexible working-hours arrangements, based essentially on the model proposed by Gösta Rehn.

The TCO executive set up an internal working-hours inquiry in 1984 to formulate a uniform working-hours policy and indicate future strategy on this subject.[12] The committee devoted special attention to the question of flexibility and took the view that an abolition of all statutory provisions and collective agreements on working hours would deprive employees of the opportunity of influencing their own working hours. The committee found that greater liberty would have to be created and secured by means of legally binding provisions in the form of legislation and collective agreements. The committee reiterated that collective agreements are essential in order for employees to influence their working hours. TCO is urged to continue its efforts to achieve further reductions of normal working time in the direction of a 30-hour week and a six-hour normal day, as well as working-hours arrangements conducive to greater equality between men and women, and, finally, greater liberty for the individual to choose or influence his or her own working hours and to exercise a greater measure of codetermination in the working-hours context. The representative of the Swedish Foremen's and Supervisors' Association on the committee dissented from the recommendation of a 30-hour working week. The committee also recommends a shift in the emphasis of union working-hours policy toward greater individualization, as well as improved opportunities for individual accumulation of time off. The committee feels that part-time employees should be entitled by law to increase their working hours, and it proposes tightening up the Working Hours Act on several points. The proposals put forward by the TCO committee on working hours are a striking example of the difficulties which unions are now experiencing in framing a uniform policy on working hours.

The TCO executive recently advocated an expansion of parental insurance, which would provide compensation for 18 months after the birth of a child. TCO is also campaigning for better opportunities for flexible retirement, including "occupational pensions" from the age of 60 onward.

At its 1986 congress, LO reaffirmed its long-term objective of a six-hour working day and a 30-hour week.[13] At the same time LO decided to press for a normal working week of less than 40 hours for several groups with irregular and unsociable working hours. The congress resolution also requires LO to press demands for six weeks' holiday and to campaign for the prolongation of parental insurance benefits to two years.

Before the 1986 LO congress, Rudolf Meidner and Anna Hedberg published a report entitled "A Free Year in Mid-Life," which is something of an embodiment of Rehn's ideas.[14] Meidner and Hedberg proposed that all employees should be entitled to a sabbatical year after age 40, and that this should be financed by means of a general funding system. The report was given a rather cool reception by LO, which asked, for example, how an ordinary LO manual worker would be able to utilize the free year. The critics argued that the free year would mainly benefit highly educated, economically powerful groups with advanced leisure interests.

At the central level LO has hardly played any part at all in general discussions concerning flexible or individualized working hours. One of the most important issues at present where LO is concerned is that of improving opportunities of flexible retirement from age 60. LO advocates a system making it possible for workers of long standing to retire on full pension from the age of 60.

In 1986 the Metal Workers' Union and the Factory Workers' Union, both affiliated with LO, and the Union of Clerical and Technical Employees in Industry affiliated with TCO, drafted a scheme for a working-hours bank, inspired partly by Gösta Rehn's working-hours model. The idea is for each individual to decide for himself or herself the way in which working hours are to be reduced. An individual working more than the normal number of hours can aggregate leave for subsequent use. Through this scheme, unions queried, for example, whether the six-hour day is at all widely supported by their members. The scheme triggered a fierce debate with the Social Democratic Women.

In a membership survey completed recently, the Metal Workers' Union has made a closer study as to whether members want their working hours to be reduced, and if so, in what way. The results show that 46 percent prefer an increase in real earnings, 42 percent prefer shorter working hours, and the rest are undecided. In the event that working hours are reduced by two hours per week, 12 percent wanted to have a daily reduction, 42 percent wanted to work two hours less on Friday afternoons, and 41 percent replied that they would prefer to "save up" two hours a week and take time off on special occasions. Some of the observations resulting from the survey are that preferences concerning the manner in which working hours can be reduced do not differ between men and women, and also that union members working for small firms prefer Friday afternoons off, whereas those working in bigger undertakings prefer an accumulative system.

The Swedish Employers' Confederation (SAF), which represents the majority of private employers in Sweden, does not believe that any scope for a general reduction of working hours will be available within the foreseeable future. In 1987 the SAF executive took a number of stands on the subject of working hours.[15] The SAF sought, among other things, to give priority to measures aimed at reducing short-term absenteeism. The SAF also underlines the importance of flexible working hours, closely adapted to the conditions of individual industries and companies. This, the SAF argues, calls for decentralized decisions on the arrangement of working hours. The SAF considers it vitally important—for recruitment reasons—that companies should make more efforts to adjust working hours to the employees' preferences. It also considers it important that employer and employee should be at liberty to agree between themselves on part-time employment.

It is worth noting that the SAF devotes little attention to legislative measures. The SAF observes that absenteeism has grown as a result of legislation concerning leave of absence, and the organization was highly critical of the enactments when they came into force. However, it is not demanding a repeal of the legislation. Quite recently, the SAF proposed that retirement age be raised to 67, in view of the financial situation affecting the earnings-based pension system (ATP). The SAF argues that, if the present retirement age is retained, ATP contributions will have to be substantially increased. The organization goes on to point out that average life expectancy has increased for both men and women.

Public employers have not adopted such clear-cut stands as the SAF in the matter of working hours. The Federation of County Councils, which is the employers' organization representing medical authorities in Sweden, has had to contend with serious problems of recruitment in medical services during recent years. A number of local employers have suggested the experimental arrangement of a six-hour day with no reduction of pay as a means of attracting personnel for medical services. The federation, whose executive committee has a Social Democratic majority, has rejected these proposals with reference to current agreements, but in order to avoid criticism, it has referred the matter to the government and the Working Hours Committee. No experimentation has yet materialized, the Working Hours Committee having made clear at the very commencement of its activities that any experiments would require unanimity among the parties. The government, for its part, has declared that no funds are available to cover the additional wage costs that an experimental six-hour working day would involve.

At its 1987 Congress the Social Democratic Party adopted a timetable for specific general reductions of working hours. According to this timetable, the 35-hour week should be implemented by the early years of the next century. The congress also resolved on an expansion of parental insurance to one and a half years. The question of quotas between mothers and fathers availing themselves of parental leave benefit days was discussed at length, but is not included in the congress resolution.

Of the nonsocialist parties in the Riksdag, both the Centre Party and the Liberal Party, are in principle in favor of general working-hours reductions. The Conservative Party (or Moderates) advocate deregulation—as regards both legislation and collective agreements—and maintain that each employee should be able to make a personal agreement with the employer on working hours. This, the Moderates maintain, would meet demands for flexibility. The three nonsocialist parties have put forward a joint program of family policy as an alternative both to the expansion of parental insurance and to the expansion of public child care. This program provides for the abolition of state subsidies to child-care institutions and their replacement with a care allowance paid directly to parents of children under three years. The aim here is to give parents a wider choice, above all as regards child-care arrangements, but also to make it easier for parents to refrain from gainful employment.

The Left Party Communists (VPK) firmly adhere to the proposal of a six-hour working day and have introduced legislation in the Riksdag every year during the 1980s for its immediate implementation.

As the governing party, the Social Democrats are taking an exceedingly wary line on the working-hours question, as witness the appointment of the Working Hours Committee. At the same time it is abundantly clear that the question of working hours will have to be subordinated to other important policy aims, for instance, a stable, efficient labor market and good economic growth.

Young cohorts will be diminishing rapidly during the 1990s, and this is expected to result in an overall shortage of labor. In the meantime the proportion of elderly persons in the population is increasing, which means heavier demands on caring services for the elderly and on the medical sector. Against this background, working-hours reductions have already come to be challenged from within the government. The government is also working quite actively to counteract part-time unemployment and involuntary part-time work. It is exceedingly averse to demands for additional legislation on leave of absence, its attitude being that these questions should be settled through collective agreements. Demands have recently been presented, for example, for leave of absence for top-level sporting activities and for work in voluntary organizations.

One big question which will have to be settled sooner or later concerns the future of the ATP system. This issue includes LO's demands for occupational pensions from age 60, as well as the necessity of levying increased contributions from industry to finance existing commitments.

The question of working-hours reductions is closely bound up with pay developments. There is also a clear historical connection between pay developments and working-hours reductions. Since the beginning of the 1950s about one-fifth of the available scope for pay improvements has been utilized in the form of shorter weekly working hours or longer holidays.[16] The development of real earnings has been highly adverse for a number of years, and this has had a restraining effect on demands for continuing working-hours reductions. The economic recovery that has now taken place augurs the reappearance of working-hours reductions among the demands presented by employees in collective bargaining. It remains to be seen, however, exactly how these demands will be framed.

The organizational structure of trade unionism provides but a poor reflection of the existing interests of present-day members where the working-hours question is concerned. This makes future working hours a volatile question at all levels, both as between unions and employers and in political assemblies. Within the union organizations there are disagreements not only between the sexes but also between different organizational levels. Members are objecting more and more to the authoritarian attitude that still characterizes parts of the trade union movement. Labor legislation has empowered unions to represent employees. This is part of the reason for good membership growth, coupled with the fact that the union organizations today also offer their members such benefits as favorable insurance terms for individual needs. The trend toward individualization at work in society and the constant growth in the competence and awareness of the individual will probably oblige the union organizations to reconsider the axiom that "the workers don't know what's good for them." And in the long term the union principle of always going for standardized solutions will probably have to give way to more flexible arrangements, both as regards working hours and in other connections.

In political quarters there are also manifest problems where the treatment of working-hours questions is concerned. In the first place, it is unclear how much of the working-hours question is a matter of incomes policy, added to which there is an unclear line of demarcation between management-union and political questions. Second, there is a purely ideological divide between the socialist and nonsocialist camps and within the parties. The Social Democratic Party, for example, has not set any definite course to follow. Instead, there are a number of conflicting interests, *viz.*, those of the women's movement, and those of the party economists, who are more concerned with the output capacity of the economy than with social needs.

Toward a Society of Free Choice

Gösta Rehn's proposals concerning a flexible working life can be viewed as part of the efforts that were made at the beginning of the 1970s to realign the Swedish model, that is, to strengthen the position of the individual and at the same time to improve the efficiency of the labor market. Rehn's proposals were partly based on giving the individual a great deal of influence on his or her own work input by means of a general system to finance various forms of leave. In Rehn's system, opportunities for leave are geared to cyclical fluctuations, which means that the system could become a part of stabilization policy, rectifying imbalances in the labor market in different demand situations. Another important consideration for Rehn was that of facilitating further education for members of the labor force.

But Rehn looked one step further, to the restriction of individual liberty resulting from progressively stronger job security guarantees and the stabilization of each company's workforce. Rehn's model would reduce the necessity and scope of statutory rules of job security. Society, therefore, to quote Rehn's terminology, ought to promote "the security of wings," not just that of the "mussel shell," so as to counteract signs of a polarization of the labor force into "one part which can enjoy security and good earnings and another part which, formally speaking, is free from commitments but has to live in poverty, with only temporary and poorly paid jobs."

In many countries, just as in Sweden, there are today clear signs of a polarization of the labor force into those who have secure jobs and those who are constantly switching from job to temporary job. Between 15 and 20 percent of all employees in Sweden have fixed-term contracts, due partly to the many temporary jobs generated when parents of young children take leave of absence. There are a large number of young persons, especially women, constantly moving from one fixed-term contract to the next. They are often excluded from unemployment insurance and other social safeguards. Nor do they participate in corporate education activities.

The main impact of Rehn's model has been to stimulate ideological and theoretical discussion in Sweden. His visionary model combines many important components of Swedish welfare policy, the individual's freedom of choice and security of livelihood, and the need for adaptability in the economy. Developments in Sweden can now be said to be heading in the direction that Rehn had earlier indicated. His model, however, implies almost a complete transformation of the system of social insurance, which is considered one of the most vital ingredients of welfare policy. It is hard to imagine such a thoroughgoing change taking place, at least in the short term. But as the six-hour day loses ground in public opinion, Rehn's ideas of working-hours flexibility are steadily gaining adherents. Developments in working life, with progressively greater demands on the education and competence of the labor force, also lend substance to Rehn's ideas. Last but not least, Rehn's proposals may be worth testing as a means of counteracting signs of polarization in the labor market, due partly to well-meant but rigid, counterproductive regulatory safeguards.

Notes

1. Statistics on participation rates and working hours in text and tables are collected from the Swedish Labour Force Surveys, unless otherwise indicated. Concepts and definitions are essentially the same as those applied in the American Labor Force Surveys.

2. *Oregelbundna och obekväma arbetstider*, Rapport 37 i serien om levnadsförhållandena Statistiska Centralbyrån (Stockholm, 1983).

3. Riksförsäkringsverket, "Fäders uttag av föräldraledighet för barn under två år födda 1982," *Statistikinformation* Is-I (1987): 1.

4. "Att dela på föräldaledigheten—föräldraskap i förändring," socialstyrelsens skriftseries, Föräldrar och barn, no. 6.

5. DELFA published two reports during the 1970s, as well as a study of the development of part-time employment: "Kortare arbetstid När? Hur?" *Svenska Offentliga Utredningar* (1976):34; "Arbetstiderna infor 90-talet," *Svenska Offentliga Utredningar* (1979):48; "Deltidarbetets utveckling," *Departementsserierna Arbetsmarknadsdepartementet (DsA)* (1977):7.

6. "Deltidsanställdas villkor," *Svenska Offentliga Utredningar* (1976):6.

7. Marianne Pettersson, *Deltidsarbetet i Sverige* (Stockholm: Arbetslivscentrum, 1981).

A Society of Free Choice 229

8. Stig Tegle, "Part-Time Employment," *Lund Economic Studies*, no. 35 (Lund, 1985): Siv Gustavsson and Petra Lantz, *Arbete och löner* (Stockholm: Industrins Utredningsinstitut/Arbetslivscentrum, 1985).

9. Republished: Gösta Rehn, "Towards a Society of Free Choice," in J. J. Wiatr and R. Rose, eds., *Comparing Public Policies* (Wroclaw et al.: Zak ad Narodowy im. Ossolinskich/Wydawnictwo Polskiej Akademii Nauk, 1977), pp. 121–157.

10. Supplementary Guidelines to the Delegation for the Study of Working Hours, Dir. 1983:12.

11. DELFA (= Delegationen för arbetstidsfrågor), *Kan arbetstidsförkortningar användas som medel i kampen mot arbetslöshet?*, DELFA-rapport no. 1 (Stockholm: Arbetsmarknadsdepartementet, 1983); DELFA, *Önskad arbetstid*, DELFA-rapport no. 3 (Stockholm: Arbetsmarknadsdepartementet, 1984); DELFA, *Arbetstidens längd och arbetslöshet/sysselsättning i vissa OECD-länder*, DELFA-rapport no. 4 (Stockholm: Arbetsmarknadsdepartementet, 1984); DELFA, *Arbetstid och driftstid*, DELFA-rapport no. 5 (Stockholm: Arbetsmarknadsdepartementet, 1984); DELFA, *Internationell utblick*, DELFA-rapport no. 6 (Stockholm: Arbetsmarknadsdepartementet, 1984); DELFA, *Önskad arbetstid II*, DELFA-rapport no. 7 (Stockholm: Arbetsmarknadsdepartementet, 1985); DELFA, *70-timmars arbetsvecka—hur skall den fördelas?*, DELFA-rapport no. 10 (Stockholm: Arbetsmarknadsdepartmentet, 1985); DELFA, *Flexiblare arbetstid—på gott och ont*, DELFA-rapport no. 11 (Stockholm: Arbetsmarknadsdepartementet, 1985); DELFA, *Arbetstid, driftstid och socialt liv*, DELFA-rapport no. 14 (Stockholm: Arbetsmarknadsdepartementet, 1985); DELFA, *Arbetstider och sysselsättning—Vad händer i Västeuropa?*, DELFA-rapport no. 15 (Stockholm: Arbetsmarknadsdepartementet, 1985); DELFA, *Hur kan vi förbättra våra* arbetstider?, DELFA-rapport no. 16 (Stockholm: Arbetsmarknadsdepartementet, 1986).

12. *Tid att arbete tid att leva. En samlad arbetstidspolitik*, Rapport från TCO's arbetstidsutredning (Stockholm, 1987).

13. *Snabbprotokoll från* Landsorganisationens kongress 20–27 (Sept. 1986).

14. Anna Hedborg and Rudolf Meidner, *Ett friår mitt i livet* (Stockholm, 1986).

15. SAF, *Arbetstiden i framtiden—en avgörande resursfråga* (Stockholm, 1987).

16. LO, *Arbetstid i ett fackligt perspektiv* (Stockholm, 1985), p. 61.

10   The Self-Management of Time in Postindustrial Society

Carmen Sirianni

The postindustrial societies of the West today are in the midst of profound changes in the way they organize time, and the prospects for democratic change depend perhaps more than ever before on developing a coherent politics of time. The unfreezing of temporal rigidities and the blurring of temporal boundaries are evident in the organization of the workplace; in the methods of sequencing and integrating major life activities such as education, work, and retirement; as well as in the challenges being made to the gendered distribution of time in the home and time in the labor market, and to the temporal structure of the careers that provide access to opportunity in the latter. The employment crisis is partly one of the temporal distribution of work time, and segmentation in the labor market is manifest in the structure of rewards and opportunities associated with part-time and discontinuous work. The ecological crisis is reflected in a pace of production, consumption, and disposal that exceeds nature's ability to recycle wastes and renew basic resources, as well as in the mental and physical shocks of various forms of "hurry sickness" that have become endemic to contemporary life.

Changes in the way we organize our time present genuine opportunities to redefine how we think about individual autonomy and democratic participation, equitable opportunity in the labor market and responsibility in the home, the purposes of work and the meaning of affluence. But the unfreezing of temporal rigidities and the increasing flexibility of options also threaten to reinforce inequality and to generate new forms of vulnerability, marginality, and control. Will the work-time flexibility sought today particularly by women help to upgrade and legitimate diverse part-time and discontinuous options for *all* who would choose them, challenge the career model that has privileged the male with a traditional housewife, and help to redistribute work within the home, or will it be used in ways that reinforce labor-market segmentation and ratify the domestic division of labor? Will flexible retirement policy become a way of

This is a revised version of an article that first appeared in *Socialist Review* 18,4 (October–December, 1988): 5–56.

enhancing the opportunity of elders to combine work and leisure, to learn other skills and explore new ways of contributing to the community, or will it become a way to exclude them from paid work in the interests of younger hires and lower labor costs? Will the temporal and spatial flexibility of homeworking and telecommuting provide new forms of autonomy and opportunities to revalue home and community life, or will it bring different kinds of control, atomization, and exclusion? Will work-time flexibility help transform other sociotechnical dimensions of work, create new bases for collaboration, and generate increased opportunities for continual learning, or will it be used to undermine workplace solidarities and the capacity to bargain for collective interests and equitable norms? All of these possibilities are currently being played out in one form or another. In some settings the liberatory potential of new temporal arrangements is clearly evident, if not always dominant. In most, however, the new flexibility has become implicated in old and new forms of inequality, marginality, and managerial control.

Time, in short, has become a contested terrain in the reorganization of postindustrial society. And as the changes taking place affect more and more areas of social life, piecemeal adjustments and ex post facto compensations become less satisfactory. Increasingly, our own capacity to shape this terrain depends on the extent to which we develop a democratic vision of temporal organization and an integrative politics of time for a postindustrial society.

This chapter attempts to develop a framework for such an integrative approach to the democratic self-management of time in postindustrial society. The first part sketches briefly some of the important changes in temporal organization in different areas of social life (work, family, and education over the life course, new technologies, and the like) that prompt a reframing of issues of equality, autonomy, and the good life in terms of time. The second part examines several major theoretical traditions that have concerned themselves with the temporal structures of modern society. Specifically, it explores the contributions and limits of Marxism, theories of social complexity, the economics of time allocation, and feminist theory in an attempt to develop a theoretical framework for what E. P. Thompson has called a "new synthesis" of temporal organization. The third part examines the specific organizational contours of such a new democratic synthesis at the level of the workplace, and the fourth part develops this argument further in terms of welfare state programs that enhance capacities for autonomous and flexible life planning on a more egalitarian basis. Flexible and reduced working-time options reveal distinct practical possibilities for reorganizing time in a way that enhances autonomy and equality, especially when legitimated as *rights* to which people are entitled and complemented by coherent welfare state policies that make such options increasingly feasible. The last part of this chapter poses the question of how we might begin to put a more coherently democratic politics of time on the agenda. This is particularly difficult in view of the many ways in which some of the new forms of flexibility serve to enhance managerial control and reinforce inequality, and in view of recent attacks on the welfare state. Rather than a defensive politics of the workplace that resists flexibility in the name of standard temporal norms of the past, however, or a fragmented welfare politics aimed at protecting against specific market inequities, we need to develop a progressively coherent politics of temporal autonomy in work and nonwork activities, and a welfare policy that supports flexible life planning on a progressively universalistic and egalitarian basis. A *postindustrial New Deal* must have the self-management of time at its core.

Time in Transition

The linear model of full-time continuous commitment to work and career, and the rigidly gendered allocation of work time in the market and in the home have become increasingly problematic as a result of a number of recent developments. Prominent among these are changes in families, sex roles, and the labor-force participation of women. The labor-force participation rate of women has been steadily increasing throughout the century, and this has been particularly dramatic since the war, surpassing 60 percent in the late 1980s and continuing its upward trend. Men's and women's labor-force participation rates have been converging, and the concomitant increases in the total amount of family time spent in the labor market, along with the particular strains on women who try to combine family and labor-market commitments, have generated pressures for greater flexibility of working time over the day and week as well as over the life course, and have begun to call into question the dominant (male) model of a work career. And those men and women who have come to be most supportive of egalitarian and nontraditional family and sex-role patterns show the strongest interest in flexible work options in daily as well as life-course scheduling, and the greatest willingness to forego earnings for increases in free time.[1]

Further pressure for flexibility has come from developments in health and longevity among the elderly. As life expectancy and particularly healthy life expectancy have steadily increased, more elders have become capable of continued work and resistant to forced retirement. Pensions and social security benefits are often inadequate, and inflation and economic uncertainty put a premium on maintaining links to paid work. Many thus desire to continue working past official retirement ages but prefer or require less than full-time year-round jobs, or need retraining for jobs more suitable to their health status. As retirement life styles continue to diversify, the need to structure "a new life-cycle period as a flexible and multi-option stage for older persons" increases. This will require various flexible work options, and the right to phased and temporary retirement.[2] The distinction between paid work and retirement has been progressively blurred on both sides of the official retirement ages, and flexibility is increasingly becoming the norm. With greater longevity and a growing proportion of elderly in the population, care-giving functions also increase. Most of these are still performed by female relatives outside of institutional settings, and as their own labor-force participation rates continue to increase, further accommodations in work-time options will become necessary. As Bernice Neugarten and Dail Neugarten have argued, "the old distinctions between life periods are blurring in today's society," and particularly as the lines fade in the later years, our aging society is challenged with developing a *new definition of productivity and qualitative growth* that includes various kinds of volunteer, self-help, and caring work outside the paid labor market.[3]

Rigid temporal distinctions between education and work at the other end of the work career are also becoming progressively blurred. As a growing proportion of youth go on to higher education, it becomes more common for many (especially those from less privileged backgrounds) to combine education with paid work, often facilitated by part-time and other flexible arrangements. Industrial restructuring and technological change displace increasing numbers from their jobs and shorten the half-life of skills and credentials that once seemed as if they might serve for a lifetime of opportunity and security in the labor market. Skill renewal and retraining thus become increasingly necessary throughout the work career if the labor force is to adjust to change. The most optimal use of new technologies in postindustrial work settings requires opportunities for continuous learning and often blurs the distinction between time learning on the job and time learning off the job.[4] Longer life spans make career changes in midlife more feasible and often desirable, and many blue- and white-collar workers have come to see recurrent education and "second chances" as a *right*. For those in low-opportunity jobs this can imply a "deferred right to education" and a rejection of the idea that failure to acquire appropriate training at the earliest possible stages of the life course should permanently disenfranchise the individual from further education and the opportunity that it might bring.[5] But even for those with some advanced schooling, recurrent education becomes an avenue to further mobility and career change. This is consonant with more general value changes that have occurred since the 1960s with regard to work: much greater stress on work as a source of continued growth, self-realization, and personal autonomy. The transition to adulthood has itself become more extended, diversified, and individualized over the past few decades, and psychology has become more oriented to personal development and human plasticity over the entire life span. Educational institutions have responded to these changes with a varriety of adult education, "lifetime learning," and "flex degree" programs.[6]

The lockstep progression from education to work to retirement as three distinct and temporally well-defined stages of the life course also appears problematic when viewed in light of the decline in the total proportion of lifetime hours that the average male nonprofessional worker must spend at work in the advanced societies. A male employee born in the mid-nineteenth century spent roughly 30 percent of his lifetime hours in paid work, whereas his grandson born at the end of the century spent 20 percent, and his grandson, born in the 1950s, will spend only 10 percent.[7] These overall reductions generate increasing opportunities and incentives for life planning in a way that challenges temporally well-defined and rigidly sequential stages in favor of more fluid, flexible, and reversible timing of major life activities. Popular guides now detail the variety of strategies by which people can accomplish this in their everyday lives.

Technological, organizational, and product innovations have also unfrozen some of the temporal as well as spatial dimensions of work. New information technologies lessen time and space constraints for coordination, communication, and service. Project teams can teleconference at long distances and have quick access to on-site managers, engineers, and workers. Telecommuting increases the possibilities of work at home and blurs the boundary between the workplace and the home. It can create peculiar problems for the regulation of working conditions for some but also provide genuine opportunities for flexible work for others. High degrees of capital investment in technologies that can become obsolete quite rapidly require more continuous usage of plant and equipment, often on a round-the-clock basis, and this leads to greater use of shift systems and increasingly to reduced or flexible work-time arrangements to make such shifts more acceptable to workers. Information technologies that demand high degrees of attention require increased time away from work to recuperate. And profitability in volatile and changing markets has come to depend on more flexible combinations of work time and workplace in general, if business and industry are to be able to respond to peak demand and variations in the production cycle. In the high growth area of services, in particular, flexible and part-time schedules permit greater responsiveness to peak times and the broadening of hours when service is available. New computer technologies also make it easier to process employee information, thus reducing the costs and increasing the benefits of hiring people on nonstandard schedules—which resembles, in a way, the use of just-in-time inventories.

New technologies also make the future of employment less certain. Although little that is definitive can be said about the extent of technological unemployment in the coming decades, the trend has been for increases in labor productivity to outpace overall production growth, thus making it progressively more difficult for those displaced by technological development to find employment elsewhere. Unlike previous periods when technical advance seemed to threaten jobs, today computerization substitutes not only for physical but for mental functions in the production of both goods and services. Chips are continually reduced in price even as they become more powerful and reliable, and every indication is that the information revolution is still in its early stages. The growth of services in the private sector, which has compensated for declines elsewhere, is unlikely to be able to continue to absorb displaced workers.⁸ The problem of distributing work and income could thus become increasingly pressing, and societies that do not develop new ways of doing so face the prospect of "dualization" between those groups that retain strong links to the labor market and those that do not. Some have referred to this outcome as the "two-thirds society," where the weaker third (displaced workers, youth unable to enter the job market, underemployed women and single mothers, the elderly poor, migrants, and the handicapped) is excluded from stable employment and the rights and opportunities that come with it. As a response to the recessions of the early 1980s in the United States, for instance, many firms seem to have developed a strategy of distinguishing a "core workforce" from a "contingent workforce," whose employment could be expanded or reduced at will in response to business fluctuations.⁹

Traditional models of redistributing work through across-the-board reductions in the workweek have also become problematic. The positive employment effects of such reductions are decreased, if not in some scenarios negated, if they lead to productivity growth, or if employer costs rise (because of full wage compensation) or demand falls (because of noncompensation for the reduced hours). Likewise, as the struggle for the 35-hour week in Germany and elsewhere has shown, collective trade union strategies for such reductions in the interest of solidarity with the unemployed have also become problematic in view of the uneven distribution of benefits and risks among members, as well as the wide variety of preferences they have for the forms such reductions might take. As Karl Hinrichs has argued, whereas earlier historical phases in the struggle for shorter hours could rely on the motives of attaining sufficient time to recuperate from work and, then, time for family leisure, the new motive that has emerged is to *integrate* work with the expanded activities outside of work, and to do so over the course of one's entire occupational biography. The 35-hour week may still retain symbolic value, especially when mediated through trade union organizations, but individual life situations and preferences for working-time reduction have become highly diversified and pluralized. Unemployment continues to challenge the ways we distribute work, and yet the models for redistributing it that we inherit from the past are no longer very compelling.¹⁰

Furthermore, ecological limits to quantitative growth models that in the past served as solutions to employment have appeared, and alternative time policies have emerged as part of a broader qualitative approach to economic growth and social welfare.¹¹ The ecological critique argues that the pace of production, consumption, and disposal must not be permitted to exceed nature's ability to recycle wastes and renew basic resources, and that the pace of social and economic life must become more compatible with the temporal rhythms of ecological systems. In addition, modern industrial civilization has progressively separated human rhythms from those of nature, and, according to

Jeremy Rifkin, the "nanosecond culture" of the computer threatens to disjoin these radically. Computer-related distress manifests itself in the temporal schizophrenia of those who move in and out of computer time, and people become less tolerant of interruptions, less patient with those who cannot respond appropriately to the precision and speed of programs, less capable of slow reflection and genuine commemoration.[12] Holistic health practice, and increasingly modern medicine as well, have associated a variety of contemporary illnesses with "hurry sickness," often triggered by an exaggerated sense of urgency or time scarcity; successful therapies, from biofeedback to meditation, aim to replace these with experiences of time that are focused in the present and not relentlessly flowing.[13] In short, what economist Steffan Linder has referred to as the "time famine" of contemporary society and sociologist Barry Schwartz has called the "phobia of time waste and preoccupation with efficient scheduling" have become acute concerns not only in the variety of ecological movements that have self-consciously begun to seek alternatives, but among broad sectors of the population that have come to recognize that the quality of life is impoverished by forms of affluence and achievement that are purchased by an overriding sense of time scarcity.[14]

Profound changes are thus taking place in the temporal organization of life and work, and these open up a new terrain for redefining how we think about autonomy, equality, and the good life. Many of these changes, in fact, have been propelled by or have become linked to demands for equity and greater freedom to integrate various activities over the life course. This has clearly been true among women, who have pressed for greater work-time flexibility, the upgrading of part-time jobs, and the legitimation of job sharing, parental leaves, and reentry rights, as well as abortion rights and effective birth-control technologies.[15] It has been manifest in increased claims for recurrent education, retraining, and second chances among various age and occupational groups, and among elders for greater opportunities to combine retirement with other productive and socially rewarded activities. Indeed, over the course of the twentieth century there has been a rather consistent pattern among working people of both sexes to strive to increase their capacities for life planning, whether this be by shaping the structure of internal labor markets, decreasing working time, or expanding the kinds of social welfare and educational rights and benefits that permit choices throughout the life course that are progressively decoupled from the vicissitudes of the marketplace and human biology.

And these efforts have, for the most part, been quite successful. The considerable democratization of capacities for life planning has resulted in increasing differentiation and pluralization of life styles and work-time preferences. In the process new meanings of personal autonomy and equitable opportunity have begun to emerge that challenge some of the fixed temporal assumptions which have structured opportunity and regulated competition in the labor market, and which have informed most previous social and political theories of equality and equal opportunity: the full-time continuous job, the male career model that can make surplus claims on our time, the linear life course, the gendered distribution of time in the home and in caring work generally.

Yet increased temporal differentiation and the pluralization of preferences and options raise a distinctive set of problems for a democratic theory that would be both pluralist and egalitarian. As we seek to legitimate a plurality of options and paths to opportunity, we must thus redefine the meanings of equity and the institutional mechanisms that might make these effective. Those who lay claim to greater autonomy over their working time in the interests, say, of improving family life or enhancing equity within the home, or expanding options outside the labor market, and thereby articulate different principles of equity that should govern the distribution of opportunity in the labor market as well, are engaged in a historic process of redefining boundaries between different "spheres of justice." They are engaged in what Michael Walzer has referred to as the "continual probes and incursions through which these shifts are worked out," and through which larger sea changes in the way we redefine the meanings of justice emerge.[16] The meaning of justice in one sphere is shaped, especially at critical junctures of social reorganization, by the dialogues and conflicts of interpretation about its meaning in other spheres. This contest over boundaries is today very much one of redefining the temporal contours of different spheres of social life, the temporal premises, disciplines, and choices that operate within them and govern the relationships among them. A pluralist and egalitarian theory must today more than ever before locate at its center a critical and democratic approach to the social organization of time and temporal diversity. The problem of justice cum diversity in postindustrial and postmodern societies cannot fruitfully be addressed otherwise.

Social Theory and the Temporal Structures of Modern Society

In his now-classic essay "Time, Work Discipline and Industrial Capitalism" E. P. Thompson suggested the possibility of a "new synthesis" that would combine certain aspects of synchronized clock time, which had been used to discipline the working classes in the transition to industrial capitalism, and an enlarged sphere of free time liberated from the unremitting rhythms of the clock.[17] Several traditions within the social sciences have focused on the problem of the temporal structures of modern society, and some have posed the question of the possibility of a new economy of time explicitly. Although this brief critical overview cannot do justice to the development of the structures of temporality in the modern world, its summary of several lines of theoretical argument—in Marxist and feminist theory, and in various sociological theories of complexity and economic theories of time allocation—can help to clarify what such a new synthesis might entail, particularly in view of the changes that are much more evident today than they were in 1967 when Thompson first issued his provocative challenge.

Marxism and the Critique of the Commodification of Time

Marx's analysis of the commodity form and the dynamics of capital revolves fundamentally around the organization of time. The riddle of value is *how* and *why* concrete human labor comes to be represented as abstract labor expressed in temporal units that are homogeneous, infinitely divisible, and mathematically measurable. Under capitalism, time develops an autonomous dynamic as part of a system of alienated labor and commodity fetishism, where the social relations among people producing in concrete time appear as relationships among things measured by abstract and disembodied labor time. Society becomes an elaborate exchange dance of abstract time taking place independently of the will of the actors, and individual producers appear as objects rather than subjects of their own expenditure of abstract labor time. "Time is everything, man is nothing; he is at most the incarnation of time," Marx noted."[18] Here the Renaissance aspiration expressed by Leon Battista Alberti, that he who knew how to exploit time would become "the master of all things," is turned on its head by Marx: the exploitation of rationalized time has transformed the producers into the servants of abstract temporal relationships expressed in the exchange of their products through value. Value relationships establish what is socially necessary labor time for producing specific use values in a way that imposes on producers, behind their backs as it were, a generalized temporal norm, or a form of quasi-objective temporal necessity. Increases in productivity that are generalizable raise the norm of what *all* must produce per hour if they are to receive the value of their labor time, and all must dance to the rhythms of this increasing temporal compulsion if they are to survive in the marketplace. The actual temporal disciplining of workers, and the later refinement of the time disciplines of scientific management, are but manifestations of the more general dynamic of temporal necessity and heteronomy that commodity exchange relations entail.[19]

Value relations not only confer an abstract and heteronomous dynamic to time, according to Marx, but they obscure and distort the historical choices for an alternative conception of real wealth as reduced and redefined labor time. In the *Grundrisse* Marx presents what he sees as the central contradiction of capitalist development in temporal terms:

> The *theft of alien labour time, on which the present wealth is based*, appears a miserable foundation in face of this new one, created by large-scale industry itself. . . . The free development of individualities [becomes possible], and hence not the reduction of necessary labour time so as to posit surplus labour, but rather the

general reduction of the necessary labour of the society to a minimum, which then corresponds to the artistic, scientific etc. development of the individuals in the time set free, and with the means created, for all of them. Capital itself is the moving contradiction, [in] that it presses to reduce labour time to a minimum, while it posits labour time on the other side as sole measure and source of wealth. Hence it diminishes labour time in the necessary form so as to increase it in the superfluous form; hence posits the superfluous in growing measure as a condition . . . for the necessary.[20]

The resolution of this contradiction can occur, according to Marx, only as workers assume control of production and recognize that freely disposable time is a form of wealth per se, and that the development of the productive, intellectual, and scientific capacities of all individuals itself becomes the greatest productive force that society has at its disposal. As this happens, the antithesis between free time and labor time breaks down, and free time—as both idle time and time for higher activity—transforms the human subject of production. The capacity for creating material affluence is thus enhanced, while free time itself becomes the greatest form of wealth. And while Marx later abandoned the rustic imagery of the *German Ideology*, where one could "hunt in the morning, fish in the afternoon, rear cattle in the evening, [and] criticize after dinner," he never relinquished the idea that flexibility, variation, and the combination of mental and manual skills were not only essential to human freedom and equality but would increasingly become requisites of work organization in technologically advanced industry.[21]

This is a powerful analysis of the temporal dynamics of industrial capitalism, many aspects of which are more relevant today than they were in the nineteenth century. But it is nonetheless an analysis that needs to be modified in fundamental ways. To theorize the conditions for an alternative economy of time, we must recognize more consistently than Marx does that there is no utopia beyond the *relative* scarcity of time, nor any utopia beyond the ex post facto verification and valuation of economic activity that market mechanisms provide. A critical theory of temporal organization must reject both the *post-scarcity* and the *ex ante* illusions that underlie Marx's idea of a marketless utopia of material and temporal abundance.[22] Furthermore, the critique of the commodity form, while articulating important dimensions of temporality, presents a very limited perspective on the ways we organize time in complex industrial and postindustrial societies.

Complexity, Pluralism, and Choice

Various theorists of social complexity have examined temporal organization from a different angle. Sorokin, while recognizing the Marxian insight that time is commodified in capitalist society, nonetheless reminds us how partial commodification remains, and how much qualitative measures of time in everyday life resist the abstract homogenization of the clock.[23] An equally important insight, however, is that the relative scarcity of time cannot simply be traced to a specific mode of production but is a function of the level of demand or the possibilities for its use. Thus the greatest scarcity is often experienced by those most enmeshed in the "rich fabric of a pluralistic social order," who have extensive networks of social relationships and expansive possibilities for using their time.[24] The clock and the schedule are thus not simply *disciplinary* instruments, but *diversifying* ones that permit us to synchronize and coordinate a broad range of activities and relationships in dense and pluralistic social networks, and that can expand the possibilities for individual and organizational flexibility within them. In fact, the view of time as scarce, antagonistic, and requiring precise measurement, which emerged during the Renaissance, reflected not only a desire to "master all things" but indicated as well a renewed urban vitality and a passion for variety that required more rational temporal techniques to enjoy fully.[25] The "rich individuality" and productive diversity that Marx posited as the ideal of a free society could, from this perspective, be achieved, not by eliminating the techniques through which time is rationalized, but by appropriating them for more plural and individualized choice, rather than for conformity and control.

Niklas Luhmann shares the view that the "temporalization of complexity" expands choice, but he also recognizes some not-so-benign unintended consequences. As time becomes increasingly scarce as a result of rising demands and possibilities for its use, as well as of complex interdependence as such, the more complex that societies become the more time they need to find rational solutions to problems and to build consensus. A manifest discrepancy thus develops between the time available and the time required for rational reflection, processing information, and evaluating alternatives. Administration thus tends to supplant democratic deliberation. Consensus is purchased at a discount and dissensus tends to be suppressed. An open and abstract future orientation becomes increasingly dominant, since it serves as a way of managing the surplus of possibilities and competing social claims, but in the process our capacity to reflect on concrete values and past traditions recedes further and further. In complex societies deadlines become increasingly pervasive, interlaced, and self-generative, revealing an autonomous dynamic of their own—similar, in a way, to Marx's commodity fetishism, but rooted in social complexity as such and not in commodity relations. The setting and meeting of deadlines come to be privileged over deciding on values, and the urgent continually drives out the important. Hierarchies of value are preempted by levels of urgency, and time is parceled into slices too small for prolonged reflection. Projects that are long-term, or to which deadlines cannot be meaningfully attached, tend to be sacrificed in favor of the short-term and delimitable. Under the pressure of time scarcity, preference is given to that which is already recognized, to paths already tried, to information and communication channels readily accessible and utilizable. Hurry is not only pervasive, but it is itself beyond discussion. And the very idea of an abundance of time must be censured, even morally forbidden, as fundamentally incompatible with complex interdependence.[26]

Luhmann's analysis alerts us to the ways in which the temporal dimensions of complex interaction can circumscribe the possibilities for rational decision making at an individual and collective level. Even as our choices expand, we seem to have less time to decide what it is that we want. Yet his formulation of the problem as primarily one of complexity makes it impossible to determine the extent to which the scarcity of time and the pervasiveness of deadlines are a function of those forms of complexity that are not subject to change in advanced societies, and those that are the result of particular work-time arrangements, career line structures, and power distributions that we can imagine quite differently. He thus cannot distinguish between those forms of time scarcity that are entailed by an increased complexity of interaction and richness of choice, and those that reflect specific distributions of power and opportunity, and serve repressive ideological functions of restricting democratic choice and censuring alternative views of the good life as a greater abundance of time rather than simply of goods.

Affluence and Scarcity in the Economics of Time Allocation

In his much discussed book *The Harried Leisure Class* Steffan Linder addresses the problem of time scarcity from the perspective of a neoclassical economics of time allocation. Linder attempts to explain why there is an apparent "time famine" in advanced industrial societies, and how economics might benefit from a bit of "utopian inspiration and guidance" in reformulating the problem of wealth in terms of a possible affluence of time. His basic premise is that people economize on time because it is scarce and cannot be accumulated, and they do so in such a way as to obtain an "equal yield" on their various forms of time use. Time spent in consumption, for instance, has a shadow price that individuals consciously or unconsciously apply, and this is determined by the wage rate they would receive in the market economy were they working instead of consuming. As labor productivity and wages increase, the yield on time spent working increases, and thus the yield on time devoted to other activities must also be raised if an equilibrium—reflecting an optimal use of time overall—is to be reestablished. The rational economic actor continually transfers time from activities with a low yield to ones with a higher yield, until such an equilibrium is reached and the overall yield is thus maximized. In a sense, the quasi-objective temporal compulsion that Marx noted in his analysis of value has found its analogue *across* the boundary between labor time in the market and time spent outside the market. The orbit of temporal constraint, in other words, has been widened by neoclassical time-allocation theory to embrace all activity.

One of the chief ways that people can increase the yield on consumption time is to "accelerate" consumption by enhancing its goods intensity. The higher the value of the goods consumed per unit of time, the higher the yield. This can be achieved by consuming more expensive versions of the same commodity, by consuming more goods simultaneously, or by consuming successively a number of commodities, each for a shorter period of time. As labor productivity and incomes increase, mandating higher yields on other forms of time use, those activities will tend to thrive that have a higher capacity for goods absorption, and those that cannot be made goods intensive will tend to wane. In the latter category are the ancient and venerable pleasures of reading, eating, lovemaking, visiting friends, and contemplation. These are inferior activities from the point of view of higher yield on time, especially when compared with activities that lend themselves to expensive goods, or activities such as cocktail parties where one can consume food and make many professional contacts in a short period of time.

Time not only becomes scarcer, but its distribution thus becomes skewed to certain kinds of activities at the expense of others. In fact, for the average income earners in the richer countries who make up the harried leisure class, the throwaway culture and the "decline of service in the service economy" become increasingly rational from an economic point of view, since it becomes relatively cheaper to replace goods rather than repair them, to repair bodies rather than maintain them, to eat at fast-food counters rather than take high-yield time away from work to cook a meal. This calculus of relative time values also leads to the "decline of decision making in a decision making economy," similar to what Luhmann observes, since it is cheaper to make mistakes by deciding quickly than to pay the higher time costs of deliberating more carefully. This applies to the way we buy our products, pick our leaders, and choose our lovers, Linder argues. In fact, the increasing yield on time in production makes it progressively irrational for us to spend time reflecting on its meaning and purposes. The mastery of time, one might say, has thus come to master its very subjects.

Linder is disturbed by these developments, but he cannot see his way toward an alternative economy of time except through vague appeals to a change of heart and the recognition that time itself imposes limits on the extent to which we can consume and maintain the vast amount of goods we are capable of producing. In an earlier but neglected book, economist George Soule developed a more elaborate argument for a new economy of time. He noted that the very progress of market society, and in particular the vast increases in productivity made possible by technological change and forthcoming computerization, has generated new needs (and revived old ones) that can be met only outside the market. As the industrial revolution drew into the commercial sector activities formerly done in the home, so now is the process being reversed, as people are beginning to use their own hands and brains to satisfy wants that were never adequately registered in the market and to cultivate the arts and graces of living. A new democratic leisure class has begun to develop—one composed of people who have struggled over the decades to gain greater control of their time, and who are increasingly unwilling to barter all of it for marketable goods and services. The very meaning of work and leisure will gradually be transformed, as expanded free time becomes the basis for increased social and cooperative production outside the market, greater attention to the arts of homemaking and child care by men, and a variety of renewed commitments to gardening, travel, sports, aesthetic pursuits, and the hardest work of all, thinking.[27]

Linder and Soule have posed important questions about the sources of time scarcity, the relative distribution of time to different sorts of activities, and the possibilities of an alternative economy of time devoted less to goods consumption and more to community and self-development. Neoclassical time-allocation theory, however, does not suffice for answering these questions. Insofar as it articulates the criteria for the efficient allocation of time in monetary terms, it is indeed indispensable. In market societies where opportunities and incentives for calculating the monetary costs of time are pervasive, if incomplete, and the costs of not doing so are generally evident, then Becker's concept of "full income" (the monetary equivalent people would earn if all their time were devoted to work) and Linder's notion of seeking equal yields on time to achieve a maximum overall yield can serve as a baseline against which to measure optimizing behavior in the pecuniary sense. But, as other economists have pointed out, such narrowly optimizing behavior does not account for many of the forms of harriedness in our society (including those that derive from what Albert Hirschman has called "obituary-improving activities"), nor can it explain why time-intensive activities such as meditation, camping, running, or handicrafts have increased in recent years. And as Gordon Winston's very important neoclassical reformulation notes, Becker and Linder have reified time as a thing that gets allocated as easily as temporally footloose money does, whereas many activities are time-specific and hence determined by more than Becker's "full income constraint."[28]

More importantly, even in market societies the monetization of time has been incomplete—and, in fact, for centuries there was much open resistance to it, even by those who stood to gain higher incomes. How we choose to distribute our time and sequence our activity, while constrained to varying degrees by concern for pecuniary optimality, is also determined by implicit and explicit moral codes and shared norms. Time serves as a sign of caring and commitment, of attention and respect. And many of the decisions we make about the time we spend with family and friends are hardly optimizing in the pecuniary sense. Time allocation theory thus requires a nonreductionist theory of values and culture. It must recognize that decisions about allocation and sequence are embedded in dense moral economies of time and constrained by institutional structures. Time-allocation theory simply assumes that effective institutional means for increasing and decreasing work time exist, that the tradeoffs of reduced hours are purely monetary, and that work time is infinitely divisible independent of career line and labor market structures. But, in fact, rather limited institutional mechanisms are available for determining working hours or the terms on which tradeoffs can be made, and the structure of jobs and career lines often imposes opportunity costs for reduced hours that are highly disproportionate to their numerical quantity. An economic theory concerned with the possibilities of an alternative economy of time must thus investigate how decisions about allocation and sequencing are embedded in and constrained by culture and institutions, and how we might expand the opportunities for choice and more freely determine the terms on which tradeoffs can occur.[29]

Gendered Time

Feminist theory has addressed these problems most fruitfully over the past decade or so. In particular, it has analyzed the profoundly asymmetrical structure of the distribution of time between men and women in market labor and household labor, and the relationship between this temporal asymmetry and inequality in the labor market. It has uncovered the gendered biases inherent in the temporal structure of the dominant career model, as well as the symbolic power that gendered conceptions of temporal ordering exercise in everyday life. And it has posed the issue of expanded choice over time in terms of autonomy, equality, and moral economy. Although it by no means supplants the important insights of the other theories considered here, it compels us to reframe them considerably.

Not only do tasks within the home tend to be sex-typed and gender segregated, but time in household labor is asymmetrically distributed. Women contribute the major share of time required by household labor, and even as total household labor time increases in response to children (the more and the younger), husbands' contributions do not seem to increase proportionately. Some earlier research reports their relative contributions to be virtually inflexible, but more recent data reveal a significant trend toward redistribution over the past decade or so—although there nonetheless remains a long way to go to equality.[30] The imperatives of domestic labor may lead wives, but generally not husbands, to withdraw from the labor market completely or to reduce their commitment to it considerably. These patterns reinforce, and are reinforced by, labor-market segmentation. All things equal, the economically rational household reduces the market time of the wife in response to increases in total household labor time, since her wages and promotional opportunities are likely to be less than her husband's. Domestic responsibilities, on the other hand, generally leave women with less time than men for a variety of activities that might enhance their position in the labor market, such as study and training, union participation, and overtime work, and with less leisure time to renew their energies. And the amount of domestic labor time negatively influences earnings for both sexes, with the greatest relative losses suffered by women in non–working-class occupations—probably because of the higher threshholds of time commitment necessary to obtain and maintain access to opportunity in middle-class and professional careers.[31] Even in the case of dual-career couples, wives have more absences from work due to child care than do husbands, are more likely to interrupt their careers, work part-time, follow their spouses' geographical moves, and suffer wage and rate-of-advancement penalties as a result. Women experience work-time demands as more disruptive of their family roles than do men, and they are more likely to experience each set of demands simultaneously, whereas men enact them sequentially—first work, then family.[32]

Part of the historical explanation for this gendered asymmetry between market and household labor time lies in the temporal regime imposed by early industrial capitalism. The factory system not only removed work spatially from the home and imposed extremely rigorous time demands on workers (12- to 14-hour days and more), but it removed control of the work process and its temporal rhythms from them as well. The biological rhythms of reproduction (pregnancy, childbirth, lactation) became incompatible with the new regime of factory time, whereas various forms of preindustrial work had been better able to accommodate them.[33] Over the past century this incompatibility has gradually lessened as a result of shorter standard working hours, more effective birth-control technologies and reproductive rights that give women greater control over the timing of childbirth, welfare state programs that assume some of the responsibility for care of dependents (children, aged parents, the sick and disabled), and state and private programs that provide maternity (or parental) leave and work-time flexibility. Yet the asymmetries remain profound, and one important reason is that the dominant model of a "career" that provides access to power and opportunity on the job disadvantages women in significant ways.

The temporal structure of what feminist thinkers have called the male career model has perhaps been best portrayed by Hanna Papanek, Arlie Hochschild, and Rosabeth Kanter.[34] Such a career hoards the time of the individual for itself and requires that family and other commitments be canceled, interrupted, or postponed if need be. Competition is temporally tight and age-graded, and many of the most vigorous pressures and key promotion stages occur during childbearing years, thus disadvantaging those who cut back on work in order to bear or care for children. Continuous and uninterrupted progress along a linear time line is the ideal of serious career pursuit. And the willingness to devote surpluses of time above and beyond what is formally required serves as a sign of seriousness and trust in organizations greedy for employees' commitment and uncertain how to measure their real contributions.[35] The time of wives is directly and indirectly enlisted by husbands and their employing organizations, and wives' availability for housework and child care permits the husband to pursue his career and respond unhindered to organizational demands that require unplanned late nights at the office or time away for business travel. Men and women who do not have such wives to provide the temporal, emotional, and material supports for a "two-person single career" compete at a disadvantage with those who do. Some women choose to remain single, not have children, or delay the choice indefinitely in order to remain competitive, while others are cooled out and lower their aspirations in a way that least threatens the ideology of equal opportunity embedded in this career ideal. And the caretaker functions within the home are often reproduced within work organizations as well, as women who are not on a career track where they are going anywhere very quickly become responsible for the nurturing work and serve as the gatekeepers of their superiors' more valuable time by screening intrusions and interruptions.

This career model exercises hegemony insofar as it is accepted as defining the main legitimate route of access to high opportunity in the labor market even by those who are unable (or unwilling) to live up to the terms it establishes, and who blame themselves for such failure, and insofar as those who reject the model have insufficient power to alter those terms. The hegemony of this male model of structuring a career is *simultaneously* undermined *and* reinforced by the recent democratization of access to jobs and education for women. The greater number of women pursuing higher education and professional and managerial careers has created strain for a career model that requires continuous and high levels of time commitment, and some changes have been achieved. At the same time, however, the democratization of access increases the competition for high-opportunity jobs, and thus, on the supply side, puts a greater premium on employees' utilizing steep levels of time commitment as a method of competing and signaling worthiness, and on the demand side, strengthens the hand of employers to require such commitment from their employees.

The hegemony of this career model seems to operate at a deeper symbolic level as well. It reproduces the symbolic antinomies that associate man with culture and woman with nature. Man, who lacks natural life-giving functions, transcends nature through goal-oriented action that creates lasting values, thus reducing his vulnerability to nature and depriving repetition of all value. Woman, on the other hand, as a result of her physiology and social role of rearing children, is associated with nature, the vulnerability of life, and the regeneration of life through repetition. Like Penelope, the wife in the two-person single career learns to wait in repetitious labor for her Odysseus to return from the adventures and adversities in the outside world through which he forges his identity—although return to the family often comes only with midlife crisis.[36] The ideal of a male career as linear, continuous, cumulative, and ever devouring one's time thus not only precludes in a practical fashion equal responsibility for the repetitious labors of raising children, the interruptions of caring for the sick and elderly, or the rituals of bedtime and breakfast, birthday and holiday; it perhaps functions at a deeper symbolic level as a form of male heroism and power, as transcendence of (female) nature and repetition, as protection against vulnerability, limits, and death. Research on the significance attributed by men to the intensive time demands of careers in medicine and high-tech engineering, for instance, reveals many elements of this symbolic constellation.[37]

The rationalized view of time inherited from the Renaissance, which promised that those who knew how to exploit time would become "the master of all things," has embedded itself deeply into the male career model, and even in its origins excluded or marginalized women's experiences and representations of time. In their idealization of progeny (i.e., sons) as a way of transcending time, for instance, the great male Renaissance writers never concern themselves with the everyday temporal rhythms and time investments involved in actually caring for children. And time is often represented as a strict father figure, watching lest precious moments be wasted, or as an antagonist that men heroically battle.[38] And one suspects that such marginalization of female experience of time was true as well of the Protestant preachers who sermonized against "empty, unaccounted for time" and the "idle chatter" of visiting with neighbors, who upheld continuous labor in a single calling as the ideal path to salvation, and who equated time with money and diversion with lost opportunity in the market. Feminist theory has increasingly challenged these representations, although in some cases (e.g., Mary Daly) there is a failure to appreciate that the techniques of time rationalization can also serve liberating functions in complex societies of expanded choice. And feminist utopian fiction portrays images of time where process and promise and patience and presence prevail, where the eternity of the dream shapes the reality of the moment, where time is not wasted when it is not enemy, and where "the search for pleasure is circular, repetitive, atemporal."[39]

Feminist theory thus challenges gender-free utility maximizing and human capital models of time allocation and their accounts of inequality, and has revealed the profound institutional bias and symbolic marginalization embedded in the dominant model of a career. And rank-and-file women, unions with significant female membership, and feminist organizations and legislators have begun to legitimate and implement a range of alternative time policies, thus redefining equity and autonomy in terms of plural and diverse temporal models for achievement and recognition in the labor market. This has been occurring in the framework of a feminist redefinition of a moral economy of time that both revalues and degenders caring and nurturance, and circumscribes the identification of time with money and market opportunity. A "new synthesis," as Thompson conceived of it, must locate the insights of feminist theory and practice at its heart.

A New Economy of Time?

Redefining a new economy of time on democratic and egalitarian foundations, however, must further recognize a number of permanent tensions and problems. In complex societies of interactional richness and pluralistic choice, the techniques of time rationalization are necessary tools of individual autonomy and democratic participation. Diversity of choice in dense and plural social networks cannot be conceived without them. The finer arts of democratic participation, even at the grassroots level, also require such techniques for rationalizing limited time, lest undefined and open-ended boundaries for discussion and decision undermine the willingness or ability of citizens to participate, narrow the spheres of social life in which they might effectively do so, or provide the opportunity for unrepresentative minorities to determine agendas and outcomes by unilaterally escalating the time costs of "voice."[40] And yet democratization requires that time be freed for participation, and that the threats posed to democratic deliberation by the pervasive scarcity of time, which both Luhmann and Linder note, be kept in check. And although the problems have shifted considerably since the shorter hours movements in the early nineteenth century first made the connection between expanded free time and democratic citizenship, the possibilities for rejuvenating participation and revitalizing public space remain linked to our capacities to gain more control of our time and redefine the terms of its relative scarcity.

Although the relative scarcity of time and its rationalization remain inevitable, Luhmann's claim that complexity itself requires that we censure the very idea of time affluence serves ideologically to obscure the choices that we *do* have to redefine the boundaries of this scarcity in favor of greater time affluence. We have much to learn from preindustrial cultures that reject haste as a lack of decorum or a sign of diabolical ambition, that have developed the art of taking their time and passing time without specific goals or expensive inputs, and that have developed rich techniques for "properly interpreting the day." Multiple ways of keeping time are possible simultaneously, and relative scarcity does not preclude a variety of forms of affluence where the rigors of the clock and the deadline do not invariably intrude.

To be sure, rationalized forms of temporal discipline have historically served purposes of domination. Marx, Foucault, and Giddens have amply demonstrated this. And yet such forms have also helped refashion psychic structures in ways that have made it possible to manage complexity and diversity in pluralist societies rich in possibilities for utilizing time, as Norbert Elias has argued.[41] They have been central to the moral projects of Protestantism (in particular), where incessant activity has been extolled as godly and idleness proscribed as degeneracy; and yet the very objects of such moralizing have repeatedly asserted claims to a different kind of time governed by alternative moral norms of responsibility to friends and workmates, family and community. However, recovering spaces of time affluence in a complex and democratized society more abundant in possibilities for time use may require not only structural reforms and cultural reenrichment, but other kinds of time discipline. As the terms of material and temporal abundance and scarcity shift with more effective claims to free time, the problem of time discipline does not necessarily disappear. Rather, its own terms also shift, and what is required is not the moral discipline to fill all idle time in frenetic activity, but the discipline to know when to "just say no" to yet more busyness, consumption, and obituary-improving activity, and not to be enticed by plentiful opportunity simply because it is available. A new economy of time, as Linder suspected, cannot rest on the premise of the satisfaction of all wants. It is not, in this sense, a post-scarcity economy. Redefining affluence thus requires redefining discipline in a way most appropriate to the dilemmas posed by the *permanent tendency* of the demand on our time in complex societies to outrun the supply. It requires becoming ever more adept at distinguishing when rationalizing techniques serve to make us more responsible and free, and when they restrict and repress choice, and indeed excuse our failures and rationalize our guilt. The dilemma of action in complex societies is that such techniques can almost always serve multiple purposes, and we often cannot know beforehand which might predominate.

Furthermore, in an open and democratic society that preserves a role for markets, time is still money. Opportunities and incentives for calculating the monetary value of time, and the opportunity costs of time spent *not* making money, cannot be eliminated in an open and complex society. But the opportunity to convert time into money is not itself the issue for a new economy of time. The issue is, rather, the terms on which this conversion occurs, and the effective chances—*symbolic* as well as *institutional*—for refusing it. The limits of the Becker-Linder approach lay in its not adequately recognizing the normative and institutional factors that define and circumscribe the processes by which people are actually willing and able to put a dollar value on their time. Historically, the monetization of time has been a difficult and incomplete accomplishment. And the maximizing assumptions of the Becker-Linder time-allocation models have not been able to understand how or why this is so. The central issue of a new economy of time is to recognize that time can be (and always has been) valued in diverse and often irreducible ways, and to explore the institutional mechanisms and symbolic resources that might permit such diversity to flourish more fully and freely.

This entails, first of all, that the mechanisms for effectively choosing alternative work-time options, and for allocating our time between work for income and other forms of activity, be expanded. Work-income tradeoff options must become an essential component of our conception of individual autonomy and moral economy. Second, the terms of such tradeoffs must be open to democratic determination. In other words, the nature and the range of the "bargains" effectively available, and their cost-benefit schedules, must be established politically and be made as transparent as possible through unrestrained discourse in a variety of public spheres. Local communities, democratic workplaces, and the welfare state have capacities (partially developed already) to structure the terms of work-income tradeoffs in ways that are more conducive to a new economy of time based on democratic, feminist, and egalitarian values.

Restructuring the choices available cannot fully eliminate the problem of value, as Marx identified this. Time is still monetized in the market, as concrete human labor time is transformed into the abstract time of value categories, at least in those spheres where markets prove indispensable as regulators of economic activity. Yet the problem shifts radically once there exist effective mechanisms for reflective discourse and democratic control over the ways in which concrete time is monetized, and the terms on which this occurs. Once there is a broad and effective array of options for both *choosing* and *refusing* to monetize one's time, and for regulating the secondary consequences of such decisions, temporality no longer can function as a heteronomous force in an overarching system of commodity fetishism and alienated labor. The power of capital—whether social or private—to posit living labor as the only source of wealth is radically restricted. Wealth no longer automatically appears as the endless accumulation of abstract labor time, nor superfluous labor time as its necessary condition. Rather, wealth can now be effectively "represented" as the development of "rich individuality," as the diverse abundance of time uses within and outside the market, in productive activity, in cultural and scientific pursuits, in nurturance and play. The legitimation of individual options and democratic control permits time to serve less as an excuse in everyday life, or as a rationale for gendered inequality. Thus we can more rightly demand of each other the time for nurturance, commitment, attention, and civility that we think we deserve. With the increased warrant to make such demands, and the freedom to respond to them, *moral* wealth emerges more fully as a central category of the political economy of time.

Toward the Self-Management of Time at Work

Over the past two decades a great diversity of options for organizing time at work and over the life course has emerged, and these reveal some of the possibilities for self-managing time in complex societies. The innovations, of course, are often limited in scope and constrained by the larger relations of power and inequality in which they are embedded, and thus present real problems for a democratic politics of time, as I will discuss in the final section. Of immediate concern here, however, is their *promise*, which is strikingly apparent for those who would integrate time into a theory of democratic self-management. A lively debate has begun to thematize these questions in terms of what an influential French report has referred to as "la révolution du temps choisi," and some in Germany have called *Zeitsouveränität*. In the United States most attention has been focused on specific work-time options and new forms of scheduling, although policy analysts such as Fred Best have recognized the broad significance of such alternatives in "flexible life scheduling" that can be shaped in the interests of greater autonomy and equity.[42] The practical experience reveals a variety of ways in which time flexibility can become linked to the process of redefining moral economies of time in everyday life and reducing gendered inequalities. It also indicates how such flexibility can become part of a larger process of reorganizing the sociotechnical dimensions of the workplace and sustaining a process of continuous learning in ways that reinforce autonomy and reduce segmentation.[43]

Enhanced autonomy is clearly one of the main promises of flexible and reduced working-time options. Job sharers (i.e., people who share joint responsibility for a single position, often a professional one), for instance, repeatedly note how sharing arrangements permit greater control over their own time and an enhanced ability to balance work and other commitments. Not only do they feel capable of allocating their time better, but also of reflecting more carefully and critically on how they use their time, and the relative value of the different ways of doing so. Job sharing thus becomes a way to "gain perspective" in one's life and work, a way to have "time to take a deep breath and know yourself again." The enhanced perspective and autonomy permit sharers to feel able to perform better at work and at home, or in other activities in which they are engaged, and to have a sense of shaping their lives as wage earners and integrated social beings in a more responsible fashion. Job sharing, as well as other forms of reduced time, become ways of restoring "balance" in one's life. Flexitime (i.e., varying starting and quitting times, sometimes with banking and borrowing of hours over the course of a week or longer) likewise improves personal time management in a variety of different life activities, and can become a tool for those (exempt) employees expected to put in unpaid overtime to lay claim to compensatory time off. It enhances the sense of personal autonomy and, as a result, improves self-esteem. It thereby reduces the symbolic power of heteronomous control over one's time and makes people feel more like adult citizens of the workplace—which in itself is not an insignificant contribution to democratic culture.[44]

As a result of increased flexibility, reduced time, or larger blocks of time off, people are able to integrate with their work a variety of other activities with greater ease and freedom than otherwise, and often with less overall stress in trying to manage multiple commitments. Various kinds of recreational and leisure activities become increasingly possible to schedule around or within work hours, and at times when facilities are not in peak use. The new consciousness of health and bodily fitness, and the holistic integration of these into everyday life, is facilitated by greater personal control over time, and is one of the factors that motivates concern for increased flexibility. And this extends to mental health and spiritual well-being as well, as some choose flexible and reduced hours to enable them to meditate, pray, or engage in community religious services. Various forms of community and political participation and volunteer work, as well as travel and hobbies, also become more available as options, and the fears of some moralists that additional free time will be used in degenerate and destructive ways appear to be borne out no more today than at earlier periods of working-time reduction.

Balancing work with family life is one of the key opportunities that alternative work-time options provide. This is particularly true for working mothers who retain primary responsibility for child care and housework, and for whom flexible schedules and part-time or job-shared positions reduce stress, enhance psychological well-being, and provide a greater sense of being able to perform both roles adequately and responsibly. And where there are children with special needs, or elderly parents requiring care, this is even more the case. Spouses also seem to be able to use flexible options to arrange better time together.

Part-time and flexible schedules also can facilitate other life transitions, such as the gradual integration of youth into the labor market, sometimes under conditions that permit their pairing with more experienced workers or their continued participation in formal school programs. Phased and partial retirement programs allow workers to test the extent to which they desire continued work in the labor market in view of their interests in leisure, family, and community involvement, as well as the changing state of their health. Divorce and separation often lead to coparenting arrangements that require increased work-time flexibility to manage effectively. And work careers themselves can be viewed as developmental sequences that entail different levels and types of commitment at different stages. Alternative work-time options provide a range of ways of shaping these sequences more autonomously, of responding to life crises with a greater capacity for control and insight, and of fashioning life plans and transitions with greater integrity.

Flexible work-time options not only ease the burdens of balancing work and household responsibilities, and facilitate life transitions, but they provide the opportunity for undoing some of the gendered inequalities associated with them. Rigid work schedules often reinforce gendered stereotypes and inequalities in the distribution of household and market labor time, whereas flexible and reduced options provide the possibility of altering these, as well as the occasion to reflect on their seeming immutability. Flexibility seems to have the overall effect of orienting men more toward the home and women more toward the labor market. Even the limited options of flexitime or shift work facilitate change where there are demands from working wives and a value shift among spouses, and fathers tend to spend more time in child care if not always in other domestic tasks as a result.[45] Job sharers and those in permanent part-time positions—the term *permanent* refers to the legitimation of the option and often the recognition of long-term career commitment, not the permanence of a particular employee in such a position—also note that time options enable them to reduce gendered inequalities. They eliminate for women the all-or-nothing choice of work or full-time motherhood after the birth of children, thus making job continuity and the accumulation of seniority more possible, or late entry and reentry into the labor market more feasible. Late entrants and reentrants can find job sharing particularly conducive to their needs, since dated or incomplete skills and shorn confidence can be compensated by partners.

Alternative work-time options can also facilitate, trigger, or reinforce other transformations in modes of supervision and distributions of knowledge and skill within and outside the workplace. Greater employee control over the timing of work reduces the symbolic power of managerial time discipline, and this seems to be true even in cases where sophisticated measuring devices, such as electronic time accumulators, regulate employees' overall hours. Under these conditions a more democratic workplace climate becomes possible, and groups excluded from time flexibility often make equity claims on the basis of the symbolic upgrading they perceive others to have achieved. Supervisors whose schedules no longer coincide fully with those of workers often must deemphasize direct oversight and monitoring in favor of consultative modes and trust-building strategies, and they must become willing to delegate authority more widely. The petty supervision of women employees, in particular, can lessen considerably. Workers themselves assume greater responsibility for maintaining coverage, and this, along with the heightened expectations of autonomy, empowerment, or intrinsic job satisfaction that often accompany flexible time options can lead to further claims for participation. The latter can also arise through the more circuitous route of enhanced freedom in nonwork life that results from alternative schedules, since this makes the restricted autonomy of the workplace seem even less necessary and less tolerable. Thus time flexibility both within the workplace and in the arrangement of other activities can help erode more rigid and authoritarian forms of supervision.[46]

And time flexibility can occasion upgrading in skills and redesign of task structures themselves. Flexitime, compressed workweeks, innovative shifts, and sabbaticals often create problems of staff coverage, which can be resolved only by permitting or encouraging workers to learn other tasks and to rotate responsibilities among themselves. Such cross-training and multi-skilling are sometimes consciously planned as a prerequisite for introducing flexible schedules or as part of a larger sociotechnical redesign of the workplace. But they often emerge in the process quite unintendedly, as employees and their immediate supervisors come to realize that they must be able to do a broader range of tasks and even perform higher level functions if time flexibility is to be made workable. Retaining new options over time thus becomes a motivator for workers to continue learning and to develop informal mechanisms for teaching each other, and it induces a new organizational flexibility over the definition of jobs and the distribution of skills. And this new learning and responsibility can open up new paths of mobility in the firm.

A particularly innovative shift system at the Shell Canada specialty chemicals plant in Sarnia, Ontario, for instance, rotates workers more equitably through the different shifts and provides more compressed hours, informal swapping of shifts, and periodic mini-vacations of nine days off in a row twice over every eighteen-week scheduling cycle (i.e., approximately six times per year), in addition to regular vacation time. The plant itself was redesigned with union participation to encourage multi-skilling and cross-training within self-managed teams, with expanded opportunities for career paths that combine a range of other technical skills, and a computer system designed to provide full access of all teams to the technical and commercial information necessary to run the plant flexibly and with an integrated view of its overall operations. Sociotechnical redesign, though motivated partly by the suboptimal use of the new technologies that resulted from previous Taylorist conceptions of work organization, became a prerequisite for equity and flexibility in scheduling. The Oil, Chemical and Atomic Workers union (now the Canadian ECWU), once invited into the planning process, was willing to negotiate the radical reduction in job classifications in exchange for increased opportunities for meaningful work, continuous learning with various career paths, participation in self-managed teams with limited external supervisory structures, and the elimination of the traditional management-rights clause in the contract. It thus became a full-fledged partner in the redesign process, giving voice to worker discontent over limited skill and learning opportunities under the existing system, and developing career modules with open-ended learning options and a schedule that responded to worker interest in flexibility and equity simultaneously. Management secured the prerequisites for flexible specialization, and workers gained greater participatory rights and the recognition of unimpeded individual learning as the basis for effective organizational learning. Time flexibility, skill upgrading, and more ambitious sociotechnical redesign can thus come to reinforce each other synergistically. And even workers who initially view time innovation in terms of what it permits outside work—education, child care by men as well as women, home renovation, gardening—come to recognize the peculiar potential it has in transforming the nature of work itself.[47]

Although time flexibility creates problems of coverage and coordination, workers often develop new forms of communication, collaborative decision-making skills, and enhanced team spirit to manage these problems effectively. Reciprocal norms of covering for each other develop to enable workers to respond to the requirements of the work process while preserving individual flexibility. And where group cohesiveness is stronger, not only are there greater opportunities for flexibility, but the productivity benefits of such flexibility seem to be more fully realized.[48] Here again the interactive effects of flexible individualization and team collaboration are apparent. Of course, there are limits to this, and too much flexibility can disrupt teams, hinder mutual learning and trust within them, and create obstacles to informal socializing and common meeting times upon which effective worker participation depends. Some of this

can be mitigated by using core hours or overlapping days for important meet-
ings, by using various computer and telephonic devices, and by cultivating a
common participatory culture throughout the organization. Such a culture can
help make flexibility in the deployment of human resources serve innovative
and integrative purposes across organizational boundaries, while minimizing
disruption as members enter and leave work teams.[49]

Job sharing provides a number of distinctive opportunities for continued
learning and upgrading on the job. Partners can train each other in areas in
which they have greater expertise and serve as continual sounding boards for
problems they each confront, thus enhancing each other's sense of competence
and confidence. Sharers often feel greater support for making difficult decisions
or taking risks. Sharing can facilitate retooling by one member who has been
away from a particular job for an extended period of time (e.g., administrators
returning to teaching, as in some San Francisco Bay area schools that have
implemented job sharing). Or it can be used directly to apprentice less skilled
workers with the more skilled. One chemist in a food-processing plant, for
instance, who wanted to cut back hours so that she could return to graduate
school, worked out a sharing arrangement with another woman from the production floor, whom she trained as her technician. In cases such as these, job
sharing can facilitate upgrading at two different levels of the skill and professional hierarchy simultaneously, and narrow the gap between mental and manual labor.

When time for learning is freed up during working hours, a similar dynamic can occur. Some participatory and quality-of-worklife programs, for instance, have developed "time incentives" for workers who increase productivity
or reach their quotas in less than the standard time allotted. In the case of
Harman's automobile rearview mirror plant in Bolivar, Tennessee, in the
1970s, for instance, the joint union-management program allowed workers to
receive "earned idle time" if they achieved their quota, and this could be taken
by going home early, by resting idly or socializing, or by participating in one
of the many in-plant educational and cultural programs developed by the
workers themselves. These ranged from ones that were specifically job- and
career-related (such as computer and high school equivalency courses), to ones
that challenged traditional gender roles (such as car care for women), to yet
others that were more broadly cultural (such as art appreciation and Bible
classes, theater groups and square dancing). The earned time thus hardly remained idle, and participation in the various activities spawned a virtual "cultural renaissance" in the plant.[50]

Alternative work-time options are a crucial component of a model of continual learning over the life course, and they have facilitated education and
training on and off the job. Many job sharers see sharing as a way to enable
them to continue education while working at a regular job, and in some cases
the sharing arrangements develop out of college-sponsored internship pro-

grams. Some use permanent part-time or voluntary reduced time (i.e., temporary reductions for a specific period of time) for the same purposes. At one particularly innovative apprenticeship program at the Hewlett-Packard Computer Systems Division in Cupertino, California, nonexempt employees (half of whom were female production workers and secretaries) were permitted to work part-time at regular pay while they returned to school full time in preparation for entry-level engineering positions within the firm. Here, time policies were directly linked to significant upgrading among employees not usually viewed as suitable for professional jobs. Some compressed workweek schedules have also facilitated return to school by blocking out larger amounts of time for classes and study, and a special weekend shift system (12-hour day shifts on Friday, Saturday, and Sunday) at one company has been particularly successful at enabling students in need of a full-time income, who might otherwise not be able to attend college, to pursue higher education nonetheless. Flexiyear programs (i.e., where a certain number of hours for the entire year are negotiated and arranged with varying degrees of flexibility) also permit scheduling around the yearly rhythms of study and course attendance. Flexitime permits scheduling of classes before and after work and with less waiting time in between. And various types of informal flexibility and released time, or educational leaves, sustain ambitious training and educational programs that link learning to job mobility and career advancement, as well as to broader cultural development.[51]

Flexible and reduced options, in short, reveal considerable potential for facilitating continued learning and second chances over the life course in ways that could have important implications for breaking down labor-market segmentation and enhancing equality. Within the workplace they can function to reduce oppressive forms of supervision, democratize culture and communication, and trigger or reinforce innovative sociotechnical designs that upgrade skills and encourage participation. They can help reduce certain aspects of gendered inequality both within the labor market and within the home, and they can enhance capacities for the autonomous allocation and timing of various life activities in accordance with people's varying conceptions of freedom and responsibility within larger moral economies of time. They can also serve as a way of delimiting commitment to certain jobs in the interests of pursuing other jobs with more promise or avocational activities of greater passion. Indeed, this has been an important motive for many in flexible and reduced work-time options, especially those in routine jobs, some of whom seek creative outlets for craftlike work outside the formal labor market, and others of whom choose routine work with flexibility in order to pursue artistic interests. To the extent that not all jobs can be significantly redesigned or upgraded to satisfy the aspirations for self-development of all workers, even under the most favorable assumptions, this aspect of work-time innovation becomes quite important for a general egalitarian approach to the division of labor and the distribution of opportunities within and outside formal labor-market boundaries.[52]

The State and the Democratization of Time

Flexible options developed at the workplace can be complemented, legitimated, and subsidized by the state. Indeed, welfare state programs have been perhaps *the* most important instruments for democratizing
control over time and enhancing the capacities for life planning on a more
egalitarian basis over the course of the twentieth century. Social security and
welfare systems, scholarship and student loan programs, unemployment insurance and retraining programs, day care and parental leaves—all have increased
the capacities of ever broader groups of people to *construct* and *revise* their
occupational biographies and life plans more deliberately and with less vulnerability to the vicissitudes of the market and of human biology. Options to
delay initial entry into the labor market in favor of further education, to wait for
a longer period for a better job offer, to interrupt labor-market participation in
response to health problems or family responsibilities, or to terminate paid
work at a certain age have been progressively made more available and on
terms more favorable to groups previously disadvantaged by the temporal structures that govern market society. Welfare state programs, in short, have enhanced individual citizens' capacities to plan more deliberately, over longer
periods, and with greater security, predictability, and opportunity to recover
and revise. And while some of this has been achieved in collective bargaining
or through the private firm—more so in some countries than others—it has
been the welfare state that has come to provide the basic infrastructure and
financing to make such temporal options effective.

A democratic and egalitarian politics of the self-management of time
would further build upon these achievements, enhancing simultaneously the
features of *choice* and *security*, and linking them innovatively to the flexibility
that is achievable at the local workplace and community level. In three ways, in
particular, the state can intervene to enhance capacities for the democratic management of time: legislating and legitimating "rights" to work at freely chosen
time, partially financing reduced-time options, and subsidizing the further development of an infrastructure for activity outside the formal labor market.

The state can legislate and legitimate rights to work-time options in a
number of ways. Most directly, it can mandate that such options be made
available to its own employees. In the United States, for instance, the Federal
Employees Part-Time Career Employment Act of 1978 made reduced-time options available to all federal employees from GS-1 to GS-15, while guaranteeing their continued access to promotion opportunities, proportional salaries, and
prorated benefits. Many state and local governments in the United States do
likewise. Second, employers receiving significant public assistance or contracts
can also be required to institute such options, as physician residency programs
have been in the United States. In some cases, minimum quotas of reduced-
time positions might be established in bargaining between public employers and

unions, as occurred between Service Employees International Union (SEIU) locals and Santa Clara County, California. The requirement to provide flexible and reduced options might also be established universally for all employers beyond a certain size. A limited version of this strategy is represented by parental leave legislation now being debated in the United States, which guarantees options and return rights at the same or equivalent jobs. In July 1990, however, President Bush vetoed the bill passed by Congress, and the House failed to override the veto.

The state can also play a major role in helping to finance reduced options to make them more attractive to employees and employers. This is the case, for instance, with parental leaves and phased retirement in Sweden.[53] Educational leaves, or support for those who combine part-time work with education and training programs (such as the transitional educational schemes targeted at youth by the French socialist government in the early 1980s), also encourage flexibility. Income tax policies could also be designed to make voluntary time and income tradeoffs more attractive. And "equity subsidies" (which are used in Sweden in a variety of ways to encourage balanced male-female training and hiring) might be granted directly to employers to encourage innovative options and reduce their cost (e.g., of extra training, benefits, and the like). The innovative social service leaves that some companies in the United States have developed might also be encouraged by state financial support. In one company an engineer developed the computer systems for the regional and then national Muscular Dystrophy offices on successive leaves, and others have engaged in alcohol and drug rehabilitation work. A system of competitive grants, as now exists for support of the arts, could be expanded, and targeted differentially at those in routine or low-opportunity jobs for creative projects in a great variety of areas—thus helping to loosen the segmentation entailed by such jobs, while providing incentives to perform them, if only on a part-time basis. A system of national and local labor-market boards providing detailed information (perhaps even accessible from home and office computers) on actual or projected job openings, sabbatical replacements, sharing options, and the like would facilitate individual choice within a framework of enhanced security and predictability.

Gösta Rehn, architect of Sweden's highly flexible postwar labor-market policy, has proposed the most ambitious and comprehensive scheme for state support of flexible time options. Rehn's model envisions a single comprehensive system for financing *all* periods of voluntary or age-determined withdrawal from paid work, which would replace the fragmented programs for youth training, adult education, parental leave, vacations, sabbaticals, and partial and full retirement. Such a system would provide general income insurance, with individual drawing rights throughout the life course, limited only by certain minimums that must remain for retirement, and ceilings on the amount one can overdraw at specific ages. The income that is transferred across different phases of our lives, which is what social insurance and other such programs largely represent, would be treated as *individual property* that each person could freely dispose of in response to particular life needs at particular times, and thus be liberated substantially from bureaucratic supervision and elaborate categorical regulation. Individual life-planning capacities, enhanced greatly by the postwar development of the welfare state, would thus be raised to a new level of individual freedom and security—a "security under wings" rather than a "security under shells," as Rehn calls it. Such a policy could be fine-tuned to the cyclical ups and downs of labor demand through *additional* financial incentives provided by the state for individuals to use their drawing rights for reduced time or temporary withdrawal at specific times, in specific industries, or with specific retraining goals. And, as I have argued elsewhere, it could have an additional voluntary and tax-deferred component, similar to Individual Retirement Accounts (IRAs), which would permit individuals to save at a rate that reflected their own individual preferences for time and income over different stages of their lives. This model would provide integrated self-management of time over the entire life course in a way that would maximize individual choice within a framework of greater equity and security. And it would do so in a way that would enhance our capacities for spontaneous activity, the revision of individual life plans, and responsiveness to the moral requirements of nurturance and care.[54]

A third component of state action to secure a democratic and egalitarian politics of time is its financial and administrative support for activity outside the formal labor market. Such support could direct itself to creating or enhancing the conditions for individual and community self-help and service, ecologically sound cooperative and craft production, as well as aesthetic and leisure pursuits (e.g., through public parks and studios). The richer the opportunities for such activities are, and the lower the cost of engaging in them (in individual or household capital investments in tools, supplies, space, or in training and networking time), the more likely that reduced work-time options will be utilized broadly, thus unburdening the labor market and helping to distribute opportunities more equitably within it. Also enhanced are opportunities for creative work that cannot be satisfied in the market, for community activities that reinforce local solidarities and *gemeinschaftliche* relationships, and for the provision of service and care in less bureaucratic ways.[55]

A number of very interesting proposals and ongoing experiments have been developed in recent years along these lines, from community and craft centers, union-sponsored workshops, and housing renovation collectives, to the state-subsidized *Kooperationsring* proposed by Claus Offe and Rolf Heinze. The latter would unite several hundred households in an elaborate exchange of services (care, transport, cleaning, and the like) through the medium of non-monetizable vouchers that represent voluntary labor contributions and equivalent drawing rights. The Service Credit Volunteer System, funded by government and foundation sources in a variety of states in the United States, allows for voluntary service contributions among the elderly that can later be drawn upon in the form of credits for needed services—a model that is being tested for child care, housing renovation, and job training as well. André Gorz has proposed to distribute administratively some minimum number of each individual's lifetime work hours to produce the social necessities, in return for a guaranteed income, and to organize the formal economy (the "sphere of heteronomy") to serve the continual expansion of production outside its boundaries (in the "sphere of autonomy"). Fred Block and others argue for a basic citizen wage or guaranteed income, independent of work in the formal economy, as the best way to foster voluntary and creative forms of nonmarket work and service.[56]

The rich experience of voluntary forms of cooperation, and the possible ways of facilitating these with state support, warrant a more extended discussion than I can provide here. Some of these recent proposals, however, present serious problems—problems of equity and the segmentation of opportunities between formal and informal economic spheres, as well as various problems of accountability, continuity, and quality of service.

An alternative model of state support for voluntary and informal activity outside the labor market that would minimize some of these problems would, first of all, build the infrastructure for such support on the basis of formalized public service roles that provide regular jobs and career opportunities, as well as administrative accountability for the use of resources, and the continuity and quality of service. Second, these formal roles would be explicitly defined in such a way as to facilitate voluntary service, self-help, and individual and small-group productive activities, thus debureaucratizing service considerably and reducing dependence on professionals for the delivery of many of the things that people might choose to provide for themselves. Third, such state services would be embedded in local communities that participate in defining the kinds of services and modes of delivery, thus reinforcing community control.

For example, a state-subsidized craft or housing renovation center could be staffed by professional carpenters, architects, and the like, whose job would be to maintain the equipment, account for its use (e.g., by restricting it to nonprofit activities, ensuring equitable access), facilitate community involvement, and teach skills to local community members. In cases where those engaged in do-it-yourself activity decide to enter the market, the center could also provide specific financial, technical, and marketing services. But the formalization of their activity would place them in a different category in terms of the extent to which they can draw freely on the subsidized services of the center, and in terms of the taxable status of their activities.

Another example: the delivery of home care to the sick and elderly could be organized by social service agencies to ensure dependability and proper professional qualification. But they could be debureaucratized with the help of sufficient resources to ensure that, say, visiting nurses had enough time to spend with their clients to provide decent care, as well as to involve clients and those closest to them in developing ways of caring for themselves and each other. Such social services could also be linked creatively with a broader voluntary exchange of services, such as the Service Credit Volunteer model.

A democratic politics of time would seek to integrate the various forms through which choice and equity can be secured and made mutually reinforcing. The local workplace provides rich opportunity for alternative time options to be incorporated into sociotechnical and participatory reforms that empower employees, upgrade skills and opportunities, and encourage learning. These options can, in turn, be anchored in and encouraged by a more generalized system of legal rights to work-time options, financial and administrative supports, and the social and material infrastructure for self-help and the voluntary exchange of service outside the market. Some version of the Rehn model seems to represent, over the long run, the most promising ideal around which a pluralist time politics might be progressively integrated—although it is not necessarily the only one, and we can imagine various routes to such integration, including those that place greater emphasis on basic income supports for activity outside the formal labor market. The Rehn model, however, is consistent with the broadest range of choices within the labor market and does not depend on dubious distinctions between necessary and non-necessary goods and work, or administrative distributions of labor that are questionable both from the point of view of effectiveness and of freedom—problems that flaw Gorz's model, perhaps fatally. It creates the basis for enhancing individual control of time and integrated life planning in a way that is freed considerably from bureaucratic classification and supervision. It provides a comprehensive system of social security and choice yet permits a variety of additional voluntary forms of savings of time and income. As an accounting procedure linking drawing rights to contributions, it has substantial capacity for legitimation on the basis of its transparency and equity—a real problem with guaranteed income–informal activity models. It has flexible application in response to labor-market vicissitudes and imperfect information. It can serve as a component of a system that guarantees formal labor-market roles for all, while encouraging voluntary participation outside the labor market and the debureaucratization of social services. It provides, in short, many of the components for a genuinely *postindustrial New Deal*.

Toward a Politics of Time

Needless to say, in countries such as the United States with much less developed and more fragmented welfare states than Sweden, and where the attack on the welfare state has been much stronger in the 1980s, we are far from being able to put such a comprehensive model of social security and choice directly on the agenda. Even in Sweden the working-time debate has only gradually—although by now quite decidedly—been framed around Rehn's proposals. Nevertheless, in the arenas of both industrial relations and the welfare state, opportunities are present for us to begin to redefine the democratic vision in terms of a more explicit and integrative politics of time.

There is increasing awareness among trade unions of the need to respond to the new forms of temporal flexibility and to incorporate less-than-full-time workers in the processes of collective bargaining. In view of the acute hazards of this, however, most unions have been very hesitant, or overtly hostile, to rethinking the model of the full-time worker on standard hours. They fear that increased diversity of schedules will increase competition among workers, and that employers will be able to use part-timers to erode the pay, benefits, and job security of full-timers. As the workforce becomes increasingly fragmented, the solidarities built upon shared time and place will also erode. And part-timers are perceived as more difficult to organize because of competing interests outside the workplace or less long-term commitment to a paid job or career. Unions—including many women in them—also fear that various flexible and part-time options will be used to further segment the labor force, thus ratifying rather than reversing the inferior status of women in the labor market as well as within the home. Flexibility that enhances employer responsiveness to demand fluctuation and market uncertainty often takes forms that reduce rather than increase workers' temporal autonomy. Flexible and reduced options are also seen by many unions as a distraction from the overriding goal of reducing the workweek for all with no reductions in pay.[57]

And, of course, even though many alternative work-time options have demonstrated rich possibilities for enhancing autonomy and equity, this has *not* been the dominant pattern of flexible and reduced options. Employers have made increasing use of part-time, temporary, and home-working options as a way of reducing wage and benefit costs, unburdening themselves of long-term employment commitments in uncertain markets, and staffing in response to irregular demand rather than employee preference. And the flexibility preferred by employers has generally had little to do with sociotechnical reform or flexible specialization.[58]

The fears of the unions also reflect a deeper recognition of how important common time standards have been to the unions' capacity to represent collective interests effectively. Such standards were a difficult historical achievement and came to serve several crucial functions for the unions. By removing individual bargaining over the number of hours one was willing to work, common standards limited competition among workers. They also established the normative foundation for a full income and served as a ratchet for further progress on both wages and hours by removing upward revisions of hours from later rounds of bargaining over wage increases. And they established the basis for foresight and regularity in workers' management of their own time by delimiting employers' claims on it.[59]

But the crisis in temporal organization, described in the first part of this chapter, has made it increasingly difficult to represent workers' interests effectively as we cling to the common work-time standards of the past. Markets and technologies have been transformed, employer strategies have changed, and employee work-time and lifetime profiles and preferences have themselves become increasingly pluralized. The traditional trade union strategy of generalized work-time reductions for all has serious limits as an employment strategy, and it fails to respond creatively to the diversity of preferences among the workforce. And in those European countries where it is progressing in increments, it has not been able to avoid the issue of increasing flexibility, which even those unions most committed to general reductions are coming to recognize as an issue that will not disappear. The organization of time, in short, has again become a problematic element on the contested terrain of workplace politics, and unions now confront the task of responding to it in innovative ways that enhance worker autonomy and choice, and reduce the forms of segmentation and vulnerability that have accompanied most temporal options that deviate from the full-time—and male—norm.

Some unions—especially those in service areas, including public services, and those with greater numbers of women—have begun to develop policies that indicate alternative ways of regulating diversity and flexibility in the interests of democratic equality. These include a number of important elements: (1) Wages and benefits should be comparable to those of full-time workers. This might mean wages and salaries equal to those of full-time workers, and some combination of full and prorated benefits, and inclusion in social security and pension systems. Some unions, for instance, have been successful in winning full health benefits for those on reduced time, and prorated pension contributions, sick days and the like. (2) Seniority, promotion, and training opportunities should be available for those on reduced-time options, specified in union contracts, civil service regulations, and company personnel policies. (3) There should be negotiation of rules and procedures determining the choice of options, the conditions under which management can refuse to grant worker requests or can require flexibility (including overtime) to meet scheduling needs and vicissitudes in demand; these issues must be included in grievance procedures as well. Specific procedures must be developed to protect the voluntary nature of options such as the pairing of partners in job-shared positions, to specify the rights of workers to become eligible for full-time positions, or to allow part-timers to switch back to comparable full-time positions they once occupied. Options must be gender neutral, unlike current "mommy track" proposals, and choices must be generally reversible, thus permitting employees to move back and forth between full-time and reduced-time options and limiting the segmentation effects of temporal diversity. (4) There could be negotiated quotas—both minimum and maximum—to ensure the availability of nonstandard options in appropriate amounts. Some SEIU locals in Santa Clara County, California, for instance, negotiated such minimum quotas in the late 1970s, even though the number of requests, as well as the number granted, generally exceeded this minimum. (5) Flexible and reduced options should be integrated into other sociotechnical reforms that upgrade skills generally and enhance the possibilities for worker participation. Many unions in the United States have already begun to face the necessity of shifting away from common-rule strategies and job-control unionism in the interests of the quality of worklife and sociotechnical reform, and they have thus begun to develop the capacities for regulating flexibility to workers' benefit—although this has clearly not been without its pitfalls. And increasing numbers of nonunionized plants have developed a variety of participation programs, formal grievance procedures, and flexible time and work-sharing options.[60]

In addition to a strategy at the level of industrial relations, we can begin to develop a social welfare politics that progressively links rights and income supports *both* for those who would withdraw partially or temporarily from the labor market *and* for those who have been excluded and wish to enter it. In other words, options to enter or leave, increase or reduce labor-market participation should be viewed as complementary, legitimated in progressively universalistic terms, and articulated as part of an integrated politics of time. For those already in the labor market, such programs could include parental leaves and flexible retirement with income supports that at least partially make up for the loss of earnings and accumulation of pension rights. The tax code could be revised to favor voluntary time-income tradeoffs, which can be done by increasing its progressivity, reducing the tax incentives for other fringe benefits relative to extra free time, and raising or removing earnings ceilings for the unemployment insurance and social security contributions of employers, which encourage them to hire fewer workers for longer hours in order to maximize nontaxable hours of work. More ambitious, yet also more costly, programs aimed at developing an integrated politics of time are also possible: publicly funded sabbaticals (including ones with variable levels of voluntary contributions and benefits), paid educational leaves, and subsidies for those who spend their time outside the labor market in voluntary social service activities. However, even when the most optimal levels of funding for these various time policies cannot be achieved, it remains critical that we legitimate and facilitate a wide range of *voluntary time–income tradeoffs* as the centerpiece for a democratic politics of time that can sustain a broad public discourse about the meanings of autonomy and equity, responsibility and affluence.

Policies that support and legitimate options for temporary and partial withdrawal from the labor market by the employed make it much easier to legitimate an adequate level of supportive services for those desiring inclusion in the labor market. It seems more likely that programs such as workfare, for instance, will receive adequate child-care and health-care support services if there exists a universalistic policy to support child care, parental leave, and health benefits from which the employed working and middle classes also derive advantage. (And universal health care would eliminate another barrier to employees' choosing reduced-time options and employers' instituting them on more favorable terms.) Likewise, a job training and placement system for all, especially if accompanied by the expansion of work-time options that facilitate continual learning, makes it easier to legitimate the services necessary to integrate into the labor market those who have suffered from long-term exclusion. David Ellwood's recent proposals for welfare reform, which include institutional supports for a norm of half-time work in the labor market for women with young children, are quite consistent with this approach.[61]

In addition to a less punitive system of workfare with greater child-care, training, and other supportive services, a democratic and egalitarian politics of time requires a policy of full employment, even if that means that only part-time jobs can be guaranteed and that other basic income supports are necessary. Full employment is perhaps the most effective way of enhancing the bargaining power of those who not only earn low wages but are most vulnerable to employer strategies to shape work-time flexibility in ways that diminish genuine choice and equity. The possibilities for workers and unions to reshape alternative options and to organize effectively among those groups that today most desire them would be enhanced greatly by full employment. Full-employment policies maintain the link between work and entitlements, which most citizens recognize as the basis of fairness, and thus enhance the capacities to legitimate a broad range of services that can facilitate increased options outside the labor market for all. And the public-sector component of a full-employment policy could be directly aimed at developing the infrastructure to support this—day care and home health care services, community craft centers for do-it-yourself activity, professional social services that facilitate self-help and voluntary exchange of service, parks and recreation facilities, community art and performance centers, and the like. Such a policy recognizes the centrality of work in personal development and the reciprocal obligation among citizens, without at the same time fetishizing the traditional work ethic. And it recognizes the indispensability of effective means for guaranteeing inclusion into the labor market as the basis of equal opportunity, without narrowly predefining equity in terms of a specific mix of labor-market and non–labor-market activities. In short, *full employment policies are a crucial means for legitimating plural temporal options on a universalistic basis and for providing the institutional infrastructure to make such options effectively available.*[62]

A welfare-state politics that is progressively integrated around a democratic and egalitarian vision of temporal organization can legitimate itself in rhetoric and symbols that have deep resonance in American culture. Policies that ensure rights and enhance options outside the labor market for all citizens—rather than just for women or deviants from the "normal" worklife profile—can be framed in terms of the rich traditions of community, neighborhood involvement, and voluntary activity that persist in the United States. And the provision of social services to facilitate self-help and the voluntary exchange of services can serve to undermine the ideological antinomy between state and neighborly initiative that Reagan had been able to appeal to in his attack on the social welfare role of government—and that some have unfortunately accepted in the renewed discussion of the role of self-help in the black community. Work-time options and social services that reduce the conflict between work and family can be legitimated in terms of the deep concern for the integrity of family life and the equity of job opportunity for women. Policies that facilitate options to trade income for time can be formulated in terms of the profound religious and secular traditions that have refused to accept the vision of the good life as an endless accumulation of material goods or the frenetic search for opportunity and achievement, as well as in terms of ecological sensibilities that recognize the need for stewardship over the earth that sustains our life together. And the expansion of individual choice over the temporal parameters of our work and nonwork activities resonates deeply with the values of individuality, moral autonomy, and self-realization in American culture. An explicit and integrative politics of the self-management of time provides the richest rhetorical opportunities for moving beyond the symbolic antinomies of instrumental individualism and collective provision that impaired the development of the welfare state in the United States,[63] and for legitimating a postindustrial New Deal in terms of the very diverse, yet potentially complementary and mutually enriching traditions of individuality and community, of family and nation, of freedom and equity.

An integrative politics of the self-management of time provides the basis for reframing the terms of moral renewal, since it recognizes that one reason for expanding autonomy and redefining equity—and perhaps the one that grounds all the others—is that we constitute ourselves as moral actors through the ways that we structure time. How we choose to parcel our time, slice it up among different activities, how we make and revise our commitments to each other over time, are all matters of profound moral import in our everyday lives. The opportunities to reflect, renew, remember, and repair are structured by the organization of time. The relative scarcity of time and its different forms shape the ways we make our commitments, excuse our failures, rationalize our guilt. Time not only structures the opportunities we have and the plans we make but the attention we distribute and the recognition we grant. It serves as a sign of respect, a measure of responsibility, an index of care and commitment in our everyday work relations and in our homes, in the shops, and in the streets. The ways that we time and sequence and ration our activities, in short, are essential to the ways that we construct and present and rationalize ourselves as moral actors. Political economies of time are thus moral economies in a very fundamental sense. An important prerequisite for enhancing moral responsibility is the ability, indeed the *right*, to structure our time more freely and deliberately. This is particularly important as our complex societies generate demands on our time and rich possibilities for its use that continually outrun our supplies and thus invariably present us with dilemmas of moral import. The condition of postmodernity is one of proliferating action alternatives in a variety of spheres of life, and more complex and individuated choices of how to sequence and apportion our time. This does not so much displace the autonomous self as make its task of constructing a moral life through time and over time that much more of a free and complex project.[64] To legitimate a broader range of choice over how we organize our time opens up to individual, interpersonal, and public reflection the reasons and rationalizations that underlie the choices that we do make. It introduces a reflective moral pedagogy into the process of apportioning and sequencing our time, making and remaking our commitments. In this sense, the self-management of time becomes a process of permanent moral education about the value we place on the time we spend together—producing goods, delivering services, giving care, having fun. It provides indispensable means for nurturing processes of critical reflection and public discourse about the kind of people we want to be, and the kind of society—indeed, the kind of wealth—we want to create.

Notes

1. Janet Zollinger Giele, "Changing Sex Roles and Family Structure," *Social Policy* (Jan.–Feb. 1979): 33; Fred Best, "Changing Sex Roles and Worklife Flexibility," *Psychology of Women Quarterly* 6 (1981): 55–71.

2. Malcolm Morrison, "Work and Retirement in the Aging Society," *Daedalus* 115 (Winter 1986): 272; "Flexible Distribution of Work and Leisure," in B. Herzog, ed., *Aging and Income* (New York: Human Sciences Press, 1978), 95–127.

3. Bernice Neugarten and Dail Neugarten, "Age in the Aging Society," *Daedalus* 115 (Winter 1986): 33, 46; Hilda Kahne, *Reconceiving Part-Time Work: New Perspectives for Older Workers and Women* (Totowa, N.J.: Rowman and Allenheld, 1985), 53.

4. Fred Block and Larry Hirschhorn, "New Productive Forces and the Contradictions of Contemporary Capitalism: A Post-Industrial Perspective," *Theory and Society* 7 (1979): 363–395; and Larry Hirschhorn, *Beyond Mechanization* (Cambridge: MIT Press, 1984).

5. Centre for Educational Research and Innovation, *Development in Educational Leaves of Absence* (Paris: OECD, 1976), 21.

6. Daniel Yankelovich, Hans Zetterberg et al., *Work and Human Values* (New York: Aspen Institute for Human Studies, 1983); and Marlis Buchmann, *The Script of Life in Modern Society* (Chicago: University of Chicago Press, 1989).

7. Bernhard Teriet, *Neue Strukturen der Arbeitszeitverteilung* (Göttingen: Verlag Otto Schwarz, 1976), 8–9; B. Hof, "Erwerbsbiographien im langfristigen Vergleich," *IW-Trends*, no. 1 (March 15, 1986), 34–48.

8. Wassily Leontieff, "Technological Advance, Economic Growth, and the Distribution of Income," *Population and Development Review* 9; no. 3 (Sept. 1983): 403–410; and idem, "The Distribution of Work and Income," *Scientific American* 247, no. 3 (Sept. 1982): 188–204; Wassily Leontieff and Faye Duchin, *The Future Impact of Automation on Workers* (New York: Oxford University Press, 1986); Colin Gill, *Work, Unemployment and the New Technology* (Cambridge: Polity Press, 1985), chap. 4.

9. The aging of the baby-boom generation and the decline in the number of younger cohorts coming into the labor force may very well ease employment problems. But labor shortages would also increase employee bargaining power, and there is every reason to believe that this would lead to an increase in flexible working-time options, but on terms more favorable to employees themselves. Some human resource managers in the United States are already planning for such shortages and exploring more innovative temporal options to attract and retain staff, especially women.

10. Karl Hinrichs, in this volume; and *Motive und Interressen im Arbeitszeitkonflikt* (Frankfurt: Campus, 1988). On various models of weekly work-time reductions and their likely employment effects, see Lucy Kok and Chris de Neubourg, "Working Time: Length, Past and Future: An International Comparison," in Alfred Kleinknecht and Tom van Veen, eds., *Working Time Reduction and the Crisis of the Welfare State* (Maastricht: Presses Interuniversitaires Européenes, 1986), 12–80; and Ronald Schettkat, "Employment, Economic Growth, Productivity and Working Time," 81–98 of same volume.

11. This is especially true in Europe. See Claus Offe, *Disorganized Capitalism*, ed. John Keane (Cambridge: MIT Press, 1985), 61ff.; and Peter Glotz, "Forward to Europe," *Dissent*, Summer 1986, pp. 327–339.

12. Jeremy Rifkin, *Time Wars* (New York: Holt, 1987); and Craig Brod, *Technostress* (Reading, Mass.: Addison-Wesley, 1984).

13. Larry Dossey, *Space, Time and Medicine* (Boulder, Colo.: Shambhala, 1982).

14. Steffan Burenstam Linder, *The Harried Leisure Class* (New York: Columbia University Press, 1970), 22; Barry Schwartz, *Queuing and Waiting* (Chicago: University of Chicago Press, 1975), 2; and the Harris Poll data cited in Rifkin, *Time Wars*, 207.

15. On life planning, the timing of births, and equitable access to labor-market opportunities in the prochoice movement, see Kristin Luker, *Abortion and the Politics of Motherhood* (Berkeley: University of California Press, 1984); on the integration of work and family, see Kathleen Gerson, *Hard Choices* (Berkeley: University of California Press, 1984).

16. Michael Walzer, *Spheres of Justice* (New York: Basic Books, 1983), 319.

17. E. P. Thompson, "Time, Work Discipline and Industrial Capitalism," *Past and Present* 38 (1967): 96; see also Michael Young, *The Chronometric Society* (Cambridge: Harvard University Press, 1988), who notes (p. 261) that "a new approach to time could be the key to a new enlightenment."

18. Karl Marx, quoted in Georg Lukacs, *History and Class Consciousness*, trans. Rodney Livingstone (Cambridge: MIT Press, 1971), 89; Marx, *Capital*, vol. 1, trans. Ben Fowkes (Harmondsworth: Penguin, 1976). Moishe Postone articulates the temporal dimensions of Marx's critique most fully, although I do not share some of his conclusions. See "Necessity, Labor and Time: A Reinterpretation of the Marxian Critique of Capitalism," *Social Research* 45, no. 4 (Winter 1978): 739–788.

19. Lukacs and Giddens develop various aspects of this argument. See Anthony

Giddens, *A Contemporary Critique of Historical Materialism* (Berkeley: University of California Press, 1981).

20. Karl Marx, *Grundrisse*, trans. Martin Nicolaus (Harmondsworth: Penguin, 1973), 705–706.

21. Ali Rattansi, *Marx and the Division of Labor* (London: Macmillan, 1982).

22. See Carmen Sirianni, "Production and Power in a Classless Society: A Critical Analysis of the Utopian Dimensions of Marxist Theory," *Socialist Review* 59 (Sept.–Oct. 1981), 33–82; and Alec Nove, *The Economics of Feasible Socialism* (London: Allen and Unwin, 1983).

23. Pitirim Sorokin, *Sociocultural Causality, Space, Time* (Durham, N.C.: Duke University Press, 1943); Georges Gurvitch, *The Spectrum of Social Time*, trans. Myrtle Korenbaum (Dordrecht: Reidel, 1964).

24. Wilbert Moore, *Man, Time and Society* (New York: Wiley, 1963); Georg Simmel, "The Metropolis and Mental Life," in *The Sociology of Georg Simmel*, ed. and trans. Kurt Wolff (New York: Free Press, 1950), 412–413; and Eviatar Zerubavel, *Hidden Rhythms* (Chicago: University of Chicago Press, 1981).

25. Ricardo Quinones, *The Renaissance View of Time* (Cambridge: Harvard University Press, 1972); and on similar motives in the Middle Ages, see David Landes, *The Revolution in Time* (Cambridge: Harvard University Press, 1983), 72.

26. Nilklas Luhmann, "Die Knappheit der Zeit und die Vordringlichkeit des Befristeten," in *Politische Planung* (Opladen: Westdeutscher Verlag, 1975), 143–165; "The Temporalization of Complexity," in *Sociocybernetics*, ed. R. F. Geyer and J. van den Zouwen, vol. 2 (Leiden: Martinus Neijhoff, 1978); and "The Future Cannot Begin: Temporal Structures in Modern Society," *Social Research* 43 (1976): 130–152.

27. George Soule, *Time for Living* (New York: Viking, 1955). Soule's analysis of time as the scarcest resource and as limit to endless consumption predated the contributions of both Roy Harrod and Gary Becker, and anticipated a number of important themes in contemporary Green movements. It offered a democratic alternative to de Grazia's elitist ideal of leisure and articulated themes that were widely discussed in labor, religious, and liberal reform circles in previous decades. See Gary Becker, "A Theory of the Allocation of Time," *Economic Journal* 75 (Sept. 1965): 493–517; Sebastian de Grazia, *Of Time, Work and Leisure* (New York: Doubleday, 1962); and Benjamin Hunnicutt, *Work Without End* (Philadelphia: Temple University Press, 1988).

28. See the symposium on Linder in *Quarterly Journal of Economics* 87 (Nov. 1973): 629–670; and Gordon Winston, *The Timing of Economic Activities* (Cambridge: Cambridge University Press, 1982). The critique of time geographers of the Lund School has also been most important. See Tommy Carlstein, Don Parkes, and Nigel Thrift, eds., *Human Activity and Time Geography* (New York: Wiley, 1978), especially the Afterword.

29. On the concept of embeddedness in economic action, see Mark Granovetter, "Economic Action and Social Structure: The Problem of Embeddedness," *American Journal of Sociology* 91, no. 3 (Nov. 1985): 481– 510.

30. Sarah Fenstermaker Berk, *The Gender Factory* (New York: Plenum, 1985), and much earlier research see little change. Compare Joseph Pleck, *Working Wives, Working Husbands* (Beverly Hills: Sage, 1985). For a qualitative study of gender strategies in the distribution of household labor time, see Arlie Hochschild, *The Second Shift* (New York: Viking, 1989).

31. Shelly Coverman, "Gender, Domestic Labor Time and Wage Inequality," *American Sociological Review* 48, no. 5 (Oct. 1983): 623–637. For feminist critiques of some of the temporal dimensions of human capital theory and the new home economics, see Paula England, "Socio-Economic Explanations of Job Segregation," in Helen Remick, ed., *Comparable Worth and Wage Discrimination* (Philadelphia: Temple University Press, 1984), 28–46.

32. See Anne Seiden, "Time Management and the Dual-Career Couple," in Fran Pepitone-Rockwell, ed., *Dual-Career Couples* (Beverly Hills: Sage, 1980); and Jeff Bryson and Rebecca Bryson, "Salary and Job Performance: Differences in Dual-Career Couples," in the same volume. On women's more contingent (and hence denser, more simultaneous) temporal worlds, compared with men's more linear ones, see David Maines and Monica Hardesty, "Temporality and Gender: Young Adults' Career and Family Plans," *Social Forces* 66, no. 1 (Sept. 1987), 102–120.

33. Johanna Brenner and Maria Ramas, "Rethinking Women's Oppression," *New Left Review* 144 (March–April, 1984): 33–71.

34. Hanna Papanek, "Man, Women and Work: Reflections on the Two-Person Career," *American Journal of Sociology* 78, no. 4 (1973): 852–872; Arlie Hochschild, "Inside the Clockwork of Male Careers," in Florence Howe, ed., *Women and the Power to Change* (New York: McGraw-Hill, 1975), 47–80; and Rosabeth Moss Kanter, *Men and Women of the Corporation* (New York: Basic Books, 1977). See also Gerson's *Hard Choices* for how the structure of careers influences the choices and worldviews of diverse groups of women.

35. See Lewis Coser, *Greedy Institutions* (New York: Free Press, 1974).

36. Sherry Ortner, "Is Female to Male as Nature is to Culture?" in Michele Rosaldo and Louise Lamphere, eds., *Women, Culture and Society* (Palo Alto: Stanford University Press, 1974), 67–87; Simone de Beauvoir, *The Second Sex* (New York: Random House, 1953), 58–59; and Max Horkheimer and Theodor Adorno, *Dialectic of Enlightenment*, trans. John Cumming (New York: Herder and Herder, 1972), 32–35, 43–80.

37. Lane Gerber, *Married to Their Careers* (London: Tavistock, 1983), 59, 66ff., 158ff.; and Gideon Kunda, *Engineering Culture* (Philadelphia: Temple University Press, 1991).

38. Quinones, *The Renaissance View of Time*.

39. Ursula LeGuin, *The Dispossessed* (New York: Avon, 1974); Dorothy Bryant, *The Kin of Ata Are Waiting for You* (New York: Random House and Moon Books, 1976).

40. Robert Dahl, *After the Revolution?* (New Haven: Yale University Press, 1970), 40ff., 50–51; Carmen Sirianni, *Participation and Society* (New York: Cambridge University Press, forthcoming).

41. Michel Foucault, *Discipline and Punish*, trans. Alan Sheridan (New York: Vintage, 1977), 157; Norbert Elias, *Power and Civility*, trans. Edmund Jephcott (New York: Pantheon, 1982), 247ff.

42. Échange et Projets, *La Révolution du Temps Choisi* (Paris: Albin Michel, 1980); Bernhard Teriet, "Die Wiedergewinnung der Zeitsouveränität," *Technologie und Politik* 8 (1977); Fred Best, *Flexible Life Scheduling* (New York: Praeger, 1980).

43. Some of the better overviews of the practical experiences are Stanley Nollen, *New Work Schedules in Practice* (New York: Van Nostrand Reinhold, 1982); Simcha Ronen, *Alternative Work Schedules* (Homewood, Ill.: Dow Jones-Irwin, 1984); Gretl

Meier, *Job Sharing* (Kalamazoo: Upjohn Institute, 1979); Maureen McCarthy and Gail Rosenberg, *Work Sharing: Case Studies* (Kalamazoo: Upjohn Institute, 1981); Harald Bielenski and Friedhart Hegner, eds., *Flexible Arbeitszeiten* (Frankfurt: Campus, 1985); and Barney Olmsted and Suzanne Smith, *Creating a Flexible Workplace* (New York: AMACOM, 1989), for a practical guide.

44. Meier, *Job Sharing*, 58, 150; Ronen, *Alternative Work Schedules*, 94–95, 108–109.

45. Robert A. Lee, "Flexitime and Conjugal Roles," *Journal of Occupational Behavior* 4 (1983): 297–315; R. A. Winnett and M. S. Neale, "Flexible Work Schedules and Family Time Allocation," *Journal of Applied Behavioral Analysis* 14, no. 1 (1981), 39–46; Kathleen Gerson, "Men's Changing Commitments to Family and Work: The Price of Privilege," talk at Harvard University, Feb. 29, 1988. Of course, the gendered structuring of part-time options today often occasions an *accommodation* with asymmetrical responsibilities and opportunities in the home and in the labor market, as Gerson has shown in *Hard Choices*. But it is not at all clear that this effect is greater than would be the case if such part-time options were not available at all.

46. Robert Golembiewski, Carl Proehl, Jr., and Ronald Fox, "Is Flex-Time for Employees 'Hard Time' for Supervisors?" *Journal of Management* 5, no. 2 (1979): 241–259; Jon Pierce and John Newstrom, "The Design of Flexible Work Schedules and Employee Responses: Relationships and Process," *Journal of Occupational Behavior* 4 (1983): 248–249; as well as Ronen, *Alternative Work Schedules*, Nollen, *New Work Schedules*, and McCarthy and Rosenberg, *Work Sharing*.

47. Janina Latack and Lawrence Foster, "Implementation of Compressed Work Schedules: Participation and Job Redesign as Critical Factors for Employee Acceptance," *Personnel Psychology* 38 (1985): 75–92; Nollen, *New Work Schedules*, 81–102; Louis Davis and Charles Sullivan, "A Labour Contract and the Quality of Working Life," *Journal of Occupational Behavior* 1 (1980): 29–41.

48. V. K. Narayanan and Raghu Nath, "The Influence of Group Cohesiveness on Some Changes Induced by Flexitime," *Journal of Applied Behavioral Science* 20, no. 3 (1984): 265–276; Ronen, *Alternative Work Schedules*; and Golembiewski, Fox and Proehl, Flex-Time," 255.

49. Rosabeth Moss Kanter, *The Change Masters* (New York: Simon and Schuster, 1983), 264–265; Richard Walton, "Establishing and Maintaining High Commitment Work Systems," in John Kimberly, Robert Miles and Associates, eds., *The Organizational Life Cycle* (San Francisco: Jossey-Bass, 1981), 236–237.

50. Daniel Zwerdling, *Workplace Democracy* (New York: Harper, 1980), 48ff.

51. Gretl Meier, *Worker Learning and Worktime Flexibility* (Kalamazoo: Upjohn Institute, 1983); Nollen, *New Work Schedules*, and Ronen, *Alternative Work Schedules*.

52. Sirianni, "Production and Power in a Classless Society," and Offe, *Disorganized Capitalism*.

53. See Ulla Weigelt, in this volume. Currently under parental leave policy, both parents are entitled to full-time leave of absence until the child is 18 months old, and both can work at 75 percent of normal working hours until the child is eight years old or has completed the first year of school. The parents can share between themselves 360 parental insurance benefit days over the course of their leaves.

54. Gösta Rehn, "Towards a Society of Free Choice," in Jerzy Wiatr and Richard

Rose, eds., *Comparing Public Policies* (Wroclaw: Ossolineum, 1977), 121–157; Carmen Sirianni and Michele Eayrs, "Tempo e Lavoro: Razionalizzazione, Flessibilità e Uguaglianza," *Rassegna Italiana di Sociologia* 26, no. 4 (Oct.–Dec. 1985): 523–567.

55. State support of activities outside the labor market, as well as various forms of flexibility and time banking, can, in short, shift the relative attractiveness of money and time as media for individual satisfaction more in the direction of the latter. Money tends to be privileged relative to time—i.e. the two are asymmetrically convertible—as a result of the inherent characteristics of each, as well as specific social arrangements. For instance, money can buy time (via services that save time), whereas time cannot so easily be converted into money, goods, and services. Money can be saved and transferred much more easily than time. Extra units of free time often cannot be used optimally and can even produce negative utilities such as boredom, without money or different social arrangements for productive activity and leisure. It is also the case that, without anticipated time options and effective ways for time banking, spending tends to ratchet itself at levels that later become difficult to reduce, thus further privileging individual preferences for money over time. See Karl Hinrichs, Claus Offe, and Helmut Wiesenthal, "On Time, Money and Welfare-State Capitalism," in John Keane, ed., *Civil Society and the State* (Cambridge, England: Polity Press, 1988), 221–243; and Rolf Heinze and Claus Offe, "Zur Requalifizierung von Zeit," unpublished paper, 1988.

56. See Claus Offe and Rolf Heinze, "Am Arbeitsmarkt vorbei: Überlegungen zur Neubestimmung 'haushaltlicher' Wohlfahrtsproduktion in ihrem Verhältnis zu Markt und Staat," *Leviathan* 14, no. 4 (1986): 471–495; Michael Opielka, "Perspektiven von Arbeit und Einkommen in der Wohlfahrtsgesellschaft," *Aus Politik und Zeitgeschichte* B 36/86 (Sept. 6, 1986): 37–51; Michael Opielka and Georg Vobruba, eds., *Das garantierte Grundeinkommen* (Frankfurt: Fischer, 1986); Andre Gorz, *Farewell to the Working Class*, trans. Michael Sonenscher (Boston: South End Press, 1982); *Paths to Paradise: On the Liberation from Work*, trans. Malcolm Imrie (Boston: South End Press, 1985); Fred Block, *Postindustrial Possibilities* (Berkeley: University of California Press, 1990).

57. Kahne, *Reconceiving Part-Time Work*, chap. 8; Nollen, *New Work Schedules*, chap. 4; Bureau of National Affairs, *The Changing Workplace: New Directions in Staffing and Scheduling* (Washington, D.C.: Bureau of National Affairs, 1986), 101.

58. Eileen Applebaum, "Restructuring Work: Temporary, Part-Time and At-Home Employment," in *Computer Chips and Paper Clips*, vol. 2, ed. Heidi Hartmann (Washington, D.C.: National Academy Press, 1987).

59. Hinrichs, in this volume.

60. On the latter, see Thomas Kochan, Harry Katz, and Robert McKersie, *The Transformation of American Industrial Relations* (New York: Basic Books, 1986).

61. David Ellwood, *Poor Support* (New York: Basic Books, 1988).

62. Needless to say, this does not respond to all of the arguments of those who believe we should abandon full employment as a strategy in favor of more generous transfer programs for those not working. See particularly the debate between Fred Block and Juliet Schor in *Socialist Review*, nos. 75/76, 81, 84 (1984–1985); and Opielka and Vobruba, *Das garantierte Grundeinkommen*. Karl Hinrichs addresses some of the problems with the Kooperationsring approach in his *Zeit und Geld in privaten Haushalten* (Bielefeld: AJZ, 1989).

63. Theda Skocpol, "America's Incomplete Welfare State," in Gösta Esping-Anderson, Lee Rainwater, and Martin Rein, eds., *Stagnation and Renewal in Social Policy* (Armonk, N.Y.: Sharpe, 1986); and James Holt, "The New Deal and the American Anti-Statist Tradition," in John Braeman, Robert Bremner, and David Brody, eds., *The New Deal* (Columbus: Ohio State University Press, 1975), 27–49.

64. See Buchmann, *The Script of Life in Modern Society*, 70–76. For the best theoretical overview of the structures of temporality, see Simonetta Tabboni, *La Rappresentazione Sociale del Tempo*, 2d ed. (Milan: Franco Angeli, 1988).

About the Contributors

Susan Christopherson is an Assistant Professor in the Department of City and Regional Planning at Cornell University. Her most recent research focuses on the implications of the expansion of service employment and the service economy. She has published a series of articles on media industries and on labor flexibility and contingent work. As a consultant to the Organization for Economic Cooperation and Development she participated in multi-country studies of changing patterns of employment in services and of women's employment in services. Her current research concerns the spatial pattern of service provision in sectors such as banking, retail, and the public sector.

Chris de Neubourg is Associate Professor of Economics and Sociology at the University of Limburg, Maastricht, the Netherlands. His research focuses on international comparative studies of labor economics and applied macro- and microanalysis of labor markets. He has recently published a number of books and articles on full employment and unemployment in Europe and on labor market flexibility.

Annik De Rongé has been a Research Assistant in the Department of Political and Social Science at the Catholic University of Louvain, Belgium. Her research interests focus on the sociology of employment, and she has published "Les jeunes et le transitoire: les nouveaux contextes de la socialisation," with Michel Molitor in 1987.

Christoph Deutschmann is Professor of Sociology at the University of Tübingen in Germany. He has written widely on industrial relations in Germany, labor-market segmentation, and working time, and is now examining the relation between decentralization of firms and industrial relations. He has been a Research Fellow at the Institut für Sozialforschung in Frankfurt, at the Wissenschaftszentrum in Berlin, and in the Faculty of Economics at Tohoku University in Japan. His book *Arbeitszeit in Japan* was published by Campus in 1987.

Karl Hinrichs is Research Associate at the Zentrum für Sozialpolitik at the University of Bremen in Germany. In 1989–90 he was John F. Kennedy Memorial Fellow at the Center for European Studies at Harvard University. His latest publications include *Motive und Interesse im Arbeitszeitkonflikt* (Frankfurt and New York: Campus, 1988), *Zeit und Geld in privaten Haushalten*

(Bielefeld: AJZ, 1989), and various articles on labor-market problems and policies. He is currently working on a comparative study of challenges to the welfare state as a result of structural modernization.

Jean-Pierre Jallade is Program Director at the European Institute of Education and Social Policy, University of Paris IX-Dauphine. He has edited several books, including *The Crisis of Redistribution in European Welfare States* (Trent on Stoke: Trentham Books, 1988), *L'Europe à Temps Partiel* (Paris: Economica, 1982), and *Employment and Unemployment in Europe* (Trent on Stoke: Trentham Books, 1981). He is currently working on vocational education and training policies in a cross-national European perspective.

Michel Molitor is Professor in the Department of Social and Political Sciences at the Catholic University of Louvain in Belgium. His research interests include social movements, trade unions, and qualitative methodologies. Among his recent publication are *Le mouvement et la forme* (Brussels: Éditions des facultés universitaires Saint-Louis, 1989), and "L'hermeneutique collective," in *Au-delà du quantitatif*, ed. H. Gérard and M. Loriaux, in 1989.

William Roche received his Ph.D. from Oxford University, where he has also served as a Research Fellow of Nuffield College. He is currently Senior Lecturer in Industrial Relations at University College Dublin and Director of the Masters Program at the Michael Smurfit Graduate School of Business. He has published extensively in industrial and economic sociology and industrial relations. His specific interests have been in union membership, organization, and militancy; sociological theory and industrial relations theory; and the politics and economics of working time. He has published a number of articles on working time in *The European Sociological Review, The British Journal of Industrial Relations*, and in several edited collections.

Carmen Sirianni is Associate Professor of Sociology at Brandeis University and Visiting Associate Professor of Social Studies at Harvard University. He co-chairs the Labor Study Group at the Minda de Günzburg Center for European Studies at Harvard, and coedits the Labor and Social Change series for Temple University Press. In 1985–86 he was a fellow at the Institute for Advanced Study at Princeton, where he began work on the political and moral economies of time. His current interests are in alternative work organization, service work and postindustrialism, and the sociology and political theory of participation. His publications include *Workers Control and Socialist Democracy: The Soviet Experience* (Verso, 1982), *Work, Community and Power*, edited with James Cronin (Temple University Press, 1983), *Critical Studies in Organization and Bureaucracy*, edited with Frank Fischer (Temple University Press, 1984), and *Worker Participation and the Politics of Reform* (Temple University Press,

1987). He is currently completing a book entitled *Participation and Society*, to be published by Cambridge University Press.

Ulla Weigelt is a researcher in the Ministry of Environment and Energy in Stockholm, Sweden, and has served in a similar capacity in the Ministry of Labor and the National Board of Occupational Safety and Health. She has served as secretary to the Working Hours Advisory Committee (DELFA), as well as to other committees for annual leaves and new working hours.